Contents

Part 1

Some Professional Issues

Teaching in Europe: The challenge, the issues and the problems

TEACHING IN EUROPE: THE CHALLENGE, THE ISSUES AND THE PROBLEMS

'1992 - just around the corner', 'A frontier-free Europe', 'Deadline '92', 'Countdown to 1992'. Such headlines, and many more, are appearing in the press, in European Community background pamphlets, in school literature, in European Parliament documentation and elsewhere. We are told that the end of 1992 will see Europe genuinely "open for business", that some hidden barriers will be overcome and that the beginnings of an integrated economic area, with complete freedom of movement of persons, goods, services and capital, combined with other integrating forces, will be in operation. A utopia on the move?

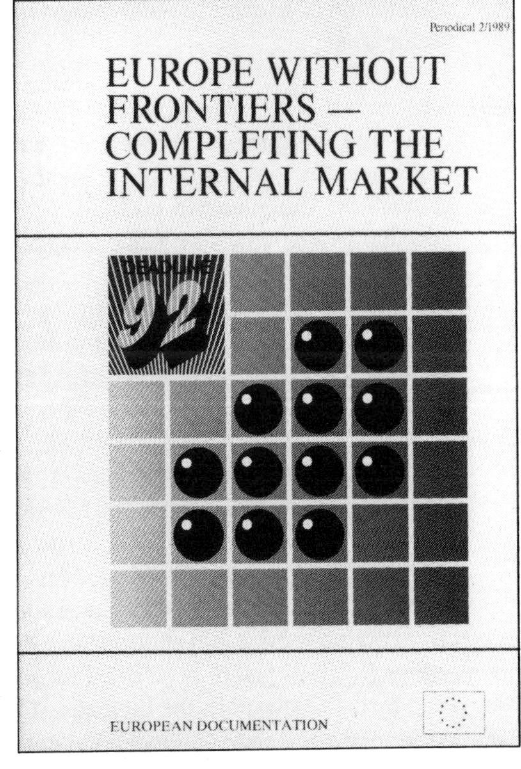

Certainly the 1957 Treaty of Rome set itself the target of abolishing tariffs and quotas between the six original partners within 12 years, but the years that followed were often more preoccupied with sluggish growth, with unemployment issues, with quarrels about payments and subscriptions, and with the Common Agricultural Policy. The new impetus, stimulated by the former French finance minister Jacques Delors, was identified in 1984 with the appeal of a truly free and open market. Such a market would counter the economic strengths and advantages of Japan, and the U.S.A. The ambitious blue-print for a large frontier free area, with some 320 million players (as consumers, businessmen, small savers, tourists, parents) is the grand design which informs our thinking.

To quote Delors:
"The countries of Europe are staking their survival in a world race against the clock. They have to find a common objective that could transcend daily routine, unite their forces, and harness their energies. On my arrival at the Commission, I therefore proposed to the European Parliament and the Heads of State or Government that between now (1984) and 1992 we should create an integrated economic area based on solidarity...."

Delors succeeded Gaston Thorn as President of the Commission on 1 January 1985.

The key to this publication, and the chapters that follow, is that The Commission of the European Comunities has presented the proposals it considers necessary for the creation of a frontier-free area, and attaches particular importance to Community nationals being free to work wherever they like in the Community and without having to go through discouraging formalities. Some important changes and developments, with consequences for education and for teachers, have already taken place. Thus:

(i) a person qualified to practise a profession in one country was frequently required to requalify in order to continue the same profession in another country. The Commission has introduced a directive (proposed on 9 July 1985) by which higher education diplomas will be recognised in all member states;

(ii) the recognition of professional qualifications already exists for a small number of professions, including Architecture, Medicine and Dentistry. New arrangements will extend this recognition to all professions, including Teaching. In late 1988 M. Marin, the Commission's Vice-President, argued strongly for the elimination of barriers to the free movement of teachers and others in certain public sector areas.

(iii) the removal of internal barriers will also have the effect of creating a single communications market, community-wide controls on consumer protection, freedom of movement for capital and encourage the establishment of European banks and insurance companies. Communication about such issues in a revamped and better-adapted education system must be a sine qua non of such changes.

(iv) additional to such developments are the programmes supported by the Community to facilitate movement, exchanges, the cross fertilisation of ideas and the increased awareness which should result. ERASMUS (European Action Scheme for the Mobility of University Students); COMETT (the Community Action Programme for Education and Training for Technology); DELTA (Developing European Learning through Technological Advance), and other programmes dealing with research are currently important. Since 1987 (when the ERASMUS programme was launched) it has been possible to finance more than 1000 inter-university co-operation programmes, and some 16,000 students have been able to study abroad.[1] The COMETT programme has been operational since 1987, and by late 1988 over 300 projects involving some 2,400 students and 125 university enterprise training partnerships (EUTPs) had been selected for support. The success of these programmes was noted by the Ministers at the Education Council (November 1988) and decisions were taken to upgrade their quality and to extend their scope.

(v) The LINGUA programme, to promote the teaching and learning of languages in the European Community, was adopted by the Commission in 1988. This strategy for action involved a common set of guidelines, applied by Member States and with Community activities drawn up support initiatives. Included in the guidelines was encouragement for young people "to study at least one foreign community language during the period of full time compulsory education, and to acquire a working knowledge of two Community languages".

Such a brief catalogue of activity cannot do justice to the range of individual and corporate initiatives that have been taken, and will continue throughout the 1990s, personal contacts and exchanges of all kinds, and the contributions made by the Euro-institutions, including the

European Schools, the College of Europe, and the European University. Alongside, the information network, EURYDICE, has been designed to underpin the developing programme of educational co-operation within the Community. Each member state has designated at least one National Unit to participate within the network, to contribute information on innovations and changes, and to help increase the flow of information within the area of educational policy.[2]

Complementary to the information provided by EURYDICE are the policy overviews developed by EPIC (European Policy Information Centre) Europe.[3] For an even broader context the regular reports and seminars arranged by The Council of Europe, and the Newsletters published quarterly by The Documentation Centre for Education in Europe[4] provide additional and overlapping information and data.

Thus far the growing range of initiatives - whether for information, survey, exchange or analysis - are symptoms of the desire to know better the educational contexts of different member states, and the broader backloth of change. Of a complementary nature are those initiatives which focus upon the incorporation of the European dimension into educational systems, into teacher training programmes, and in relation to personal contacts and exchanges arranged between pupils and teachers from different countries.

The European Association of Teachers (*Association Européene des Enseignants. A.E.D.E.*), without whose co-operation and help this publication would not have been possible, is one major teachers' organisation concerned with promoting a European consciousness. Its main purpose is to create amongst teachers an awareness of European problems and a deeper understanding of those essential qualities which are characteristic of European civilisation, as well as to support international contacts at the personal level.

Founded in Paris in 1956 by a group of French and German professors (many of whom had worked in wartime resistance groups) its membership has spread to all EC member countries and beyond, including Switzerland and Austria. The co-operation and information supplied by members of the various AEDE sections, and the help and support of other teachers, has made these chapters possible. (see also appendix I)

The work of AEDE/EAT is, in fact, complemented by the May 1988 resolution of the Council and Ministers of Education meeting on the subject of the European dimension in education. The resolution includes objectives and action at the level of Member States, and at the level of the European Community (see appendix II). The European Teachers' Association, at its congress in Njmegen in 1989, considered its own strategy for supporting such resolutions within its membership. Parallel or related organisations (including such groupings as The Centre for European Education; and The Association for Teacher Education in Europe (A.T.E.E.)) have made their own plans and priorities for action.

This publication looks especially at dimensions of the teaching profession in the different countries. Matters related to recruitment, training, recognition and status, probation, teaching conditions, career advancement and inservice opportunities are identified and developed. The mosaic is colourful and by no means automatically duplicated, or easily transferable from one country to another. The cultural envelopes remain strong.

Nonetheless, in June 1988 the Council of Ministers agreed the text of a directive which will come into force in the 1990s. This directive states that one member state should treat the professional qualifications of another on a par with its own. Adaptation to a different context, career prospect, or professional status is nevertheless inevitable.[5]

The discussions will not end. Indeed, "The Profession of Teachers" is a priority for the Commission, and meetings of the Ministers of Education in 1991. There is also likely to be further commitment to promoting co-operation between teacher education institutions; to the mobility of students and their teachers; to the development of the European dimension in teacher training, in teaching, and in school curricula.

It is hoped that this volume will enable teachers who contemplate moving from one country to another, and those interested in the permutations and interpretations of training and teaching elsewhere to become more aware and knowledgeable about the prospects and problems. We may also become involved in a tour of insights into the nature of the teaching profession and, indeed, how a professional is defined and recognised.

The changing face of Europe has been dominant news in the late 1980's and in the early years of the 1990's. The chapters that follow have been written against a background of West European integration, and all that this entails and implies. In addition to the Community member countries, Austria and Switzerland have also been included (and where AEDE sections exist). The experiences of Sweden have also been added. For long a country of political stability, and rolling reforms, teachers in Sweden have become increasingly concerned about pay and working conditions. Austria has applied for EC membership, and Sweden has announced that it will apply, formally, on July 1st 1991.

By the end of the 1990's it is likely that an enlarged European home, and openings to the East will cause us to rethink many of the chapters that follow. Nevertheless 1992 represents a crucial year in the momentum towards integration, and a basis upon which to contemplate further enlargement and accommodation of interests.

Footnotes

1 Useful publications include: The Student's Handbook in the European Community; The ERASMUS Newsletter; and the ICP Directory giving details of inter-university co-operation programmes.

2 The Eurydice European Unit (Rue Archimede 17/B 17, B-1040 Brussels) has published source data on such areas as: Initial Teacher Training in the Member States of the European Community (1987); The Education Structures in the Member States of the European Communities (1986); Employment and Status of Teachers in State Schools in the European Community (1987); Tables on the School Year (1987).

3 Policy overviews of relevance to this publication, and published over the period 1986-1988, include Headteacher Appointment; Parental Participation in Education); Recruiting

Teachers of shortage Subjects; Assessment and Promotion of School Pupils; Access to information on schools, pupils and teachers; and Educational Provision for pupils with physical handicaps.

4 *Obtainable from: Council of Europe, Documentation Centre for Education in Europe, BP 431 R6, F - 67006, Strasbourg Cedex.*

5 *France offers a pointed example of discrimination against non-nationals. Only French teaching qualifications are recognised and non-nationals are usually employed only in private schools or in adult education centres on vacataire contracts with low hourly rates of pay. Hopefully this practice will change before 1993.*

Professional identity and recognition

PROFESSIONAL IDENTITY AND RECOGNITION

What is professional identity? Are there any common denominators? What key issues emerge? What are the problems in terms of the mobility of teachers?

Undoubtedly these are shared concerns and, despite the variety of political systems and life styles, governments face broadly similar problems within the educational field. The implications of new technology, changes in family structure, linking schools more closely with industry, problems of teacher status and pay levels, and matters of school attendance and classroom discipline are all generally shared. There are also agreed priorities, including the expansion of inservice training and professional development opportunity, and the need to enrich and inform the expertise needed by school heads and principals.[1] Above all the need to attract the right kind of candidate into teaching is generally recognised.

In the late 1980's such matters were the focus of Education Ministers, gathered in Helsinki to face the problem of "New Challenges for Teachers and their Education".[2] This conference, bringing together Education ministers from 18 European countries, agreed on major reforms which should be implemented at national level in their different countries. As such their blueprint could become an important common denominator in the development of professional identity in European countries in the 1990's.

The measures proposed include the following:

- The image of teachers should be improved to attract suitable candidates from other professions; more women teachers should be recruited.
- Inservice training should be seen as an integrated whole, and a form of permanent education.
- Teachers should take the main responsibility for appraising their own professional performance.
- Appraisal should not be based upon narrow educational objectives, such as academic achievement, but should take account of aims such as fostering the personal development of pupils.
- The recruitment of teacher trainers, head teachers, inspectors and administrators should be reviewed.
- Measures should be taken to alleviate unemployment, such as improving job mobility, counselling, retraining, job sharing and increasing the opportunities for part-time and short-term contracts.

A further matter to be considered is the context of demographic change in the EC member states, and the impact upon matters relating to recruitment and the professional development of teachers in the different countries. With the exception of Éire all member states have faced a sustained decline in their birth rates, leading to a fall in the numbers of young people in the school system, and a contraction in the demand for teachers.

Community-wide studies indicated a halt in the overall population decline in the UK, Luxembourg, The Netherlands and France by the late 1980's.[3] As a consequence some countries anticipate the implementation of special policies designed to attract the necessary numbers of students into teaching in the 1990's.

These include making a payment to student teachers whilst training within schools; programmes and provision to attract the more mature student into teaching; a concern for increasing the percentage of women teachers in promoted posts of different kinds; and an overall pre-occupation with maintaining quality in a profession identified as 'top heavy' in terms of years of service and distance from initial training.

Such matters have been recognised in the medium-term perspectives published by the Commission for the years 1989-92. These highlight the need to extend inservice training and the professional development of the teaching force. To quote from the Commission,

> *"Given the demographic context of mainly stable, or falling, school populations and a similarly stable teaching force, with low turn over and recruitment levels, the main emphasis for action to enhance performance must lie in extending participation in in-service training and ensuring that it is of high quality."*

There is recognition also of the wide differences which exist in terms of the length and nature of initial training, and of the nature of education offered in compulsory schools. In such respects it is recommended that:

> *"Strong encouragement should be given, at Community level, to promoting dialogue and cooperation amongst teacher-training staffs, to promote faster convergence of philosophy and practice in this area. This in turn could help reduce differences in approach to each age level of the compulsory school in the different countries and thus contribute to easier mobility between countries for pupils and their families, and for teachers themselves".*[4]

Placed against such a background the professional identity of teachers working in EC, and other countries included in this publication, may be addressed from a number of standpoints, viz:

1. Is the teacher recognised as a civil servant and thereby able to enjoy, the status and 'rewards' (such as lifelong tenure) of being a civil servant?
2. Is the teacher required to undertake a period of probation and/or temporary status, subject to review, before being granted a teacher's licence?
3. Is the teacher accorded status by virtue of being granted a title, or level within the profession following success in a competitive examination?
4. Is the teacher subject to regular review?

1. Professional Identity as a Civil Servant

The growing list of studies on the training and conditions of service of teachers, and on the quality of education, will provide the reader with a wealth of further data and detail.[5] In the context of this analysis we may note that recognition of teachers in EC member countries is predominantly given by the appropriate Ministry of Education, following the acquisition of the appropriate teaching diploma and (in some countries) following success in a competitive examination.

One exception is in Scotland where teachers must be admitted to the Register of The General Teaching council (GTC), which gives the teaching profession self-governing status.

Teachers seeking provisional registration with the GTC are expected to possess an appropriate teaching qualification and the completion of a satisfactory probation period will allow the teacher to become fully registered with the Council. Without this registration it would be impossible to teach in a publicly maintained school. Broadly similar procedures have been proposed for England and Wales, and for the Republic of Ireland (Éire).

Whatever the process of recognition or registration it is not always the case that civil servant status is granted to teachers. For EC member countries it is accorded to those who are recognised by their Ministry of Education (or registered with the Inspectorate, as in The Netherlands), and is evident in the countries of Denmark, France, Germany, Greece, Italy, Luxembourg, The Netherlands, Portugal and Spain. No such recognition is accorded to teachers working within the U.K., in the Republic of Ireland (Éire), nor in Belgium.

The country studies that follow will give further illustration of the civil service status and any conditions related to this. Clearly, being a civil servant has consequences for such matters as union membership and salary negotiations. It has also been closely tied to the idea of nationality, and has been a major issue in the discussions related to teacher mobility within the Community (see below).

2. Professional identity confirmed through a probation period, or by serving a satisfactory period as a temporary teacher.

Within the European Community a number of countries insist upon a period of work as a probationer, at least as a condition for employment in state schools. In general terms it may be noted that:-

a) only certain countries insist upon a period of probation; that this varies in length between the countries, and is subject to varying conditions in relation to the support and help available, and the form of assessment given; and that
b) satisfactory completion of such a probation period can give the teacher a specific status, or level of recognition within the profession.

In 1986 an analysis undertaken by the Eurydice European Unit[6] indicated that 9 countries provided some form of probation period for their teachers, viz:

Belgium: a minimum of 240 days;
FR Germany: variable in relation to the marks obtained;
France: 1-2 years;
Eire: at least one year;
Italy: 1 year practical training "in ruolo" after national competition;
Portugal: two years, including inservice training;
England and Wales: One year;
Scotland: 2 years;
Spain: 6 months 'practical trial'.

Such an analysis relates to the length of the probation period, but it is evident that there are further variations in the interpretation of 'probation', and in relation to such issues as:

- assessment procedures;
- support formally offered by 'mentors';
- a possible lighter teaching load;
- teaching of a smaller range of classes; or
- other provisions which might ease the beginning teacher into teaching in a supportive and helpful context.

The case studies in Part 2 will illustrate these differences more clearly, and at greater length. At this point, however, selected examples can be used to show something of the variety of practice that exists in relation to entry to professional status as a teacher, thus:-

a) In Germany, where a probation period might vary in relation to the mark (or grade) received;
b) In Scotland, where two years is the minimum period required, and where satisfactory performance is assessed by the school headteacher;
c) In Belgium, where all intending teachers are required to undertake a period of work in a temporary post;
d) In Luxembourg, where the intending teacher will receive some recompense as a "surveillant" or general supervisor of classes, and be able to teach a small number of lessons each week;
e) In The Netherlands, where no formal probation period exists.

Undoubtedly these are matters which may well be reviewed in the light of the concerns for high quality teachers, the greater prospects for mobility between countries, and the pressures for change coming from international bodies. Even in 1966 the World Confederation of Organisations of the Teaching Profession (W.C.O.P.T.) supported the UNESCO/ILO recommendations relating to the status of teachers. Amongst other matters, these state that:

> *"access to pre-service and inservice education, of sufficient quality to permit the teacher to function competently and confidently, effective induction procedures, and fair and impartial assessment are all pre-requisites to the maintenance of a good school system".*

More recently we may note that the Council for cultural Co-operation has produced recommendations which include the concern that, for any new teacher,

> *"there should be a reduction of the number of lessons to be given by the new teacher during his first years and that colleagues and superiors should help newcomers settle down "harmoniously" in the life of the school."*[7]

3. Professional identity and competitive success

We have already noted that many countries accord a civil service status to teachers. some will also award teaching posts as a result of success in competitive examinations. Two examples may be cited at this stage. In Italy, where professional status is enhanced by success in a series of examinations; and in France, where status and working conditions can be considerably affected by success in competitive examinations.

In the case of Italy a complex situation may be summarised as follows:
Primary school teachers, awarded a state diploma (*Maturita magistrale*) at the end of their course in an *istituto magistrale*, will enter for a competitive examination at provincial level. Secondary school teachers must normally possess a university degree and may also have a further qualification in the *abilitazione* examination - in essence a minimum professional preparation.

In all cases such teachers will apply to be entered on temporary teacher lists drawn up by the local provincial government representative, the *Provveditori*. Ranking on these lists will reflect the teacher's status, temporary teaching experience to date, pass level in a degree examination and other matters. The competitive examination (or *Concorso)* will be arranged from time to time in relation to the permanent jobs that become available.

Success in the written and oral tests of the *Concorso* will normally enable the temporary teacher to be placed upon the permanent list (*"di ruolo")*, and be offered a teaching post. Satisfactory teaching during a one year probation period, judged by the school headteacher (*preside*), will lead to the status of *Ruolo Ordinario*. For a secondary school teacher, therefore, the progression of professional status might well be as follows:

- possession of degree only: non *abilitate*;
- possession of degree and abilitaxione: *abilitate*;
- temporary teacher: *precare*;
- success in concorso examination: *Ruolo straordinario*;
- success in one year probation: *Ruolo ordinario*

In such a progression professional status is enhanced through success in examinations and by a successful probation period. Furthermore, the degree of success will influence placing within lists and the prospects of a teaching job being offered in locations which might be deemed more or less desirable.

The example of French practice also involves the organisation of highly competitive examinations, related not only to job availability (and therefore as a means of controlling numbers) but very obviously to status and working conditions within the secondary school sector. The competitive examinations will relate to a specified number of posts, and will not immediately reflect teaching proficiency nor practical classroom skills. Before competing, however, the candidate will normally undertake preparatory work for at least one year, and undertake to serve the State for a period of 10 years. In exchange the government is bound to offer a post to the successful candidate.

The examination will be either for the CAPES (*Certificat d'Aptitude Professionelle á l'Enseignement Secondaire*) or for the higher level *Agrégé*.[8] Normally the CAPES holder will teach for 18 hours each week, and the *Agrégé* for 15 hours.[9] It can also be noted that the location of employment, and especially at the beginning teaching stage, may be influenced by the level of pass obtained in the examination. Certain other conditions, such as marital status, number of children, and teaching experience as a temporary teacher may be taken into account. Given the massive teacher shortages facing the Education Minister at the end of the 1980's and the slim chances of success in these highly competitive examinations, the current policy has been to offer more passes. A 40% increase was announced for 1989, for example. Even so, not all successful candidates take up the offer of a post. In 1988 a quarter of CAPES posts, and 15% of *Agrégation* posts were turned down.

4. Is the teacher subject to regular review?

We have already noted that the Standing Conference of European Ministers of Education (Helsinki, 1987) included amongst its proposals that:

- teachers should take the main responsibility for appraising their own professional performance, and that
- appraisal should not be based upon narrow educational objectives.....but should take account of aims such as fostering the personal development of pupils.

For the EC the main emphasis for action - in terms of the professional development of teachers - is on extending participation in inservice training and ensuring that it is of high quality.

The country studies will illustrate the nature and purpose of teacher review, where this exists, and it is evident that the introduction of teacher appraisal schemes has been a feature of discussion in some areas. Pilot schemes have been introduced in parts of the U.K., for example. For the general European context we may also note the recommendations of the ILO (International Labour Organisation) - UNESCO members, and those of the WCOPT (World Confederation of Organisations of the teaching profession).

The ILO/UNESCO recommendation was adopted in 1966 and in relation to the status of the teaching profession. Paragraphs 63,64 and 65 on the rights and responsibilities of teachers, and their right to professional freedom, are of particular relevance:

- *"Any system of inspection or supervision should be designed to encourage and help teachers in the performance of their professional tasks and should be such as not to diminish the freedom, initiative and responsibility of teachers.*

- *Where any kind of direct assessment of the teacher's work is required such assessment should be objective and should be known to the teacher.*
- *Teachers should have the right to appeal against assessments which they deem to be unjustified.*

- *Teachers should be free to make use of such evaluation techniques as they may deem useful for the appraisal of pupils' progress, but should ensure that no unfairness to individual pupils results".*

The WCOPT study, drawing upon responses from 16 organisations, indicated there was very often no official assessment of teachers; in the few countries where such an official system exists (as in Cyprus; Finland; France; Germany; Ireland; and Malta) the assessment is mostly done by inspectors; headteachers and educational officers.[10] A number of key clarifying principles, drawn up by the WCOPT in 1988, include the following:

- *"that the purpose of appraisal is to improve the overall quality of the educational system.....in particular by assisting the process of staff development;*
- *that the appraisal of teachers is accordingly only one element in the appraisal of the efficiency and quality of teaching;*
- *that appraisal should not be used as a means of encouraging competition between teachers nor lead to a reduction in each individual teacher's independence and responsibility in the classroom. It must on no account be linked with disciplinary measures which might lead to the reduction of status or salary of the individual teacher. Similarly, appraisal should not lead to the classification of schools".*

The country descriptions in Part II contain details illustrating both the wide variations in policy and practice, and also the procedures, where these exist, for assessing the competence of teachers beyond probation or beyond the initial temporary period of service. Some indicators are therefore available in terms of how competence is defined, who is involved, the frequency of assessment and what - in the event of poor or high level competence - might follow upon a formalised review process.

Examples may now be taken from France, Belgium, The Netherlands, Germany and the UK. In France, where there exists a distinct hierarchy in the teaching force, initial advice and help may come from the school inspectors. From time to time, throughout their career, teachers will be inspected and the result expressed in a '*note*' or mark given for their performance in pedagogic and administrative duties. On a scale of 20, the grading of performance is as follows:

Bad..........................	less than 10
Mediocre...............	10-11
Fairly Good..........	12
Good....................	13-14
Very Good............	15
Exceptional..........	16

To take the example of a secondary school *(lycée)* the Headteacher *(Proviseur)* is required to complete a "*Notice Annuelle de Notation*" which will include a mark (or *note*) on such issues as professional behaviour, punctuality, disciplines, authority, general professional bearing, and relationships with parents and with the community in general. An annual comment *(appréciation générale)* is also written. In addition the beginning teacher will normally be inspected by the *département* inspector and given a mark on the scale 1-20. Frequency of inspection may subsequently depend upon the initial mark given and other pressures upon the inspector.

Particularly significant for the teacher will be the effect that a high or low mark will have on acceleration or delay in moving up the salary scale. A good mark may well mean that promotion from one salary step to another will be about every two years; a poor mark perhaps over every 3-4 years; and the maximum salary step being reached after some 30 years instead of possibly 20. A further issue will be related to a change of school, and where the inspector's mark, the annual "*note*" and other criteria will be taken into account. In the most sought after schools the inspector's opinion will be very important indeed.

In Belgium, once nomination has occurred it is likely that the established teacher will receive less frequent formal visits from either the headteacher or a school inspector. In general terms the Headteacher will be responsible for reports on temporary teachers and *stagiers*.[11] Beyond this level an inspection might take place every five years or so, unless there are other circumstances (e.g. where a teacher is deemed to be exceptionally poor, or where a request has been made in connection with possible promotion).

In contrast to earlier inspections, where recommendations are made on a three point scale, these later inspections will result in the award of points to the teacher, according to the following pattern:-

Professionalism...	(maximum)	10 points
Influence on the education of the child.........	(maximum)	10 points
Personal presentation..................................	(maximum)	5 points
Use of language...	(maximum)	5 points
Professional commitment.............................	(maximum)	5 points
Responsibilities undertaken..........................	(maximum)	5 points
		(total 40 points)

Points will result in a grade or achievement level reached, in relation to the following scale:-

less than 24 points..................	Unsatisfactory
24-32......................................	Good
32-36......................................	Very good
more than 36 points...............	Exceptional

An exceptional award will normally justify a personal letter of congratulations from the General Inspector. An unsatisfactory report may be accompanied by suggestions for improvement in teaching method and general professionalism. There are no penalties nor more rapid increases up the salary scale, but a series of very good or exceptional marks as a nominated teacher will be helpful in relation to promotion prospects.

Broadly similar to the practice in Belgium and France, it is likely that German school inspectors will visit all teachers, and see them teaching at least once every six years. This will continue until the teacher reaches the age of 55, or thereabouts - depending on the state concerned.

In Bavaria, for example, inspections are usually held every three years, following which a grade will be awarded on a 5 point scale, viz:-

Highly satisfactory;
Satisfactory;
Satisfactory with some deficiences;
Minimally satisfactory;
Unsatisfactory.

Examples of the appraisal of teacher's duties are given below (see Teaching in Germany). Those teachers who are deemed to be unsatisfactory in their performance could eventually lose their job and those who are shown to have some deficiences will be required to take further courses arranged specifically for them.

Within the UK, and related to the context of promotion it may be argued that some form of internal assessment, mock interview or evaluation has often been exercised by Headteachers for the benefit of staff who are interested in promotion. For the period of probation a teacher in England or Wales is normally assessed by a local school inspector and in co-operation with the headteacher.

Additionally, and throughout the late 1970's, a number of Education Authorities in England and Wales also introduced checklists to aid school and self evaluation processes. In some cases these local publications were to help heads prepare reports, and instigate school review procedures related to the demands made by school governing bodies.

In Scotland there have been similar developments. Some of the Regional Authorities have devised school-evaluation schedules and there are firm proposals to implement a system of teacher appraisal by 1992. Teachers are now resigned to the fact that successful completion of the probationary period is not the end of the assessment process. Individual teacher competence will require to be demonstrated at regular intervals, just as schools overall will be expected to meet certain performance criteria. Staff who are not performing as well as they might be will be identified, and help will be offered. Training vouchers might be made available to undertake inservice training courses appropriate to personal needs, to job satisfaction, and to career development.

To summarise, it is evident from the foregoing examples that the notion of teaching competence is interpreted in a variety of ways. In some countries regular school reports and/or external inspection are quite evident and continued at intervals throughout the teacher's career. These can have an effect on salary, status and possible advancement. In other countries (Sweden, Eire, Italy, Greece may be cited) there is little evidence of similar practice or policy.

The issue of maintaining inservice training and staff development as a major priority area, albeit with many unsolved problems, is a key issue for EC member states. Many new initiatives are at an early stage, for example, new structures to co-ordinate inservice training include -

- *'Missions'* in each French Academy or administrative region to co-ordinate inservice work;
- *Centres* (IRRSAE) in each region of Italy to organise inservice activity, and to act as a focal point for regional and national initiatives;
- growing contributions from teacher training institutions in Denmark;
- a multi level grand plan in Scotland, to include certificates, advanced diplomas, and Master's degrees.

Nonetheless it is also the case that studies related to the involvement of teachers in inservice training indicate that in all EC countries there is a significant number who never participate, and that the organisation of inservice provision is very different in the member states - in terms of scale, scope, and coherence.[12] Improvement in the quality of teaching, and the enhanced professionalism of the teaching force in the Community countries remains a key challenge for the 21st century.

Teaching as a Career

Thus far we have noted some of the many variations in policy and practice which relate to matters of probation, temporary or provisional employment, teacher assessment, appraisal policy, and advancement through success in different kinds of competitive examinations.
It is inevitable that there are also different perspectives on teaching - as a career - and that there will be variation in terms of opportunities for promotion and advancement.

Several categories of professional opportunity exist. At one extreme there are countries such as England, Wales and Scotland where a clear hierarchy of promoted posts is evident. In these circumstances the ambitious teacher may aim for advancement up a professional 'ladder'. In the UK some 40% of staff hold promoted posts and not to have won promotion after a number of years teaching may even be seen as a mark of failure. Rewards can be high and the Headteacher of a school may earn more than twice the salary of an unpromoted teacher.

At the other extreme are systems where there is little or no sense of career development through promotion. In these cases administrative tasks may be carried out voluntarily and without extra remuneration. Nor are the 'top' posts of 'Director' or 'Secretary' much sought after. In Spain, for example, such appointments are the result of a vote by staff; the appointment is for a limited period, and the financial rewards are negligible. In The Netherlands it is evident that "duty points" can be awarded to a member of staff to undertake some administrative duties.

Elsewhere, as we have seen, success in a competitive examination may lead to a further qualification, and increased status - often leading to a reduction in the number of teaching hours, and an increased level of pay. France provides a good example of such practice. There are also countries where competitive examinations are set for a small number of posts at Headteacher or Inspector level, and where success might lead to nomination to such a post. Generally, these arrangements are in line with normal civil service procedures existing in those countries.

Readers may also wish to refer to other studies, undertaken during the 1980's, related to the appointment and training of school headteachers.[13] It may added that for many countries (including Belgium, Denmark, France, Germany, Italy, Luxembourg and The Netherlands) neither the individual school nor its governing body (where this exists) will have much influence upon the choice of a new headteacher.

Career prospects for women

A related issue is that of opportunities for women to continue their professional advancement, perhaps to the rank of Headteacher/Principal or to becoming a School Inspector.

It has long been the case that equal treatment for women has been a priority. Within the European Community The Treaty of Rome provided for equal pay, and an EC Directive on equal pay has been in force since 1976. Further EC legislation covering equal access to employment, vocational training and promotion, and equal treatment in social security matters has been in place since 1978. Other documentation includes:

- *The Position of Girls in the Second Level of Education*: European Action Programme at Community level (1976)
- *Equal Opportunity for Women*: European File (1984)
- *You and the European Community*: Making Equal Opportunities Work. Background Report (1987)
- *Sex Discrimination is Unfair*: The Equal Opportunities Record of the European Community (1987)

Thus, for the European Community, the elimination of sex discrimination is a long-term challenge, and continues as a priority for the 1990's. In May 1990 the Council of Ministers formulated draft conclusions on the promotion of equality of opportunity in education, and through the initial and inservice training of teachers. Nonetheless, Commission figures indicate that job segregation is as rife as ever. Some 73% of women work in the service sector; 20% in industry; and 8% in agriculture. Given the huge demographic changes in Europe in the 1990's, with fewer young people entering the labour markets, it is likely that more women will be returning to work, with massive implications for retraining schemes and increases in child care provision. Against this general background it can be added that the percentage of women involved in work as school Heads, School Inspectors or similar is small, compared with males.

Career expectations, social conditioning and education itself mean that in many EC countries less than 25% of secondary school Headteachers and School Inspectors are women and, in some cases, the percentages are far smaller. In Spain and Portugal 34%-35% of School Inspectors are women, and in Greece 43.5% of its secondary Headteachers are women. Where the Primary school is clearly defined (e.g. Belgium, Spain, Greece, France, Eire) about 40%-47% of primary Heads are women. In Scotland the figure is 61%, and in Portugal 90%.[14]

In 1988 there was evidence that some countries were adopting promotion policies which would give positive discrimination in favour of women. In the Irish Republic, for example, women teachers had been urged by their union, The Irish National Teachers' Organisation, to apply for top jobs in primary schools. In that country three out of four teachers are women yet only one woman teacher out of every 10 becomes a school head compared with 4 out of every 10 male teachers. The Union has prepared a pamphlet on promoting gender equality in primary school teaching.

Other policies include the provision of better childcare facilities in order to attract women teachers with children back to the classroom. Some countries are making plans for this. In

England it is possible that an Education Support Grant will be given to authorities for setting up school-based crèches, and in London the local authorities are making serious efforts to retain working mothers by making more money available for childcare schemes. By contrast the French Education Ministry has done little to encourage mothers to take up teaching, but the long established and well organised child care system is an important contribution. Nursery schools in France have crèches so that working mothers can deposit children early in the morning and pick them up late in the evening. Teachers also have public servant status, and this entitles them to attractive benefits. These include bonus payments per child, and also the right to choose to work between 50% - 80% of the normal number of hours, with a corresponding cut in salary. In addition mothers with three or more children have been exempt from the age limit normally imposed on teachers for the two secondary teacher qualifying examinations (i.e. the *Certificate d'aptitude au professorat d'enseignement secondaire*, and the *Agrégation*).

Retirement from Work:

Closely linked to the matter of equal opportunities for men and women is the possibility that the retirement age for women could be raised. In mid 1989 discussions resumed within the European Community on a draft directive which would require member states to bring forward legislation to equalise state pension ages. Legislation was envisaged as being introduced six years after the directive is agreed, and then implemented over a 10 year period. Implementation may well take longer, and well into the 21st Century. Nonetheless, in some countries, Ministers have been studying ways of phasing in an increase in the retirement age for women.

In mid 1989 Pension ages in the European Community were as follows:

	Men	Women		Men	Women
Belgium	65	60	Italy	60	55
Denmark	67	67	Luxembourg	60-65	55-65
France	60	60	Netherlands	65	65
Germany	65	65	Portugal	65	62
Greece	65	60	Spain	65	65
Ireland	66	66	UK	65	60

Against this background a particularly significant decision was that taken by the European Court of Justice in May 1990. In effect the Court ruled that pension benefits and retirement ages for men and women must be the same. The European Court decided that occupational pensions were part of the wide concept of "pay", within the guarantee of equality between the sexes in Article 119 of the Treaty of Rome, and that the use of different age requirements for men and women as a condition for obtaining those benefits is contrary to Community law. The Court also held that every element in an employee's remuneration must be equal to the remuneration of a comparable employee of the other sex.[15]

Footnotes

1. *See, for example: Buckley, J. The Training of Secondary School Heads in Western Europe. Council of Europe/N.F.E.R. - Nelson 1985*

2. *Conference of Education Ministers, Helsinki 1987 "New Challenges for Teachers and their Education". Council of Europe Standing Conference of European Ministers of Education.*

3. *See also: The Patterns of Demographic Change in the Education Systems of the European Community. EC monograph 1983 and, Europe in figures. Luxembourg 1988. Section 9 Demographic Trends.*

4. *Education in the EC Medium-term perspectives: 1989-1992 (Section d. Professional development of the teaching force.) Commission of the European Communities. Brussels, 18 May 1988.*

5 *For Example*
   - *Commission of the European Communities. Studies. Education Series No. 8 Inservice Education and training of teachers in the European Community 1979*
   - *Regulations concerning Compulsory Schooling in Member States of the European community. 3rd Edition. Eurydice European Unit 1985*
   - *The Education Structures in the Member States of the European Communities. Eurydice 1986*
   - *Employment and Status of Teachers in State Schools in the European Community. Eurydice 1986*
   - *Initial Teacher Training in the Member States of the European Community. Eurydice 1986*
   - *Tables on the School Year in the Member States of the European Community. Eurydice 1987*
   - *The Conditions of Service of Teachers in The European Community. Commission of the European community 1988*
   - *Education in OECD Countries. 1987 - 1988. A Compendium of Statistical Information. OEDC 1990.*

6 *Employment and Status of Teachers in State Schools in the European Community Eurydice European Unit, Brussels. 1986*

7 *Second Council of Europe Teachers' Seminar. "The newly-qualified teacher: the first years". Council for Cultural Co-operation. Donaueschingen, October 1978*

8. *For further details of these examinations readers should refer to the country section on France.*

9 *A teacher with the agrégation need only put in a maximum of 17 hours actual teaching per week; a teacher with the CAPES only 20 hours. Both are paid overtime for any extra teaching, as well as bonuses for attending school meetings and acting as a form master or mistress.*

10 *Report on Appraisal of Teaching. Joint WCOPT - Council of Europe Seminar.. Strasbourg, France. April 1988*

11 *A full explanation of the conditions related to these levels of teaching is given in the chapter on Belgium.*

12 *The Inservice Training of Teachers in the twelve Member States of the European Community. Commission of the European Communities. Eurydice Education Policy Series. V. Blackburn and C. Moisan. 1986.*

13 *Appointment of Headteachers. Procedures in selected Member States of the European Community. Joanna Le Metais. EPIC Europe. (Revised) August 1987.*
The Training of Secondary School Heads in Western Europe. John Buckley. NFER - Nelson 1985 School Management Training in Europe. Report. Council of Europe/Council for Cultural Co-operation. Strasbourg 1983

14 *See also: Breakdown by Sex of the Numbers of Inspectors and Headteachers in the Education System of the Member States of the European Community. Eurydice European Unit. 1987.*
It may be noted that these figures represent the position in the mid 1980's. Very small percentages of women were employed as secondary Headteachers in the UK; Luxembourg; Denmark; and The Netherlands. For Inspectors Italy; Ireland; Greece; Scotland; and Denmark employed 15% or less of their workforce as women.

15 *At the end of 1990 The European Commission proposed a new action programme on equal opportunities for men and women (1991-1995). This follows the adoption by the Community of the Charter of Fundamental Social Rights for Workers, which provides for the implementation of an action programme to promote equal opportunities.*

The new action programme is the third in the line of medium term programmes begun in 1982 to promote equality of opportunity for men and women. It is expected to mark a new stage in equal opportunities policy with a more integrated and more comprehensive strategy for action, promising to build on Community achievements in the area and on the experience gained to date, and to develop new schemes to assist women in the field of vocational training and employment.

In essence the third action programme laid down three priority courses of Action:
- *application and development of the legal framework;*
- *promoting the occupational integration of women;*
- *improving the status of women in society.*

For teachers it is highly likely that the development of 'womens' studies', and the promotion of innovatory programmes and material which challenge traditional female stereotypes, will be part of pre-service and/or inservice programmes. Indeed, some institutions have already developed higher degree programmes for teachers involved in such issues.

Teacher mobility

TEACHER MOBILITY

The Community's internal market, which will remove political and fiscal barriers to trade and free the movement of capital and people between member states, is due for completion in 1992. Crucial to the free movement of manpower, as well as improved language training (with the aim being a knowledge of several Community languages by as many citizens as possible) is the mutual recognition of the different qualifications on offer in the various states.

There are other difficulties which have already been illustrated - the decline in demand for teachers, reflecting the demographic trends overall, and a growing concern that the professions in general (including nursing and the medical profession) will be competing for fewer well qualified teenagers as they finish school in the early 1990's.

Some general points may be noted. At least 6 million citizens now live and work in ECMember States other than their state of birth; 45 million workers live in frontier zones and either work in a different Member State than the one in which they live, or are affected by conditions pertaining to that neighbouring state.

Community legislation (Directive 64/221; Regulation 1612/68; Regulation 1251/70; and Directives 73/148 and 75/34) relates respectively to matters controlling restrictions on foreign nationals; access and residence for workers; the right to retire; and the rights of access, residence and retirement to the self-employed. Every citizen has a right to leave his country and to enter another Member State to take up employment.

Alongside such matters we may recall some of the many achievements in developing a "People's Europe". The common format European passport is gradually being introduced in all Member States; the Resolution on the removal of customs signs; use of the European flag and Anthem; the introduction of an EC National channel for entry at ports and airports. Such a context is one for enhanced student, teacher, and researcher mobility.

Over the years there have been very effective measures adopted in order to facilitate academic mobility. The European Conventions on the equivalence of Diplomas leading to Admission to Universities; on the Academic Recognition of University Qualifications; on the Equivalence of Periods of University Study; and on Continued Payment of Scholarships are all milestones of significance. The European Network of National Information Centres on Academic Mobility and Equivalence (set up by the Council of Europe) meets annually, and discusses the problems raised by mobility and equivalence in a "greater" Europe, which includes the Council of Europe's Community and non-Community member states, as well as Finland and Yugoslavia.

There has also been important growth and recognition given to the ERASMUS programme adopted in June 1987, and COMETT, which is launching a further 5 year phase from January 1990.

All the member states, as well as representatives of the former German Democratic Republic and Poland, have shown a marked interest in the ERASMUS programme. Described as "a programme of hope for the young people of Europe" the action programme for the mobility of students and for co-operation in higher education devotes a major proportion of the annual budget for student mobility grants.[1]

COMETT (Community Action Programme for Education and Training for Technology) was operational from January 1st 1987 for university-enterprise co-operation in the field of training for technologies and their applications. The first results obtained in 1987 and 1988 saw: 125 university-enterprise training partnerships (UETPs); almost 400 exchange programmes involving 2,500 students (and more than 120 university and enterprise personnel); and almost 200 joint continuing training projects.[2]

For matters specifically pertaining to teachers it is important to remember that the different processes for recognising teachers; the varying lengths of probation; different attitudes to continued competence and/or appraisal; different career structures and pay scales - all these, and other factors, ensure that mobility is not simply a matter of recognising a qualification, but also recognising and adjusting to different 'cultural envelopes' surrounding the 'teacher and task'.

One significant development, in 1982, was the agreement amongst the Nordic countries (Denmark, Finland, Iceland, Norway, and Sweden) that enabled a class teacher qualified in one of those countries to be appointed as a teacher of general subjects in any of the other four countries. Any teacher taking up such a post would be expected to have command of the language in which he or she would work.

In the context of the European Community the following are the key reports, and a summary of the steps taken in the 1980's, and leading towards a teacher's right of access and employment in any Member State.

(i) **February 1984 European Parliament Working Documents, Report on the academic recognition of diplomas and periods of study (Rapporteur: Mr O. Schwencke)**

Amongst other things, this report pointed out that freedom of movement within the community, as guaranteed by the Treaties, must also apply to students, teachers, and those engaged in research, and should be promoted by facilitating mobility in the field of higher education.

We are also reminded that Article 3(c) of the Treaty of Rome states that the activities of the Community shall include 'the abolition, as between Member States, of obstacles to freedom of movement for persons, services and capital'.

(ii) **November 1985 European Parliament Working Documents. Report on the proposal from the Commission of the European Communities to the Council for a Directive on a general system for the recognition of higher education diplomas. (Rapporteur: Mrs N. Fontaine)**

This report, and its motion for a resolution, was based on "mutual confidence between the States concerning the professional value of the diplomas which they issue, verify, and validate", and asked the Commission (as early as possible) to take additional measures to ensure academic recognition of diplomas issued during or at the end of courses of university study - so as to facilitate student mobility within the Community and the recognition of all vocational proficiency certificates.

(iii) **October 1986 European Parliament Working Documents. Report on encouraging teacher mobility in the European Community (Recognition of teaching qualifications and a Community status for teachers). (Rapporteur: Mr W. Münch)**

In October 1986 the European Parliament adopted the Münch Report on Teacher mobility with the European Community.

The main recommendation was the removal of teaching from the exceptional provisions of Article 48 (4) of the Treaty of Rome, by which some member states excluded foreign teachers from permanent employment in their public education sector on grounds of nationality. Additionally, the commission was urged to "examine the different aspects of status which affect the possibility of being employed as a teacher, (and) to work out the aspects to be covered in a community statute on these matters..........."

By the mid 1980's, therefore, increased urgency was being given to a policy for mobility and exchange which could affect more than 5 million teachers working within the Community, and in daily contact with some 70 million young people, school children and students. The complexities related to differences between qualifications; security of the rights to return; career progression; and the retention of acquired rights to retirement pensions. Alongside this was the challenge of recognising the effects of the single market upon teachers who, in effect, were to become promoters of European awareness.

By 1988 some optimism was being expressed over reaching agreement on a proposed Europe-wide system of mutual recognition of higher education diplomas with the implication that lawyers, accountants, teachers, surveyors, bankers, actuaries and secretaries would be able to practise within the EC without having to totally re-qualify in their chosen country of residence.

(iv) **21 December 1988 Council Directive 'On a general system for the recognition of higher-education diplomas awarded on completion of professional education and training of at least three years' duration'.**

In 1988 this Directive indicated that detailed rules would be laid down regarding any adaptation period, and aptitude tests would be determined by host member states "with the aim of assessing the ability of the applicant to pursue a regulated profession in the Member State".[3]

Such developments inevitably raise further questions. The Council Directive was concerned with the recognition of qualifications and not with the right to employment; suitably qualified professionals should have the right of access - subject to any adaptation mechanisms to the regulated activities in other Member States. Where the migrant's training area of activity is 'significantly different' (a condition to be determined by the Member State) the adaptation mechanism would be brought into force. One factor to be taken into account is the age range of the pupils to which the training relates. Another is that a period of probation could be required where this was a condition of employment.[4] Linguistic ability is also relevant.

Hitherto a language test (except in the case of the Irish Republic) cannot be imposed as a barrier to freedom of movement, under Community law, and migrant teachers are not required to take a specific test. Nonetheless, language ability would be evident from any written application, and in any oral interview that might take place.[5]

FREEDOM OF MOVEMENT IN THE COMMUNITY
ENTRY AND RESIDENCE
by Jean-Claude SÉCHÉ
COMMISSION OF THE EUROPEAN COMMUNITIES

One further point relates to the initiatives that have been started to help teachers recruited by another EC country to prepare for their professional life within that new setting. Language assistants have usually received some orientation, but other initiatives have also been evident.

At the University of Amsterdam, for example, a course was started in session 1989-90 designed to give Dutch teachers recruited for London some idea of English teaching methods, and other professional matters. A 10 day course included intensive study of the English education system, from the examinations used to teaching techniques. Given increased mobility such initiatives are likely to grow.

Finally, we may be reminded that the desirability of teacher mobility has been further recognised by the WCOPT (World Confederation of the Organisations of the Teaching Profession). In 1982 this body adopted a recommendation for action, stating that:

"WCOPT, in cooperation with UNESCO, the International Bureau of Education, and regional organisations, should continue to work for the international recognition of teacher education qualifications on a regional and worldwide basis, thus allowing for the fact that it is highly desirable that teachers have the maximum mobility across national boundaries. WCOPT should do all it can to further the process which will render this ideal possible".

In the WCOPT Dublin conference report (1988) many factors were identified, and which may act as a hindrance to mobility of teachers.[6] Apart from language; differences in degrees, and level of professional qualification, a number of other factors included: salaries and conditions of service; family ties and marital status; socio economic conditions; teacher status; and differences in teacher education systems. Another important issue was the wide disparity existing between teachers' salaries and working conditions.

In spite of all such difficulties it is nonetheless apparent that WCOPT European member Unions are deeply interested in, and concerned with, the issue of mobility and the completion of the European internal market.[7] Whether a significant number of teachers will seek the wider opportunities available remains to be seen. The country case studies that follow provide a snapshot of the prospects, conditions of service, and career posibilities available.

Footnotes

1 *Further information is available from:*
ERASMUS Bureau, Rue d'Arlon 15,B - 1040 BRUSSELS, Belgium.

2 *Information is available from: COMETT Technical Assistance Unit, Avenue de Cortenbergh 71, B - 1040 Brussels.*

3 *A regulated professional activity was deemed to:*
- *award a diploma to its members;*
- *ensure that its members respect the rules of professional conduct which it prescribes;*
- *confers on them the right to use a title or designatory letters, or to benefit from a status corresponding to that diploma.*

At the end of 1990 the Commission proposed a further Directive which sought to complement the system established in Directive 89/48/EEC. When a Member State regulates the performance of a given activity by restricting it to those with a particular national qualification, then the proposed Directive would lay down the procedures for enabling Community nationals from other Member States to have recognised or taken into account:

- *qualifications achieved by higher education courses lasting less than 3 years, and qualifications recognised as equivalent to these:*
- *qualifications achieved by courses of secondary studies in general or technical education establishments, and qualifications recognised as equivalent to these;*
- *professional experience.*

The proposed Directive would not apply to regulated occupations which are the subject of specific Directives introducing mutual recognition of training courses completed before taking up the occupation (such as those covering doctors).

4 *We may note, from the UK standpoint, that the stance of the Government was to support in principle the inclusion of teachers within the European Council Directive, subject to agreement on full reciprocity and the adequate safeguarding of professional standards. The UK view of the aptitude test was that it should be sufficiently flexible to meet the particular needs of the profession (i.e. not only factual knowledge but linguistic competence and professional skills); that its contents should be decided by the host country; and that it should be sufficiently rigorous to protect consumers.*
Within Scotland, the General Teaching Council would no longer be able to reject teachers' qualifications solely because of their (possible) shorter duration when gained in

other Member states. Through the aptitude test, the work of its committees, and the special position of the GTC it is inevitable that this would be the "competent authority" for Scotland. Future procedures regarding "Exceptional Admission to the Register" are likely to include a probation period, as well as the knowledge and qualifications required for performance of the job on offer.

5 *In late 1989 The European Community Court of Justice backed Irish Government regulations which stipulate that teachers in public-sector schools must be able to speak in Irish. The Court rejected a discrimination claim by a Dutch born art lecturer who was refused a permanent post because she did not have a Certificate of competency in Irish. This ruling may have implications for other EC member states such as Luxembourg, where certain jobs and promotion depend upon knowing a minority language.*

6 *Draft Report on Teachers' Mobility in Europe. WCOPT report. Dublin European Conference Report. September 1988.*

7 *Readers are reminded of European Documentation specifically concerned with the general implications and challenges resulting from the completion of the internal market. In particular we may refer to:*

(i) *A General System for the Recognition of Higher Education Diplomas. Bulletin of the European Communities. Supplement 8/85 (1985)*

(ii) *Séché. Jean Claude: Freedom of Movement in the Community. (Luxembourg. 1988). This draws together key texts relating to right of entry and residence, and to inform the reader in what circumstances the right arises and what restrictions can be imposed on it. Matters relate to Entry and Residence (and the right to remain) for workers in paid employment; entry and residence (and the right to remain) for the self employed; and to matters concerning refugees.*

A fundamental provision is Article 7 of the EEC Treaty which prohibits any discrimination on grounds of nationality in the fields covered by the Treaty.

(iii) *Europe without frontiers: Completing the internal Market (Third Edition) (European Documentation. 2/1989. Luxemborg 1988).*

This booklet sets out to explain the main aspects of the Community's programme and to show what progress has been made. Matters relate to the removal of physical barriers to mobility, and to the removal of technical and fiscal barriers. In particular we may be reminded of the adoption, by the Council of Ministers, of the proposal on the mutual recognition of higher education diplomas (see above). This would enable individuals holding the relevant qualification from one Member State to practice in the field of their expertise in another Member State under the same conditions as individuals holding the relevant qualification of that other State(called the "home State").

(iv) *The European Community and Recognition of Diplomas for Professional Purposes. European File. Commission of the European Communities. 13/89 (October 1989).*

Teacher concerns and the unions

TEACHER CONCERNS AND THE UNIONS

Causes for Concern

Teachers individually and collectively, perhaps through their unions, express concern about a whole range of issues affecting education and affecting the profession. Among other things, teachers in at least some of the various European countries complain as follows:-

(i) The job is becoming too difficult; new demands are continually being foisted on teachers and the pace of change is too great.

(ii) Teachers are underpaid and undervalued; in some countries they take second jobs to make ends meet.

(iii) Working hours are being extended and working conditions are deteriorating.

(iv) Schools are under-resourced and under-financed.

(v) Too much control is exercised by non-professionals sometimes through excessively bureaucratic procedures, and educational planning is ineffective.

(vi) The pressures on teachers to accept programmes of re-training or staff development pose a threat, especially when these are not adequately resourced.

(vii) Often there is no proper career structure for teachers.

The fact that these are sometimes shared concerns reflects common background factors. Some of the factors are there because of the advent of 1993 and the moves towards closer economic and political union; other factors are more broadly-based.

That **education is in a state of flux** has become almost a cliché. Yet it is true. The 'explosion of knowledge' is well and truly with us; and the impact of information technology is radically altering both the teaching/learning situation and the role of the teacher. The school curriculum is becoming overcrowded as more and more is added: a balance between depth and breadth becomes harder to achieve. Underlying these matters, and perhaps more important, are uncertainties about the nature and purpose of education; to say that there is a crisis of values is not to overstate things. At a fundamental level, merely to re-iterate that society is (or ought to be) multicultural and pluralistic is at best an oversimplification, at worst a side-stepping of the problems. Education needs clear, practical aims and perhaps these are missing. At a time when compulsory education is being extended in a number of European countries this is particularly unfortunate. There are serious consequences at school level. A Scottish writer, when speaking of the 'prolonged period of teenage dependency', when 'parents are expected to give bed, board, limitless pocket money and near-adult freedoms to their teenage children, while expecting nothing in return but a load of cheek and a home rendered uninhabitable by disco-noise', continued as follows:-

*"The classic argument for it (teenage dependency) is that human children need a long, sophisticated education in order to achieve their full potential; in reality, a frightening proportion of British kids spend the years of compulsory education between 13 and 16 wasting their time, longing for the day when they can get out into the world, wrecking the prospects of other kids who seriously want to study, and making life hell for the unfortunates who have to keep the lid on their youthful energy and frustration throughout the school year - I mean **the Teachers**."*

(Joyce MacMillan The Glasgow Herald August 18th 1990).

This is by no means an exclusively British phenomenon. Others in EC countries say the same.

A second factor or set of factors is that of **demography**. This has already been referred to above: the population in the so-called advanced industrial societies has declined. School rolls have fallen. Teaching posts have been lost, and newly-trained teachers more often have been offered temporary contracts. There are also difficulties in actually recruiting new teachers as the various professions compete for smaller numbers of school-leavers.

A third factor is that of **the role of government in relation to education**. In most cases in one way or another this is being modified or at least it is under review. One trend is towards devolved decision-making; in a number of countries traditional tight control from the centre is being loosened ,at least as regards day-to-day administration. This may have consequences for teachers, especially in the case of England & Wales where a market forces view is leading to financial autonomy for individual schools: the numbers of teachers to be employed and the salaries bill become very important.

The market forces view is gaining favour, and it is seen as perhaps providing a much-needed equilibrium between the supply and demand for teaching posts. In conjunction with this goes an almost universal **attack on the public sector**: it is wasteful and expensive. Services such as education (which is particularly expensive) should be made more accountable. Employees in the private sector (i.e. industry etc) prefer not to bargain alongside employees in the state sector because their hand may be weakened.

Following from the demand for greater accountability are the arguments which **challenge the validity of current approaches to teacher training**. These arguments underline the importance of practical help and school experience for trainees while doubting the value of the more theoretical elements contained in professional studies programmes. Again, a more extreme version of this model where 'licensed' or 'articled' teachers are to be provided for in schools, without the participation of the training institutional. One can see why such approaches are attractive to central administrators with urgent problems of teacher shortage to contend with: long 4 or 5 year concurrent courses in expensive colleges do not easily find favour. Alternative modes of entry (e.g. recruiting scientists and mathematicians from now redundant military personnel) are sought after.

A sixth factor of importance to teachers has already been mentioned - the demand that **teacher competence** be demonstrated. The first step is to make sure that all employed teachers have been trained in the first place. Some extra stresses and strains are being placed on the teaching force as a consequence. Emergency measures are being taken (e.g. in Portugal where the newly-established Open University is playing its part).

A final background factor concerns the schools themselves. In most EC countries there is not the same awareness of schools as institutions requiring good management as there is in the UK. But this is slowly changing. Diplomas in school management are being established. The future may mean more, **better defined school management posts.** This could help satisfy teachers' demands for an overall improved career structure.

Teacher Unions

How are these concerns to be acted upon and by whom? One thinks first of all of the teacher unions - are they pursuing the same role as trade unions? In a sense they are the same although they have an interest in a broad range of professional issues, going beyond what are though of as usual union business. At least one union, The Educational Institute of Scotland, awards degrees for distinguished educational work!

However, teacher unions do participate in salary negotiations and they may attempt to put pressure on employers and another controlling authorities. This may not always be to the satisfaction of members. Take Sweden as an example, and the words of an Swedish colleague:-

"Most teachers are members of a Teachers' Union, (there are two of them) not so much of conviction as on account of loyalty and peer pressure. I do not think, however, it is too much to say that there is a widespread discontent among the members with the Unions. The fees we pay to the Union (c.1.600 Sw Kr a year) make it tempting to leave the Union, especially as they seem incapable to really do something for us - paywise or otherwise. Compared to what it was like in the 60's, which was a good decade, we - they say- lag behind by 20% in real wages. In Finland (where they have a school system very similar to ours) the terminal pay amounts to 18.000 Sw kr a month while in Sweden a teacher of a comparable status has 14.000 Sw kr a month, not to mention that there are other differences are regards professional prestige in the eyes of the public and differences in the actual working conditions." (1989 figures).

On the face of it the evidence from some other countries seems different. In **Germany**, the G.E.W. (Gewerkschaft Erziehung and Wissenschaft) which is also the biggest union, has sought conditions for teachers which are essentially similar to the public sector settlement and (in 1989) launched a campaign for workload reductions.

In **France** strike action has been prompted by a number of unions. Thus, the second largest of the teaching unions (SNES. Syndicat National des Ensignements du Second Degré) has demanded improved working conditions - notably in the lycées, and where teachers often face classes of 35 or even 40 pupils. The main union (the Syndicat National des Instituteurs et Professeurs d'Ensiegnement de College) and which includes both primary and secondary teachers has stressed that any changes in teachers' working conditions should not mean working longer hours.[1] Within **The Netherlands** the Union of Teaching Personnel (ABOP

Algemene Bond van Onderwijzend Personeel) has continued to press for teachers to be given the possibility of early retirement from the age of 56, thereby reducing the logistical problems within schools, and as a solution to create the problem (soon to pass) of how to create more jobs in the profession. In **Italy** teachers unions have agreed to the introduction, from September 1990, of a more flexible working week. Teachers should be able to chose between full time (currently 24 hours a week for primary teachers; 18 hours for secondary teachers); part-time; and a "super" full time position which will involve an extra three hours per week with a corresponding pay increase. Teachers who opt for such an extended working week would not be allowed to have other jobs.

Within **Belgium** economic cuts brought on by government economy measures in the mid 1980's prompted the francophone Federation of Christian Teachers (F.I.C.) - with support from parents and others teachers' bodies - to take legal action against the government at both national and European levels. In particular, changes in calculating subsidies for children of parents not subject to Belgian taxes caused the F.I.C. to start proceedings at the European Commission - against the government - for breaking the Treaty of Rome, which forbids discrimination on grounds of nationality, and lays down the principles of free movement of workers. In **Denmark**, the Danish National Teachers' Union (Danmarks Laererforening) has repeatedly called for strike action, and amassed strike funds in anticipation of difficulties, in the light of decreasing incomes amongst teachers compared with other wage groups.

The overall picture regarding teacher unions in EC countries is therefore very complex and unions may differ according to the sectors they represent - primary, lower secondary, upper secondary vocational, etc. There may also be separate unions representing university staffed teacher training personnel. A further division may be on the basis of religion; thus there are Catholic and Protestant unions and groupings, while linguistic differences may also determine affiliation as in Belgium and Spain. Private school staff can also have their own separate unions. The overall numbers for each country are as follows:-

Belgium (French speaking)	:	7
(Dutch speaking)	:	10
Denmark	:	14
F.R. Germany	:	3
Greece	:	4
Spain	:	12
France	:	24
Eire/Ireland	:	6
Italy	:	8
Luxembourg	:	3
Netherlands	:	4
Portugal	:	17
U.K. England and Wales	:	9
Scotland	:	4
(Further Education)	:	5

It has to be noted that unions may also be organised in federations, thus uniting forces when engaged in consultative or negotiating processes with government. The scene may not be as divided as it seems.

Furthermore, at an international level there are several significant groupings, including:-

World Confederation of Teachers (W.T.C.), with its HQ in Brussels; International Federation of Free Trade Unions, based in Amsterdam; and World Confederation of Organisations of the Teaching Profession (W.C.O.T.P.), based in Switzerland.

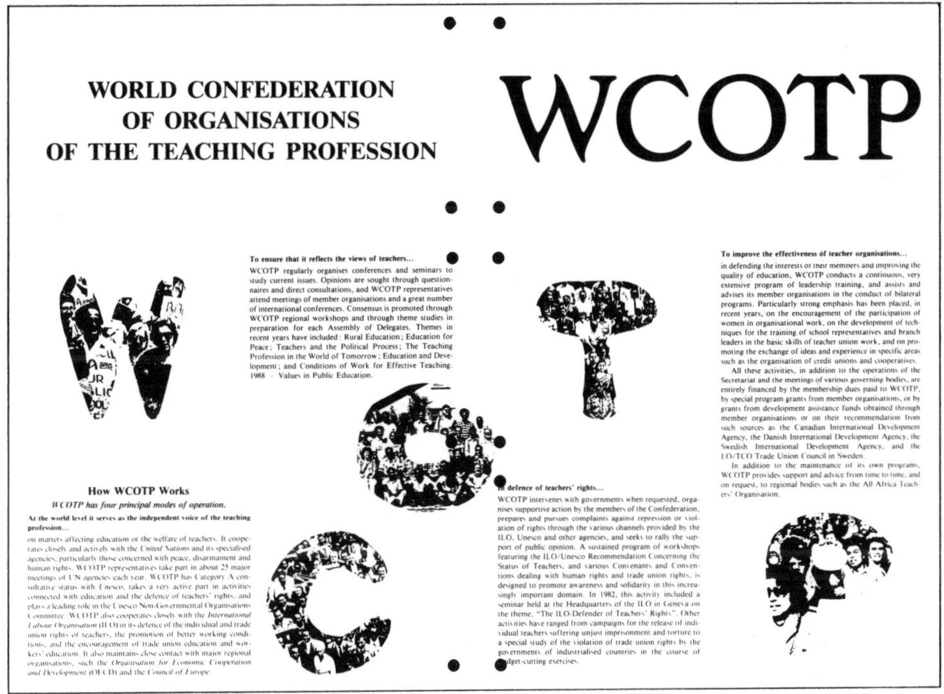

WORLD CONFEDERATION OF ORGANISATIONS OF THE TEACHING PROFESSION

WCOTP

How WCOTP Works

WCOTP has four principal modes of operation.

At the world level it serves as the independent voice of the teaching profession...
on matters affecting education or the welfare of teachers. It cooperates closely and actively with the *United Nations* and its specialised agencies, particularly those concerned with peace, disarmament and human rights. WCOTP representatives take part in about 25 major meetings of UN agencies each year. WCOTP has Category A consultative status with *Unesco*, takes a very active part in activities connected with education and the defence of teachers' rights, and plays a leading role in the Unesco Non-Governmental Organisations Committee. WCOTP also cooperates closely with the *International Labour Organisation* (ILO) in its defence of the individual and trade union rights of teachers, the promotion of better working conditions, and the encouragement of trade union education and workers' education. It also maintains close contact with major regional organisations, such the *Organisation for Economic Cooperation and Development* (OECD) and the *Council of Europe*.

To ensure that it reflects the views of teachers...
WCOTP regularly organises conferences and seminars to study current issues. Opinions are sought through questionnaires and direct consultations, and WCOTP representatives attend meetings of member organisations and a great number of international conferences. Consensus is promoted through WCOTP regional workshops and through theme studies in preparation for each Assembly of Delegates. Themes in recent years have included: Rural Education; Education for Peace; Teachers and the Political Process; The Teaching Profession in the World of Tomorrow; Education and Development; and Conditions of Work for Effective Teaching. 1988 - Values in Public Education.

In defence of teachers' rights...
WCOTP intervenes with governments when requested, organises supportive action by the members of the Confederation, prepares and pursues complaints against repression or violation of rights through the various channels provided by the ILO, Unesco and other agencies, and seeks to rally the support of public opinion. A sustained program of workshops featuring the ILO/Unesco Recommendation Concerning the Status of Teachers, and various Convenants and Conventions dealing with human rights and trade union rights, is designed to promote awareness and solidarity in this increasingly important domain. In 1982, this activity included a seminar held at the Headquarters of the ILO in Geneva on the theme, "The ILO-Defender of Teachers' Rights". Other activities have ranged from campaigns for the release of individual teachers suffering unjust imprisonment and torture to a special study of the violation of trade union rights by the governments of industrialised countries in the course of budget-cutting exercises.

To improve the effectiveness of teacher organisations...
in defending the interests of their members and improving the quality of education, WCOTP conducts a continuous, very extensive program of leadership training, and assists and advises its member organisations in the conduct of bilateral programs. Particularly strong emphasis has been placed, in recent years, on the encouragement of the participation of women in organisational work, on the development of techniques for the training of school representatives and branch leaders in the basic skills of teacher union work, and on promoting the exchange of ideas and experience in specific areas such as the organisation of credit unions and cooperatives.

All these activities, in addition to the operations of the Secretariat and the meetings of various governing bodies, are entirely financed by the membership dues paid to WCOTP, by special program grants from member organisations, or by grants from development assistance funds obtained through member organisations or on their recommendation from such sources as the Canadian International Development Agency, the Danish International Development Agency, the Swedish International Development Agency, and the LO/TCO Trade Union Council in Sweden.

In addition to the maintenance of its own programs, WCOTP provides support and advice from time to time, and on request, to regional bodies such as the All Africa Teachers' Organisation.

The last-named describes itself as having four principal modes of operation:-

(i) At the world level it serves as the independent voice of the teaching profession.
(ii) It organises conferences and seminars on current issues to ensure that it reflects the views of teachers.
(iii) It helps to defend the rights of teachers.
(iv) It attempts to improve the effectiveness of teacher organisations.

Returning to the broad European context the European Trade Union for Education (ETUCE) groups together some 53 unions representing the teachers of 18 member countries of the Council of Europe. These unions have some 3 million members, of which about 2.7 million come from Member States of the European Community. [2]

The ETUCE aims to ensure that the material and moral interests of its members and of the professions are defended in the various institutions of the European Community and the Council of Europe. ETUCE also aims to encourage the development of initial and inservice education. Its programme of action is defined annually by the general assembly of the ETUCE. Amongst other issues, its objectives are being pursued in:-

a campaign against young people's unemployment;
a campaign for equal opportunities for boys and girls;
campaign against the discriminatipm against women;
campaign against the privatisation of teaching.

Within the context of teacher mobility, the ETUCE also seeks to play an important role. A number of working groups are involved also in such matters as the COMETT and ERASMUS programmes, the transition from school to working life and matters related to post compulsory education.

In addition, and pertinent to this study, the Association Européenne des Enseignments (AEDE) is an association of teachers at all levels, with thirteen sections. AEDE is concerned with activities at both a European level and with activities at the national level organised by the different sections. By contrast with unions that are concerned with protecting the rights, working conditions, and salaries of their members the AEDE is concerned more specifically with ways of presenting Europe to school pupils, while seeking generally to introduce the European dimension into education.

Indeed, some years ago, under the auspices of the French Section of AEDE, a Charter for the European Teacher was produced. Some key extracts are as follows:-

A Charter for the European Teacher: Some Extracts

Article 1 The questions of education and training represent the basis for the future of Europe. They must therefore be specifically included in a new Treaty of European Union.

The priorities for European co-operation in this field must aim particularly to improve the reception, development and fulfillment of young people. At the same time the patterns and content of education are changing within our societies, and we should be reducing cultural ethnocentricity and giving to the citizens of Europe the desire to become united, to achieve their common destiny in a world in which their continent must act in concert to maintain peace and innovation for the good of mankind.

In order to ensure that the steps taken to achieve these aims are publicised and implemented fully, it is essential to involve closely educational administrators and teachers at all levels. Similarly, greater cooperation in this whole area must be reached between the institutions of the Community, other European organisations and the national, regional and local authorities of each country.

Article 3: Every educator and educational administrator has a right to initial and in-service training. He should share in defining the aims of his training.

Article 5: It is important that those teachers who come from the academic world should be given some experience and insight into the commercial world, and conversely that those who come from the world of commerce should receive academic training and teaching skills. Hence, familiarising themselves with the world of work outside school ought to be a constant concern of teacher so that they may give pupils appropriate guidance in their choice of career, which must be suited to their needs, interests and abilities. These periods of industrial training and work experience, or of study in an academic institution, could be spent outside the teachers' own countries.

Article 6: Any training for future teachers should include a component of comparative education which would comprise two elements: theoretical, covering an analysis of other national systems, and practical, which would cover, during time spent in linked training institutions, classroom observation and discussion with other training personnel from the host country, and in addition solid information about other teaching and administrative systems.

Article 7: If the training of future teachers of a foreign language - even at the Primary level - requires specially planned courses in a country where that language is spoken, then courses must also be provided for all other teachers so as to enable them to handle a language other than their own. This encouragement of language-learning is a necessary pre-condition for developing communications, access to information and links of all kinds and for creating a Europe in which there is mutual understanding.

Article 8: In-Service or regular retraining must be meshed in with the initial training that precedes and paves the way for it, and this integrated training must be considered as essential in any career development and it must be supported by all available means.

In this regard teachers and administrators could be allowed a paid "research year", possibly renewable for a further period, to enable them to complete work relevant to their professional activity and preferably in a country other than their own.

This arrangement does not preclude the organisation of sabbatical periods which should be granted to teachers at all levels and disciplines, at intervals and for periods to be decided upon, to enable them to retrain and refresh their experience both at the national and international level.

Article 9: There should be recognition of the personal initiatives taken by teachers both within their own education system and outside their country by the granting of material assistance with the organisation of courses, training periods, refresher courses, and by the reimbursement of costs, the creation of a system of bursaries, the arrangement of international insurance, especially against illness, and for career enhancement and security of tenure.

Article 11: A European Institute or a European Foundation for Educational Sciences needs to be set up to collaborate with existing international and national bodies, and to coordinate, disseminate and develop research which is already in progress or which it would itself promote.

Article 12: It is essential that free circulation should be guaranteed for people and ideas in the educational world, not only for inspectors, administrators and teachers, but also for students and pupils.

In addition to courses of training and periods of residence abroad, it is important that exchanges should be encouraged between schools, and that regular contacts should be formally set up between administrators or heads of each kind of institution training teachers for schools, for work outside school and after compulsory schooling.

Article 13: A European Bulletin of information and teacher exchanges is vital so as to enable European teachers to have access to adequate information regarding research and pedagogical practice, both in methodology and materials - that they can use also quite freely, whatever the provenance of the material in Europe might be.

The data banks of the European information networks and all other means of communications, whether already in existence or planned for the future, must be available for everyone, and must allow everyone to contribute to their enrichment, so as to create a real democracy of information.

Article 15: The European teacher must be able to have his national qualifications recognised, which allow him to work as a teacher at different levels. This recognition which will of course be simplified by a harmonisation of training patterns, must be based on the idea of comparability.

Conditions of Service and Pay

In a number of respects some issues which relate to conditions of service have been described in earlier chapters: probation, the assessment of teachers, the process of nomination, and the prospects of promotion are all matters which have influence upon teachers' work in one or more of the countries under review.

Additionally, however, we may consider the following matters:

a) requirements for appointment;

b) appointment procedures and contract;

c) teachers' workload;

d) teachers' pay.

a) **Requirements for appointment**: in many countries teachers have the status of civil or public servants and, as such, are normally expected to provide proof of good conduct, a satisfactory medical certificate showing fitness, the qualifications required for teaching and (generally) they must satisfy an age qualification. Belgium, Denmark, Germany, France, Greece, Italy, and Luxembourg, may be included within this category. For other countries (including England and Wales, Éire, Scotland, and The Netherlands) requirements will usually include proof of good conduct and a medical declaration. In Scotland a teacher must be registered with The General Teaching Council: in the Irish Republic it is necessary to pass an oral test of competence in the Irish language.

b) **Appointment procedures and contracts**: in many countries it would be possible to apply directly to a school when an advertised post arises. England and Wales, Belgium, Germany, Denmark and The Netherlands provide us with examples. In some countries, and notably Italy and France, appointments will be made in relation to regional procedures and (in Italy) placings in the lists of results following the competitive examinations. In Scotland teachers in state schools must always be registered with the General Teaching Council, and applications for jobs are made to the appropriate regional authority.[3]

c) **The Teacher's workload**: as a general background point we may note that some European countries operate a school day whereby pupils start school at 8.00 am, or even earlier, and finish at or around 2.00 pm, giving children the afternoon for recreation or homework study. Some countries (notably Sweden, outside the EC) have introduced an extended school day whereby children may stay on at school to complete homework and further studies and activities.

Denmark, West Germany, and Italy will typically start school at 8.00 am - or possibly earlier; French schools tend to start at 8.30 am, breaking for lunch between 11.30am and 1.30pm., and closing at 4.30pm. In Denmark schools are open from 8.00 am. until 2.00pm. By contrast schools within the UK will generally start at about 9.00am, and continue until 4.00pm (for secondary school pupils) and with a lunch break or about 1.5 hours.

In Portugal some large secondary school buildings accommodate two or even three schools, one in the morning, one in the afternoon, and one in the evening for adult returners. Teachers usually staff one of these sessions, but it is possible to contribute to more.

The teacher's workload increasingly reflects national agreements and in some countries teaching loads related to a rank achieved following success in competitive examinations. France provides a good example of this. Agreements on hours of work will also reflect levels within the school system (i.e. primary or secondary); extra requirements (such as time designated for staff development; attending parent meetings); and other matters.

Some examples may be cited as follows.

> In West Germany teachers are contracted to teach a given number of periods per week, averaging 26. As most teachers will have civil servant status their terms of employment will be determined by regional statutes. Up to three extra lessons per month can be required without additional pay. Teachers are not required to be in school for periods when they are not teaching.[4] (It should be remembered that teachers' hours in Germany will vary from Land to Land. In North Rhine Westphalia they are expected to teach 28 periods (21 hours) in a Grundschule or Hauptschule; 27 periods (20.25 hours) at a Realschule; and 25 periods (18.75 hours) at a Gymnasium.
>
> In France, as already noted, teachers work a certain number of hours in terms of their qualification (viz: from 25 hours for a primary teacher to 15 hours for the highly qualified agréges). A pool of special replacement teachers will be available to cover for those teachers who are absent from school as a result of illness.
>
> In Denmark full-time Folkeskoler teachers expect a normal working week of 40 hours (of which some 27 will be in class teaching). Extra salary can be earned by standing in for absent colleagues for up to five hours a week, on top of the normal teaching load.
>
> In Scotland teachers have to be in school for a full week, from 9.00am to 3.30 or 4.00 pm daily. For most of this time they are teaching, apart from 4 periods of preparation time. Promoted staff are allocated more non-teaching time according to seniority. However, this 'free' time can be reduced by the need to take the classes of absent teachers. Agreements with teachers' organisations also determine the maximum sizes of classes to be taught.

Teachers' Pay

Throughout the 1980's numerous strikes and disruptions characterized the teaching profession in many European countries, reflecting the low level of reward that many considered to be the case. In every country detailed negotiations also led to changes related to inflation awards; new conditions of service; or special allowances. Special additions to salary are sometimes made to compensate for the higher costs of living in cities, or remote areas.

Despite this complexity key studies made in the 1980's may indicate the broader trends and issues apparent within the European Community countries [5], and case studies can illustrate the nature of pay and status within specific contexts.

Detailed procedures for establishing a teacher's salary vary considerably between countries but, in general terms, the criteria used will include: level of responsibility; years of teaching experience; relevant work experience before teaching; and level of qualification.

One major area of contrast, however, is the salary range within the profession itself. In the Scandinavian countries a unified salary scale, with a narrow range, reflects the overall income policy of those countries.[6] More "traditional" countries (e.g. Italy; France; Austria) have a more hierarchical salary structure - with high rewards for the best qualified in the senior positions. In some countries changes over the 1970's and 1980's have both reduced the number of salary scales related to qualification obtained, and also reduced the number of years normally taken to reach maximum salary as an unpromoted teacher. Scotland is a good example of this change.

Studies of comparability between teachers and others are fraught with problems. ILO surveys have related teachers' salaries to the average salary of all people working in industry. At the end of the 1970's, by this measure, beginning teachers were deemed to be worst off in Italy, Austria, England and Wales, and Norway - where their starting salary was 58% ; 66%; 75% and 95% respectively of the industrial average. The countries where teachers were best paid (or the industrial workers worst!) included Switzerland, The Netherlands, West Germany and Denmark. In Switzerland the lowest paid teachers earned 128% of the industrial average and the highest paid teachers received 312% of the industrial average.

In the mid 1980's yet more comparisons were made by the UK Labour Research Department. Comparing teachers across England and Wales, France, West Germany, and Italy with the annual pay of male manual industrial workers (1985) the teachers' pay was indicated as a percentage of industrial pay. Thus: England and Wales 108%; West Germany 129%; France 116% (for primary and middle school teachers) and 168% for senior secondary level teachers.[7] At that time English graduate teachers could reach the top of the basic scale in II years; in France progress through the salary scales (each with II increments) was related to assessment (see above); for most West German teachers there were 14 increments from the bottom to the top of their grade scale. In West Germany this could take 30 years to accomplish. A further feature was that West German and Italian teachers were paid a 13 month salary on top of the normal 12 monthly payments.

The survey carried out by the European Commission, and published in 1988, was the first official survey of its kind undertaken by the Commission. One reservation, however, is that it is based upon 1985 pay levels; the other caveat is the great complexity of trying to compare pay and conditions between countries with differing cultures, currencies, and economic systems.

One method of calculating teachers' salaries was to convert gross annual salaries into ECUS, the European Currency Unit, another method was to use the Purchasing Power Standard (PPS), a cost of living index which measures comparative purchasing power of national currencies. In the comparison based upon ECUS, classroom teachers aged 32 would be paid the highest if working in Luxembourg, West Germany or Denmark and the lowest if working in Scotland, Belgium, France and Italy.

The complexities of comparisons of such a nature are unlikely to end any debate as to whether employment conditions in one country are better or worse than elsewhere. Other matters, including bonuses, family allowances (as in Luxembourg), qualification allowances (as in Greece, or in France), and special duties supplements must all be considered carefully.

Some country "snapshots" reveal that , for many European teachers, the salaries and opportunities are far from ideal. In Éire, high taxes as well as lack of career opportunities are seen to be the main reasons why many professionals are leaving the country. Fewer than 150 of the 2000 teachers qualified to teach in primary or secondary schools in 1987 obtained permanent jobs in Irish schools. In Greece mass walk outs by primary, secondary, and tertiary teachers seeking increased pay paralysed schools across the country in late 1988. State school teachers, considered to be amongst the lowest paid in Western Europe, are frequently involved in second jobs - including teaching in private "cram" schools or *frontisteria* - to boost their meagre earnings.

Similar problems were evident in Italy, where disputes caused disruption to schools for much of 1988. Yet again, in 1991, teachers marched the streets - demanding a new contract, and seeking improvements in salary. In France teachers have also resorted to strike action in support of salary increases and improved working conditions. As in many other EC countries teacher shortages are likely to get worse as retirement accelerates. Outside the Community - in Sweden - many teachers are reported to be leaving the profession attracted by higher salaries elsewhere. One associated development, reflected in the above snapshots, is an increased political sophistication among teachers and the abandonment of the view that teachers are "professionals" and, as such, do not strike.[8]

Footnotes

1. *At the beginning of 1989 there was fierce opposition from teachers and union members to the proposal for a new corps of teachers who would be attracted by superior pay and career prospects. Both the FEN and SNES demanded substantial rises for all their members. Further demonstrations were called for the spring of 1989, with some of the fiercest action coming from teachers acting independently of the unions who were demanding instant withdrawal of LM. Josplin's proposals, and the projected "loi d'orientation".*

2. *Specific details of unions affiliated to the ETUCE are given in the Directory of Teachers' Unions in the European Community. Eurydice European Unit, Brussels. 1987.*

3. *Further details can be obtained from : The Conditions of Service of Teachers in The European Community. (Commission of the European Community, Luxemburg 1988).*

4. *It should be remembered that teachers' hours in Germany will vary from Land to Land. In North Rhine Westphalia they are expected to teach 28 periods (21 hours) in a Grundschule or Hauptschule; 27 periods (20.25 hours) at a Realschule; and 25 periods (18.75 hours) at a Gymnasium.*

5. *For example: Teachers' Pay. International Labour Organisation (I.L.O.) Geneva 1980. "Rotten Apples for British Teachers; how Europeans Compare". Labour Research Labour Research Department. London 1985.*
   The Conditions of Service of Teachers in The European Community. Commission of the European Communities. Luxembourg 1988.

6. *An example may be taken from Sweden. In 1986 salary scales, per month, were:*

Junior level class teacher monthly salary (Sw. Kroner)	*7612 - 10999*
Middle Level	*7763 - 11244*
Upper Level	*8379 - 12109*
with Ph.D	*9380 - 13361*
Headteacher, basic school	*11455 - 14575*
Principal, upper secondary school	*11882 - 15112*

7. *In this comparison the figures taken for teachers' pay were averages for France, and England and Wales, and the mid point of the most common scale for West Germany and Italy.*

8. *In the UK a Government pay deal to teachers in England and Wales, announced in February 1989 promised better rewards to Headteachers and their deputies, and to those going to work in high cost areas. Nonetheless six teacher unions all complained that the increases were going too little too late and would do nothing to solve the growing crisis in teacher recruitment in the 1990's. "The Teacher Today" (OECD Paris 1990) has further highlighted the common experience of a loss of status, falling morale and lessened overall attractiveness of the teaching profession, leading in turn to growing difficulties in ensuring adequate teacher supply.*

Part 2

Country Case Studies

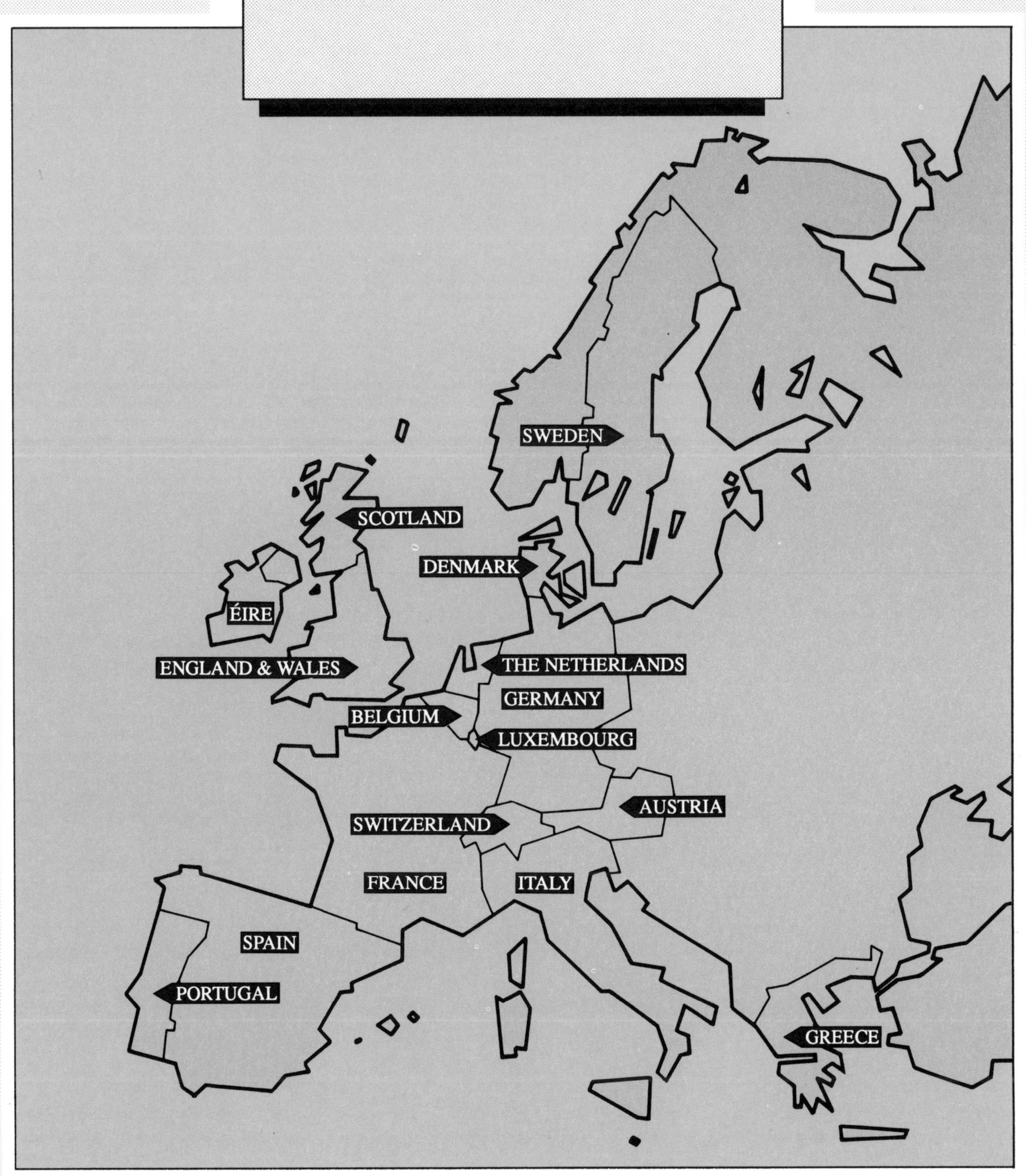

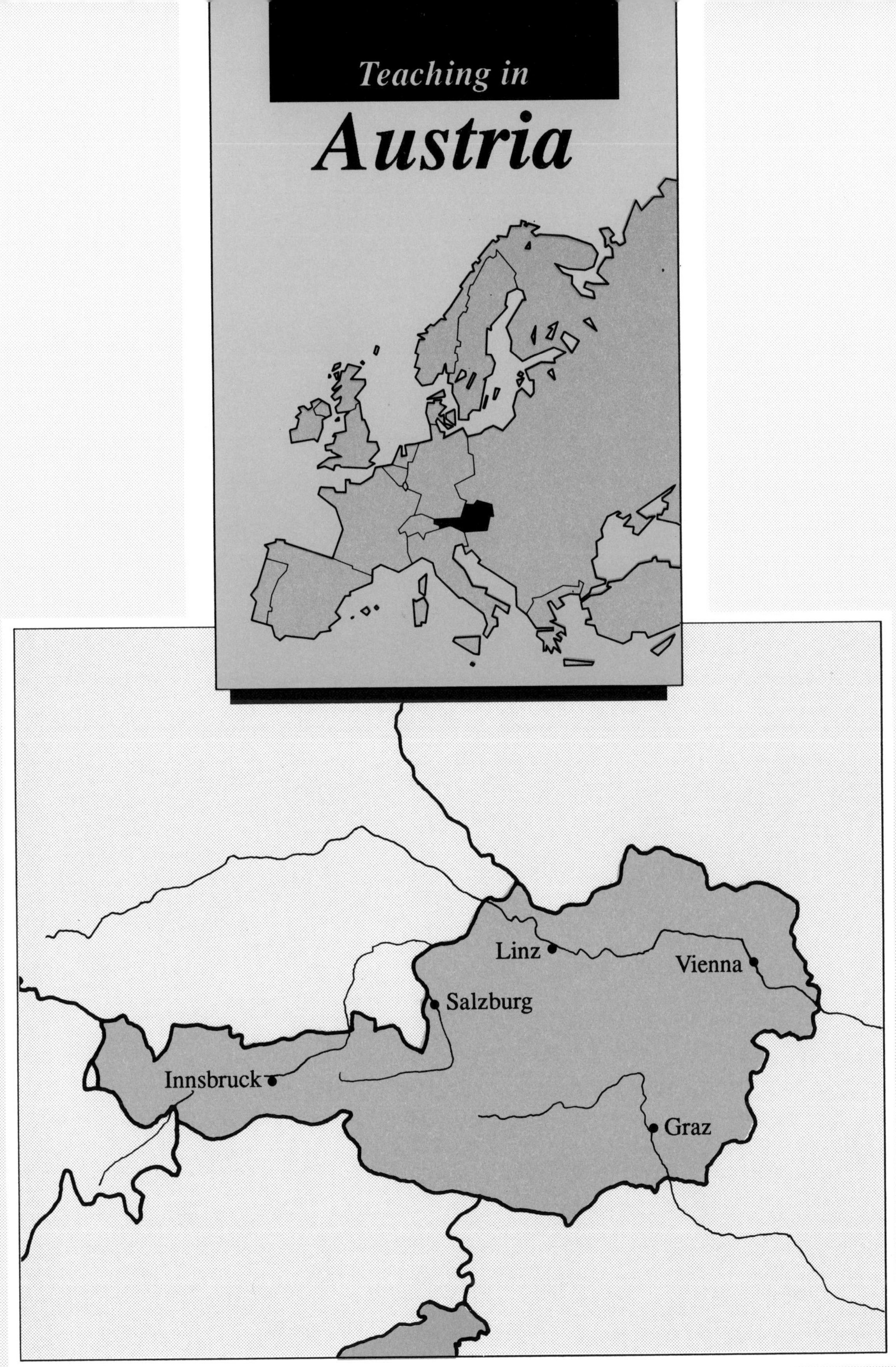
Teaching in
Austria
Linz
Vienna
Salzburg
Innsbruck
Graz

TEACHING IN AUSTRIA

The Republic of Austria occupies a central position in Europe, the shortest journey to the sea being to the Adriatic, either through Italy or Yugoslavia. To the east lies Hungary and to the north Czechoslovakia and Germany, Liechtenstein and Switzerland being to the west. Austria, therefore, is subject to influences from many quarters. While wanting to maintain its policy of 'active neutrality' the *Republik Österreich,* a member of EFTA, is likely to seek membership of the European Community.

The physical geography of the country is sharply contrasting, extending from the alpine and mountainous regions of the western 'finger' to the low-lying broader lands of the east. There are great variations in the climate as a consequence.

Economic factors relate closely to the geographic. With a GNP per capita of $16,600 in 1988 Austria is among the more prosperous European countries. Most of its trade is with EC countries thus underlining the need to consider joining the Community. The economy depends mainly on manufacturing while agriculture continues to decline. Mineral production (lignite; iron, lead and zinc ore) is of considerable importance e.g., Austria is one of the largest sources of graphite. Forestry also remains important and tourism requires special mention. In winter the main attraction is the Austrian Alps, for skiing, and in summer the country as a whole has much to attract foreign visitors - some 16 $1/_2$ million visited Austria during 1988. Hydro-electric and nuclear power remain highly controversial in Austria and a great deal of power is imported, mainly from the east.

The population in 1988 was 7.6 million, the vast majority being German-speaking. Since then there has been an influx of people from East European countries, at least on a temporary basis. Almost all Austrians profess Christianity and they are predominantly Roman Catholics. Since 1867 however, the State not the church, has exercised authority over schools.

Modern Austria dates from 1955 when the four occupying forces left a sovereign and independent country. It is a democratic federal republic, with 9 *Länder*. Power rests mainly with the elected National Council to which the Federal Chancellor and the Council of Ministers are responsible. Education is under the charge of the Minister for Education, The Arts and Sport, while higher education is administered by the Ministry of Science and Research. Educational legislation requires a two-thirds majority before changes can be enacted, thus every reform is a 'forced compromise'. While curriculum is controlled centrally, a new syllabus is only accepted after wide consultation.

The Education System

The basis for the system is found in the school Organisation Act of 1962, which reads as follows:

> "It is the task of the Austrian school to foster the development of the talents and potential abilities of young persons in accordance with ethical, religious and social values and the appreciation of that which is true, good and beautiful, by

giving them an education corresponding to their respective stages of development and to their respective courses of study. It should give young people the knowledge and skills required for their future lives and occupations and train them to acquire knowledge on their own initiative.

Young persons should be trained to become healthy, capable, conscientious and responsible members of society and citizens of the democratic and federal Republic of Austria. They should be encouraged to develop an independent judgment and social understanding, to be open minded to the philosophy and political thinking of others. They should be enabled to participate in the economic and cultural life of Austria, of Europe and of the World and to make their contribution, in love of freedom and peace, to the common tasks of mankind".

The system of schooling is controlled and administered in different ways and at different levels. Legislation and matters of principle, including curriculum matters, are, of course, a federal responsibility, while implementation of the system is delegated to the *Länder*. Day-to-day administration of lower-level schools may be delegated in turn to district education committees. It should be added that parents and pupils, through community councils and school committees, are able to influence the system.

The diagram below illustrates the system in general; it also considerably oversimplifies the situation. While age 6 years is the starting time for pupils, many will have attended *Tagesmutter* and *Kindergarten*. These may be provided by the state or they may be private, but fees are always charged.

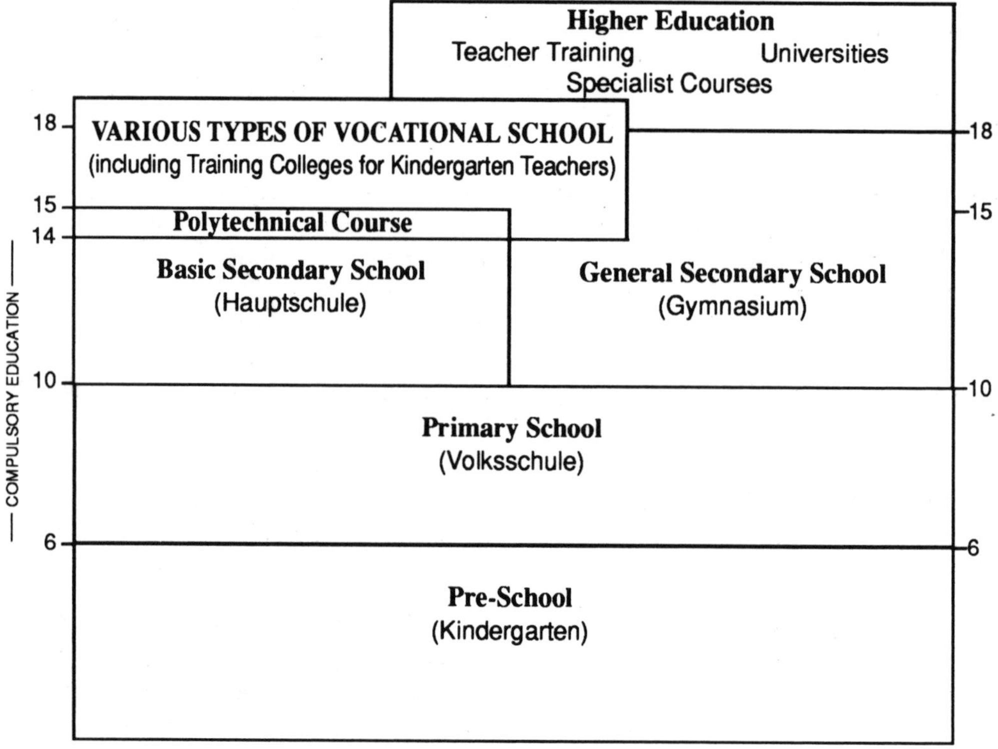

As the diagram indicates, compulsory schooling lasts nine years, from age 6. The first four years are spent in a primary school after which parents choose between two types of secondary education, on the advice of primary school staff. Basic secondary school (*Hauptschule*) with its three streams may be followed by a vocational year and then an apprenticeship. Others at age 14 may enrol in intermediate or longer vocational courses, including training courses for kindergarten teachers - there is a firm commitment to vocational education within the Austrian system.

The more academic pupil may choose to enter *Gymnasium* or *Realgymnasium* at age 10 years, leading to the *Matura* at 18, and then to university or other form of higher education. While this suggests a divided and divisive system, this is not intended, and movement between streams and courses is always seen as possible.

WIR SIND EINE KLEINE SCHULE, BEI UNS KENNT JEDER JEDEN!

Teacher Training

Teacher training is by category of teacher. Training is seen as an essential pre-requisite except in the case of teaching in further education where practical experience of the trade or job comes first and the training later.

Future **Kindergarten** teachers choose from a range of vocational opportunities at age 14 years. The content of the course is predominantly practical, alongside continuing personal education.

For those students who wish to teach in **primary** schools (*Volkschulen*) or **lower secondary** schools (*Hauptschulen*) - following the *matura* - there are 3-year courses in a Teachers' Training College (*Pädagogische Academie*). Course content aims at a balance between theory and practice while devoting full attention to the personal and academic development of the trainees.

During the first semester classroom contact is largely restricted to observation, with perhaps some teaching of small units lasting 10 minutes or so. From the second semester onwards classroom teaching plays an increasingly important part in the course. Usually there are schools attached to the *Akademie* and early experience of classrooms takes place there. Later, students will be placed in various schools in the area.

Some 6-8 hours each week are spent on the basic subjects of the primary school (i.e. reading, writing, mathematics, art, physical education etc.). A similar amount is devoted to the 'human sciences' (*Humanwissenschaften*) i.e. psychology and sociology. Methodology, lesson analysis and teaching techniques complete the programme.

Akademie staff are experienced and of proven teaching ability. This ensures that standards of training are satisfactory. Assessment is generally informal, with little by way of a checklist of competencies. Grades are determined in consultation by school and *Akademie* staff, the final grade on the diploma being either Excellent, Good or Satisfactory.

Those with the highest grades on their diploma have tended to fare best as regards getting a post although now, in the early 1990s, all are likely to find employment. In any case the first year's teaching is a trial period if not a probationary year in the full sense. This year must be carried out successfully before further progress can be made along the road from contract teacher to tenure. Even when permanent (*Pragmatisiert*) employment can be in any school. Full tenure comes after 15 years or so, and teachers may achieve the right to a job in a particular school for life (*Schulfeste Stelle*). About 50% of the staff of a school have this tenure at any one time. Tenure also means that a tenured teacher has priority if a post becomes vacant elsewhere and if she wishes to move.

Training for Upper Secondary School (*Gymnasium*) teaching rests with the Universities. The degree course lasts at least 9 semesters and usually longer. Two subjects are taken except for Biology which counts as two. Training for teaching occurs from the 5th semester onwards and consists of Pedagogy (*Pädagogische Ausbildung*), Subject Studies (*Fachdidaktik*) and School Practice (*Schulpraktik*). The general belief seems to be that the university provision is too theoretical and too remote from the practical. However, the universities take their role seriously and they defend the value of the practical element as provided by them jointly with the school staff (*Betreuungs Lehrer*) to whom students are attached during school experience.

A probationary year follows. Again the probationer may be attached to a *Betreuungslehrer* who coordinates and oversees a varied pattern of teaching taking in a variety of classes. The probationer (*Probelehrer*) may not yet have a class of her/his own. One semester is devoted to each of the two subjects. On one day a week the probationer attends the *Pädagogische Institut* for seminars with other probationers, and periodically they may sit in on each other's lessons in groups. Final assessment results from a discussion involving the *Betreuungslehrer,* the Headteacher, a School Inspector and staff of the Institute.

Career Development

The mechanism for obtaining a post involves the appropriate school directorate. Trainees may not always be successful in obtaining a post in the area of their choice and Magdalena's story below illustrates the issues. Success is dependent upon a number of factors, including teaching performance and also political affiliation. A major factor must be supply and demand and in the early 1990s it seems that all trainees are likely to find a post quite quickly.

The idea of teaching as a career in Austria is not perceived in terms of promotion, more in terms of satisfaction as a classroom practitioner. Obtaining a post and achieving tenure are critical steps and after that regular increases in salary can be expected. There are few promoted posts in a school anyway - Head Teacher and one other, probably - and these are not seen as an objective by many, perhaps because Heads do not have much room for manoeuvre. However, a really ambitious teacher can aim to become a Head Teacher, or perhaps a School Inspector in due course. Some may seek to advance their careers in the *Pädagogische Akademie* or in the *Pädagogische Institut*, while others may aspire towards university teaching.

Inservice training has an increasingly important part to play in career development. Official thinking here is unambiguous: there should be a continuous review of the system at all levels and improvements made. In the vocational field (i.e. through the *Berufs-pädagogische Institut*) this has been particularly apparent, with general education moving in the same direction. While inservice education is not yet compulsory, there are strong pressures on teachers to keep up to date and to extend their skills into new areas. Courses are usually offered by the *Stadtschulrat* or the *Landesschulrat*. There are no supply teachers in Austria at present and attendance at courses is dependent upon the agreement of the Head and the willingness of colleagues to cover for a teacher who is absent on a week's course.

A Teacher in a Vienna Grammar School

Magdalena wurde 1960 in Wien geboren. Ihre Eltern führten eine Bäckerei in einem Dorf ungerfähr eine Stunde von der Hauptstadt entfernt. Im Zuge des Wirtschaftsaufschwunges Anfang der Siebziger Jahre vergrösserte sich das Unternehmen zusehends.

Nach der Volksschule besuchte Magdalena ab ihrem zehnten Lebensjahr das Gymnasium, obwohl sie ihre Eltern eigentlich lieber in die Hauptschule geschickt hätten, da sie doch eines Tages das Geschäft übernehmen solltes. Den Ausschlag für die Entscheidung gaben Magdalenas Lehrer. Sie selbst hatte jedoch andere, höherfliegende Pläne für sich selbst: nach ihrer Matura - sie war 18 Jahre alt-inskribierte sie Vergleichende Literaturewissenschaft und Englisch an der Universität Wien. Von allen Seiten bekam sie zu hören, dass sie wohl kaum auf eine Stelle als Literaturwissenschaftlerin hoffen konnte, aber Magdalen war das egal. Ihren Eltern war es wohl nicht so egal, sie unterstützten sie aber trotzdem. Österreichische Studenten müssen keine Studiengebühren bezahlen, aber in Wien studieren bedeute für Magdalena natürlich, dass sie nicht mehr zu Hause wohnen konnte. Magdalena bekam auch kein Stipendium, da ihre Eltern zuviel verdienten (ungefähr 10% aller Studenten in Osterreich bekommen ein Stipendium, das ca. 4600 0S im Monat beträgt). Nach ihren beiden ersten Jahren an der Universität machte sich Magdalena das erste Mal Sorgen um ihre Zukunft, und beschloss, das Lehramt als ihren zukünftigen Beruf zu wählen (im Grunde fiel ihr auch gar nichts anderes ein, obwohl ihr auch diesmal von allen Seiten gesagt wurde, dass die Arbeitslosenrate unter Lehrern bei zehn % lag und sie nicht reich damit werden würde). Sie wählte Deutsch und Englisch als ihre Fächer, so dass sie zumindest ihre Zeugnisse aus Englisch anrechnen lassen konnte. Magdalena war sehr eifrig, und konnte daher ihr Studium nach vier weiteren Jahren abschliessen, wahrend nicht wenige ihrer Studienkollegen acht oder neun Jahre für ihr Lehramtsstudium brauchten. Ihr Studienplan beinhaltete eine gründliche theoretische Ausbildung (jeder, der in Österreich an einem Gymnasium unterrichten will, muss für jedes seiner zwei Fächer - mit der Ausnahme von Biologie, das allein unterrichtet werden kann - einen universitären Abschluss vorweisen können), aber auch einen praktischen Teil, der allerdings etwas mager ausfiel: während ihres Studiums verbrachte Magdalena ungefahr zehn Wochen in Schulen, selbst unterrichten konnte sie sechs Stunden. Letzteres gefiel ihr sehr gut. Ihre Betreuungslehrer halfen ihr bei der Vorbereitung, und die Schüler reagierten wohlwollend und liebten wohl auch die Abwechslung.

Nach Abschluss ihres Studiums Beschloss Magdalena als Assistentin für ein Jahr nach England zu gehen - einerseits um ihr Englisch zu ve bessern, andererseits aber auch, um das englische Schulsystem kennenzulernen. Selbstbewasst und guter Dinge harrend kam sie aus England zurück, um ihr Probejahr im Herbst zu beginnen, für das sie sich vor einem Jahr beworben hatte (beim Wiener Stadtschulrat - jedesder neun österreichischen Bundesländer hat einen eigenen Stadt - bzw. Landesschulrat; dieser ist jedoch nur für Gymnasien bzw. andere höhere Schulen zustandig - die Volks - und Hauptschulen unterstehen dem Bund; sämtliche Lehrplane gelten jedoch bundesweit).Magdalena hatte drei verschiedene Gymnasien angegeben, an denen sie gerne arbeiten würde, wurde im Endeffekt jedoch für eine andere Schule zugeteilt, die noch dazu am Stadtrand von Wien lag und Michaela wohnte zentrumsnah.

Sie wusste, dass sie je eine Klasse fur jedes ihrer Facher selbständig führen wurde. Dass es sich in ihrem speziellen Fall um eine 5. Klasse handeln würde, die sie in beiden Fachern unterrichten würde, erfuhr sie jedoch erst an ihrem ersten Schultag. Eine 5. Klasse bedeutete 4 Deutsch - und 3 Englischstunden pro Woche. Schule ist in Osterreich gewöhnlich von Montag bis Samstag (von 8 bis 1.30). Um auch den Lehrern eine 5-Tage-Woche zu garantieren, haben sie ein Anrecht auf einen freien Tag. Magdalena hatte Glück und hatte den Samstag frei. Den Rest ihrer Zeit an der Schule veebrachte sie mit Stundenbeobachtung bei ihren Betreungslehrern, die sie am Ende des Schuljahres auch benoten würden, gemeinsam mit dem Direktor der Schule, dessen grosser Einfluss auf die Note kaum gerechtfertigt ist, da er nur wenige Male überraschend ins Klas enzimmer des Probanden kommt.Magdalena begann (möglicherweise das erste Mal überhaupt) zu realisieren, wie wichtig Geld eigentlich war. Ihre Freunde/innen, die Fächer wie Ingenieurwesen order Wirtschaft studiert hatten, verdienten selbst als Trainees ungefähr dreimal so viel wie sie selbst. Mit ihren 8000 ÖS im Monat (Gehalt wird in Osterreich immer als monatliches Gehalt genannt und in den meisten Berufssparten 14mal ausgezahlt) konnte sie sich noch immer nicht die Miete für ihre recht grosszügig angelegte Wohnung leisten. Als sie selbst noch Studentin war, hatte sie zwei Untermieterinnen gahabt, jetzt nur mehr eine, die jedoch mehr als die Halfte der Miete von 4700 ÖS bezahlte. Öffentliche Verkehrsmittel in Osterreoch sind vergleichsweise billig in Wien - ein Monatsticket beispielsweise kostet 450 ÖS - und die Verbindungen sind auch recht gut. Um zu ihrer Schule zu gelangen hätte Magdalena jedoch über eineinhalb Stunden gebraucht. Ihre Mutter schenkte ihr altes Auto und bot ihr sogar an, Versicherung und laufende kosten zu übernehmen, was sich Magdalena von ihrem Gehalt ohnehin nicht hätte leisten konnen und daher das Angebot gerne annahm.

Unterrichten machte Magdalena Spass, und sie war auch ziemlich beliebt an der Schule. Die Schule selbst befand sich in einer Siedlung, und die meisten Schüler/innen litten unter sozialen Problemen, ausgelöst durch Umgebung und Familie. Magdalena kapierte recht schnell, dass sie hier mit der deutschen Klassik oder mit mittelalterlichen Reimschemen keinen Erfolg haben würde, und setzte daher auf Klassendiskussionen über Themen, die den Schulern am Herzen lagen, und wo sie sich auch eifrigst beteiligten, oder Artikel aus Jugend - magazinen. Die Schüler/innen waren auch durchaus bereit, Rechtschreiben oder Grammatic durch machen. Im Englischunterricht ve suchte sie ihre Schüler durch Popsongs, aktuelle Nachrichten, u.a. zu motivieren.

Sowohl Magdalenas Betreungslehrer als auch der Direktor entschieden, Magdalenas Probejahr mit 1 zu bewerten.

Magdalena was sich natürlich bewusst gewesen, dass die Wartelisten für eine volle Lehrverpflichtung lang sein würden, aber als sie horte, dass si e mit vier Jahren Wartezeit rechnen musste, war sie doch einigermassen geschockt. Sie glaubte jedoch immer noch, dass Qualifikationen zählen wurden, was sich jedoch als Irrtum herausstellte: sowohl die ÖVP als auch die SPÖ legten ihr nahe, ihrer Partei beizutreten, um dadurch schneller auf der Warteliste vorzurüchen. Jeder Lehrer/jede Lehrerin in Osterreich muss irgendwann (politische) Farbe bekennen und einer Partei beitreten: Die Parteiangehörigkeit des Direktors (Direktorinnen sind hochst rar in Osterreich!) bestimmt gewöhnlich die politische Richtung der Schule und widderspiegelt auch die politische Gesinnung der meisten dort tätigen Lehrer.

Magdalena brauchte dringendst eine Anstellung, und beschloss daher, Mitglied einer der beiden grossen Parteien zu werden. Trotzdem hatte sie zu Beginn des nächsten Schuljahres - noch keine Anstellung bekommen. Erst als es bereits zu spat dafür war, erzählte ihr jemand, dass sie sich als Stützlehrerin in Voks - und Hauptschulen hätte bewerben konnen. Diese Stützlehrer/innen waren dazu da, den kindern, deren Muttersprache nicht Deutsch war, im Unterricht zuhelfen. Sie bewarb sich also für das darauffolgende Jahr und arbeitete in der Zwischenzeit bei der Post, etwas, das sie früher als Sommerjob gemacht hatte. Nicht, dass es ihr grossen Spass machte, aber sie hatte wohl keine andere Wahl, nachdem ihre Arbeitslosenunterstützung lacherliche 3000 ÖS betragen wurde. Danach arbeitete sie zwei Jahre als Stützlehrerin, um dann mit 28 Jahren endlich eine volle Lehrverpflichtung zu bekommen. Die Schule war diesmal in der Nähe ihrer Wohnung, und die meisten der Kinder kamen aus stabilen Familienverhältnissen. Der Direktor war recht liberal und die Kollegen recht nett. Sie hatte fünf verschiedene Klassen zu unterrichten - vier Deutschklassen und eine Englischklasse: insgesamt ein Umstand, der sie tief betrübte, aber es war nichts zu machen. Sie musste 18 Stunden pro Woche unterrichten, wobei eine Schulstunde 50 Minuten dauert (die Anzahl der zu unterrichtenden Stunden hängt vom jeweiligen Fach ab. Das Anfangsgehalt betrug 15 000 ÖS netto im Monat und stieg von da an kontinuierlich. Nach ungefahr acht Jahren würde sie pragmatisiert werden, d.h. ihr war damit der Job auf Lebenszeit garantiert (frauen gehen in Österreich mit 55, Männer mit 60 Jahren in Pension Karriere hatte sie keine vor sich: da es in österreichischen Schulen keine einzelnen Abteilungen ('departments') gibt, konnte sie nicht einmal Abteilungs leiterin werden. Die einzigen höheren Posten in der Schule sind die des Administrators und des Direktors. Das einzige, was sie zusätzlich tun konnte, war am Nachmittag freiwillige Übungen wie Bühnenspiel order Kreatives Schreiben anzubieten.

Ihr letztes Gehalt könnte möglicherweise rund 30 000 ÖS brutto betragen, die monatliche Pension würde ungefähr 20 000 ÖS betragen.

Obwohl Magdalena ihren Beruf liebte, und auch die langen Ferien nicht missen mochte (neun Wochen im Sommer, zwei zu Weihnachten, eine Woche im Februar, zwei Wochen zu Ostern), und darüberhinaus auch nicht wusste, was sie sonst tun konnte, beneidete sie doch manchmal ihre Freunde aus der Studienzeit, die sich weit mehr als sie selbst leisten konnten, obwohl sie deswegen auch nicht weniger arbeitete und eininge ihrer Kollegan unter der Arbeitslast und sonstigem Druck zusammenbrechen sah.

Was wir jedoch nicht in Erfahrung bringen konnten ist, ob sie es wohl jemals bereut hat, nicht das Geschäft ihrer Eltern ubernommen zu haben...

Magdalena was born in 1960 in Vienna. Her parents had a bakery in a small town about an hour's drive from the capital. With the economic boom in Austria in the early 1970s they were able to extend their business considerably.

After primary school Magdalena started attending the Gymnasium at the age of ten, although her parents would rather have sent her to a Hauptschule, because they intended her to take over the business one day, if it hadn't been for the advice of Magdalena's teachers. Magdalena herself had very intellectual ambitions and after her Matura at the age of 18 she enrolled for Comparative Literature and English at Vienna University. Everybody kept telling her that there were no jobs in Austria for literature experts, but Magdalena didn't mind. Her parents did but they nevertheless supported her. Students in Austria don't have to pay university fees, but studying in Vienna meant living away from home, and Magdalena didn't get a grant because her parents were too well-off (about 10% of all students in Austria get a grant of approximately £230 a month). After two years of studies Magdalena gave more thoughts to her future, and decided she might like to be a teacher (she couldn't really think of anything else she would like to do, although again everybody kept telling her that the unemployment rate among teachers was around 10% and that she wouldn't earn a lot of money). She chose German and English as her subjects which meant that she could at least make use of the certificates she had had already acquired in English. Magdalena was studious and therefore able to finish her degree in another four years' time, whereas many of her fellow students took up to eight or nine years for their degrees. Her studies involved a very thorough theoretical training in her field (everyone aiming to teach at an Austrian Gymnasium has to have a university degree for each of his/her subjects - the only exception is Biology: Biology teachers don't have to have another subject). The practical training on the job was rather poor, as it involved only a total of about ten weeks in schools and the small number of six lessons to teach by yourself. This Magdalena however enjoyed immensely. The teachers whose classes she taught helped her with the preparation and the pupils were very tolerant towards students in general and also liked a bit of change.

After she had finished her studies Magdalena decided to go to England for a year as an assistant teacher - to improve her English as well as to get an impression of what teaching in England would be like.

Having become self-confident and looking forward to her first "real" job Magdalena came back to Vienna to start her probationary year for which she had applied a year earlier at the Wiener Stadtschulrat (=Viennese Education Authority for Gymnasien - every one of the nine

Austrian provinces has its own authority for Gymnasien, but this is not the case for primary schools or Hauptschule, which have a national authority still; there are national curricula for all school-types). Magdalena wasn't appointed to a school of her choice: she would have preferred a school in the centre of Vienna near to which she herself lived, but instead she had got a job on the periphery of the city.

She knew she would have to teach one form in each of her subjects. Only on the day when school started, however, did she learn that she was to teach a fifth form, which meant 4 German lessons and 3 English lessons a week. The rest of her time in school she spent observing the teachers whose classes she taught and who would eventually decide on a mark for her probational year, together with the headmaster, who would base his decision on little more than the odd unexpected visit to the classrooms. Schools in Austria are usually in session six days a week (from 8 till 1.30), teachers having one day off. Magdalena was lucky and had the Saturday off.

Magdalena now began to realise (probably for the first time in her life!) how much money mattered. However friends who had studied subjects like engineering or economics at university had a starting salary, even as trainees', about three times as high as her own. With her £400 a month (salaries in Austria are usually given in monthly amounts and paid 14 times a year in most professions) she still couldn't afford to pay the rent for her rather big flat just on her own. As a student she had had two lodgers, now she had just one who paid more than half of the £250 a month rent. Transport is fairly cheap in Vienna (£23 for a monthly ticket) and connections are quite good, it would have taken her an hour and a half to get to the school by means of public transport. Her mother ordered her her old car and even offered to pay insurance and repairs, which Magdalena couldn't have afforded and therefore gladly accepted.

Magdalena enjoyed teaching and became quite popular at school. The school was situated in an estate and quite a few pupils had a lot of social problems at home. She understood quickly that the pupils would not respond to the German classics or medieval verse (both of which are in the national curriculum for German in the Gymnasien) but they were quite willing to participate in classroom discussions about topics that interested them, would read articles out of popular magazines and were keen on improving their spelling and grammar. In her English lessons she tried to motivate them by using pop-songs, BBC news, etc. However teachers and the headmaster decided on Grade 1 when assessing her teaching.

Magdalena had known that waiting lists for a full-time job were long but when she was told she had to wait for four years she was quite shocked. She still believed that qualifications counted, but it proved wrong. She was approached by both the Conservative and the Socialist Party to join them and thus get quicker to the top of the list. Every teacher in Austria has at some stage to decide for one party or the other if he/she wants to get a safe job: the party-membership of the headmaster (there are very few headmistresses around!) usually tells you the political opinion of the teachers working at the school.

Magdalena, desperate for a job, agreed to become a member of one of the parties. Still she had no job by the end of the summer. Only then somebody told her she could have applied for a job as a support teacher (Stützlehrer) in a primary school or Hauptschule, designed to help children whose mother-tongue wasn't German, but it was too late for this year. Magdalena

went temporarily back to one of her former summer-jobs and worked at the Mail Exchange for a year. She didn't enjoy it, but there was no choice; her unemployment benefit would have been a ridiculous £150 a month.
The following two years she worked as a support teacher, and finally got a job at a Gymnasium. She was 28 years old then. This time the school was near her home and most of the pupils had quite a stable social background. The headmaster was liberal and the colleagues nice enough. She had five different classes to teach (four German classes and only one English class, which she deeply regretted but couldn't help it). She had to teach 18 lessons a week, one lesson lasting 50 minutes (depending on your subject teachers have a different number of lessons to teach). She was earning £750 a month in her first year and her salary would rise every year. After about eight to ten years she could expect to be "pragmatisiert", which means that her job was secured until her retirement (women retire at the age of 55 in Austria, men at the age of 60). There was no career ahead of her: there are no departments in Austrian schools, the only higher posts are those of the headmaster and the administrator. The only thing she could do was work more, i.e. offer afternoon lessons like drama, creative writing, etc. Her last salary would be as high as £1500 a month, her pension about as high as £1000 per month.

Although Magdalena liked her job, the long holidays (nine weeks in the summer, two weeks at Christmas, one week in February, two weeks at Easter), and couldn't imagine doing something else, she sometimes couldn't help envying her old friends from university who could afford much more than her, although she certainly didn't work less than them and had to experience quite a few nervous breakdowns among her colleagues, who simply cracked up under the amount of pressure.

We don't know, however, if she ever regretted not having taken over her parents' business...

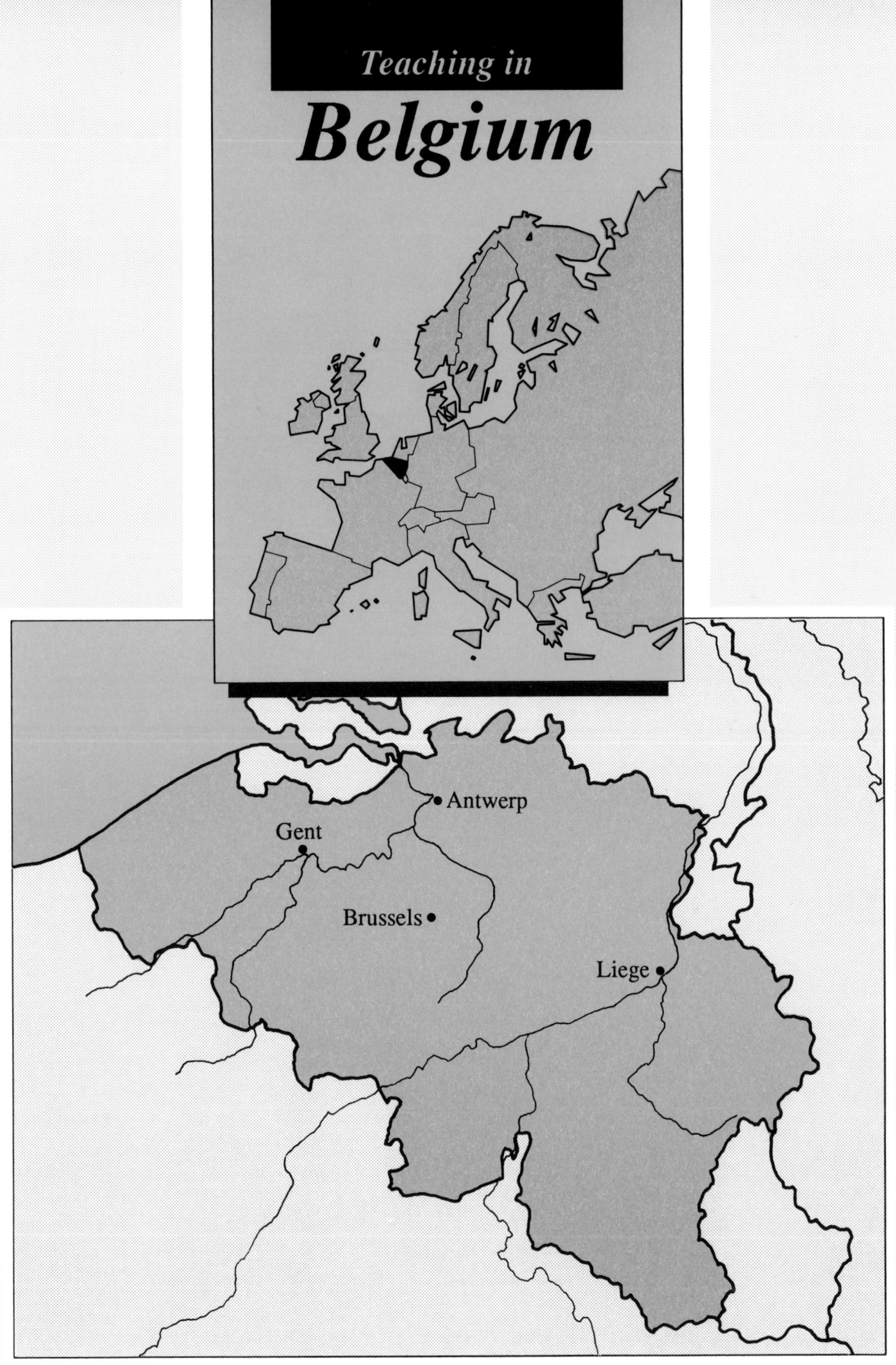
Teaching in
Belgium
Antwerp
Gent
Brussels
Liege

TEACHING IN BELGIUM

Belgium, one of Europe's most densely populated countries, is bordered by France, The Netherlands, Luxembourg and West Germany. Until 1970 the structure of the Belgian State remained unchanged since its creation in 1830; it was based on the principle of unity of legislation and government for the whole of the territory. The laws of 1970, 1971 and 1980 put an end to the unitary system in Belgium, and initiated the system in which powers are divided between the central State, the cultural communities, the regional, provincial and local authorities.

Belgium has about 10 million inhabitants, linguistically and culturally split between the majority who speak Flemish (a dialect of Dutch) and the large minority who speak French. The two predominant groups live in separate areas and communities, even in Brussels - which is officially bi-lingual - and both guard their linguistic traditions jealously. In the late 1980's 57% of Belgian children attended Flemish schools, and 43% were taught in French. The educational provision of the small German community was administered by the French community. In 1988 Belgium was preparing to devolve the control of education from national government to linguistically-determined community authorities, following the formation of a new coalition government. From January 1st, 1989 the Flemish and French speaking communities took over responsibility for education. Compulsory school ages; conditions for awarding diplomas and organisation of boarding facilities are still determined at national level.

Schooling

Article 17 of the Belgian Constitution declares that:
"there shall be freedom of education; any measure hindering such freedom shall be prohibited; penalization of infringement shall be governed by law".

In this context the organising power for education lies with various bodies, private and official. The private or 'free' institutions are dominated by the Catholic group (see below).

Compulsory education lasts from 6-16 years, but is being progressively increased so that attendance until the age of 18 years is likely to be compulsory. A Royal Decree, issued in July 1984, provided for the organisation of 90 centres for part-time education (for the 16-18 year olds) and aimed essentially at improving and extending vocational education.

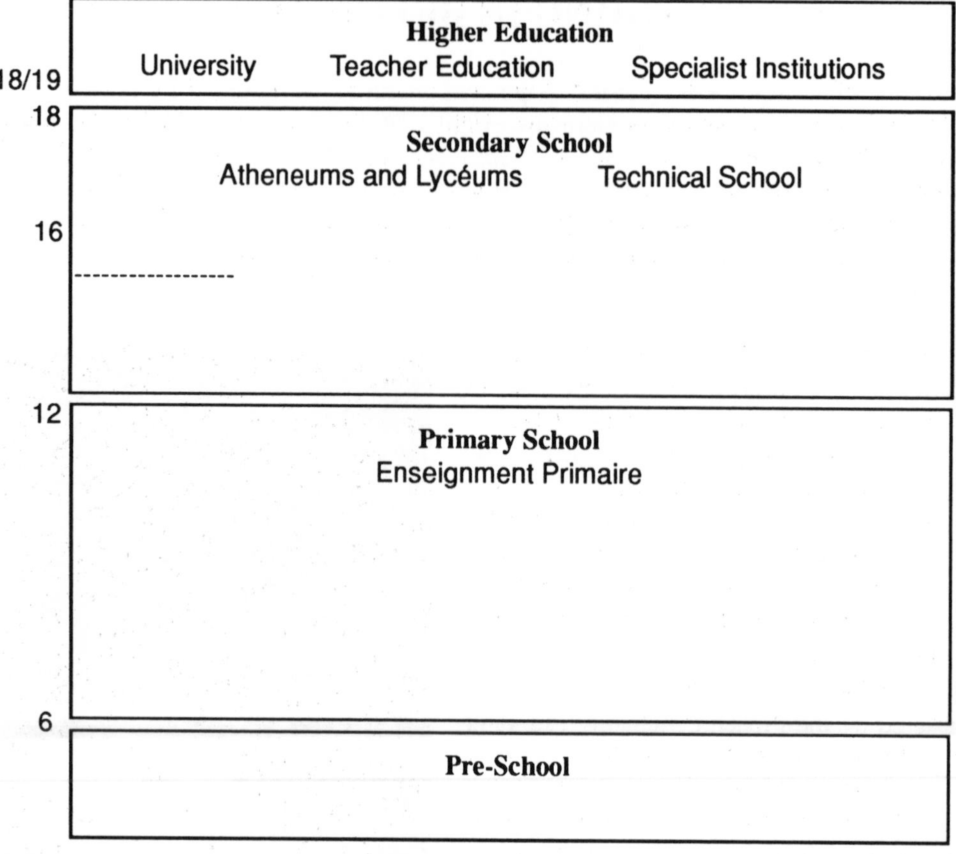

Prior to attendance at primary school there is high attendance at pre-school level, with well over 90% of 2½-3½ year olds attending. As a rule co-education is applied to schools organised by the State. Among schools subsidized by the State (especially in relation to religious education) many are still divided according to sex.

Primary education, compulsory from age 6 to 12 years provides for a weekly timetable devoted to the mother tongue; arithmetic; religion or ethics; environmental studies; physical education; and music. From 1971 a second foreign language was being introduced into primary schools. From the 1970's, also a revised system of education was introduced to give secondary school students more flexibility in their choice of subjects. Secondary schooling is divided into three stages, viz:

an observation stage (12-14 years); an orientation/pre-specialisation stage (14-16 years), and a determination stage. In effect this means that pupils will initially take a common syllabus and later (in the determination stage) follow general (academic), technical, vocational or artistic studies - on the basis of teachers' observations and on pupil's own preferences and abilities.

ATHÉNÉE ROYAL MIXTE DE SAINT-GILLES

FICHE MATRICULE

N° matricule : ....

Inscrit(e) le ....

Religion catholique, islamique, israélite, protestante.

Morale.

Allemand ou Espagnol.

Nom et prénoms : ....

Né(e) le .... à ....

Etudes antérieures : ....

Etablissements antérieurs : ....

Chef de Famille.

Nom et prénoms : ....

Profession : ....

Adresse : ....

Téléphone : ....

Départ de l'élève.

Date : ....

Motif : ....

Etudes poursuivies : ....

Profession choisie : ....

Mariage et nouvelle adresse : ....

Année scolaire	Classe	
19..........		
19..........		
19..........		
19..........		
19..........		
19..........		
19..........		
19..........		
19..........		
19..........		
19..........		
19..........		
19..........		
19..........		

Signature du Chef de famille,

Mère, Père,

656-76

In 1986 it was proclaimed by the then minister for French national sector education that the revised system had made "everyone progress at the slowest speed possible - the strongest as well as the least clever", and announced an end to the revised system. By 1988, however, the socialist party had taken over education again from the right-wing Liberals in a new five-party coalition government.

Inevitably, some concerns have been expressed about the rapidity of change and the instability within State education. Between 1978 - 1986, for example, there had been a succession of seven ministers, from three different political parties, in charge of the French-speaking Ministry of National Education. Each change of minister had brought changes in timetables, in programmes and teaching options. Such situations have prompted proposals, and formulas for making State education less dependent upon the personal views of a particular minister. If carried through this could introduce profound changes in the management of education in Belgium, and especially with respect to programmes and teaching methods.

Teacher Training:

Entry into teaching in Belgium will involve students in a course provided in a teachers' college, or in university studies, followed by a period of teaching as a temporary teacher.

In the 1980's the training possibilities included:

a) *école normale* (a teachers' college) providing a programme of training over 3 years and leading to a certificate (and title of "*instituteur*") for teaching in the elementary school (6-12 year olds);

b) a course of training (lasting 3 years from 1985) preparing candidates for teaching in the lower secondary school (pupils aged 12-15), and giving the intending teacher the title of "*agrégé*" for lower secondary education; *(diplôme d'agrégé de l'enseignement secondaire inférieur)*[1]

c) preparation at university level for teaching at the upper secondary level (with pupils aged on average 15-18 years). Alongside the study of academic subjects such intending teachers are expected to follow a course in pedagogical studies which might typically begin the the third year of university attendance. Such studies, both of an academic and practical nature, will include such items as: study of school history; educational theory; visits to schools; school visits; watching a mentor teacher (appointed and paid a small subsidy by the university) and some teaching. The last might typically be for at least 10 lessons. Completion of university studies will lead the successful student to the title of "*licencie*", and after at least four years of study. Successful completion of the pedagogical studies will lead to the title of *Agrégé* *(diplôme d'agrégé de l'enseignement secondaire*

Supérieur). Invariably this may be seen as a further diploma awarded at the same time as the "licence".

Current discussions related to teacher training indicate that a full year of pedagogical training is desirable, and that present preparation is somewhat superficial.

It may be noted also that intending teachers who have not undertaken their pedagogical studies concurrent with other (academic) university studies can return to such work at a later stage, and undertaken this on a part-time basis for 6-7 hours per week, and usually over a two year period.
Upon completion of the initial period of study the intending teacher will be obliged to undertake a period of teaching on a temporary basis. Given a general shortage of teaching posts available it will mean that the temporary teacher must be prepared to move and also re-apply each year for the same, or another temporary post.[2]

Such conditions are carefully regulated in relation to entry to the level or status of "*Stagier*" and, ultimately, to become nominated to a permanent teaching position. These conditions are set out by the Ministry of Education, and related to the age of the candidate seeking to enter the level of "*stagier*", viz:

- for primary schools the teacher must be at least 21 years old, and have served 240 days as a temporary teacher;
- for lower secondary schools the teacher must be at least 23 years old, and have served 240 days as a temporary teacher;
- for upper secondary schools the teacher must be at least 25 years old, and have served 240 days as a temporary teacher.

Temporary teachers are paid at the "full rate", and not at any reduced scale because of their temporary status. Nonetheless the condition of becoming a *stagier* reflects the fierce competition for jobs; a "temporary" status for 600-700 days is not uncommon, and it could well be that a wait of up to 5 years is possible. Much will depend on ministerial decisions which can affect curriculum provision and opportunities are currently more readily available in chemistry, and physics; a longer waiting period is evident for history and physical education.

No special facilities or concessions are accorded to the temporary teacher, such as a reduced teaching load, or special classes. He/she is fully engaged, and on a full time basis. In addition to fulfilling the minimum time allocated (see above) it is also necessary for the temporary teacher to obtain a good report on his/her teaching abilities. This report will indicate the teacher's name; hours/subjects taught; and an appreciation or summary of the work undertaken. A recommendation will be made for one of three categories: Satisfactory; Partly Satisfactory; Unsatisfactory. Usually this report will be signed by the teacher; the headteacher concerned, and a Ministry official and will apply to temporary teachers who have been in a school for a minimum specified period.

Headteacher's Report on Temporary Teacher

Ministerie van Nationale Opvoeding en Nederlandse Cultuur

Onderwijsinrichting : (School)

Leden van het bestuurs- en onderwijzend personeel, van het opvoedend hulppersoneel en van het paramedisch personeel van de rijksinrichtingen voor kleuter-, lager, buitengewoon middelbaar, normaal, technisch en kunstonderwijs

Verslag over de wijze waarop het tijdelijk aangesteld personeelslid zijn opdracht heeft vervuld

Naam en voornamen van het tijdelijk personeelslid (1) (Teacher's Name)

Diploma

Ambt (Level)

Gepresteerde diensten (2) (Hours/Subject taught)

Omstandig verslag van het inrichtingshoofd (3) :

(Appreciation)

Advies van het inrichtingshoofd (4) :

1. De betrokkene heeft mij volledig voldoening gegeven. Satisfactory
2. De betrokkene heeft mij gedeeltelijk voldoening gegeven. Partly satisfactory
3. De betrokkene heeft mij geen voldoening gegeven. Unsatisfactory

Handtekening van het inrichtingshoofd : Datum :

50 10

Dit verslag werd aan het personeelslid overhandigd op

Handtekening van het inrichtingshoofd | Handtekening van de betrokkene

---

De ondergetekende heeft kennis genomen van het verslag en van het advies van het inrichtingshoofd en stemt ermede in (4) - niet mede in (4) om volgende redenen

Datum | Handtekening van de betrokkene

(Agree/Disagree)

(Teacher's signature)

Dit verslag werd aan het inrichtingshoofd overhandigd op

Handtekening van het inrichtingshoofd | Handtekening van de betrokkene

---

Dit verslag werd gestuurd naar het Hoofdbestuur van het Ministerie van Nationale Opvoeding en Nederlandse ...

Handtekening van het inrichtingshoofd

---

(1) Voor de gehuwde vrouw vermelden : meisjesnaam, voornamen echtgenote van

(2) Moeten worden vermeld : de gepresteerde diensten waarvoor dit verslag wordt opgemaakt : van ... tot ... voor ... uren per week

Criteria: professionalism; influence on children, personal presentation, speech communication, commitment socially and to extra activities.

(3) Dit verslag moet nauwkeurig zijn en alle gegevens vermelden over de wijze van dienen van het tijdelijk personeelslid. Het vermeldt inzonderheid de volgende punten : beroepsbekwaamheid, invloed op de opvoeding, houding en voorkomen, taalzuiverheid, toewijding aan het onderwijs en aan de inrichting, verantwoordelijkheidsbesef.

(4) Het onnodige doorhalen.

The Stagier

To become a *stagier* is generally dependent upon one's age; completion of the minimum period if temporary teaching; a good report from the Headteacher; and a vacancy being available in one's subject specialism, and at the level of teaching (i.e. upper or lower secondary). Such a vacancy could be anywhere within Belgium, and opportunities for choice are becoming noticeably thinner.[2]

Once appointed as *stagier* it is now necessary to serve a further full teaching year, with particular responsibilities for a class. There are no special teaching conditions, reduced timetable or other forms of support normally given.

To become "nominated" (see below) it is also necessary that the *stagier* is inspected and unsatisfactory performance over the year may lead to this "stage" being lengthened for a further year, or to a recommendation that the *stagier* is not nominated, and should therefore consider leaving the profession. One difference is that school inspectors are obliged "to inspect", and to give priority of attention to the *stagiers*, as opposed to temporary teachers. Teacher's diaries; schemes of work; homework assignments and marking will be included in the inspection process. In addition to this, and over the year concerned, the Headteacher receiving the *stagier* in his/her school will compile a dossier/file noting good and/or bad points in the teacher's professional contribution, and the dates where appropriate. This form must be signed by the teacher, and can be seen by the inspector and/or a ministry official.

Rapport sur la manière de servir des stagiaires

Nom et prénoms du stagiaire : (1) ______

Diplôme : ______

Fonction : ______

Prestations hebdomadaires dans l'établissement : ______

______ **heures.**

Date d'admission au stage : ______

Interruptions de service (périodes, motifs) : ______

Rapport circonstancié du chef d'établissement (2).

Proposition du chef d'établissement (3).

1. Je propose de nommer le stagiaire à titre définitif.
2. Je propose que le stage soit prolongé d'un an.
3. Je propose de licencier le stagiaire.

Signature du chef d'établissement : Date :

(1) Pour la femme mariée, indiquer nom, prénoms, épouse de ______

(2) Ce rapport doit être précis et porter sur tous les éléments relatifs à la manière de servir du stagiaire. Il porte notamment sur les points suivants : aptitude professionnelle, action éducative, tenue et présentation, correction du langage, devouement à l'enseignement et à l'établissement, sens des responsabilités

(3) Biffer la mention inutile.

Ce rapport a été remis au membre du personnel en date du

Signature du chef d'établissement Signature de l'intéressé :

Pris connaissance du rapport et de la proposition du chef d'établissement.

D'accord (3). Pas d'accord pour les motifs suivants (3) :

Date : Signature de l'intéressé :

Ce rapport a été remis au chef d'établissement en date du

Un recours écrit est/n'est pas (3) joint au rapport.

Signature du chef d'établissement : Signature de l'intéressé :

Ce rapport et le recours (3) a (ont) été adressé(s) à l'administration centrale du Ministère de l'Education nationale et de la Culture française, en date du

Signature du chef d'établissement :

(4) Avis de la Chambre de recours : ______

Date : Signature du président :

(4) Décision du Ministre : ______

Date : Signature :

(4) A remplir uniquement s'il y a recours.

In summary, this period will be one of significant inspection, viz:

a) there will be an inspector's report, which will include comment on lessons watched; on the professionalism and personal qualities of the teacher; on issues of teaching method and pedagogy;
b) a headteacher's report on the *stagier*, giving general comment; in both a) and b) there will be the recommendation for nomination or recommendation for a further year as "*stagier*" or an unsatisfactory report or a recommendation for withdrawal;
c) the headteacher's file/dossier on the teacher concerned.

Clearly, when the inspector's visit may last for up to a day there is close consultation with the headteacher concerned on the performance and professional qualities/capabilities of the *stagier*, prior to nomination.

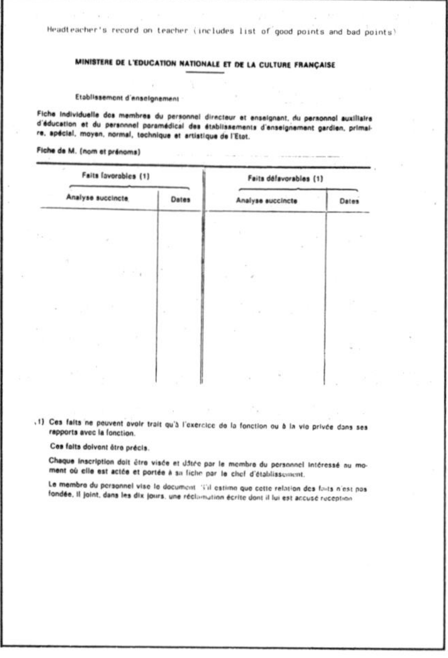

Headteacher's record on teacher (includes list of good points and bad points)

MINISTERE DE L'EDUCATION NATIONALE ET DE LA CULTURE FRANÇAISE

Etablissement d'enseignement

Fiche individuelle des membres du personnel directeur et enseignant, du personnel auxiliaire d'éducation et du personnel paramédical des établissements d'enseignement gardien, primaire, spécial, moyen, normal, technique et artistique de l'Etat.

Fiche de M. (nom et prénoms) ______

Faits favorables (1)		Faits défavorables (1)	
Analyse succincte	Dates	Analyse succincte	Dates

(1) Ces faits ne peuvent avoir trait qu'à l'exercice de la fonction ou à la vie privée dans ses rapports avec la fonction.

Ces faits doivent être précis.

Chaque inscription doit être visée et datée par le membre du personnel intéressé au moment où elle est actée et portée à sa fiche par le chef d'établissement.

Le membre du personnel vise le document. S'il estime que cette relation des faits n'est pas fondée, il joint, dans les dix jours, une réclamation écrite dont il lui est accusé réception

Upon award of the nomination the teacher is accorded status as a civil servant, and will normally be assured of a permanent job in the same (or another) school. Undoubtedly this is the most significant hurdle to be overcome for entry into the teaching profession, and it is obtained only after considerable 'temporary' teaching experience, which must be satisfactory, and upon successful completion of the "stage" described above.

The Assessment and Inspection of Teachers

After receiving nomination it is likely that the teacher will receive fewer formal visits from either the Headteacher or school Inspector. The Headteacher can request a school Inspector to visit a teacher if the situation is deemed to be sufficiently bad. It is possible that a teacher could be placed in another school or, at worst, lose the status of being a nominated teacher.
A teacher may request an inspection in connection with possible promotion to the post of Headteacher, or school Inspector, but in general terms it is possible that teacher inspection may occur every five years or so.

In distinction to earlier inspections, where recommendations are made on a "three point" scale (e.g. for satisfactory; partly satisfactory; or unsatisfactory performance) these inspections will result in "points" awarded to the teacher, according to the following pattern:

Professionalism	maximum 10 points
Influence of the education of the child	maximum 10 points
Personal presentation	5 points
Language use/usage	5 points
Professional commitment	5 points
Responsibilities undertaken	5 points
	(total 40 points)

Following assessment the points will be totalled, and a "grade" of achievement awarded as follows:

Less than 24 points	unsatisfactory
24-32 points	good
32-36 points	very good
more than 36 points	exceptional

Where a grade/award of either unsatisfactory or exceptional is awarded this must be accompanied by a further detailed report justifying the grade given. An exceptional award will normally justify a personal and private letter of congratulations from the General Inspector. Such an award will typically be given in the month of May, but will not make a difference to salary, or more rapid mobility up the salary scale. Where there is an unsatisfactory report on a teacher, given by a Headteacher, it can be suggested that the person concerned watch senior teachers, for advice and example. In addition a subject inspector could visit the teacher, and complete a further form, giving information and comment on professionalism, teaching method, and suggestions for improvement.

Inservice, Staff Development and Promotion Possibilities

Various activities are offered to teaching staff who can choose according to their needs, and the particular conditions prevailing within the school in which they work. Such activities include pedagogical or re-training days; visits to teachers' centres; residential courses lasting two or three days; longer residential courses. In the French language area the State organises an educational week for teachers in pre-school and primary education. A recent development within the Flemish speaking area is for teachers to work in a company for 4-8 months in order to become acquainted with the industrial world, and the new technology. These seconded teachers will still receive their normal salary and are replaced by temporary staff.

As there are no department (i.e. subject) heads within Belgian secondary schools any promotion possibilities will be primarily related to becoming a Headteacher or school Inspector.

Currently regulations indicate that such promotion would only be considered once at least 10 years of teaching has been undertaken, after the nomination has been obtained, and the candidate is at least 35 years of age. Clearly a good mark (and a series of good marks) as a nominated teacher will be helpful in this process.

It is also necessary, however, to pass an examination - whether for entering the Inspectorate or a Headship, and where the content of the former has more emphasis upon pedagogy, and for the latter more emphasis upon a knowledge of school law, and upon administrative issues. A Headteacher will not teach, as such, on receiving an appointment.

For entry to the Headteacher grade the following elements comprise the examination (which is spread over a period of time):

i) written and oral examination on issues of school law and school administration;
ii) a lengthy "interview" related to a range of educational issues, problems, and recent (up to $1^1/_2$ hours) initiatives touching upon the life and work of the compulsory school;
iii) an assessment of the teaching of two, or more lessons, undertaken by teachers in another school; one lesson will be in the subject of the examinee; another lesson in a different subject. a jury (of school inspectors, and a chairman, as well as an administrative secretary) will also be in attendance, and will examine a written report (or reports) completed by the examinee who has watched, and is assessing the teacher(s) concerned. This report would be in terms of "If I were an inspector; if I were a headteacher...", and is clearly related to the future tasks of assessing teachers, whether at temporary, *stagier*, or nominated 'levels'. Preparation for such examinations can involve attendance at courses run by teachers' trade unions, university specialists, and possibly over a period of up to 2 years, with attendance on a part-time basis. Candidates are not obliged to attend preparatory courses, but it is advisable. Given the limited number of jobs available it may also be the case that some successful candidates will be "temporarily designated" headteachers, waiting for a post.

The Private Sector

Traditionally, private education receives more political support in the Dutch-speaking part of Belgium, while public education is stronger in the French-speaking community. There are significant differences to be noted with respect to teaching and teachers, when comparing the state sector with the private sector in Belgium. Viz:

a) the nomination for permanent status can be given as a private contract, and without the special features and procedures above;
b) subject inspectors, and general inspectors will not be authorised to inspect the methodology and teaching of teachers in private schools, but only advise and comment on more general issues;

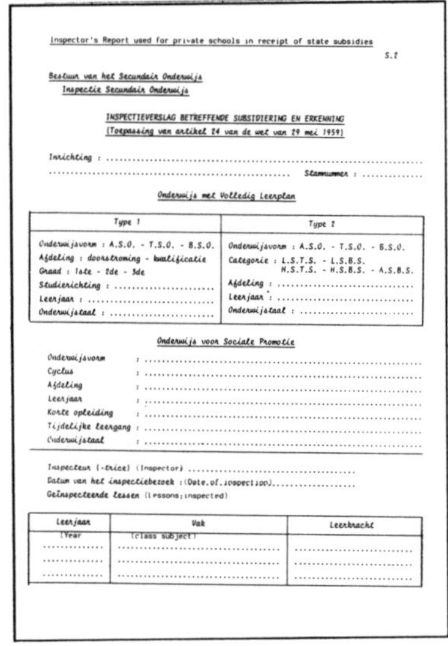

Inspector's Report used for private schools in receipt of state subsidies

S.1

Bestuur van het Secundair Onderwijs
Inspectie Secundair Onderwijs

INSPECTIEVERSLAG BETREFFENDE SUBSIDIERING EN ERKENNING
(Toepassing van artikel 24 van de wet van 29 mei 1959)

Inrichting : ....
.... Stamnummer : ....

Onderwijs met Volledig Leerplan

Type 1	Type 2
Onderwijsvorm : A.S.O. - T.S.O. - B.S.O. Afdeling : doorstroming - kwalificatie Graad : 1ste - 2de - 3de Studierichting : .... Leerjaar : .... Onderwijstaal :	Onderwijsvorm : A.S.O. - T.S.O. - B.S.O. Categorie : L.S.T.S. - L.S.B.S. H.S.T.S. - H.S.B.S. - A.S.B.S. Afdeling : .... Leerjaar : .... Onderwijstaal : ....

Onderwijs voor Sociale Promotie

Onderwijsvorm : ....
Cyclus : ....
Afdeling : ....
Leerjaar : ....
Korte opleiding : ....
Tijdelijke leergang : ....
Onderwijstaal : ....

Inspecteur (-trice) (Inspector) ....
Datum van het inspectiebezoek :(Date.of.inspection)..............
Geïnspecteerde lessen (Lessons;inspected)

Leerjaar (Year	Vak (class subject)	Leerkracht
....	....	....
....	....	....
....	....	....

c) private schools organised by the Catholic church have their own inspectors who will report to the Bishop; private management; and any other authorities concerned;
d) where private schools receive certain subsidies from the state they will be inspected in connection with specified areas, such as school buildings and structures; materials and resources used; curriculum provision.

Footnotes

1 *For pre-school and primary education professional training includes practical training periods in schools, and preparatory exercises within the school of the teacher training college.*

Training for lower secondary school training includes:
Compulsory courses (general courses; pedagogy and practical training) in a specified subject area; an extra optional subject; and further optional courses. As in primary education the time devoted to teaching practice increases over the 3 year course to about half the training time.

2 *From late 1986 anxiety created by economic measures related to reducing the budget contribution for secondary schools had provoked strikes, protests and demonstrations from teachers' and parents' organisations. Economy measures had threatened job losses amounting to around 6,500 teaching jobs in secondary schools. Proposals included changing the pupil-teacher ratio from 15:1 to 18:1 in the primary schools, and from 9:1 to 11:1 in the secondary schools, with a freeze on new appointments. By early 1987 the Government was redeploying teachers who had lost their jobs, and in a programme designed to tackle rising unemployment. Various measures undertaken in the 1980s included early retirement opportunities (in certain cases permission was given to receive pension at 55, with credit for the years not served); the lifting of certain barriers so that career interruption for personal reasons could be increased from two to five years; and provision for the recruitment of non-statutory supplementary staff to carry out replacements on a temporary basis.*

A Primary School Teacher

Een onderwijzer lagere school heeft in zijn klas alle lessen, uitgenomen turnen en muziek, van maandag tot en met vrijdag, woensdagnamiddag vrij. Een klasdag begint om 8.30 uur, wordt van 12 tot 13.00 uur onderbroken en eindigt om 16.00 uur. Er komen bij het vernieuwd onderwijs wel wat vergaderingen bij. Het salaris is ongeveer 30.000 BF, is afhankelijk van de indesxtijgingen en verhoogt om de twee jaar tot het maximum na 12 jaar vit is een netto-bedrag. De afhoudingen voor sociale zekerheid, ziekteverzekering en pensioen zijn zeer hoog (1/3 tot 1/2).

De lessen duren 30 minuten en er is een speeltijd van 15 minuten om 10.00 uur en 14.30 uur, verschillend volgens de school.

Voor bewaking op de speelplaats wordt niet extra betaald, wél in de meeste scholen voor bewaking bij het middageten.

Het onderwijzersberoep is de laatste tijd niet erg in trek, daar men in privé-bedrijven veel meer kan verdienen. Maar er zijn de vrije dagen en lange vakanties! (Kerstmis en Pasen twee weken en vanaf 1 juli tot 31 augustus).

A primary schoolteacher has to give all lessons in his class, except (in most schools) gymnastics and music, from Monday till Friday - Wednesday afternoon and Saturday being free. A school-day starts at 8.30, has a break of about 10 to 15 minutes; from 12 to 1300 hrs for lunch, and ends at 1600 hrs. In the comprehensive system there are plenty of conferences after school-hours. The salary is at the start about 30.000 BF, dependent from the rise of index, and being raised every two years, till maximum after 12 years. Deduction for social assurance, sickness-assurance and pension are very high (one-third to one-half). There are 30- minute periods.

There is no extra pay for watching the children during playground hours, but some towns pay extra for watching during the lunch-time. The teaching profession is not regarded as popular in recent times, as a bigger salary can be had 'in private'. But still, there are the free days and long holidays (Christmas and Easter: two weeks) and the summer-holidays from July 1st till August the 31st!)

A Teacher in a Lower Secondary School

Ik ben 35 Jaar en onderricht Nederlands en Engels in een Middelbare school, Lagere graad aan jongens van 14-15 jaar. Wekelijks geef ik 22 lessen van 50 minuten, en voel mij bij de jongens niet gelukkig, daar de basiskennis voor verder onderricht ontbreekt en ook daar het inspanningen vraagt om ze tot tucht en studiegeest te brengen. Onze jongens zijn producten van de welvaart-maatschappij, die nooit zoals wij - door gevolgen van de oorlog, ontberingen hebben gekend, dus niet weten wat een frank of een boterham waard is, en altijd maar met minimum-inspanninngen rekenen. Mijn salaris begon met ong. 3500 BF en jing tweejarlijks met ong. 2000 BF omhoog. Veel collega's verlaten het onderwijs omdat er in de privé-industrie meer te verdienen is, maar als men voor het onderwijs geroepen is, blijft men erbij, ook als het moeilijker wordt. Er wordt op heden minder gestudeerd: huiswerken en notities laten de jongens fotokopiëren, er wordt afgeschreven om illegaal de nodige punten te halen, en het is voor veel leraren geen plezier meer te blijven onderwijzen. Ik weet niet of ik in het onderwijs blijb.

I am 35 and am teaching Dutch and English at a Secondary School, Lower Grade, to boys being 14-15 years old. I have to give 22 periods a week (50 minutes), and do not feel so happy doing this, because the basic knowledge for further teaching is not there and also because from the teacher immense energy is required to bring the pupils to a certain grade of discipline and studying spirit. Our boys are a product of prosperity, who do not know of the impact of hunger or the worth of money, and only act by minimum activity.

My salary was raised every two years by about 2.000 BF. You can live by this, but many colleagues leave the school sector because there is more money to be earned in the private sector. But when you feel yourself called to be a teacher, you stay, also when difficulties arise. Studying today is not popular with the boys: they try to get their house-tasks and notices copied in order to get their marks illegally, and plenty of teachers have no more pleasure in teaching. I do not know whether I will continue teaching.

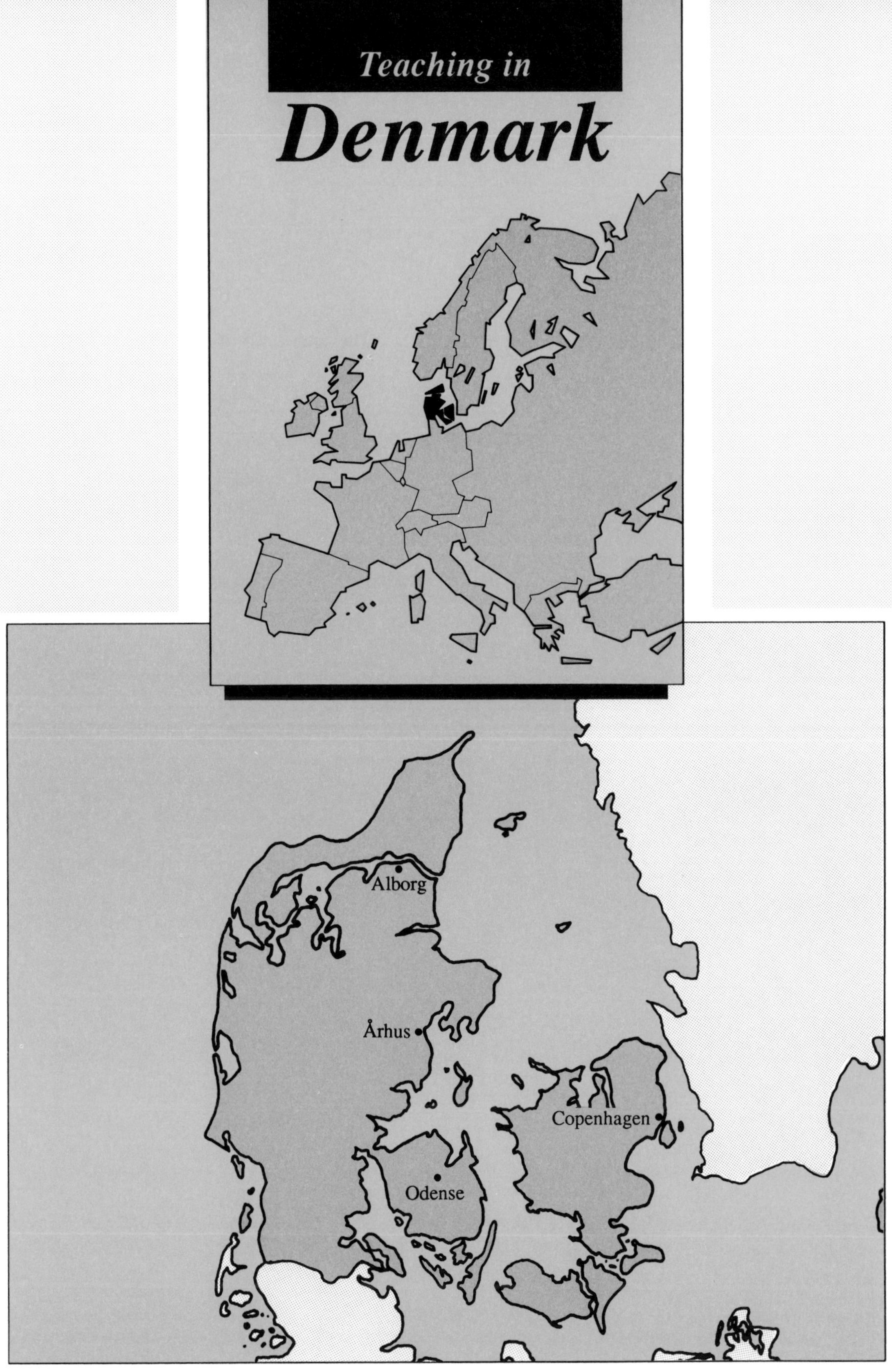
Teaching in
Denmark
Alborg
Århus
Copenhagen
Odense

TEACHING IN DENMARK

Denmark consists of the Jutland peninsula, between the North and Baltic seas, and 482 islands off the peninsula - the largest being Zealand and Funen (or Fyn), and also the Faeroe Islands and Greenland.

As the smallest of the Scandinavian countries it has a history dominated by farming life, and as a centre of Viking expansion. Denmark has a highly developed state education system, and advanced social security schemes. Recent years have witnessed increasing concern that fertile farmland is being swallowed up by urban development.

Schooling

The Danish school system is one which is distinguished by decentralisation, with local autonomy highlighted in the 1980's by increased political effort to delegate the administration from the Ministry of Education to local authorities, and from the local authorities to the individual schools. Concurrent with this is the effort to strengthen the influence of parents and pupils in the day to day running of the school. Each school has a school board (normally of 5 or 7 parents, a member of the municipal council, two teachers, two pupils, and the Head); a teacher's council; a pupil's council; and a head.

All Danish children attend school between the ages of 6-7 years, and 15-16 years, with optional pre-school classes being provided for children of 5 and 6 years. Education in state schools is free but, at the beginning of the 1980's some 14% of all schools were private, and accounted for less than 10% of the compulsory school age group.

In 1976 a new Education (*Folkeskole*) Act came into effect, making nine years of primary and lower secondary education compulsory for all, with an optional pre-school year and an optional tenth year. The Danish Ministry of Education issues guidelines relating to curricula, and, within this context, the Danish teacher will have freedom to use the teaching method(s) he or she wishes. From 1990 it will be possible for the school's Board of Directors to give advice regarding detailed curricular content, but the teacher will retain the decision as to classroom teaching and organisation.

Children are able to enter the optional one-year pre-school classes in the year of their sixth birthday and, from 1980-81, all the municipalities were required to make such classes available. At the beginning of the 1980's over 80% of all children attended pre-school classes.

The aim of the *Folkeskole* is to give pupils a possibility of acquiring knowledge, skills, working methods and ways of expressing themselves, all contributing to the all-round development of the pupils. In principle the *Folkeskole* is a comprehensive school, and pupils will follow a broad range of subjects, with optional choices available to them in the last three years of their compulsory schooling. In the first 5-6 years Danish, Arithmetic/Mathematics, Physical Education and Sport, Sound Subjects, Creative Art and Music are at the core of the curriculum. English is studied from the fifth year, with indications that children will begin learning this foreign language at an earlier age in the future.

Age		
	Further and Higher Education Courses Age 19+	
19 16	GYMNASIUM (Academic)	YOUTH EDUCATION (Vocational) apprenticeship training, basic vocational courses, basic courses at technical and commercial schools, government services teaching courses
7	(+ optional 10th year) FOLKESKOLE age 7-16	
0	PRE-SCHOOL CLASSES KINDERGARTENS DAY NURSERIES	

Administratively the school year begins on August 1st, with actual teaching beginning in the second week of August. 200 school days normally comprise the school year.

A key feature is the 'class teacher' system whereby a class teacher will have the social responsibility for a particular class and quite possibly from the 1st to the 10th grade. This gives a very close contact between the class and a teacher, and establishes the teacher as an important link between home and school.

The period of compulsory education is over when a pupil has received 9 years of instruction (i.e. normally after completion of the 9th form, or grade). At this point there are several possibilities for continuing education, including attendance at the general upper secondary school, or entering into vocational education and training. For the former the pupil will be able to attend the three year *Gymnasium*, and take courses leading to the Upper secondary school leaving examination - or *Studentereksamen*. About one third of all *folkeskole* students will complete the optional 10th grade and take the examination (*udvidede prøve*) available at the end of that year.[1]

Other possibilities include entering basic vocational education; commercial studies; or taking courses leading to technical or agricultural qualifications. It is likely that there will be changes within the pattern of vocational-further education, and implementation of these changes by late 1991.

Teacher Training

At the end of the 1980's teacher education in Denmark was characterised by the concurrent model for the training of *Folkeskole* teachers, and was essentially similar in all the colleges other than *Den Frie Laererhojskole* at *Fyn*. It is distinguished further by a unified teacher education system for the whole period of compulsory schooling.

The training of teachers for the *Folkeskole* is provided in teacher training colleges (*'Seminarium'*) over a period of 4 years. With rationalisation and closure the numbers of such colleges have been reduced but remain fairly evenly spread across the country. To enter the four year course a student would require either:

a) the *Studenteksamen* , (Certificate of General Education) or

b) the *HF examen*. Other possibilities may also be acceptable, provided that a minimum of 12 years previous schooling is attained.

Once accepted into the 4 year programme, a student teacher will take a common core course which includes pedagogy; psychology; didactics and the wide range of *Folkeskole* subjects. In addition specialisation will enable the student to focus upon two subjects which will be taught in greater detail to the older age groups within the compulsory school. Other opportunities include courses for teaching the handicapped; specialising in teaching a particular age group; or working with adults.

In addition students will be closely involved in a practice school or schools, for observation and teaching practice, with at least 16 weeks being given to such experiences.

For those wishing to work in the *Gymnasium* or as *HF* course teachers it is first necessary to obtain an appropriate university degree, and also to complete a short (i.e. 5 month) post graduate course in educational theory and practice (the '*Paedagogikum*').[2] Teachers at the vocational schools will undertake short courses, usually on an inservice basis, at the State Institute for the Educational Training of Vocational Teachers.

Employment

Upon obtaining the *Folkeskole* teaching diploma, or a university degree and '*Paedagogikum*', the teacher will seek employment with full civil service status; with probationary status; or as a contractual employee. Other opportunities will be available perhaps as temporary teachers, and filling short term vacancies. Given a major decline in the birth-rate the 1980's had been witness to an increasing number of teachers who had never attained full civil servant status and the security attached to this. Such problems may well change in the 1990's, as elsewhere, with predictions that there may be shortages of teachers to fill all the posts available.

As a qualified *Folkeskole* teacher one is qualified to teach any subject from the 1st up to the 7th year of the *Folkeskole*. In the 8th-10th years a teacher will usually only teach the two main subjects which were the specialist focus in the *Seminarium*.

Probation

Entry into teaching service in the *Folkeskolen* is usually on a probationary basis, and after two years of satisfactory service, full civil servant status is achieved. Within the process the Headteacher will be an important figure; he/she will be responsible for informing the School

Board of the school about performance and other professional qualities related to the probationer. It will be the School Board which will decide whether the probationer teacher becomes permanently engaged. However in recent years, there have been very few permanent appointments.

Given the decentralised nature of the Danish school system there are no standard or formalised procedures for evaluating probationer teachers. The Headteacher will make decisions in relation to his or her professional judgement, and will make formal and informal visits to the probationer's classroom. Information will also be sought on the commitment and contribution to broader and social aspects of the life of the school. Depending upon the location of the probationer it might also be possible to attend a short course or seminar organised within a college and designed to help those still in their probationer years.

Career Development and Inservice Training

The decline in demand for teachers has already been noted. Within the *Folkeskolen* the possibilities for promotion would lie in becoming a deputy Headteacher, or a Headteacher. Other possibilities will include those of entering into school administrative work at a district level, and the great majority of those working in school administration have already served as teachers within the *Folkeskole.*

Teachers might also be seconded for work on a part-time basis within the *kommune*, in order to give special help and support as a consultant.

For the great majority the career possibilities would be related more obviously to attendance at various inservice and refresher courses organised by The Royal Danish School of Educational Studies. Attendance is largely voluntary and much is therefore left to the individual teacher's enthusiasm and discretion.[3] The recommendation and support of the Headteacher would usually be required.

There is also the prospect of reaching the maximum pay level for a classroom teacher, after 20 years service, with progression through 10 salary steps, each of two years duration.

Footnotes

1 A further possibility includes taking a two year course leading to the 'Higher Preparatory Examination' (the HF examination) which includes some of the Studentereksamen subjects and gives an entry qualification to Higher Education. Originally introduced in the 1970's to enable adults to obtain an entry qualification for higher education it is now mainly used by young people after the 10th class. Adults will also take the HF examination over several years of part-time study, and perhaps passing one subject at a time.

2 *In order to obtain this teaching diploma the trainee must attend a course in educational theory and teaching methods. Theoretical training consists of a general course including educational theory and methodology, and a subject specific course in methodology and area specific theories. Practical classroom training is supervised by both experienced teachers in the school, and who help support and guide the trainee by discussing methods and aims. In addition a 'studielektor' (a senior teacher in the school) will give general support to the trainee, and co-ordinate the guidance given by the subject teachers concerned.*

3 *There will also be opportunities to attend locally organised courses at the "Amtscentral". Denmark is divided into 275 kommunes, and these are grouped in 14 Amter, each of which have an "Amtscentral". Teachers are able to borrow resources, AV materials, and other classroom aids from these centres, and short courses are often arranged for the purpose of helping or improving methods of teaching and communication in the classroom.*

A Teacher in the Danish Folkeskole

I left a Danish "Folkeskolen" when I was 17 and then I worked as an au-pair for about a year. I wanted to be a nurse, and I took a preliminary course at the nurses' training school. I didn't finish training because of marriage and children.

I stayed at home with our two boys for about 4 years, and then I felt like having an education. I wavered between being a social worker or a teacher for a long time, but finally decided to start at the Teachers Training College. Before that I had to take a H.F. course (two years) because my exam from 1963 was too old. I was lucky to get in at the Teacher Training College, the first time I applied.

The education takes four years and my specialities were Danish and art and I also specialised in teaching children with special needs. Finishing the education in 1977 it had already begun to be difficult finding a job. I started applying for jobs in the town where I lived, but it was impossible to get anything but substitute teaching. I finally got employment at a medium sized school in a small town about 20 kms away.

It wasn't the job I desired, but better than nothing I thought. The first year turned out to be absolutely terrible and I almost felt like giving up teaching. I taught 10 different classes during that year and I also taught subjects which I didn't feel competent at. I didn't teach any Danish or art and neither did I teach pupils with special needs. Besides, some of the classes were really difficult. The only subject I enjoyed teaching was English, so I decided to "give teaching a chance" and to improve my qualifications at the Royal Danish Institute.

In my second year as a teacher I succeeded in getting my own 1st class, and everything changed. I now enjoyed teaching and felt really enthusiastic about my work. The first two years were a probationary period, and I was now among the permanent staff which made me feel confident. It's normal for a form teacher to follow a class all the way through "Folkeskolen", and so I did. I came to know the pupils very well and sometimes I almost felt as if they were my own children. I still see them although they left school three years ago.

When I had finished my class after 9 years I didn't feel like starting a new 1st class, and in some ways I felt that I needed a change. There's no possibilities for promotion in our system, unless you want to be a headmaster or a deputy head, and neither of these posts appeals to me. Fortunately I was able to arrange a one-term exchange with a teacher in the UK

I feel that the exchange has been very successful, and I've returned to Denmark with renewed strength and new inspiration.

After 13 years in teaching I still like being a teacher although I find the pay much too low! I'm lucky to have a husband who earns a great deal more as an architect so I haven't had any economical problems which a lot of other teachers have.

A Teacher in a Danish High School

I have been asked to write about what it is like to be a teacher in Denmark, and find it rather difficult to do so.

There are many kinds of schools and you have a different job if you teach youngsters than you have if you teach adults. But one thing is the same - you are not very well paid - and consequently if you like neither your job nor your students you are in a rather awkward position.

Teachers in Denmark have freedom of choice in teaching and they can use the books they want.

The teacher has a frame and can do what she/he wants to do within this frame.

You teach in a friendly atmosphere - you and the students use christian names - hardly ever surnames. Like in some other countries we have two different ways of addressing people the "du" to those you know and the "De" to those you do not know or to whom you want to keep a distance. Students and teachers always use the "du".

Danish students have a questioning attitude - they are not afraid of telling the teacher if they disagree - or do not understand what she/he says. They do not accept everything, and if they disagree they want to know why the teacher has a different solution to a problem. This is of course more the case if you teach civics rather than languages.

It is a hard and challenging job to be a teacher in a Danish school. If you look at statistics you will find that the percentage of suicides is the highest for teachers - could this be a hint saying that there is too much freedom?

It is hard work every day not forgetting the heavy burden of homework - but it is an inspiring challenge too.

A Teacher in a Danish High School

After taking my school certificate exam in the summer of 1965, I began my studies at the University of Aarhus; German Studies being my main subject and Greek my secondary subject. I had studied modern languages for my School Certificate. However, I soon had to come to terms with the fact that my knowledge of Greek, which I had acquired from private lessons during my schooling, was not sufficient for the level required at University, so I changed over to studying Scandinavian languages and Literature.

I had the good fortune, that my parents were in a position to finance me for a considerable period of my studies, so that I did not have to apply for a state grant, loan or turn to teaching for an income until my last year of study. This meant that I did not have the large amount of debt to repay, once I had finished at university, unlike many of my fellow students.

I got a lot of pleasure while at university from studying my main subject, but a lot less from my subsidiary subject which I had turned to from necessity, as I thought that this particular combination would lead to a job later on. During my time at university I was very involved in other aspects of university life, organising activities in a general way and also within my department. In the winter of 1971/70 I concluded my studies in my main subject and two years later in my second subject.

From the Autumn of 1971 till December 1978 I worked as an assistant at the Institute of Germanic Studies, a job which solved some of my economic problems and at the same time gave me a lot of satisfaction, as the teaching of new German Literature was largely handed over to the assistant. For a long time I could not decide whether I should aim for a career at university or in a High School. However the possibility of getting a permanent position at university was fairly remote, as only very few posts were available. For that reason I decided to concentrate on securing a post at a High School.

The Danish High School covers three years and in some of these in particular the teaching has no connection with that of the main state secondary school. To teach at a High School you must have an appropriate university education and have completed a teaching course at a High school. Before this was possible in my case, I had to undergo my military service. As I am a refuser of military service (a conscientious objector) I served my twelve months as an all-purpose assistant in the Aarhus Museum of Art. From August 1975 till February 1976 I completed my teacher training at a high School in Aarhus. I stayed in Aarhus because I had also married in the meantime.

The teacher training course is set up so that the trainee teacher is under the direction of teachers at the school and (in fact) in his main subject as well as in his secondary subject. The main teaching points to be learnt from here arise from a general discussion of the problems which appear in the course of the lesson. The value of such a course depends so much on the particular teacher the trainee is working under. I had no great luck with the teachers in my main subject, as one of them felt less qualified academically than I was and the other had hardly any time available. Many of the discussions had to take place in the intervals, a system which does not lend itself to very thorough worth while discussions. I had better luck with the teachers in my second subject, with whom I got on very well. At the end of the session a short theoretical piece of work had to be written. I must add that, having taken part in the teacher-training from the angle of the teacher, the training side of the professional High School teacher is still very neglected.

From February 1976 till April 1976 I was out of work, which is not particularly surprising, as at that time there were no jobs available in the High Schools. I should mention that during my so called unemployment, I was busy with my new offspring of one year - but this unfortunate period ended in August 1976, when I acquired a post in a High School in Aarhus. During the next three years I worked as a teacher almost entirely in my second subject in a non-permanent appointment. I was a so-called 'supply teacher', i.e. only working for the periods when I was needed in the course of a year. The situation gradually became unbearable to the point that I was almost only taking classes for Danish (in fact an experience which later turned out to be very useful, but was not what I had hoped for). As there was little chance of any change for the better in that school, I applied to another High School in Esbjerg finally in the summer of 1979, as there was an opportunity there for my wife to continue with further education.

For eleven years I have been working at the State School in Esbjerg, and although I have got no particular connection with the town, I am very happy with my work here. I value the personal contacts I have with the pupils. It can be a bit hard when the pupils stay for only three years and then have to leave. Also for seven years I have been a school guidance teacher. This work takes up one third of my timetable, which means that I have only three classes (for four years, entirely German). There are 5 guidance teachers at our school of 600 pupils approximately. We attend to the personal problems of the pupils, help them with their choice of subjects for advanced study and also advise them about career choices etc. I am very interested in this work, also for the reason that I am in close touch with the administration of the school.

I have not had much to do with administrative work, but have taken part for four years in an extensive educational development project in the school as the leader. Apart from this I am responsible for contacts with schools abroad, which at present consist only of one close connection, with a high school near Hannover.

Teaching in

Éire(Ireland)

TEACHING IN ÉIRE (IRELAND)

The Republic of Ireland (Éire), a member of EC since 1973, consists of 26 of the 32 countries which comprise the island of Ireland, the rest being in Northern Ireland (UK). Éire with its population of some $3^1/_2$ million enjoys a mild climate as determined by its location in the Atlantic Ocean some 80 km to the west of Great Britain.

Economically the country has faced difficulties but prospects for the future are brighter. Agriculture, forestry and fishing have been overtaken in importance by the industrial sector. Among the principal products are food and beverages, metals and engineering goods, electronic products, chemicals, tobacco and textiles. Some oil has been discovered and there are indications of good supplies of natural gas.

Éire is a predominantly Roman Catholic country. Irish, the official first language, survives as a vernacular only in some areas, mainly in the west of the country. English is universally spoken. The personal social services, including education, are seen as vital to the welfare of the country.

In the Republic of Ireland (Éire) the authority of the State in education is vested in the Minister for Education, who is a member of the government. The Department of Education is the administrative agency.

Schooling

In the 1937 Constitution of the Republic of Ireland it is acknowledged that the family is the first and natural educator of the child. The State's constitutional duty is to provide free primary education in National Schools which are under local control and patronage - predominantly of the Roman Catholic church. Usually the Patron is the Bishop, who will apply for grant aid from the State.

From 1975 local Boards of Management have been responsible for the day to day running and maintenance of the National School and for the appointment of teachers.

Ireland is virtually unique amongst European countries in that it is possible for children aged 4 years and above to attend the public primary school. The compulsory attendance of children is required from age 6-15 years, with the great majority of children transferring to the post primary junior cycle at about 12 years of age.

Primary education covers a period of 8 years, and the main components of a child-centred curriculum include: Irish language; English language; mathematics; social and environmental studies; music; art; and craft; physical education; religious education.

The post primary Junior Cycle (for 12-15 year olds) can take place in a secondary school; a vocational school; a comprehensive school; or a community school. The majority of secondary schools are run by religious communities (e.g. The Christian Brothers) which receive financial assistance from the State, amounting to almost 100%. Vocational schools are administered by local committees and have been traditionally associated with preparing young people for trades. Since 1966 a full range of second level courses have been available. Almost 100% of the running costs of these schools is paid for by the state, with a small contribution from the local administrative authority.

Comprehensive schools were first established in 1966, essentially combining academic and vocational opportunities. Like the Community schools there are financed almost entirely by the State and are run by Boards of Management. By the end of the 1980's there were some 15 such schools in the Republic.

Community schools, established since 1972, often had their origins in the amalgamation of secondary and vocational schools due for renovation, and are seen to be a focal point for community activities, alongside their normal teaching function for post primary pupils.

Central Government influence, via the Department of Education, is to be found in regulations relating to teacher qualifications, probation, and the assessment of teacher performance by school inspectors. All schools are subject to inspection, and school inspectors are centrally appointed for primary, and post primary schools. For primary (National) schools a full school inspection may take place at intervals of approximately once every four years, and every school is expected to have a plan, involving schemes of work and related matters.

After inspection a copy of the school inspector's report will be sent to the Chairman of the Board of Management, and also to the school.

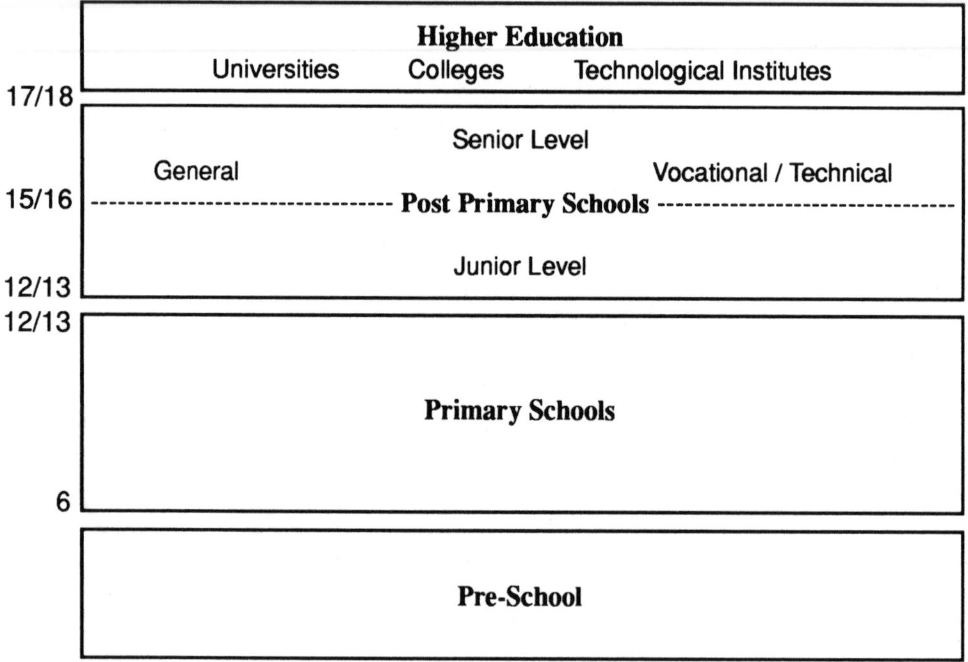

Periodic inspection, of a less frequent nature, will be applied to Post Primary schools, and it is also the case that a school inspector will visit all probationary teachers (see below).

Teacher Training

From 1974 the preparation of National School teachers has been within the context of a university validated degree course. Prior to 1974 teacher preparation took place within a non-university context and resulted in the award of a teaching diploma. The change to a more complex three-year degree course, validated either by The National University of Ireland or by The University of Dublin, effectively synthesised both university standards and values and the acquisition of practical classroom skills and experience.

The result of the changes taking place from 1974 meant that intending National School teachers had to matriculate at either the National University or at the University of Dublin, and pursue a course leading to the degree of B.Ed. (Bachelor of Education). For those associated with the University of Dublin it was likely that the more theoretical components of the course were taught at the university while matters related to classroom competence and practice were the concern of associated colleges. Courses validated by the National University were taught entirely by staff of colleges associated with the university.[1]

An open competitive examination for entry to Colleges of Education is held annually.

Candidates must have passed six subjects in the School Leaving Certificate, of which three are obligatory: Irish, English and Mathematics, and three are optional.

Minimum grades required are

a) Grade C (Hons.) on a higher level paper in not less than three subjects, one of which must be Irish.

b) Grade C on a lower level paper, or Grade D on a higher level paper in English.

c) Grade D in Mathematics.

d) Grade D in the three other optional subjects.

Because of competition for entry to Colleges of Education successful candidates will often have examination passes far exceeding the minimum level required.

The number of places available in the Colleges of Education creates the first competitive hurdle. Only a proportion (on an order of merit basis) of those who have satisfied the school Leaving Certificate examination requirements are then called for interview, and also for Oral Irish[2] and Music tests. Successful candidates will also be required to attend a course in the Gaeltacht area of Ireland - mainly in the west - where the Irish language is the normal language of the home.

Within their degree course students will study Education, and specialise in an academic subject. They will also be competent in the Irish and English language and be able to teach at any age level within the National School.

Course Content: Over the three year education course a typical combination of studies would include Theoretical, Curricular, and Practical elements.
Theoretical studies would include the study of issues in the Philosophy, History, Psychology, and Sociology of Education as well as Curriculum Theory.
Curricular studies would be related to specific teaching methods in the primary school curricular areas (for example, in Mathematics; Social and environmental studies; Art and Craft) along with specialisation in selected curricular areas (e.g. drama; early childhood education; Children's language).
Practical work would include observation and teaching practice in a range of classes.

Teacher training for the post primary school level involves the consecutive model as the predominant mode. Thus, for those wishing to work in the post primary schools it is first necessary to possess a university degree, recognised by the (Irish) Registration Council for Secondary Teachers. This Council was established in 1918 and is the agency which accords official recognition to most post-primary teacher education courses. To be admitted to the register as teachers candidates will have to be graduates; have undergone a teacher training programme, and have successfully completed a probationary period of teaching (see below). Such teachers must also have passed a proficiency test in the Irish language, administered by the Department of Education.[2]

The post-graduate teaching diploma is known as the Higher Diploma in Education (H.Dep.Ed.) and within this one year course there will be a minimum of 100 hours devoted to teaching practice in schools. Further studies will be related to Educational Theory, and Foundations of Education; subject methods courses; elective courses.

Employment

Opportunities for teaching have been dominated by difficulties and, throughout the 1980s, there have been strikes and stoppages related to teachers' pay and conditions. In 1987-88 sharp cuts in educational spending raised the likelihood of larger classes in both the national and post-primary schools, and voluntary redundancies in the teaching profession. Following recognition of the Irish teaching qualifications many teachers have been employed within the UK and particularly in the London area.

At the end of 1989 it appeared that the prospects for the 1990s were likely to be dominated by a decline in the birthrate and therefore a decline in the school population. However, in January 1990 a new economic deal agreed by the Government and spelled out in the policy paper 'Programme for Economic and Social Progress' gave education top priority. Teachers will have wide ranging benefits including a 10% pay rise; there is a commitment to reducing the pupil-teacher ratio; and the promise of additional ancillary staff for schools. Estimates are that Ireland must recruit between 1450 and 2250 teachers by 1993, and much may depend on winning teachers back to Ireland. Recruitment for teacher training, particularly in the primary sector was cut by about 70% in the 1980s.

Probation

Circular R.O. 153446 (1983), addressed to Boards of Management of National Schools and Principal Teachers is entitled "Teachers on Probation". This document sets out the conditions for the completion of a satisfactory probation period, viz:

(i) in the case of continuous service, satisfactory service of not less than one year's duration; in the case where service is not continuous satisfactory service of not less than 300 days in the aggregate;

(ii) probation must be completed within five years of the first permanent appointment;

(iii) in the case of continuous service there are required reports to be furnished on the teacher's work; a *Beagthuairisc* report is normally done during the first school term (i.e. September-December) and a second report, a *Mórthuairisc* is normally done before the end of the school year.

Such reports contain records of the teacher's employment; the classes and number of pupils in his/her care; dates of visits from the school inspector; and a record of the school inspector's comments at the time of visiting the probationer. The initial visit will normally be of an advisory nature; the *Mórthuairisc* - or General Inspection - could lead to an Inspector recommending that a teacher's probationary period be extended.

MORTHUAIRISC

Ceantar.......... Contae.......... Uimhir Rolla..........

Ainm 7 Seoladh na Scoile..........

Ainm 7 Seoladh Cathaoirligh an Bhoird Bhainistíochta..........

....

Oide.......... Post sa Scoil.......... Ar phromhadh: Tá/Níl

Coláiste agus Blianta Oiliúna.......... Dáta Breithe..........

Dáta a cheaptha mar oide (i) Anseo.......... (ii) Faoin Roinn..........

Dáta an mhórfhiosraithe..........

An mhórthuairisc í seo a leanann fógra sé mhí..........

Dáta na mórthuairisc is déanaí..........

Breithmheas ar obair an oide sa Mhórthuairisc sin..........

Na ranganna agus líon na ndaltaí atá faoi chúram an oide..........

Dátaí na mbeagchuairteanna a tugadh ar an oide le bliain anuas..........

Don Roinnchigire:

Má tá an t-oide ar a phromhadh an moltar don Roinn an diploma a bhronnadh air..........

Síniú..........

Dáta..........

Don Roinn:	Inisleacha	Dáta
Breithmheas scr. san ROI	....	....
Sleachta curtha amach	....	....
Cóip curtha chuig an gCigire	....	....
Cuireadh fógra chuig an R.I.	....	....
I dtaisce (ag an R.O.I.)	....	....

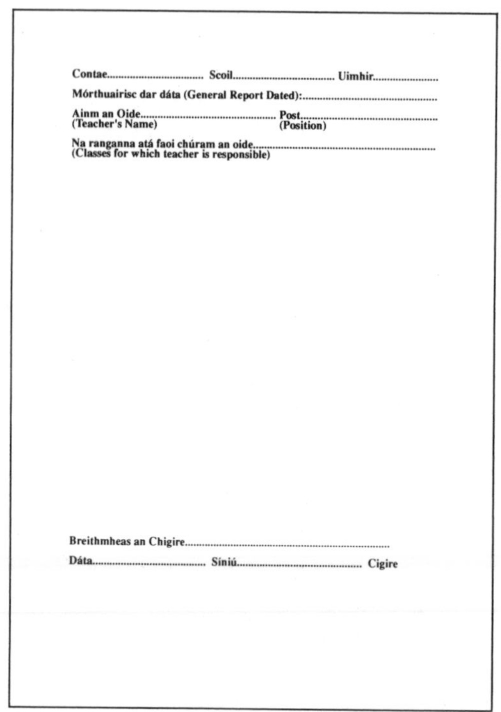

Contae.......... Scoil.......... Uimhir..........

Mórthuairisc dar dáta (General Report Dated):..........

Ainm an Oide.......... Post..........
(Teacher's Name) (Position)

Na ranganna atá faoi chúram an oide..........
(Classes for which teacher is responsible)

Breithmheas an Chigire..........

Dáta.......... Síniú.......... Cigire

Having completed a satisfactory probation teachers are awarded the Department's Diploma which certifies that they are fully qualified National School teachers and are eligible for appointment in any National School.

It may be noted that there are no special conditions attaching to the probationary period, such as reduced teaching load or specified support in school. Occasional courses may be provided in a Teachers' Centre but, in general, these are not obligatory.

Such conditions have been applied to other groups, from September 1983. These include primary teachers trained in Northern Ireland (or abroad) who have not previously completed a probationary period. Those teachers who are involved in the secondary level are also required to undertake a probationary period of one year and must satisfy a school inspector as to their proficiency in the classroom. Headteachers (usually called Principal Teachers) are expected to help and support the process of probation but do not formally report upon or appraise probationers.

Once probation has been successfully completed, continued teacher competence and performance is assessed on an irregular basis by the appropriate school inspectors.

Career Development and Inservice Training

With recruitment into the teaching profession in Ireland considerably diminished, and school staffs becoming more stable, opportunities for promotion are limited. Certain conditions are attached to eligibility for appointment as a Principal Teacher (i.e. Headteacher) in National Schools, and related to years of service as a teacher.

In 1981, following negotiations and a national wage agreement, the teachers' common basic salary ranged over a fourteen year incremental span. Extra allowances are paid for qualifications (e.g. degree; H.Dip. Ed.,Ph.D.). Posts of responsibility are categorised A and B, commensurate with the level of responsibility involved.

It is generally accepted that the present inservice provision in the country is uneven and unco-ordinated. In the early seventies, twenty-one Teachers' Centres were set up and financed by the Department of Education. These provide inservice courses, lectures, workshops and induction programmes for serving teachers. In addition the Department of Education provides occasional day seminars and summer courses of one week's duration for teachers. These courses, which are free of charge to teachers, focus on curricular, practical and theoretical areas. Colleges of Education also offer day seminars and summer courses on a fee-paying basis and primary teachers are awarded three days personal leave in lieu of attending a summer course of one week's duration. One-year part-time remedial courses for primary teachers are provided at a number of venues throughout the country.

Teachers may also be released for full-time attendance, usually for one year's duration, for Diploma and Master of Education courses directed towards greater specialisation and personal development. In most cases such teachers are expected to arrange for, and pay, substitutes during their term of absence from the school concerned.

Footnotes

1 *Colleges of Education, which are recognised colleges of the National University, include Mary Immaculate, Limerick, and St Patrick's, Dublin. Associated colleges of the University of Dublin include St Mary's College, Dublin; Froebel College, Dublin; and Church of Ireland College, Dublin.*

Teacher education for certain specialist subjects is provided in specialist colleges and the degree validated by The University of Dublin; The National University of Ireland, and The National Council for Education Awards.

2 *In late 1989 The European Community Court of Justice backed the Irish Government regulations which stipulate that teachers in public-sector schools must be able to speak Irish.*

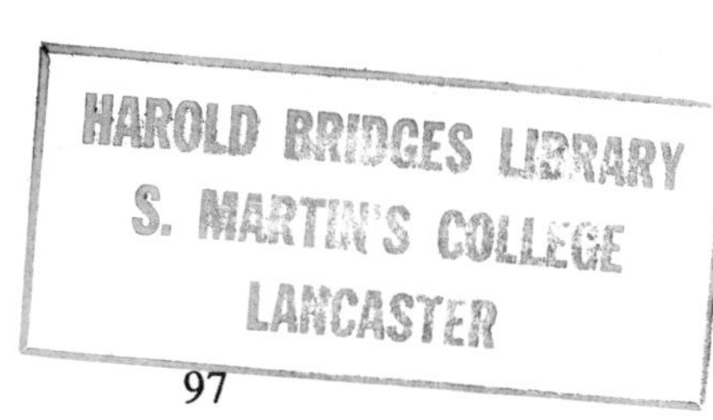

A Teacher in a Primary School

Meallann bunmhúinteoireacht in Éirinn micléinn ar ardchaighdheán a bhfuil cáilíochtaí acadúla acu a thabharfadh cead isteach dóibh i slite beatha a mbeadh luach saothair i bhfad níos brabúsaí dá mbarr. Cuireann na Coláistí Dideachais san áireamh go gcuireann an bunmhúinteoir Éireannach a chuid cruthaíochta, solais agus taithí i bhfeidhm i gceird na múinteoireachta, agus dá thoradh sin ní hé amháin go mbíonn oideachas mar ábhar céime sa B.Ed., bíonn ábhar acadúil eile ann chomh maith. Ní chuireann an curaclam náisiúnta Oideachais isteach ar an solúbacht a cheadaítear do chuile mhúinteoir ina sheomra ranga féin, ligeann sé do chumas, scil agus speiseanna an mhúinteora ar leith a theacht chun cinn. Cothaíonn sé seo saibhreas agus éagsúlacht sa mhúinteoireacht, rudaí a bhíonn in easnamh i gcórais oideachais níos cuibhrithe.

Tá farasbarr na múinteoirí an-tugtha dá gcuid oibre, is mion minic a dhéantar an t-ullmhuchán taobh amuigh d'uaireanta oifigiúla na scoile. Is mór idir na coinníollacha oibre ó áit go chéile ó thaobh achmhainí, fearas agus tacaíocht ó thuismitheoirí de. Faigheann go leor múinteoirí sásamh as a gcuid oibre, ach mar sin féin tá fadhbanna sa chóres oideachais a chuireann bac ar lán-fhorbairt an chóraise. Tá gealltanas ann an coibhneas an-ard dalta-múinteoir a ísliú taobh istigh d'achar gearr. Ina theannta sin caithfear cód oifigiúil smachta a chur ar fáil agus caithfear feabhas a chur ar sholáthar chórais siceolaíochta, teiripe chaints agus mhúinteoireacht feabhais. Táthar ag súil go mbeidh níos mó béime agus níos mó airgid ar fáil d'fhorbairt curaclaim agus d'Oideachas inseirbhíse, agus go mbeidh daoine níos eolaí faoi cheisteanna a bhaineann le gnéasnascadh le linn na nóchaidí.

Ach oiread le haon chóras Oideachais eile, tá deacrachtaí agus lochtanna ann a éilíonn aird agus cúnamh ó chuile dhuine atá sáite i gcúrsaí oideachais, ón dream atá i gceannas anuas. Fós féin léirítear scileanna agus dúthracht mhúinteoirí na hÉireann sa gcaoi a dtéann siad i ngleic leis na fadhbanna sin agus sa mbunfhiric gurb é forbairt iomlán an pháiste croí lár na bunmhúinteoireachta in Éirinn.

Primary teaching in Ireland today is a career which attracts students of a high calibre whose academic achievements qualify them for entry into many more lucrative careers. Reflecting the extent to which the Irish primary teacher brings much of her/his own creativity, knowledge and experience to bear in the practice of teaching, the Colleges of Education offer a Bachelor of Education degree which allows students to study not only Education but also a second subject to degree level. The existence of a national curriculum does not interfere with the flexibility allowed each teacher within the classroom; this permits the potential of the individual teacher's personal skills and interests to be realised, resulting in a richness of teaching perhaps absent in more confining systems of education.

The majority of teachers are very committed to their work; in many cases preparatory work is done outside official school hours. Working conditions vary greatly from area to area in terms of resources, equipment and parental support. Many teachers find their jobs fulfilling; however, problem areas exist within the education system which impinge upon its achieving its full potential. There is a commitment to lowering the currently very high pupil/teacher ratio within a short period of time; coupled with this must be the provision of an official code of discipline and an improvement in access to remedial, psychological and speech therapy support systems. Other hopes for the education system in the 1990's would include increased consideration and funding of curriculum development and inservice education and a heightening of awareness with regard to gender issues.

As with any education system, various difficulties and limitations exist which demand the ongoing attention of all involved in education - from those who control the system to those who work within its parameters. However, the skills and dedication of Irish teachers are reflected in their handling of these problems and a concern for the full development of the child remains central to Irish primary teaching.

A Primary Teacher

I never knew anything else other than being a teacher, was of much importance! Teachers abounded in our family for generations, right back to "hedge-school" days. We were the fourth generation in fact. So away back in the early fifties I had a choice to make - did I sit for the Preparatory Examination or for the County Council Scholarship Examination? The choice was easy - Preparatory of course! This success at Easter meant I could now enter a Preparatory College for the Education of future teachers. These were all Gaelic language Colleges, four in the Country. Whereas other Secondary Colleges utilised a five-year course to Leaving Certificate these Colleges used a four-year period. Having completed a high-grade Leaving Certificate I then entered Out Lady of Mercy Training College in Dublin to complete a two-year course, graduating with Honours in 1957. My teaching practice weeks were all single-class in city schools - some deprived, some middle-class, one decidedly upper class. None of these compared at all to my first teaching post.

I launched forth into a four-teacher rural school in a distinctly agricultural area. As one encouraging Departmental Inspector put it to me - "you won't get too far here with the Gaelic it's a "plantation area"! I never could fathom that out - as far as I was concerned planters learned their Gaelic same as anyone else. I had Junior and Senior Infants, First and Second Class in one room, had to prepare First Class for both Sacraments of Penance and Eucharist. I took Needlework for all the girls once a week and had choir practice once a week for the local Church. That was part of the school appointment. Church Choir each Sunday morning and evening, and also organise for Christmas and Easter ceremonies.

There was a probation period of two years after training - I had an Examination of one complete day in year one and another in year two. Many visits from Departmental Inspectors occurred in between, Infants Inspectors, Needlework Inspector, Music Inspector and also a Divisional or Higher Inspector from Dublin. One was always prepared for a call! My final Diploma was done on October 6th 1959 with 65 children in the room of a delapidated old building with many cracked windows, holed floors, and one small oil-stove in the corner. All for the princely sum of £27 per month! But I loved my new life.

One might wonder why a young teacher had so many pupils! In that area which was "seed potatoes" country all families' income came from potatoes, so the children went away to harvest the crop in early October until mid-November or later. We had to close the schools in these areas for holidays then instead of taking long summer holidays. Our Senior boys and girls also went over to Scotland in gangs to harvest the potatoes there as well, not returning to the area until Christmas. This meant that our attendance was always down for two terms and one could not gain an extra teacher - the average had to be static for three terms. My seven years in that school were the happiest perhaps of my career.

On marriage in 1964 I transferred to the West of the Country to a remote enough area. Jobs were plentiful, thankfully as I was to transfer in and out of seven schools in the next six years - due to promotion in my husband's job. I never missed a day at school in those years. Once you had a reference from both clergyman and Inspector you simply could pick up any job. Most schools in the rural West were two-teacher schools with approximately 35-40 pupils. The pupil/teacher ratio took some getting-used-to after such huge numbers. The lack of general knowledge also irked me somewhat, and the hospitality and openness of the North was lacking. These were a cunning crafty race of youngsters. I became Principal of one of these remote schools but only stayed a year.

Our new Curriculum was introduced to schools then in 1971 after much "piloting" and "trials" all over the Country. It was reasonably successful in the smaller schools where the average number of children was suitable but in the large urban areas the "swing away" from basics to Environmental Studies left a generation of children lacking in two areas - spelling and numeracy skills. However with in-service days and summer holiday courses each year that has been put to rights hopefully a long time ago.

In July 1972 I came to a large city all-girls' school, run by nuns. This was a new approach to education. I now had a single class of one sex in a shiny well-waxed new three-storey rambling building with lawns and flower-beds and classroom slippers! One wondered at times which was of more importance, a waxed floor and slippers or education! Numbers were 45+ in a class. Happily, 18 years on I am proud to say our team of dedicated teachers has raised the standard of education in our city to a very high one. I moved in and out of Infants, First and Second Standard until 1977 when volunteers were called for, to take on a new idea - a transition year from Primary to Secondary, but based in our Primary School. It was felt children were transferring at a very young age as they came to school at 4 years. I took it on a trial basis for one year. So it was back to the study for me, back to Senior Grammar, Algebra, Geometry etc. It was a tough year but a rewarding one. Here thirteen years on in 1990 I'm still there! My own children have come through the school and have completed that extra year which is of enormous benefit. They mature beautifully, catch up on areas where "gaps" might have been, take an adventure into First Year Mathematics, History, Geography and French. We find time for Music, Art, Irish Crochet, and invite visitors into our classroom. We take field-trips out. Sadly our numbers have only dropped to 40 per class in all those years, while our young teachers go around hoping to work days or weeks if they are lucky. Our financial situation improved wonderfully and these same young teacher now earn £50 a day doing temporary work. We have another National Wage Agreement on stream and at last our three Teacher Unions are getting up there and staying - "sort out our Tax - get our ratio down - get our young teachers on stream for permanent work immediately! I think things are going to improve. I hope so. The fifth generation of teachers is coming along in June 1991, to follow family tradition - my older beautiful daughter is in her final year, she did her final teacher practice with us for four weeks! Ever look at yourself in the mirror at work? I did! She is a carbon copy only better!

One note of apprehension does come to the fore. Four of our retired teachers have never been replaced - the birthrate is beginning to drop even in rural areas. This intake in 1990 to Training College - of male students - stands at six in one college, nine in another and four in a third college. Will teaching become an all-female preserve? That will be a sad day for education. But the "perks" and opportunities are obviously not there to the same extent as they are in other professions and in private enterprise. We hear mutterings abroad of late, of co-education in our city centre becoming a reality within a short time. We also have non-denominational schools appearing - change is afoot. I hope sincerely that my daughter will have as fruitful and as satisfying a life among children as I have had for 34 years this very month of October.

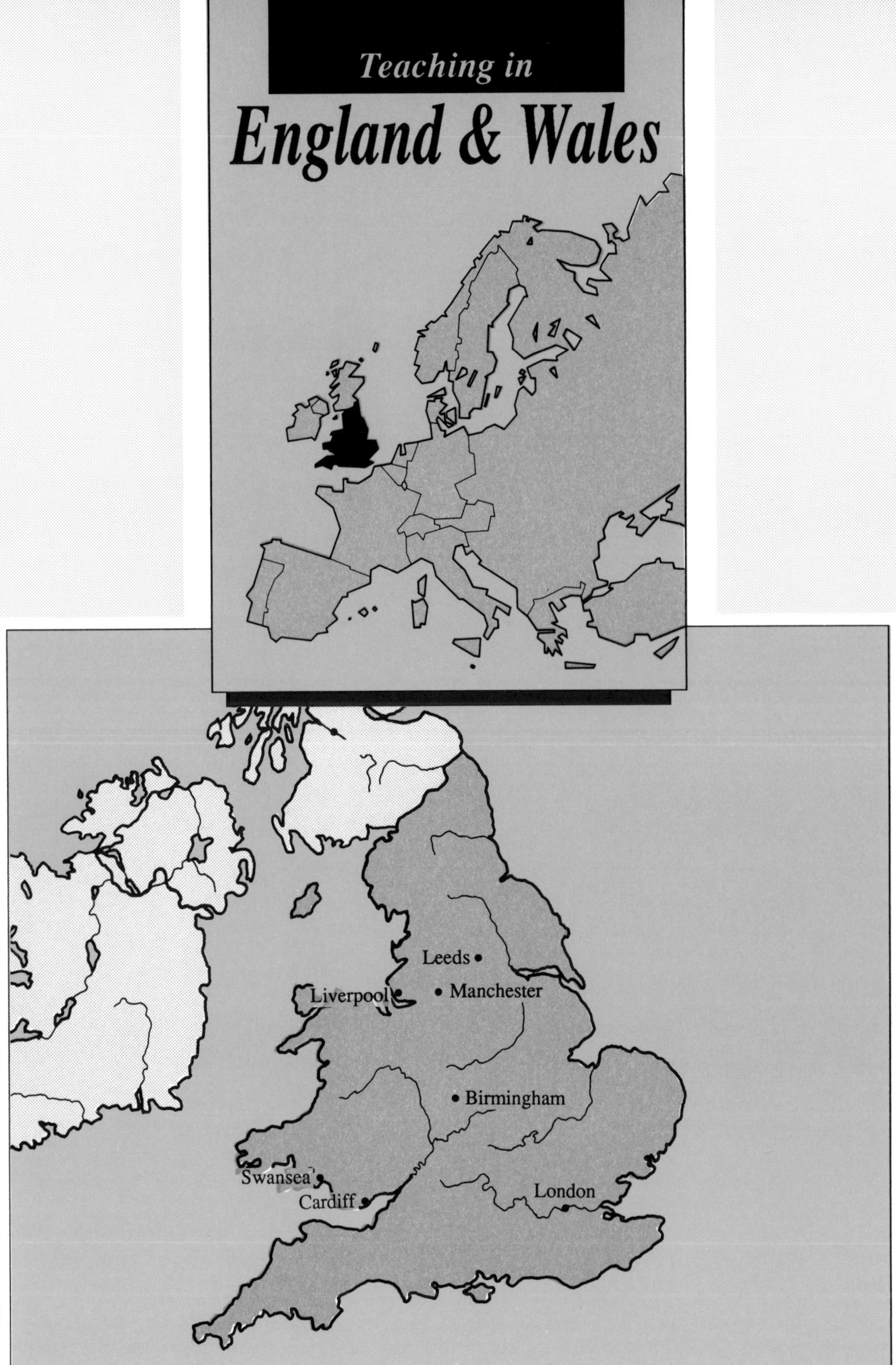
Teaching in
England & Wales
Leeds
Liverpool
Manchester
Birmingham
Swansea
Cardiff
London

TEACHING IN ENGLAND AND WALES

Geographically the British Isles stand apart from Europe, separated from the mainland by the English Channel and the North Sea, with the Atlantic Ocean to the west, where the island of Ireland dominates. The United Kingdom of Great Britain and Northern Ireland is a constitutional monarchy consisting of England, Wales, Scotland and Northern Ireland. The UK extends some 1000 kilometres, from the Isles of Scilly in the south west, to the Shetland Islands in the north east. Scotland has its own legal and educational systems and it is treated separately. Northern Ireland also has its own arrangements governing education.

The economy, although showing a decline in heavy engineering in favour of growth in high-technology industries and in the service sector, is quite broadly-based. Manufacturing remains of great importance, while agriculture, forestry and fishing make significant contributions. Major reserves of coal, oil and gas also make their impact on the economy as does a sizeable tourist industry.

Of the English population of some 46 million, the majority are urban-dwellers living in and around London and in other main cities and towns in the midlands and the north. The population of Wales is about 2 3/4 millions, one-fifth of them being Welsh-speaking. Partly because of imperial and British Commonwealth connections, there are large numbers of Moslems, Jews, Sikhs and Hindus in the country, over 1 1/2 million in all.

As already mentioned, Education in the UK is administered under three different authorities: The Department of Education and Science (DES) for England and Wales, the Scottish Office for Scotland (SOED), and the Northern Ireland Office for Ulster, the thirteen counties comprising Northern Ireland. England and Wales form the largest of the three areas.

Education in England and Wales is the responsibility of a Secretary of State at the Head of a Department, rather than of a Minister, although the Secretary of State is a member of the Cabinet. The Department has its main seat in London, with a few smaller offices in the provinces.

The most striking differences between the organisation and administration of education in England and Wales and that in most other countries lies in the strong decentralisation to the county authorities, so that much more local autonomy is found in organisational structure, funding support services, management, etc. However, teacher training is centrally controlled by the Department of Education and Science (DES) regulations, even while training institutions have the freedom to devise course patterns that may reflect needs in their area. Central direction has become more prominent under the Conservative administration, though this has been as much from political motives as from the need for harmonisation and the enhancement of standards.

Schooling

Children in England and Wales are obliged to start school at the beginning of the term in which they reach the age of five. Where there are vacancies, many will be accepted by Primary schools even earlier, if parents wish for this.

Primary education lasts for 6 years; children transfer to secondary schools when they are 11, and compulsory schooling in that phase lasts up to the age of 16. As a result, the need for sufficient teachers to provide 11 years of education is a heavy financial, logistical and recruitment burden. Primary education divides into an Infant phase of 2 years and a Junior phase of 4 years, though these are continuous, taking children from Reception classes in which socialisation and initiation into basic skills of literacy and numeracy are introduced, to preparation in the final year for the more specialised and more advanced studies of the Secondary school.

A major piece of legislation, the Education Reform Act (ERA for England and Wales) was enacted in 1988. This requires, among many other innovations, all Primary and Secondary schools to implement the National Curriculum, which prescribes not only the subjects that all pupils are to study, but also the proportion of time to be devoted to each one, and, through more detailed documents, the programme of study, attainment targets, assessment arrangements and teaching approaches to be adopted.

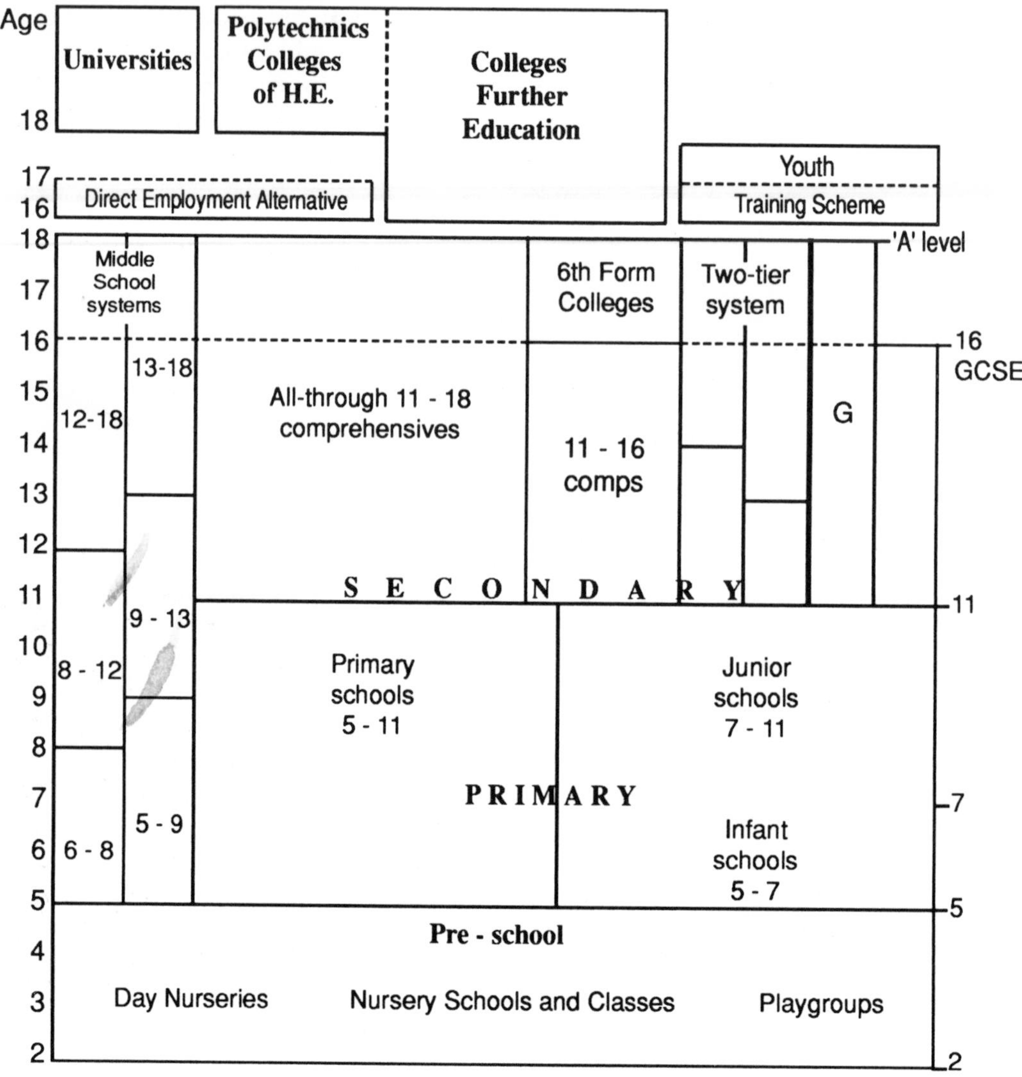

The National Curriculum for Primary schools lists three 'Core' subjects, English, Mathematics and Science, and six 'Foundation' subjects, Technology, History, Geography, Art, Music and Physical Education. Religious Education will, of course, continue to be taught in every school. In addition, the ERA requires the curriculum to cover health education, other aspects of personal and social education and an understanding of gender and multi-cultural issues, usually through subject-based studies.

INTRODUCING THE
NATIONAL
CURRICULUM
COUNCIL
NCC
NATIONAL
CURRICULUM
COUNCIL
NOVEMBER 1989
second edition

The transition from Primary to Secondary schools is automatic, although a detailed assessment of each child's achievements, skills and potential is prepared and, after discussion with the parents, a recommendation is made about the choice of school for secondary education. Parents have the right to choose the school which they wish their child to attend, although often in many parts of the country the availability of different schools is limited and does not allow for a wide range of choice. The LEA (Local Education Authority) is required to respect parental choice, however, especially where a single-sex as opposed to a mixed school is concerned, or where a religious affiliation leads to the selection of a denominational school, i.e. one with a strong religious ethos and representation on its Governing Body.

Secondary schools in the maintained, i.e. state, sector are designated by a variety of titles. Most commonly they will be Mixed Comprehensive, usually taking pupils from 11 to 18 years; some will be Girls' or Boys' Comprehensives; others may be High Schools, teaching pupils from 14 to 18 years after they have come from a Middle School (Years 9 to 13); while a very few are still selective in their intake and bear the title Grammar Schools. In addition to the range of Core and Foundation subjects mentioned in the paragraph on Primary schools, a Secondary school must offer at least one Modern Foreign Language to all pupils for the five years from 11 to 16. The National Curriculum for secondary schools requires emphasis to be given to awareness of technological advances, to the economic basis of everyday life, to the importance of relating the academic to the practical. The very detailed syllabuses for each curriculum subject have

been devised to ensure that pupils are guaranteed a recognised standard wherever they study and to ease the problem of transition when pupils change schools.

The first external examination which pupils take in English and Welsh schools is for the General Certificate of Secondary Education (GCSE), taken at the age of 16, following five years of secondary study. For those staying on after age 16 there follows a cycle of more intensive but narrower studies leading to the A Level (Advanced Level) examinations at 18, that qualifies students for entry into Higher Education.

Happily the staying-on rate has been increasing. At present (see Regional Trends 25 published by the Central Statistical Office) the proportion of 16-year olds staying on or entering further education or a Youth Training Scheme is 64.2% in England and 62.5% in Wales, both substantially lower than in Scotland where the figure is 77%. In England 12% of boys and 10.5% of girls leave school at age 18 years with three or more A-levels.

The staying-on rate is higher in independent schools, which is explained by the fact that parental expectations, the selection process on academic grounds, and the curriculum patterns are all geared to continuing education beyond 18. In 1985 a scheme for assisting able pupils from families unable to pay the high fees levied by independent schools was introduced, so that by this Assisted Places system pupils who could benefit from a more intensive and academic education, given in more narrowly homogeneous teaching groups, such as is more common in such schools, are enabled to attend them.

Teacher Training

All teachers in the maintained, i.e. state, sector of education, whether at primary, secondary or further (i.e. post-16) level, must possess a training certificate attesting to satisfactory skills, knowledge and experience for the phase concerned. University teachers, however, are not obliged to have training in teaching. Teachers in independent schools may be appointed without training, although the vast majority will have received their training through the state system or will have demonstrated their competence in the classroom by other pathways.

Students who wish to become teachers in Primary or Secondary schools may follow one of two distinct routes: either a Concurrent course of 4 years combining curriculum, pedagogical and educational studies, together with substantial practical experience of teaching in schools throughout; or a Consecutive course consisting of an academic degree programme over 3 or 4 years followed by an intensive 1-year pedagogical and practical course. In practice the majority of Primary teachers opt for the first type, leading to the B.Ed. Hons. (Bachelor of Education with Honours) degree, since they prefer the continuous and varied experience of contact with children and teachers in schools while they are extending their curricular and educational studies. Graduates from a wide range of academic disciplines may also opt for Primary training leading to the PGCE (Postgraduate Certificate in Education) qualification, but the majority will be preparing for specialist teaching (in secondary schools) in one or two subjects only. In either case, the student who successfully completes the course will be awarded QTS (Qualified Teacher Status) and a DES (Department of Education and Science) registration number, without which no appointment to maintained schools can be made. Teachers in Further Education colleges will usually be drawn from those with previous professional qualifications, so that a 1-year training course, leading to the award of the

Certificate in FE teaching and comparable to the PGCE in its design, will be the normal training programme.

Students will not be admitted to training courses unless they have three particular qualifications:

- a minimum of two satisfactory passes in A Level examinations, usually in relevant or acceptably academic subjects;
- a minimum of Grade C in GCSE in English Language and Mathematics;
- the appropriate qualities of personality, character and experience required for teaching children; this requirement is always assessed by a detailed reference from the applicant's school, by a comprehensive curriculum vitae and by an individual interview in which the candidate's ability, expression, commitment to the mission of education and potential are assessed.

Mature applicants (i.e. those over 21) are slightly increasing in number and may be given certain academic concessions if they appear to be very suitable for teaching and to have the potential to complete their training successfully.

From 1989 a new mode of Teacher Training has been introduced, designed to enhance the recruitment of teachers especially in subjects in which there is a severe shortage, and entitled the Licensed Teacher Scheme. The students selected are jointly appointed to an appropriate school in which they teach for approximately four days a week, and then receive pedagogical and educational courses on the fifth day, for a period of two years. It is too early to assess fully the impact of this scheme on the schools and training institutions, but it will undeniably appeal to those with relevant qualifications and/or maturity who feel they wish to be trained more predominantly in the context of the school classroom.

From 1990 yet another mode of Teacher Training was being introduced, entitled the Articled Teacher Scheme, similar to the above, but where the trainee teacher has a degree in a school subject and is actually appointed to the staff of a given school. This teacher receives a reduced salary (which is nevertheless considerably greater than a student's maintenance grant) and is likewise trained for a proportion of the week at a training institution over a period of two years, finally being awarded a PGCE qualification.

Teacher training is provided in various types of institutions: the B.Ed. in Polytechnics, Colleges of Higher Education or Colleges of Education; the PGCE in University Departments of Education, Polytechnics and Colleges of Higher Education; the FE Certificate in only four specialist institutions in England. The training staff are themselves experienced teachers from the relevant phase and the DES has recently moved formally to require these training members of staff to update their experience and practice by returning periodically to the classroom, so that their skills match current situations and demands and their training correctly prepares their students for entry to the profession.

While training institutions retain the right to devise their own patterns of B.Ed. and PGCE programmes, they must satisfy the DES that their courses meet the demands of the national educational system. This is particularly important in England and Wales, where trained teachers have freedom of movement and indeed seek their own posts in schools upon qualification. Training thus pays regard to general national patterns of schooling, and, in this respect as in many others, the introduction of the National Curriculum and the greater standardisation of examinations has been of advantage. On the other hand, the greater decentralisation resulting from the LMS (Local Management of Schools), and the resulting discrepancies in staffing levels, supply of materials, support services, etc. may lead to differing conditions of service for teachers from LEA to LEA and from school to school.

The structure of the training courses ensures that coverage of the five major areas of knowledge and skills, i.e. curriculum studies, pedagogical studies, education studies, special subject studies and school experience, is balanced and cumulative. The illumination of theoretical examination of a subject and its successful presentation to a class by actual contact with a group of children is ensured by a regular weekly day in a school, followed at the end of the year by a 'block practice' in the same school. Teaching experiences are so arranged that a broad understanding of problems associated with children at different ages, schools in different environments and staff with different philosophies about effective teaching approaches can be gained over the period of training. This will evidently be more easily achieved in the 4-year B.Ed. with its range of school experiences. Back in college students will be expected to attend lectures, seminars, tutorials, practical classes, etc., to write essays, prepare teaching materials and sample lessons, but, above all, to develop a self-critical approach by means of maintaining a File of notes from Teaching Practice. This will contain, in addition to essential preliminary information on the school in question, such as size, staffing, resources, structure of responsibility, pupil analysis, socio-economic data, syllabus details, a sheet for each lesson or teaching period taught and including a concise Evaluation of the lesson outcome. The creation of a habit of self-analysis is a key factor in the development of an effective and confident teacher. With the current demand for continuous development of professional skills, even good practising teachers will also be expected to maintain their cutting-edge by attendance at INSET (i.e. In-Service Education for Teachers) courses either at Teachers' Centres or within their own school. As teachers gain in experience and seniority, not only will they be expected to seek promotion to extend their skills, but they will be entrusted with supervision of younger colleagues or students in training.

Employment

As was mentioned earlier, each teacher is eligible for appointment as soon as QTS and the DES Registration is awarded. In fact, students will be making application for appointment from the beginning of the following academic year during their last year of training. For the not inconsiderable numbers who can offer "shortage" subjects, such as Mathematics, Science, Technology, Foreign Languages, and several others, they may well be offered posts from Christmas onwards, and only in very rare cases would they be unemployed, unless they chose to be. But even for teachers offering other secondary subjects and for Primary teachers the chances of being appointed are very favourable. Each student will write to the Authority advertising a vacancy for an application form. This is a comprehensive document, allowing for a personal statement covering interests and experience as well as academic and other details. A reference from at least one responsible person, generally the student's tutor at College, will be required. If the Authority, through the school, believes the applicant is potentially suitable, he or she will be included on a Short List for interview. At the Interview the Head, a senior member of staff and at least one Governor will be present and the candidates will all be given equality of treatment in terms of time, questions asked, opportunity to pose questions. The successful candidate may be informed at once if the application has been successful; otherwise, notification will be made by post. The LEA will issue the teacher with a contract of employment, usually as a Probationary Teacher in the case of a First Appointment, and the teacher will be held to accept the (generally fair) conditions of service. The level of salary will be determined according to the length of training, the other qualifications, the experience of the teacher and the responsibilities of the post to which he or she is appointed.

Career Development

During the period of Probation, which at present lasts one year, the new teacher will be inspected by the LEA Inspector, and the Head of the school will be expected to write a report on the professional progress of the probationer. Upon completion of the year, and assuming that the reports have been positive, the teacher is then given a permanent appointment and, in theory anyway, could well be in the same institution for the remainder of his or her career. In practice, this is extremely unlikely, since not only does each teacher wish to gain broader experience, acquire more responsibility by moving, or simply find that personal circumstances require a change of house, but also the Head and governors would advise a teacher who has not refreshed his or her career by a new challenge to seek another appointment.

The majority of teachers will be appointed with a starting salary at the lower end of the MPG (Main Professional Grade), but opportunities exist for supplementary payments for special responsibility and for promotion. Since the staff employed in other educational establishments are often recruited from maintained school service, there are promotion opportunities not only to Head of Department, Deputy Head and Head, but also to Lecturers in Colleges of Further Education, Colleges of Higher Education, Polytechnics and Universities. The latter posts will require evidence of substantial subject expertise acquired through responsible teaching experience but more especially through research, higher degrees and publications. However, the successful primary or secondary teacher has the great advantage of effective teaching to support his or her appointment to lecturing positions which will profit from the training and experience that school teaching has conferred. Alternatively, teachers may move into the Inspectorate, either for the LEA or for the DES, or as a local specialist Adviser, or they may transfer into education administration in the LEA. Some teachers in maintained schools may wish to transfer to the independent school sector, which may offer a more advantageous salary scale, better teaching conditions, wider experience in a boarding school, etc. The perception by parents of problems encountered in the state schools system has led to a slight increase in the percentage of pupils attending independent schools, despite the often very high level of fees. The ensuing expansion has thus created more teaching posts in these schools.

Finally we may note that plans for implementing the appraisal of teachers were well advanced at the beginning of the 1990s. Proposals made by the Education Secretary, in November 1990, indicated that all teachers in England and Wales will have their classroom performance assessed every two years. Every teacher will be interviewed, and observed teaching in the classroom. A report will be drawn up, weaknesses identified, and targets set. Headteachers and Depute-headteachers will be appraised by someone nominated by the local education authority.

A Modern Languages Teacher

I took a degree in French and Latin at Bristol University, which included a year as an English Assistant in a Lycée Technique in the Paris area. This spell in a foreign school was, on reflection, somewhat neglected, as it was not properly appraised, although I gained a lot from the experience. My training course, also at Bristol University, covered the teaching of my specialist subject of Modern Languages (though I offered French and German, rather than Latin which is very rare in state secondary schools), educational studies which included Pastoral Care of children, and a subsidiary subject, in my case drama. There was also, of course, a proportion (about 40%) of the time spent in different schools on Teaching Practice. I have to criticise the course in several respects: the methodology component consisted on reviewing, critically, the succession of teaching styles, and then promoting the "communicative approach"; current materials and aids to teaching were referred to but not always used; the educational studies lectures were also of little help to me, consisting of sociological or pastoral themes, much of which seemed obvious or unnecessary. The teaching practice consisted of one day each week followed by two whole weeks in the first term, then a whole term spent in a different school. My timetable consisted of about half of what a full-time teacher would take. My supervisor was very helpful, giving advice before and after lessons and fairly frequent observation. The school staff also gave me advice during the practices.

During the last term of my training course I applied for and obtained a post as an assistant teacher of French and German in a secondary school, teaching children aged from 11 to 18 and coming from a variety of ethnic backgrounds. I was also made a form tutor and gave, outside the curriculum, some games instruction. At the interview for the post there were four candidates and the Head of the school was supported by the head of the Languages Department, a school governor and the schools' adviser for languages. I was expected to teach the special subjects and their appropriate methodology; to support the christian commitment of the school (it was a church of England school); to maintain a positive classroom order and to provide a youthful face to the teaching staff! My first salary was approximately £9,000 per annum, which included an addition for being a "Good Honours" graduate (I obtained an "Upper Second" class degree) and for my years of study.

During my first year of teaching I was, like all teachers at the outset, a "probationer", being observed by the Head of Department for one lesson each term. There were two reports on my performance, one at Christmas and one in July. Since then I have expanded my responsibilities by introducing Spanish to the school, and am now going to be the Deputy head of a Languages Department in another school. I shall eventually hope to become Head of Department. My main interest is in teaching my subject, though I recognise that pastoral concerns are also important. I cannot predict my future career with certainty.

A Physical Education Teacher

In 1980 I completed my Scottish secondary education and moved to I. M. Marsh College of Physical Education, Liverpool, to begin a four year B.Ed. Honours Degree course in Physical Education, with English as a second subject.

My expectations of the course were high and I believed that P.E. teachers qualifying from I. M. Marsh were well received by prospective employers. Although there were various teaching practices throughout the first three years, varying progressively from the junior age range to secondary, the most valuable was the final ten week practice where the staff at the school and my supervisor were extremely helpful and gave excellent practical advice. My criticism of the course would be that actual contact time with children and instruction in the practical skills needed for my profession actually decreased throughout the four years and work gradually became completely theoretical.

Finally concluding my course in 1984, resulting in an Upper Second Class Honours Degree, I experienced great difficulty in obtaining a teaching post and worked my way through numerous applications and a total of seven interviews. Eventually I was appointed, on a one year contract - a type of probationary period - to a Girls 7-18 Independent School in the North of England, the only independent school I had applied for.

During my first year in teaching I received a gross salary of £6,700. I lived in rented accommodation near to school which, although furnished, was not comfortable, clean or warm, especially through the winter months. The cost of living in this flat was substantial and meant that I found it very difficult to save when I also had expenses incurred from being properly attired and from the purchase of books necessary to feed me with ideas for teaching material. Had my parents not helped me financially to acquire a car and later a mortgage, when I decided that this would be an investment and a more economical way of living, I would have found it very difficult to achieve a decent standard of living.

The Physical Education Department within which I worked had good status within the school and area mainly through the reputation of my Head of Department who was very thorough in all preparation, had a comprehensive specialist knowledge, used original thinking to continually increase and update her teaching material and methods and had an amazing capacity for hard work and commitment. Being very aware that my appointment was initially for a one year period I wished to prove myself worthy of the post but was only too well aware of how unprepared I was to tackle a job like this where I needed a huge amount of specialist knowledge. I was fortunate in possessing a willingness to work at the necessary pace and in return was rewarded with an incredible amount of help in terms of ideas and advice from my colleagues. By Christmas, to my enormous relief, my contract had been made permanent. However especially for the first two years of my teaching career it remained a highly pressurised task to be part of such a busy, successful department which was expected to maintain only the highest possible standards of attitude, behaviour and performance in both curricular and extra-curricular situations.

More settled in home-life and after two and a half years I received promotion to second in the department and an 'Incentive "A" Allowance' which I felt was some recognition for a great deal of effort and dedication.

I had always been aware that I was giving up a large amount of extra contact time to my job, after school, Saturdays, Sundays, holidays, and although I enjoyed this found it increasingly difficult to follow my own interests, indeed even to have a holiday when there was so much term-time administration to work through and a mountain of preparation to climb in order to be ready for the new term. Although I was very settled in terms of where I lived and conditions of pay, during my fourth year I began to become slightly discontented by the lack of appreciation from staff in other departments, the headteacher, parents and indeed from the children themselves for the opportunities they were being offered. I had also reached a point where I was called upon and able to make decisions in school yet could see myself being in an annually repetitive situation with no scope for professional development in any direction.

After a great deal of thought I decided that my best option was to gain employment in the state sector of education where I would have the opportunity to continually participate in in-service training. I also decided that I would change direction from secondary Physical Education to being a class teacher in Primary Education. Not such a surprising change since one third of the content of my five years teaching timetable had been with Junior School pupils and I felt this was where my future lay.

In September 1989 I began a one year course at Manchester University specifically designed to re-train secondary teachers for the primary sector. I hoped that while this would mean commuting from Blackpool daily for six weeks every term and to a teaching practice school elsewhere for the remainder of the term it would hopefully place me in the best possible position to enter this new field of education. Again without the financial support of my parents this would have been impossible as unlike the other members of my course, who were seconded by their Local Education Authority I had to resign from my post in order to receive this training.

I found that the security of a home and the experience I had from five years of teaching gave me more confidence and competence in my approach to the course and to the teaching I encountered. In January of this year I began applying for suitable posts.

It was at this point that I encountered a certain amount of opposition from those in positions of responsibility in primary education seemingly for two reasons: firstly because I had been a secondary teacher - 'could I cope with specific behaviour or learning difficulties of young children or was I just interested in teaching subject content?'; secondly because I had previously taught in an independent school - with 'nice girls' - which they obviously considered an easy option. These people obviously took little notice of the committment and desire to teach primary children I had shown by re-training and had little knowledge about children who are educated within independent schools most of whom are very 'ordinary' children. This opposition was not conducive to building my confidence about gaining employment especially when so many applications were turned down or in some cases not even replied to. In the end four local establishments showed interest and I begin a one year fixed-term contract in September at a large Junior school eight miles from my home. The future is as yet still somewhat insecure but as long as I can gain good experience there should be less resistance in future years.

It is an exciting and challenging prospect and although I am once again on the bottom rung I have my previous experience to draw upon and as a curriculum co-ordinator for Physical Education feel that I can make some contribution to the school, staff and pupils whilst depending on their advice and drawing a great deal of knowledge and expertise from them. I am well aware that there could be opposition to me with my teaching background but hope that those I work with have enough professionalism to accept my abilities in a positive manner and accept my willingness to adapt to a new working environment. It will take some time to regain the position I held a year ago either professionally or financially but I believe that I now have access to the facilities which will enable me to make continual meaningful progress in my chosen career.

A Teacher of Welsh

Roedd hi'n amser yr Eisteddfod ac roedd fy nhaid yn siarad â'r cynulleidfa yng Nghapel y Rhos. Diwrnod fy mhenblwydd oedd ac roeddwn i'n edrych ymlaen at fy mharti. Roeddwn i'n ddeg oed.

"Rhaid i ni weithio yn galed iawn i gadw ein hiaith a'n diwylliant ...."

Ugain mlynedd yn ôl, ond mae'r neges dal yn glir. Y noson honno, wrth wrando ar fy nhaid yn siarad, mi benderfynnais - roeddwn i'n mynd i ddysgu.

Canwyd ur emyn Saesneg 'Fight the Good Fight ......' ar ôl i Daid orffen, ac i fi, yn ddeg oed roedd yn gân symbolig iawn.

Es i i Goleg Prifysgol Cymru, Aberystwyth. Roeddwn i wedi penderfynnu iddysgu y Gymraeg i blant bach a dywedodd fy nhaid mai Aberystwyth oedd y lle gorau i wneud fy ngradd. Yn ystod y blwyddyn 'P.G.C.E.', mi gwrddais â llawer o fyfyrwyr eraill oedd yn awyddus i helpu yn yr ymdrech i wneud yr iaith Gymraeg un boblogaidd.

Yn fy marn i, doedd y cwrs 'P.G.C.E' ddim yn ddigon i'n paratoi ni ar gyfer bywyd mewn ysgol uwchradd. Cawson ni llawer o seminarau yn delio a sut iddysgu 'limericks' mewn ffordd diddorol, on basai 'survival guide' wedi bod yn fwy defynddiol.

Es i am gyfweliad i ysgol yn Mhowys.Cyfweliad hir ac anodd oedd, ond roeddwn i'n llwyddiannus. Roeddwn i ar bigau'r drain wrth edrych ymlaen at y tymor newydd.

Ddaru mi fwynhau fy mlwyddyn gyntaf yno.Ces i gymaint o help gan y disgyblion a'r athrawon eraill ac roedd y pennaeth adran yn barod i wrando a helpu pan oedd problem gennf. Arhjosais yn yr ysgol am bum mlynedd ac erbyn i mi adael, roeddwn i'n athrawes llwyddiannus a phrofiadol.

Ces i llawer a fwynhâd wrth ddysgu iaith, yn enwedig i blant dosberth un. Weithiau, pan oedd hi'n dawel yn yr ystafell, roeddwn i bron yn gallu gweld fy nhaid yn gwenu arnaf. Yn anffodus, bu farw cyn i mi basio f'arholiadau.

Ar ôl i mi briodi, roedd rhaid i fi adael yr ysgol i fagu fy mhlant. Ar adega, roeddwn i'n meddwl bod bywyd gwraig-ty yn andros o anodd i'w gymharu â bywyd athrawes.

I ryw raddau, roeddwn i'n edrych ymlaen at yr amser pan fasai'n rhaid i mi ddychwelyd i'r ysgol.

Yn anffodus, yr adeg hynny, doedd dim swyddi ar gael.

Symudais o ysgol i ysgol, yn llenwi i fewn pan oedd athrawon yn sal. Adeg uffernol oedd.

Wedyun, daeth y Cwricwlwm Cenedlaethol. Does dim llawer o athrawon i ddysgu's Gymraeg ar gael a ches i swydd o'r diwedd. Mae contract parhaol yn weth y byd!

Rydw i wedi bod yn f'ysgol presennol ers 1988 a newydd ddechrau ceisio am swyddi pennaeth adran.

Rydw i'n dal i ddysgu sgiliau'r athro a hoffwn i aros yn myd addsyg. Yn anffodus, mae fy ngwr allan o waith a dydy cyflog athro ddim yn ddigon i gadw teulu - ond, bydd rhaid aros a gweld.

Ar byn o byd, rydw i;n falch bod swydd gen i o gwbl. Yn bwysicach byth yw'r ffaith mod i'n dal i fwynhau'r gwaith.

One of my earliest recollections is of the chapel where my 'tard' or grandfather was a deacon.

The memory of his welcoming address to the Llangollen & District Chapels Eisteddfod Committee remains as vivid today as it was over 20 years ago, and I am able to feel anew the impact of his message to the assembled dignitaries and villagers:

"We must strive to preserve that most precious gift of our language and work hard to promote the cultural heritage that has made us a unique people."

This was followed by a hearty rendering (in Welsh) of the English hymn "Fight the Good Fight".

I think that the desire to teach was born at that moment - a desire to share the burden of preserving the Welsh language for future generations. At the tender age of 10 years, I had made a decision that would affect my whole future.

During my P.G.C.E. year, I met other students who shared my ideals - eager recruits in the fight to make popular an ancient language.

I must be honest and admit that the P.G.C.E. course was not an adequate preparation for life in a secondary school. Looking back, I would have welcomed a "survival guide" to my first weeks in school as a "member of staff". I feel it would have proved rather more beneficial than a three hour seminar concerned with teaching limericks in an interesting way!

My success at first interview came as something of a surprise. I had been prepared to spend the majority of my post-examination time and energy in pursuit of a suitable position. The interview was long and difficult - a barrage of questions from largely nameless faces. I viewed the approaching new term with a great deal of trepidation.

My probationary year turned out to be one of the most enjoyable of my career. I received a great deal of support from both staff and pupils. The Head of Department proved to be a goldmine of helpful advice and constructive criticism.

I remained at the school for five years, during which time I became a successful and proficient teacher. There is a great deal of personal and professional satisfaction to be gained from teaching a language and at times I could almost feel my grandfather's approval as yet another "Bore Da" issued forth from unpractised lips.

I left teaching for a time to rear my children - although I must confess that my "second" career as a wife and mother did not progress nearly so well as my teaching career. I was always slightly haunted by the feeling that I was "moonlighting" and looked forward to a return to school.

Unfortunately, my only entry back to teaching came via the supply staff roundabout and I spent many disillusioned and uncertain years without a permanent contract, moving from school to school. However, "Welsh" teachers are scarce and the advent of National Curriculum saw an increase in the demand for permanent post-holders.

I have been in my present school for two years and have begun to apply for promoted posts.

I continue to learn new skills and would hope remain within the profession, although being the only wage earner would make me consider very deeply a career outside teaching should it become financially necessary.

For now, I welcome the stability of my present position and believe the most important consideration is that I continue to enjoy the work that I do.

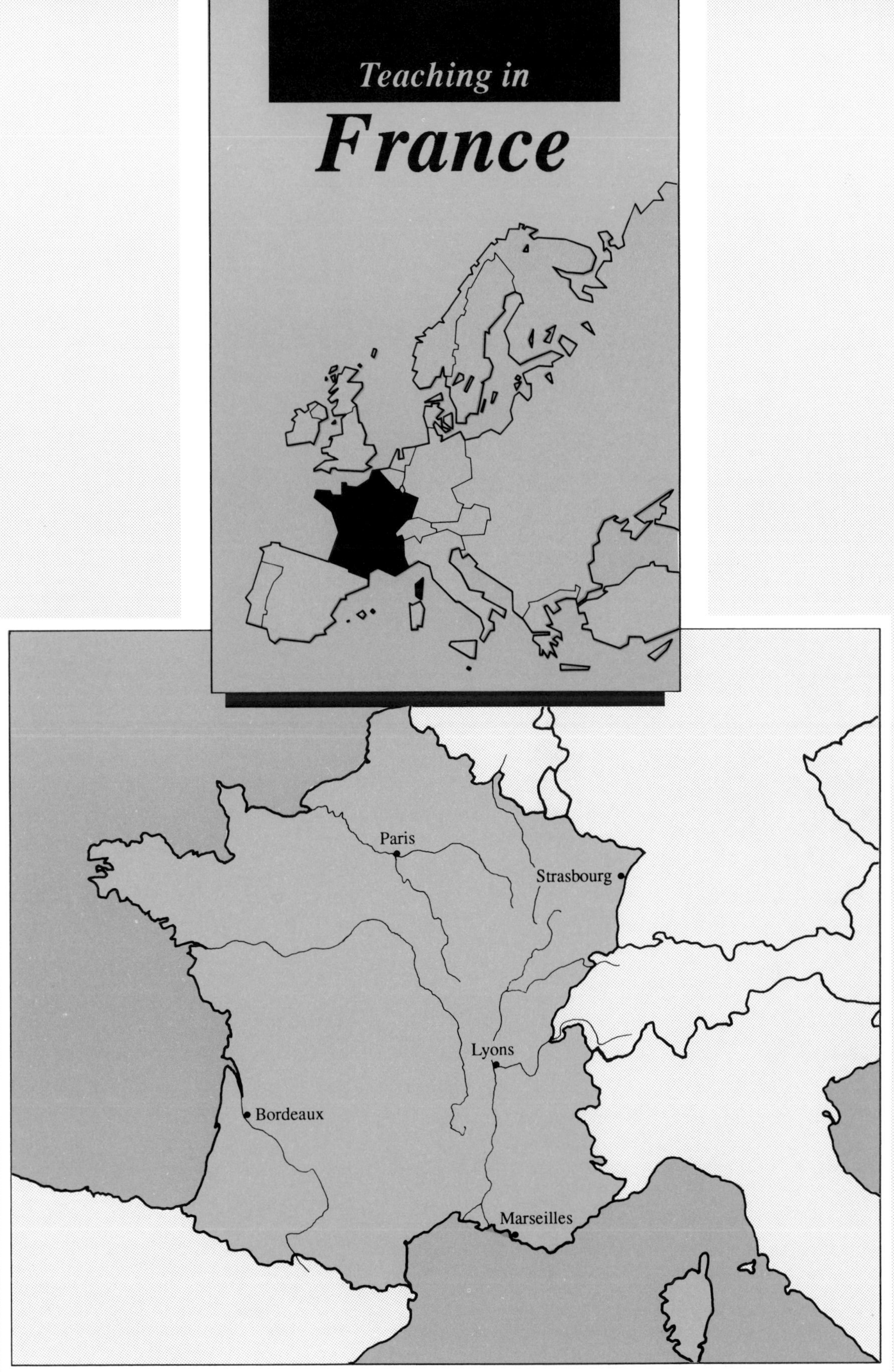
Teaching in
France
Paris
Strasbourg
Lyons
Bordeaux
Marseilles

TEACHING IN FRANCE

France, officially the French Republic, is the largest country in Western Europe. It is divided administratively into 95 departments grouped into regions. The former colonies rank as overseas departments.

France is a major agricultural and industrial country, leading Western Europe in food production. With people increasingly moving from the rural areas into the towns it is currently the case that more than 70% of the population lives in cities and towns, with the Paris megalopolis having more than 15% of the total population.

Since 1959 restructuring of the organisation of secondary schooling has resulted in a comprehensive school system, with significant implications for teacher training.

Schooling

On July 11th 1975 the Education Act No. 75 620 redefined the aims and objectives of the French educational system and reasserted the principle of the right of every child to obtain education designed to "promote the development of his potentialities" and to "prepare him for working life and the exercise of his responsibilities as a man and citizen".

Embodied within the Act was the key task, "to promote equality of opportunity" and, to this end, the stipulation that "All children should receive secondary education in *collèges*". These *collèges* would provide a common course of education, in four successive stages, and would provide a series of options and appropriate help for children who had difficulties.

The Act came into force at the beginning of the 1977 academic year and it has had considerable influence upon teachers and teaching in France.

The French education system is also distinguished by a number of key characteristics, viz:

(i) That staff in schools are state officials, with the exception of service and maintenance staff in pre-elementary and elementatary education, who are paid by the local authorities.

(ii) That the rules governing the administrative and financial organisation of teaching; the teaching establishments; the number of hours allocated weekly to subjects taught; the content of teaching and the ways whereby studies are certificated, are all based upon provisions laid down at national level.

(iii) That the state has a monopoly of the award of university degrees and diplomas, and of the organisation of examinations for the recruitment of officials, or for entry into certain schools.

(iv) That there is a highly organised regional service, based upon 27 *Académies*, with the major part of any decentralised powers administered and directed by a Rector, appointed by the Cabinet. Each *académie* contains several *départements*, and in each *département* the *Inspecteur d'Académie* is the director of services.

For long regarded as a highly centralised organisation the duty of the intermediate authorities has been to assist the State, through observations, appraisals, and opinions, in order to maintain professional oversight over the vast numbers of teachers who - as civil servants - are employed by the French Ministry of Education.

Since 1962 government policy has been such as to increase administrative decentralisation, with certain decisions regarding school management being taken by the *département*. It may also be noted that, since 1985, the financial organisation of teaching establishments has been managed at regional level - reflecting further the process of decentralisation. The Decentralisation Law has given to the *Conseils Régionaux* (concerned with the second cycle secondary schools) and the *Département Conseils Généraux* (concerned with the *collèges*) certain powers. Such powers include, for example, choice of modern languages in schools; the development of school links and exchanges; and the provision of non-compulsory aspects of the school programme. The *communes*, (organising primary schools and infant schools) also possess significant powers in terms of local decision making, and within the general context and educational principles established by the State.

Education in French state schools is secular, and religious education is not included within school curricula.[1] Relations between the State and private educational establishments are governed by the Act of December 31st, 1959, and subsequent laws. In effect, this allows educational establishments to enter into contracts. For primary schools the State may pay the salaries of teachers provided that they possess the requisite qualifications. For private secondary schools the State will pay the salaries of teachers and the running expenses of the school, provided that it gives education in accordance with public educational curricula and provided that it employs teachers belonging to the public sector or who are bound to the State by contract.

Children will be able to enter pre-school facilities *(écoles maternelles)* from the age of 2 years up until the age of 6 years. Such facilities have for long played a significant part in French education, both to ensure equality of opportunity and to assist in the early detection and treatment of handicaps of all kinds.

At the age of 6 years children will enter elementary or primary education (*enseignement élémentaire*) for a broad based education which includes: spoken and written French; simple Arithmetic and Mathematics; and Scientific, Technical, Artistic and Physical Education. Children attend the primary school for 5 years. This is organised in three stages: preparatory, elementary and intermediate.

Since 1959 the restructuring of secondary education in France has progressively developed a comprehensive school system, and children leaving the primary school at 11 years have attended the same type of school. In 1963 the creation of *collèges* enabled the different 'types' of pupil population to attend the same school, but by distinct and separate routes. From 1977 onwards these distinct educational routes were abolished and almost all the school population after leaving primary school attends the first two years of the *collège* in mixed ability classes. In the third year of the *collège* some pupils (about 25%) will attend pre-apprenticeship vocational classes whilst others will remain in the *collège* to undertake two further years of study before proceeding to the *lycée*, the professional training institutions or to work at 16.

For pupils continuing their studies beyond the *collège*, or first stage secondary level, opportunities will lie within the 3 year general *lycée*; leading to the national *baccalauréat* diploma;[2] or to a national technical diploma (*Diplôme national du brevet de technicien*). Other opportunities will include attendance at one of the vocational *lycées* (*lycées d'enseignement professionel*, or LEP) and leading to a vocational certificate (*Certificat d'aptitude professionelle*, or CAP) or possibly to a vocational studies certificate *(Brevet d'études professionelles*, or BEP).

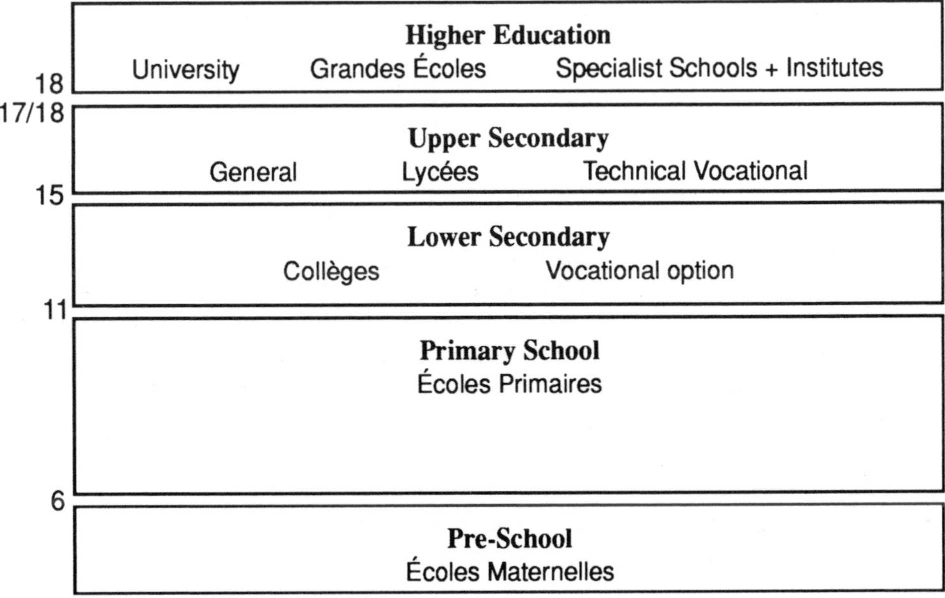

Teacher Training

There is little doubt that the teaching profession in France has long been associated with the idea of social promotion, the most accessible post in the profession being that of *instituteur.* The possibility for gradual ascent, particularly evident within the secondary sector and through success in competitive examinations, could allow the ambitious to reach the highest level - that of *agrégé.* This combines enhanced status and high pay with reduced hours of work.

An outline of the main categories of teacher may be presented as follows:

Level/Type of Education	Age of Pupils	Teacher
Pre-primary education *(écoles maternelles)* Primary education *(Enseignement élémentaire)*	2-6 6-11	A. *Instituteur* *Institutrice*
Secondary education *(enseignement du premier cycle;* taken in a *Collège d'enseignement secondaire or Collège)*	11-15	B. *Professeur d'enseignement général de collège PEGC* C. *Professeur Certifié* D. *Professeur agrégé*
Secondary education	15-18	C. *Professeur Certifié* D. *Professeur agrégé*

Before considering the issues of training and examination which relate to such levels of teaching it is valid to note the different opportunities that may be available to these teachers. As one might expect in a country with a centralised administration there are clear national guidelines relating to teachers. *Instituteurs* (primary school teachers) are *département* based, and *professeurs d'enseignement général de collège* (lower secondary teachers) are academy based. As such these groups of teachers could, under normal circumstances, only request a move within their home *département* or *academie.*

By contrast those teachers who are *certifiés* and *agrégés* (and who are more evident in the upper secondary schools) can apply to move anywhere within France.

The training of the primary school teacher (*instituteur*) has undergone considerable transformation and upgrading over the past 20 years and further plans for reform were announced in August 1989.[3] Before 1969 those hoping to teach at this level would go directly to an *École Normale* at the end of the *troisième* class (i.e. 15 years). After that date the minimum entrance of the *baccalauréat* required that all entrants had to complete their education at the *lycée* and before entering a two year course. Each *département* in France had an *École Normale* with entrance tests for school leavers with the *baccalauréat*.

By 1979 the two year course was lengthened to three years and it was based upon compulsory and optional modules of study. The *Écoles* were able to organise a range of possibilities which might respond to a locally felt need as well as student interest.

In 1984 all the *Écoles* were renamed Schools of Higher Education and were combined closely with the universities to train teachers for the pre-primary and primary level. As a result, all intending primary teachers are now obliged to attend a first cycle university education leading to the *Diplôme d'études universitaires générales* (University and general studies diploma, or D.E.U.G.) and, within this cycle, they take a professional module in educational studies. Success in this diploma (which includes such studies as History of Education, Child Psychology and Sociology) will allow the student to enter the competitive examination for entry to the École Normale.

Once accepted into the School of Higher Education the student teacher will undertake two years of professional preparation comprising courses within the areas of pedagogy and didactics, and subject knowledge, together with teaching practice and observation in schools. For this purpose the student teacher will be attached to a *maître conseiller* or tutor designated to supervise and help the student, and paid extra by the *département* concerned for these services. At the end of their course students take an examination in both practical and academic knowledge, and are awarded a mark by a 'jury' which includes members of the inspectorate, college tutors and university representatives. Success in this examination will lead to the award of a Diploma in Primary Education (*Diplôme d'instituteur/trice*).

The preparation of teachers for secondary schools (the *collèges; lycées;* and vocational *lycées*) may also be interpreted best in the light of competitive success in relation to different levels and status within the teaching hierarchy. Within the four year *collèges* may be found teachers who had previously worked in the *lycées* , and "graded" in relation to the examinations they had passed, viz: the *agrégés; certifiés*; the *adjoints d'enseignement* or *maîtres auxiliaires*. On the other hand there are those teachers who are qualified specifically for the *collèges*, viz: *Professeurs d'Enseignement Général des Collèges* (PEGC).

To simplify matters it is now possible to summarise training (and examination success) in relation to these teachers, and to other levels within the secondary school teaching force:

P.E.G.C.
Will have attended the first cycle higher education (DEUG); passed a competitive examination; and attended a training course in pedagogy and subject matter at a centre attached to an *École Normale*. This recruitment group is being phased out from the mid 1980's.

Certifiés
Such teachers will have obtained the university *licence*, have passed a competitive examination, and successfully passed the theoretical examination of the CAPES (*Certificat d'Aptitude Professionelle de l'Enseignement Secondaire*).[4] They will also be required to undertake a one year (i.e. three training sessions) in a school as a *Stagiaire*, and to pass a practical examination. This is administered by a jury comprising a school Inspector and two teachers. The *Certifié* will be expected to teach 18 hours per week.

Maître Auxiliaires
These teachers have obtained the university licence, and are recruited on a temporary basis without being selected as a result of success in a competitive examination.

Adjoints d'enseignement
These are former *maîtres auxiliaires* who have been granted tenure but who did not have any specific teacher education prior to being appointed.

Agrégé
In this the most highly academically qualified category are teachers who will normally have passed the master's degree (*Maîtrise*) and be successful in the competitive (theoretical) *Agrégation* examination. This teacher will be expected to teach 15 hours each week.[5]

For both the CAPES and *Agrégé* teachers it is a condition, set before the teacher competes in the examination, that the state will be served for a period of 10 years. In exchange for this pledge the government will provide a post for those who are successful in the examination.

Stagiaires

Following their success in the theoretical examination the teacher will be obliged to enter the practical stage of training, as a *stagiaire*. This will involve a number of hours of teaching, related to previous experience, viz:

a) for those who have taken the CAPES or *Agrégation*, six hours per week;
b) for those who have already taught in school, and have now passed the *agrégation*, up to 15 hours per week;
c) for those who have already taught, and have now passed the CAPES, up to 16 hours per week.

This teaching is paid, and on the first salary step as a *Certifié* or *Agrégé*. It is also the case that the 'beginning teacher' will be supported by a nominated teacher (the *conseiller pédagogique*) who will arrange for demonstration lessons. Attendance is also required at classes in the *Centre Pédagogique Régionale* (CPR). In each Academy it is policy that one day each week will be kept free for *stagiaires* to attend such classes, and to attend a variety of seminars related to classroom and school policy.[6]

Over the one-year period, chaperoned by the nominated teacher, the *stagiaire* will pass through two *stages*, that of

- *stage en résponsabilité* (with 6 hours teaching, or more); and
- *stage en situation* (with more responsibilities and greater time allocated to teaching duties).

At the end of this training period the candidate will be visited by the school inspector, the school tutor; and one other independent teacher. Observation of lessons taught and an oral examination on school organisation matters will complete the training period. The *stagiaire* will also be involved in a lengthy discussion (*entretien de formation générale*) related to specific school problems and issues, and to aspects of civil service commitment.

Finally, we may note that the significant reforms proposed for the 1990s will - hopefully - play a part in breaking down the barriers between different teaching groups and enable all teachers to increase their knowledge and awareness of the whole educational system (see below, footnote [3])

Employment and Career Development

It has already been noted that employment possibilities, issues of mobility and career development are closely linked to the levels of qualification, to examination level passed and to related matters. Once in employment an important factor is the process of inspection. Within a *lycée*, for example, the Headmaster (*Proviseur*) will normally be expected to administer the *Notice Annuelle de Notation*, which will include comment and a mark on matters of professional behaviour; school and classroom discipline; authority; general influence and bearing within the school; relationship with parents and the community, and other matters. This annual mark will be awarded upon the basis of:

Very Good	5 marks
Good	4 marks
Fairly Good	3 marks

Mediocre 2 marks
Poor 1 mark
(turned into a scale of 1 in 20)

An annual comment, or *appreciation générale* will also be written by the headteacher. In all the years of teaching the school subject inspector is also involved, typically on a bi-annual basis.

NOTICE ANNUELLE DE NOTATION

Année Scolaire 19 - 19

ACADÉMIE DE
DIVISION DES PERSONNELS
ENSEIGNANTS

Discipline
* Emploi :

Établissement d'exercise (No, sigle, et adresse) :

Nom: Prénom:
Nom de Jeune fille:
Date de naissance: Situation de famille:
Adresse:

Grade: Échelon: Date de promotion:

(1) EN ACTIVITÉ ☐ EN DISPONIBILITÉ ☐ Date d'affection dans l'établissement actuel:

Affection précédente:

Rappel de l'élément administratif de la note de l'année antérieure.	Année	Note	Grade	Académie	Etablissement

Numéro I.N.S.E.E. : | Note chiffrée arrêtée par le Chef d'Établissement:

OBSERVATIONS éventuelles de l'intéressé (e) ☐

Je, soussigné (e), déclare avoir pris connaissance de ma note chiffrée proposée par le Chef d'Établissement.
Date et Signature. ☐

Appréciations et propositions du Chef d'Établissement: M

	Ponctualité et assiduité					Activité et efficacité					Autorité et rayonnement				
	Très Bien	Bien	Assez Bien	Passable	Médiocre	Très Bien	Bien	Assez Bien	Passable	Médiocre	Très Bien	Bien	Assez Bien	Passable	Médiocre
*	5	4	3	2	1	5	4	3	2	1	5	4	3	2	1

entourer les codes correspondant aux appréciations

Appréciation général:

Date et signature:

Avis éventuel de l'Inspecteur d'Académie, Directeur des services départementaux de l'Education:

Date et signature:

Élément pédagogique
Élément Administratif
NOTE GLOBALE

*(1) *la notation doit intervenir dés qu'un fonctionnaire a été présent ne serait-ce qu'un jour dans l'établissement.* CATI 233

For the teacher concerned an important factor is that a good mark will lead to promotion - about every two years - to a higher step on the salary 'ladder'. With 11 steps in all, a maximum salary may be reached in about 22 years. For those who have received poor marks the attainment of maximum salary may take much longer.

Those who are teaching in primary schools, the *instituteurs*, will enjoy broadly similar prospects with a school inspector visiting them about every two years and giving a mark on a scale of 1-20. A bad mark (under 10, for example) would lead to more frequent inspection.[7]

In summary, the headteacher's mark representing 40% in weighting, and the inspector's mark representing 60% in weighting, will allow advancement up the salary scale to be accelerated or delayed.

Other opportunities are related to success as a *Certifié* or *Agrégé*, with the opportunity to move to a position anywhere within France. Given that there may be several applicants for a post selection is made on the basis of a points system. The main factors to which points are allotted include:

(i) length of service in present post;
(ii) length of service as a teacher;
(iii) teacher category;
(iv) official grading by school inspector;
(v) distance from spouse's residence or place of work;
(vi) number of children in the family.

A teachers'/administrators' panel can adjust placings and ensure that all relevant factors are considered.

A further issue relates to problems of how to attract many more teachers to cope with the sharply rising intake into the *lycées*, and when relatively low salaries, difficult working conditions and loss of public esteem have meant that there are not enough recruits for the vacancies available. Pay increases have fallen short of expectations, although extra payments are made to those who work in a difficult school or area. Extra funds are also being made available to develop an early recruitment scheme under which students intending to teach receive an allowance.[8] For those aspiring to the higher ranks of the profession an alteration in examination pass levels could provide more opportunities and more optimism..[9]

For promotion into the inspectorate or to such posts as Headteacher (*Proviseur*) or deputy headteacher (*Censeur*) it is necessary to undertake an appropriate course of training. A Headteacher, for example, would undertake an 11 week course.

Inservice Training

An important development in the 1980's has been the creation of an inservice centre (*Mission Académique à la Formation des Personnels de l'Education Nationale*) in each educational region, or *académie*. A key function is to structure and rationalise inservice training and to define regional training policy. Each year these *Missions* publish a regional training plan, together with a list of courses offered. In addition, since 1982, university summer sessions have reinforced the regional training networks in helping staff cope with the significant innovations and changes within the educational system. Increased emphasis on institution-based inservice training, and closer liaison with institutional priorities and reforms is a high priority.

Footnotes

1 *This is not the case in Alsace, and in the part of Lorraine annexed by the German Empire between 1870 and 1918. The separation between Church and State has not been applied to these "liberated" départements. Religion (i.e. Roman Catholic and Protestant) is taught in schools and the church Ministers are paid by the state.*

2 *The French government has decided that, over a phased period, 80% of an age group should arrive at the Baccalauréat level. Most critics of the baccalauréat have argued that such an examination - founded on grandiose assumptions about the nature of French intellectualism - is patently unsuited to mass education at the end of the 20th century. The examination will usually begin with a four-hour philosophy paper. Without a pass in philosophy there is no baccalauréat award, and no automatic right to a university place.*

3 *Proposals announced in the Bulletin Officiel de l'Education Nationale, No.4 (31 August 1989) indicated that future instituteurs would be recruited from those already possessing the baccalaureat, and a licence (i.e. obtained after three years of university study). Student teachers would attend an Institut Universitaire de Formation des Maîtres (I.U.F.M.) for a period of two years. During this time the students would be acting as a part-time stagiaire - under the guidance of a conseiller pédagogigue, and part-time as a student. A final examination would lead to an appointment with tenure (i.e. as titularisè). Three pilot institutions (in Grenoble, Lille and Reims) were opened in October 1990. The remainder (one per académie or education authority) are due to open in September 1991. It is hoped that this reform will not only put an end to segregated training, and break down barriers between different teaching groups, but enable all teachers to increase their knowledge of the rest of the system.*

Certain general guidelines have been set, viz:

a) all candidates for teaching must have their licence;
b) at the end of the first year students will sit an examination for either primary or secondary teaching;
c) in the second year school-based training will be a minimum of 500 hours for future primary teachers and 300 hours for secondary level teachers;
d) both years must combine theory and practice.

Within this context each IUFM is asked to formulate its own programme, and take local needs into account. In each region the Recteur (who is also a ministry appointee) will preside over the IUFM's administrative council. Close central control is likely to continue.

4 *In each case there are different texts/set books/and syllabus set each year. In the competitive examination for English, for example:*
A CAPES examination would include 4 parts, viz:

(i) a 4 hour essay on the set books;
(ii) a commentary (written in French) on the set books;
(iii) a three hour translation from French to English (on an unseen text);
(iv) a three hour translation from English to French (on an unseen text).

Given the high level of competition, and standard expected, some candidates may take the examination repeatedly, and perhaps pass only after several attempts. It is possible to take the examination up to the age of 40 years. A further "hurdle" will be an oral examination, in four parts, and related partly to the texts studied to the explanation of points of grammar and to the presentation of a short story on an unseen topic (given a two hour preparatory period).

5 *In order to obtain the Agrégation, a totally separate examination, it will be necessary to possess the Maitrise (masters degree). To take the further example of English there could be different "options" available concerning linguistics or civilization, with several set books to be studied. For the option of "literature" there will be around 10 set books for study. Lengthy examinations; a 7 hour essay on the set books; lengthy translations and oral examinations will also face the potential agrégé.*

Once having passed the theoretical part a successful candidate can, in effect, enter into teaching, but is obliged to undertake a year as a stagiaire.

6 *Matters related to subject teaching; the organisation and administration of the educational system; specific school issues, such as - teaching in inner cities; the psychology of the teenager, and drug addiction will be included.*

7 *Primary teachers are under the supervision of the primary school inspector, as well as the Inspecteur d'Academie, and are not directly under supervision from the school principal.*

8 *Allowances for teachers also include an allowance for travel to work, for examining, for helping a student on teaching practice, and for extra hours worked. By European Community standards French teachers are poorly paid. For most of the 1980s pay increases were below the rate of inflation. Private sector salaries averaged 25% less, even including summer unemployment benefit, and most teachers have to work extra hours at schools.*

The introduction of compulsory foreign language teaching in primary education forced the Education Minister to employ non-French nationals, including some British teachers, in state schools for the first time. These staff were employed under the terms of a 'vacataire' and did not have the same conditions of employment as French staff. Though this contravened EC legislation, that employees carrying out a similar job should have equal rights, no action had been taken by the end of 1990.

9 *Both the CAPES and the Agrégation have a reputation of being very difficult to pass, and they create much anxiety. Furthermore, although it is possible to obtain a teaching post on the strength of possessing a degree, that post is not a permanent one and has to be surrendered as soon as a qualified candidate appears. A further issue is that a teacher cannot be paid the full rate for the job without passing the examination. In 1982, there were 360 CAPES teaching posts in English, with 4,555 candidates. At the level of the agrégation, 1,693 candidates competed for 120 posts.*

A Teacher in a Lycée

Je suis professeur d'anglais dans un lycée d'Etat. J'avais décidé de faire carrière dans l'enseignement après un certain nombre d'années passées en entreprise. Titulaire d'une licence, j'ai pu passer le concours d'entrée dans l'enseignement secondaire: le CAPES. Suite à ma réussite au concours, j'ai passé un an en tant que professeur stagiaire, rattachée à un Centre Pédagogique Régional. Au cours de cette année de stage, j'avais deux classes en responsabilité et par ailleurs, j'assistais à diverses séances de formation administrative et pédagogique. En fait, l'essentiel de ma formation s'est fait "sur le tas" et grâce à mes conseillers pédagogiques.

A la fin de cette année de formation, j'ai été titularisée après une inspection et un entretien avec une inspectrice pédagogique.

J'ai eu la chance d'être nommée sur un poste à quelques kilomètres seulement de mon domicile. En France, les professeurs doivent accepter le poste qui leur est proposé, n'importe où en France.

Malgré mon manque d'expérience, j'ai dû faire face immédiatement à la prise-en-charge de classes très différentes, y inclus deux classes de Terminale. J'ai été surtout très frappée par le manque de moyens mis à la disposition des professeurs, qui doivent tout fournir: leurs livres et leur matériel personnel de travail, et même souvent les cassettes audio et vidéo. Mon lycée est relativement neuf et confortable par rapport à beaucoup d'autres établissements; pourtant, il est très difficile pour les professeurs d'y travailler. Aucun professeur n'a sa propre salle et la salle des professeurs est peu adaptée au travail personnel. Les très mauvaises conditions de travail, surtout les effectifs très lourds des classes, pèsent sur l'enthousiasme des enseignants.

Pour l'instant, je garde le moral et j'aime beaucoup mon métier. J'ai de la chance d'avoir des élèves motivés et travailleurs pour la plupart d'entre eux. Cependant, je constate le découragement de beaucoup de mes collègues et je me demande si, par lassitude, je ne deviendrai pas comme eux. Il est vrai que déjà j'ai du mal à faire face à la masse de travail écrasante qu'exige ce métier (préparations, corrections, réunions diverses, etc.); d'autant plus que j'ai l'impression de travailler plus qu'en entreprise, avec des responsabilités plus lourdes, pour moins d'argent.

I am an English teacher in a state lycée. I decided to go into teaching after some years working in industry. Being a graduate I was able to take the examination (concours) for entry into secondary education, leading to CAPES. After passing the concours I spent a year as stagiaire, attached to a Regional Centre for Teachers. During this year I took two classes and in addition I attended various training seminars. In fact, my training was essentially on-the-job, this the charge of pedagogical advisers.

At the conclusion of this training year, I was certificated after a classroom visit and an interview with a school inspectress.

I was fortunate to be nominated for a post only a few kilometres from my home. In France, teachers must accept a post offered to them wherever it is in the country.

Despite my lack of experience, immediately I had to take charge of very different classes, including two leavers' classes. Above all I was hit by the shortages of materials at the disposal of teachers who must provide their own books and materials and often even their own audio - and video-cassettes. My secondary school is relatively new and comfortable compared with many other establishments; however, it is very difficult for the teachers to work there. No teacher has his/her own room and the staff room makes little provision for marking or other tasks. The very bad working conditions, and above all the heavy teaching loads, tax the enthusiasm of the staff.

For the moment, my morale has not been affected and I like teaching very much. I am fortunate in having largely well-motivated and hard-working pupils. In the meantime I note the demoralisation of many of my colleagues and I wonder if, out of weariness, I might become like them. It is true that I am already encountering difficulties faced with the overwhelming amounts of work which teaching demands (preparation, marking, all sorts of meetings etc.). This is more especially so, since I have the impression that I am working much harder than ever I did in industry, with heavier responsibilities but with less pay.

A Teacher of English

De la sixième à la terminale, l'Anglais a toujours été ma matiére préférée. Ma mère, elle-même enseignante, a toujours manifesté beaucoup d'enthousiasme pour son metier. Alors une fois le baccalauréat en poche, c'est tout naturellement que je me suis inscrite à la Faculté des Lettres de Clermont Ferrand, section d'Anglais, où j'ai suivi un cursus universitaire classique: DEUG puis Licence d'Anglais. Au lieu de préparer tout de suite Le Concours de Recrutement de professeurs de l Education Nationale j'ai préféré poursuivre ma formation universitaire en préparant une Maîtrise.

L'envie d'être financièrement indépendante m'amena à interrompre là mes études universitaires et je décidai de préparer le CAPES. La préparation de ce concours représenta une somme considérable de travail. J'obtins le CAPES théorique en juin 1985, devenant Professeur Certifié Stagiaire, un statut ambigu qui fait de l'Ex-étudiant un être hybride, parfois professeur seul, face à ses classes et parfois encore élève:
- cours hebdomadaires au Centre Pédagogique Régional
- observations de séances, travail avec les conseillers-tuteurs.
Cette année de stage me sembla bien plus dure que la préparation au concours théorique. Se retrouver seule, face à une classe d'adolescents aux regards inquisiteurs sembla d'abord au dessus de mes forces: peur de ne pas savoir m'imposer, de ne pas pouvoir dominer la classe. Que d'angoisses, de cauchemars. En Juin 86 j'obtins pourtant le CAPES pratique. J'étais désormais professeur Certifié. Cela signifiait bien sûr la certitude d'un poste stable et la garantie d'un statut mais aussi, malheureusement, une affectation ministérielle, vraisemblablement sur les zones de'ficitaires de la France ou de la Région Parisienne.

Je fus nommée dans une petite ville de l'Aisne, à plus de 600 km de ma famille, un veritable déracinement. Comme la plupart des jeunes enseignants exilés loin de chez eux, je continue à "redescendre" dans ma région même aux plus petites vacances.

J'enseigne depuis deux ans dans un collège rural. Deux ans, une expérience bien courte, diront certains. Et pourtant j'ai changé en deux ans. J étais alors pleine d'enthousiasme, prête à m'investir dans toutes les directions: informatique. PAE Video etc. Je cherchais sans arrêt comment mieux faire passer le savoir que j'avais à dispenser: méthodes, supports, animation de la classe etc, pensant sincèrement obtenir de bien meilleurs résultats.

Je n'avais pas encore réalisé que l'enseignant n'est qu'un maillon de la chaîne et que la part incombant à l élève est déterminante. Je me trouve, comme mes collègues, confrontée au dur problème des élèves qui'ne travaillent pas chez eux, qui n'apprennent pas leurs leçons. Il n'est pas rare que, dans certaines classes, décidant d'un contrôle surprise de leçon, je me retrouve avec plus d'une dizaine de 0/20 dans une classe de 25 élèves.

Les punitions, les retenues, le dialogue avec les parents (souvent démissionnaires) n'y font rien. En lycée, où j'avais effectué mon stage, la situation est souvent différente, les élèves sont plus âgés, déja sélectionnés, motivés soit par le baccalauréat ou l'orientation. La motivation des enseignants doit s'en ressentir. Je continue à travailler de la même manière, dans les mêmes directions mais en sachant maintenant que je ne changerai pas grand chose et que toutes les heures passées bénévolement au collège (réunions - projets etc) ne sont que de toutes petites gouttes d'eau.

Le metier, que j'ai choisi, ou cru choisir, pourrait être tres épanouissant si nous avions des conditions de travail satisfaisantes (locaux - effectifs - matériel pédagogique etc), des relations de compréhension mutuelle avec notre administration, le soutien des parents. La plupart du temps il n'en est rien. Et qui plus est, nous sommes mal payés vu notre formation.

Triste bilan et pourtant, quand un cours a bien marché, qu'est-ce que nous sommes contents!

From 6th grade onwards English was always my favourite subject. My mother, herself a teacher, always displayed much enthusiasm for her work. So, once I had passed bacalauréat it was natural that I should enrol for a university course in English. Instead of the concours for entry into teaching at that time I chose to continue my university education and to take a Masters degree.

The desire to be financially independent led me to interrupt my university studies and I decided to aim for CAPES. Preparation for the concours meant a considerable amount of work. I obtained the theory-based CAPES in June 1985 becoming a Professeur Certifié Stagiaire. The ambiguous status of the stagiaire, makes the ex-student into a hybrid creature, partly a teacher when in the classroom, and partly still a pupil. The latter required weekly attendance at the Regional Teachers' Centre, seminars and work with professional advisers/tutors.

This year seemed to me even harder than the preparation for the theoretical concours had been. To find oneself alone, facing a class of adolescents, under the eye of tutors, at first seemed more than I could stand. There was always the fear of not knowing, of not being able to control the class. What anguish! What nightmares!

However, in June 1986, I passed the practical part of CAPES. From then on I was a certificated teacher. That meant the certainty of a steady job and the guarantee of status but also, unfortunately, allocation by the Ministry, probably to an area of deprivation or to the

Paris region.

I was nominated for a post in a small village in the Aisne area, more than 600 km from my family. Thus uprooted, and like most young teachers exiled far from home, I continue to come back to my home region even during short holidays.

For two years I have been teaching in a rural collège. Two years is a short time, you will say. However I have changed in two years. So, I was full of enthusiasm, ready to get myself involved in many things: information technology, interactive video, etc. All the time I was looking for better ways of passing on the knowledge that I had to dispense - improved teaching methods, better teaching aids, new ways of motivating the class etc., always with a sincere desire to produce better results.

I had not yet realised that the teacher is but a link in a chain and that the part left to the pupil is determined like my colleagues, I find myself confronted by pupils who never work at home and who do not learn their lessons. In classes it is not unusual, when I decide to take the register, to find only 10 or so out of a class of 25.

Punishment exercises, being kept in, discussions with often apathetic parents all come to nothing. In the lycée where I taught as stagiaire the situation is often different. The pupils there are older, selected and motivated by their courses. The teachers' motivation must be affected by this. I continue to teach in the same way, but now knowing that I shall not change major things and that all the hours willingly spent in collège (meetings, planning etc.) are only drops in the ocean.

The profession I chose, or thought I chose, could be very uplifting if we had satisfactory working conditions, a relationship of mutual understanding with management and the support of parents. Mostly, these are missing. Furthermore, we are badly paid, given our training.

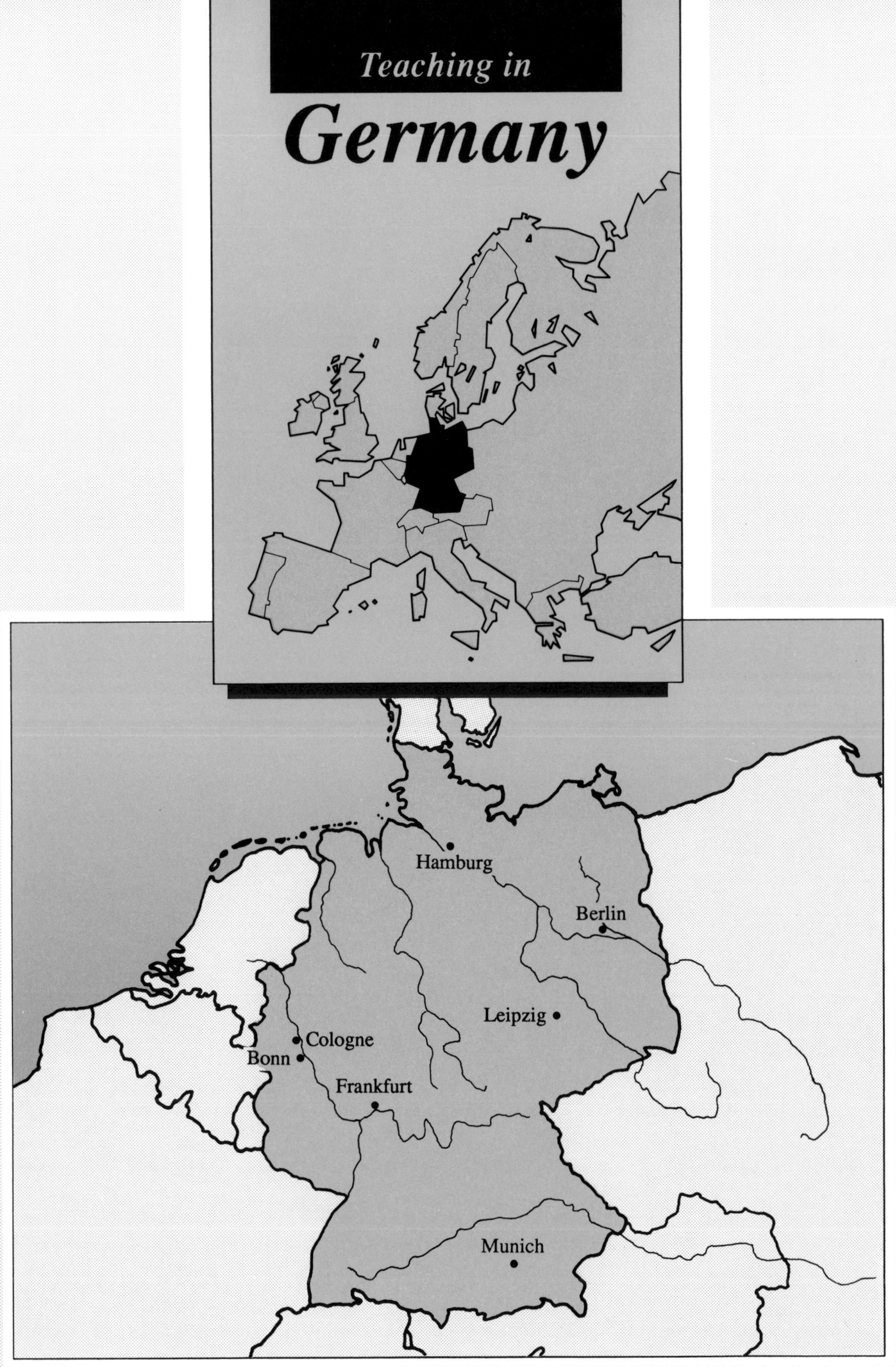
Teaching in
Germany
Hamburg
Berlin
Leipzig
Cologne
Bonn
Frankfurt
Munich

TEACHING IN GERMANY

Geographically the potentially very powerful united Germany, with a combined population of 80 million extends to the borders of Poland in the east and it includes considerably enlarged access to the Baltic Sea. Its EC neighbours are Denmark to the north and The Netherlands, Belgium, Luxembourg and France to the west. To the south lies Switzerland and Austria, two potential members of the European Community.

The integration of the 'two Germanies' is likely to take many years to complete. In the words of Jürgen W Möllemann, Federal Minister of Education and Science, 'unification implies the welding together of two completely different economic and political systems... the structure in all areas has to be changed to pave the way for a pluralist order of society and the introduction of a social market economy'. Considerable stresses and strains have been experienced and detailed outcomes are uncertain. However, what is reasonably clear is that the process will be largely that of the West assimilating the East. The reasons for this are obvious. The far greater prosperity of the FDR, makes it the dominant partner, while the new freedom won by the DDR enables it to embrace those liberal-democratic principles long enjoyed by EC countries.

Because of the above-mentioned factors, this account will be orientated towards the West German experience, sometimes taking Hamburg as an example.

Teacher professional development in West Germany has roots that are firmly in a European tradition while developing qualities and elements that are distinctive. Traditionally the educational system, and hence teacher training, has valued the theoretical and the academic. At the same time the priority given to work-related schooling and training has coloured the system overall. As a consequence the balance between the vocational and the non-vocational, and between theory and practice, takes a special form.

As regards the present situation, it is necessary to be reminded that the control of education, including teacher development, lies firmly with the *Bundesländer*, as required by the Basic Law of the Federal Republic of Germany. While there may be some kind of national framework[1] for all, emerging from the monthly meetings of the fifteen State Ministers of Education, each *Bundesland*, can be different from others.

As a consequence, the system of schooling varies from Bundesland to Bundesland, at least in matters of detail. Beyond the age of 12 years pupils who are not enrolled in a comprehensive school (*Gesamtschule*) go their separate ways according to achievement and inclination. The provision of comprehensive schooling is less in some areas and more in others, according to the political ideology of the governing party.

Both the *Gesamtschule* and the *Gymnasium* offer courses leading to the *Abitur*, the entry qualification for higher education. The alternative may be the *Hauptschule* or the *Realschule* which is more vocationally orientated. In fact, vocational education assumes great importance in the German system. Indeed, for those not taking other courses after leaving school, it is compulsory at least on a part-time basis to the age of 18. The diagram below provides a general picture.

Age	Year						
Age 19 -	13	*Neugestaltete gymnasiale Oberstufe* (reorganised upper forms)		*Weitere Bildungsmöglichkeiten* further possibilities of education			*'Abitur'*
	12						
	11						
	10	Gymnasium	*Siebenstufiges Gymnasium*	*Realschule*	*Hauptschule* (9-year elementary school)	*Gesamtschule* (Comprehensive School)	*'Mittlere Reife'*
Age 15 -	9						
Secondary School	8						
	7						
	6	*Orientierungsstufe*					
	5						
	4	*Grundschule* (basic school)					
Primary School	3						
	2						
	1						
Age 6 -	0	*Vorschule/Kindergarten*					

Allgemeinbildendes Schulwesen Bundesrepublik Deutschland
General Education in the Federal Republic of Germany

Teacher Training

Teacher Training in the Federal Republic of Germany takes the form of three phases, as follows:

Phase 1 Studies at the University (*Studien an der Universität*)
Phase 2 Preparation in a Seminarium (*Besuch des Studienseminars*)
Phase 3 Further Professional Training (*Lehrerfortbildung*)

Taking Hamburg as an example, the 7000 or so students in the Education faculty of the university come from the city and from other parts of West Germany. Many are preparing for teaching at different levels and in different institutions in the system.

Since 1988 four types of teaching 'licence' have been recognised in the training arrangements for teaching viz. :

(i) younger age groups in the *Grundschule*;
(ii) secondary classes in the *Gesamtschule* and the *Gymnasium*;
(iii) vocational courses in the *Realschule* and the *Hauptschule*;
(iv) pupils with special educational needs, in *Sonderschulen.*

Staff say that trainee-teachers are hard working students despite the fact that, locally, there may be few teaching posts annually for a substantial output of students. Some control of entry has seemed necessary although the situation may change markedly in the 1990s, even leading to teacher shortages. Here, as elsewhere, unification may have an effect.

As already noted the university course is the first stage of a 3-stage process. It lasts at least 8 semesters (i.e. 4 years) and often 11 semesters. The time taken to complete the course is partly determined by the traditional view that individuals should be free to choose when and for how long they wish to study, partly by the fact that students must make up their own time-tables according to when classes run. Students may be aged 28 or 30 before they are properly accredited teachers, and ways of reducing academic training time are being sought.

The academic specialisms, usually in two teaching subject areas e.g. Mathematics and Science, are provided for by the relevant university faculty. Teacher training as such is located in the *Institut für Schulpädagogic* and different aspects of the course are dealt with by different departments. Taking modern languages as an example, three different departments are involved, thus,

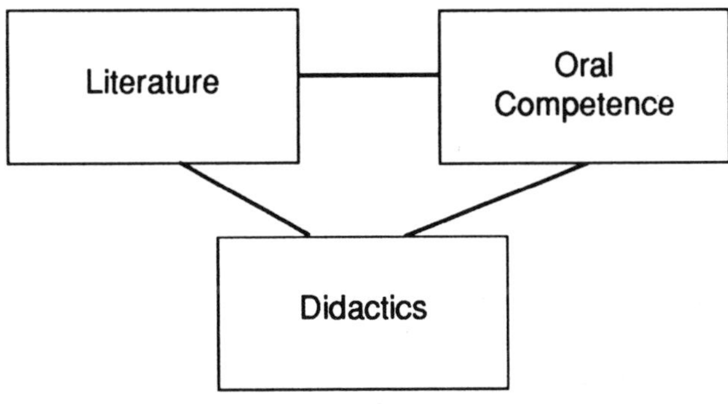

The nature of the Education course in the university is freely acknowledged to be largely theoretical, and practical only to a minor degree. Education seminars are concerned with such matters as the general principles underlying, for example, the teaching/learning of a foreign language; or with an analysis of curriculum areas; or with a discussion of the validity of different methodological procedures; and so on. Time spent in schools and in classrooms is of relatively short duration. There are organised group visits with a member of the University staff to learn from school staff about the range of teaching situations in school, followed by a few weeks observation of classes in school, arranged by students individually. There will also be a short period of teaching, with perhaps two or three lessons taught, observed and discussed.

Teaching competence is **not** assessed at this stage. The First State Examination, which has to be passed, says nothing about the ability to teach. The examination is of an academic nature, consisting of written papers on curriculum content and methodology.

The university course is followed by the **second phase**, which is predominantly practical. The graduate is now teaching and the emphasis is on developing classroom skills and teaching competence. Again taking Hamburg as an example, the base for this phase is the *Staatliches Studienseminar Für Die Lehramter An Hamburger Schulen* (SSS).

The SSS course lasts 4 semesters i.e. 2 years. It has its own permanent staff but, in the main, courses are staffed by *Seminarleiter* who teach in their own schools for half the time and they supervise the trainees (*Referendare*) for the rest. The *Seminarleiter* have been selected for their teaching expertise and for their ability to relate to young people. A higher salary is earned. In each school where there are trainees there is a Teacher Mentor (*Betreuer*), who 'guides' the trainee. This is an unpaid post.

The concern during the SSS phase is with the practicalities of teaching a subject, with lesson preparation, with discussion of teaching and the like. Usually three seminar groups of 10-15 *Referendare* are combined to form the *Hauptseminarleiter* who is a full-time member of the SSS staff, salaried on scale "A16" *Hauptseminaren* are concerned with general curriculum principles and with wider school and community perspectives. *Hauptseminaren* take place once a fortnight while subject seminars are held monthly.

Referendare spend most of their time in or near to classrooms, guided and coached by the *Seminarleiter*. Lessons taught are observed and carefully analysed afterwards. An important feature of these for semesters is that *Referendare* gain experience in 2 or 3 schools, usually teaching different age groups within their chosen field.

On completion of teacher training in Phase 2, the Second State Examination must be passed. Final assessments (*Lehrproben*) are made jointly by three categories of people (i) *Seminarleiter,* (ii) Head of the School, (iii) the Teacher Mentor (*Fachleiter*). These assessments are likely to be based on an extended piece of work, with perhaps 2 hours of teaching being observed. While individual assessors may work to systematic criteria, possibly in the form of a checklist, there are no official guidelines. There is no government model of what constitutes a minimally satisfactory level of teacher performance. However, grades are in fact awarded, usually on a 1-6 scale (1 being a high grade; 5 and 6 being unsatisfactory grades), with some variations in different *Länder*. Having good grades is important in getting a job and it also has bearing on the length of probation.

Mobility between the 'two Germanies' is not likely to be easy. Qualifications obtained in the East are not recognised initially and teachers wishing to teach in the West are required to prepare for the Second State Examination there.

In the future the Länder will mutually recognise all teachers' examinations on the basis of agreed minimum standards determined by the Conference of Ministers of Education and Cultural Affairs. The diversity in the different state systems of teacher training will remain and the five new Bundesländer can be readily included.

Probation

Getting a teaching post may not be easy although the prospects could improve in the mid-1990's. To some considerable extent present opportunities depend on the grades obtained in the Second State Examination: those with grades 1, 2 and 3 could be fortunate, others not.

Once in post, the length of probation is also determined by grades. Grade 1 will mean probation of up to 12 months duration, Grade 2 up to 15 months and Grade 3 up to two years. These rules apply to teach each week - contracts vary from 12 hours per week, to 18 hours or more.

Assessment of probation is largely in the hands of the School Inspector who pays at least two formal visits, one early in probation, one towards the end. The last visit will obviously be very important, and the Inspector is likely to see several lessons taught. The Headteacher may also be asked to report on the candidate and in the case of teachers in the *Gymnasium* this would always be so. Heads would be expected to report in broad terms - Very Good, Good, Satisfactory, Unsatisfactory.

A probationer encountering difficulties would be identified early in probation. Remedial action within the school might be recommended e.g. by attachment to another experienced teacher. There are no structured induction programmes for probationer teachers.

Inservice Training

As already described there is a Phase 3 to follow Phase 2, although it would be wrong to think in terms of a continuation. This third phase, provided at and through the *Institut Für Lehrerfortbildungen,* is concerned with **inservice training.** The institute in Hamburg, founded in 1925, is a large building, containing specialist facilities appropriate to different areas of the curriculum. There is an impressive library, a games and sports complex, and so on. The SSS is housed in the same buildings and there is some communication between the two.

Some 120 staff work in the Inservice Institute. courses on offer are varied and interesting. These are listed in a catalogue sent to all schools and they include courses of all sorts and kinds - on music, religion, sport, physics, languages, law, and so on. The needs of all categories of teacher are catered for.

These inservice courses take place in teachers' own time. They are staffed by permanent centre staff, sometimes by others, including school personnel, university staff or *Seminarleiter* from 'next door' in the SSS.

Take Modern Languages as an example. The section directrice has charge of a pleasant office, a large resource/seminar room, store-rooms and a language laboratory. Classroom and teacher materials relating to the teaching of German, English, French, Spanish etc. are held in good quantities. A main aim is to make available for inspection some of the latest language teaching texts and courses. Publishers are encouraged to conduct presentations on their materials and they are keen to get their products on the approved state list. It must be added that the teachers do not have open access as they would in some teachers' centres; access and use is by arrangement.

Institute staff are available on a consultancy and advisory basis and their services are called upon quite regularly. The demand may arise out of courses offered. These almost always take place in the evening, the one exception being an annual residential week-end for Modern Languages teachers.

Inservice training is in no way structured. The Centre offers the courses that it thinks will be seen as valuable. Attendance is always voluntary and at the teacher's expense. There is also pressure that this should take place during holidays, thus not taking teachers away from the classroom. Those who attend are the committed, enthusiastic ones. This makes for good courses with a high level of discourse and involvement. It does not affect those who are perhaps most in need of professional refreshment - the lazy, the out-of-date, and so on. Attendance at courses is not tied to career development in any formal way. However, there is evidence that teachers increasingly are obtaining records of attendance and that these are being placed on file in the area office.

Further Career Development

Successful advancement to maximum salary and to promotion depends on maintained competence and performance. School Inspectors are expected to visit all teachers at least once every six years up to the age of 55, and in some *Länder* visits could be more frequent. Headteachers and other promoted staff are included in this process. Again, grades are awarded, usually on a 1-5 scale.

In principle it is possible for 'unsatisfactory' teachers to lose their job. An intermediate step would be to arrange for remedial help to be made available, possibly including attendance at special courses.

Career development and promotion are not big issues in Germany. Not to have gained promotion is not seen as a deficiency. In any case the number of posts of special responsibility is small and there are few opportunities. Furthermore, salary differentials are not great and as one German teacher puts it, 'You always think twice about increasing your work load'.

Footnotes

1. *Federal money is used to finance particular initiatives e.g. in providing textbooks and in assisting vocational training and higher education programmes in the five new Bundesländer.*

A Primary School Teacher

Im Jahre 1978 würde die Ausbildung für das Lehramt an Volks-schulen in Bayern reformiert. Zukünftige Lehrer mußten sich mit Beginn des Studiums entscheiden, ob sie in der 1-4, Klasse (Grundschule) oder in der 5-9 Klasse (Hauptschule) unterrichten wolten. Das Studium würde stark wissenschaftlich ausgerichtet, die Studenten mussten sich nun für ein Hauptfach und drei Didaktikfächer entscheiden.

Im Wintersemester 1980/81 hat Klaudia mit dem Studium Lehramt an Grundschulen in Würzburg begonnen. Als Hauptfach wählte sie Geographie, bei den Didaktikfachern entschloss sie sich fur die Kombination Mathematik, Biologie und Sport. Sie gab diesen Fächern den Vorzug, da sie ihr persönlich gut gefielen und weil sie sich von ihnen in der Prüfung gute Ergebnisse erhoffte. Als sie nämlich zu studieren begann, waren die Aussichten auf eine spätere Anstellung schlecht. Viele rielten ihr sogar von dieser Ausbildung ab. Nun war sie aber überzeugt, dass ihr der Umgang mit Kindern sowie das Unterrichten gefallen wurden und liess sich von ihrem Vorhaben nicht abbringen. Sie wollte sogar ein paar Jahre auf der sogenannten Warteliste in Kauf nehmen. Voraussetzung überhaupt in den Schuldienst zu gelangen, waren somit gute Noten im ersten Staatsexamen. Der Druck, möglichst gut abzuschneiden, beeinflußte sogar die Auswahl zahlreicher Seminare oder auch der Dozenten.

Das Geographiestudium - stark wissenschaftlich orientiert - kostete sie viel Arbeit und Zeit. Eine intensivere Beschäftigung mit grundschulspezifischen Fächern, die eigentlich sinnvoll gewesen wäre, gelang ihr selten. Im 7. Semester schrieb sie ihre Zulassungsarbeit im Fach Didaktik der Geographie, für die sie fast 9 Monate benotigte. Nach dem 8. Semester legte sie ihr 1. Staatsexamen ab.

Glücklicherweise hatte sie durch ihren Notendurchschnitt eine gute Ausgangsposition für ihren späteren Beruf geschaffen. Ihren zweiten Ausbildungsabschnitt begann sie im Februar 1985 in einer Dorfschule in der Nähe von Marktheidenfeld. Das erste Jahr des Referendariats bestand im Wesentlichen aus Hospitieren bei einem ausgewahlten Betreuungslehrer, Unterrichtsversuchen unter Beaufsichtigung desselben und der theoretischen Ausbildung im Seminar (10 Stunden). Im zweiten Jahr besuchte sie weiterhin zweimal wochentlich das Seminar, das jedes Mal in einer anderen Schule des Landkreises stattfand. Zudern erteilte sie nun 14 Stunden eigenverantwortlichen Unterricht in einer 3. bzw. 4. Klasse. Nur noch der Seminarleiter erschien angekundigt zur Beurteilung von Unterrichtsversuchen. Im Juni 1987 legte sie im Fach Geographie ihre Einzellehrprobe ab, im Oktober 1987 ihre Doppellehrprobe in Biologie und Sport. Die mündlichen Prüfungen und die Klausur fand in der letzen Wochen in den Sommerferien statt. Hinter ihr lagen zwei Jahre in denen sie sehr viel arbeitete und wenig Zeit fur ihre Hobbies hatte. Allerdings zahlte sich dies aus, da sie aufgrund ihrer Prüfungsergebnisse schließsslich eine Planstelle in Marktheidenfeld bekam.

Vor ihr lag jetzt wieder eine neue Situation: Statt 14 Stunden unterrichtete sie 28, neben ihren studierten Fächern erteilte sie Unterricht auch in Deutsch, Musik and Kunst; austelle von Viertklässlern sassen nun Erstklässler vor ihr. Dazu kamen noch die organisatorischen Aufgaben bei einer Klassenführung sowie die Elternarbeit. Wieder war sie in ihrem Beruf so eingespannt, daß ihr wenig Freizeit blieb. Erst jetzt, wo sie diese Altersstufe zum zweiten Mal unterrichtet profitiert sie von ihren vielen Vorbereitungen and kann viel mehr als damals pädogogisch wirken. Sie weiß zwar nicht, wie sie in den nächsten Jahren die Situation beurteilen wird im Moment aber gefallt ihr die Arbeit mit den Kindern und sie ist froh, daß sie keine Mühen gescheut hat ihren Berufswunsch zu erfüllen.

In 1978 teacher training for the elementary school in Bavaria was reformed. Teachers in future had to decide at the start of their course of study whether they wanted to teach classes 1-4 in the Primary school or classes 5-9 in the Intermediate school. The course of study was made strictly academic. the students now had to choose a main subject and three teaching subjects.

Klaudia began in the winter term of 1980/81 her Primary school teacher training course in Würzburg. She chose Geography as her main subject and a combination of maths, biology and Sport for her teaching subjects. She preferred these subjects, as she had a strong personal liking for them and because she hoped to get good results in them in the exam. As she started her course of study, however, the chance of obtaining a post later on became less certain. Many even tried to dissuade her from doing the teacher training. Now however she was convinced that working with children as well as teaching was what pleased her most and so she was not dissuaded from following her original intentions. She was even prepared to take into account waiting for a couple of years on the so-called waiting list. Success in joining the teaching profession depended mainly on getting good reports in the first state exam. Pressure to do as well as possible even influenced the selection by countless colleges and lecturers.

The Geography course - which was strictly academic - gave her a lot of work and took a lot of time. She was seldom successful in the subjects specifically connected with the Primary school which she studied hard at and which had become really significant. In the 7th term she wrote her qualifying paper in the subject of the teaching of Geography, for which she had needed almost nine months to prepare. At the end of the eighth term she sat her first state exam.

Fortunately on leaving she had secured a good report taken from an average of her overall marks. The second part of her training course began in February 1985 in a village school near Marktheidenfeld. The first year of teaching probation consisted of being under a particular guidance teacher, attempts at teaching under his/her supervision and learning educational theory in seminars (10 hours). Furthermore in the second year she attended a seminar twice a week that took place each time in a different school in the region. Only the seminar tutor seemed to be informed of her teaching attempts. In June 1987 she was assessed in one teaching demonstration and in October 1987 her double teaching demonstration in Biology and Sport. The oral and written exams took place in the last weeks of the summer holidays. Behind her lay two years in which she had worked very had and had had little time for her hobbies. Anyhow it finally resulted in, due to her exam results, her getting a teaching position in Marktheidenfeld.

Once again she now faced a new situation: instead of 14 hours, she was teaching for 28. As well as the subjects she was qualified in, she had to share in the teaching of German, Music and Art; instead of class 4 children sat class 1 children in front of her. With this group came the additional work load of organising classes and dealing with parents. Once again she was so taken up with her profession that she had little free time left. Only when she took this age group for the second time could she take advantage of all the preparation she had done, and make it much more effective in the classroom than she had been able to do the first time. She doesn't know in fact, how she will get on in this post during the next few years but she enjoys working with children, and is pleased that she was not put off following her chosen career.

A Comprehensive School Teacher

Klaus ist Gesamtschullehrer und unterrichtet Englisch, Politische Weltkunde und Gesellschaftskunde (d.h. Erdkunde, Geschichte, Sozialkunde). Durch die folgende Beschreibung des Bildungs- und Ausbildungsweges wird deutlich, daß eine entsprechende Qualifikation nur durch ständige Weiterbildung, entsprechend dem Prinzip des lebenslangen Lernens, erreicht werden kann.

Klaus verließ die Schule mit 19 Jahren. Mit dem Abitur (allgemeine Hochschulreife) beendete er seine 13-jährige Schulkarierre (4 Grundschuljahre+9 Jahre Gymnasium) und begann ein Studium in Wirtschaftswissenschaften an der Universität Augsburg. Nach 4 Jahren schloß er sein Studium mit einem Diploma (dipl. ökonom) ab und nützte die Chance sofort als Referendar am Studienseminar in Giessen beginnen zu können. Die Gelegenheit, Lehrer werden zu können ergab sich aufgrund der damaligen hessischen Bildungsreform, in deren Rahmen ein neues Fach Wirtschafts- und Sozialwissenschaften an Gymnasien geschaffen wurde. So gehörte Klaus schließlich zu den wenigen Lehrern, die nach 1 1/2-jähriger 2. Ausbildungsphase die Qualifikation zum Unterricht des Faches Wirtschafts- und Sozialwissenschaften und Sozialkunde erwarben. (2. Staatsexamen)

Doch nun haben sich im Läufe der 1 1/2 - jährigen Ausbildungsphase die Zeiten geändert: Finanzielle Mittel für den Bildungsbereich wurden gekürzt (1976) und die Reformansätze verwässert bzw. rückgängig gemacht. so kam es, daß die einst so umworbenen Lehrer seines Ausbildungsfaches schließlich (nun ausgebildet!) nicht mehr gerne gesehen waren bzw. "nicht mehr eingesetzt werden konnten". Dank seiner hervorragenden Noten (mit Auszeichnung!) bekam Klaus eine befristete Anstellung auf einer 2/3-Stelle und schaffte es schließlich bald in den Berliner Schuldienst übernommen zu werden. Daß Klaus doch noch Lehrer bleiben konnte liegt an seiner Bereitschaft zur räumlichen Mobilität und an seiner Offenheit, sich neuen Anforderungen zu stellen.

In der Berliner Gesamtschule sah er sich nun mit einem völlig anderen Verhalten der Schüler konfrontiert und mußte nun in Politischer Weltkunde und Gesellschaftskunde in Fächern unterrichten, die ihm - zumindest in Teilgebieten wie Geschichte und Geographie - fremd waren. Dies bedeutete eine absolute Arbeitsbelastung, so daß eine 70-Stunden-Woche (bei 23 Unterrichtsstunden) eher die Regel als die Ausnahme war. Mit 28 Jahren wurde er schließlich Beamter auf Lebenszeit und entschloß sich, sich zum nächsten Jahr beurlauben zu lassen um neue Kraft und neue Erfahrungen sammeln zu können.

Im Rahmen der nun 5-jährigen Beurlaubungszeit lernte Klaus als Reisender und Mitarbeiter Kulturen und Producktionsweisen anderer Völker kennen, studierte an der Freien universität das Fach Amerikanistik/Englisch und studierte schließlich als Austauschstudent an der Indiana University in Bloomington, USA. Bevor er wieder in seinen Dienst als Lehrer zurückging erwarb er noch durch eine Prüfung beim Landesprüfungsamt Berlin die

Qualifikation zum Unterricht des Faches Englisch an Gymnasien.

Die Reintegration in den Schuldienst war mit einigen Schwierigkeiten verbunden. Zunächst mußte Klaus an zwei Schulen unterrichten bis er schließlich nach einem Jahr wieder an seine ehemalige Stammschule zurückkonnte. Doch auch hier hatten sich die Arbeitsbedingungen aufgrund der veränderten Politik (geringere Unterstützung für Gesamtschulen) verschlechtert. Die Negativ-Propaganda führte seit Ende der 70-er-Jahre zu einer Veränderung der sozialen Zusammensetzung der Schülerschaft.

Aufgrund seines Engagements für die Schüler und der Konfrontation mit fast unlösbaren sozialen Problemen in seiner Klasse entschloß sich Klaus-durch Gehaltsverzicht (Reduzierung der zu leistenden Unterrichtsstunden) - sich mehr Zeit und Ruhe für die Schüler zu verschaffen. Nun mit einer Unterrichtsverpflichtung von 17 Stunden hat er das Gefühl, den Anforderungen gewachsen sein zu können, ohne vollständig von der Arbeit und den Problemen "aufgefressen zu werden". Zuden nimmt er in seiner Freizeit an vielen Fortbildungs- und Weiterbildungsveranstaltungen teil, um zukünftigen Aufgaben nicht unvorbereitet gegenüberstehen zu müssen.

Klaus is a Comprehensive School teacher and teaches English, World Politics and Social Subjects (i.e. Geography, History, Modern Studies). From the following description of the educational and training course it will become clear that an adequate qualification can only be achieved through constant further education following the principle of continuous life-long learning.

Klaus left school at the age of 19. His 13 year school career (4 primary and 9 High School years) ended with the Higher leaving certificate (Abitur). Then began his university education at Augsburg, reading Economics. Four years later he completed his university studies by obtaining a diploma (diploma in Economics) and took the opportunity of starting teacher training in Giessen as a probationer. This opportunity to become a teacher was due to the educational reform which took place in Hesse at that time. It brought about the introduction of Economics and the Social Sciences as teaching subjects in the High Schools. Klaus therefore eventually became one of the few teachers, who after a training period of 1½ years gained the qualification for the teaching of the subjects of Economic and Social Sciences.

However the 1½ year period of training has been altered. Financial resources have been cut in this area of training. The reforms have either been diluted or abolished altogether. And so it turned out that these once so much sought after teachers with their new qualifications were now not looked on favourably and they could no longer be appointed. Due to the outstanding marks obtained by Klaus (with distinction), he got a teaching position, first limited to 2/3 years and then was taken on by the school authority in Berlin. What enabled Klaus to remain a teacher was his readiness to move around freely and his ability to set himself high standards.

In the Berlin Comprehensive School, he was faced with a completely different system and now had to teach World Politics and Social Subjects, areas of which, in Geography and History were completely unknown to him. This meant a huge work load, so that a 70 hour week (23 periods) was more the rule than the exception to the rule. At 28 he eventually became a fully qualified, registered permanent teacher and decided to take a year off to enable himself to renew his energy and to enrich his experience of life.

In the course of his 5 year leave as a traveller and fellow worker, Klaus got to know how other people lived and worked at first hand; studied at the 'Open University' American and English Literature and eventually studied at Indiana University in Bloomington, USA as an exchange student. Before he returned to the service of teaching, he gained the qualification to teach English in the High School in Berlin by passing the qualifying exam.

Klaus faced certain difficulties when returning to school service. Immediately on his return he had to teach in two schools until eventually after a year he could get back into his original school. Even here, there were also conditions of work he had to comply with, caused by the political changes, which worsened things. (Less support for Comprehensive Schools.) Negative propaganda has been leading to changes in the social structure in the schools.

Due to his commitment to the pupils and to confronting almost insoluble social problems in his class, Klaus decided to go for a reduction in his actual teaching periods with a corresponding reduction in his salary, to give himself more time and peace for the sake of his pupils. Now with a teaching load of 17 hours he has the feeling that he is getting nearer to being able to answer all the demands made of him without 'being completely devoured' by his work and its problems. In his free time he takes part in many teacher development courses so that he will not be unprepared for any future demands that he has to meet.

A Secondary School Teacher from Bavaria

Karl ist Hauptschullehrer und unterichtet die Fächer Deutsch, Mathematik, Biologie, Erdkunde, Geschichte, Arbeitslehre, Musik und Physik/Chemie. Wie es zu dieser Fächeranhäufung kommt, soll in der Beschreibung der Hochschulausbildung näher beschrieben werden.

Karl hat nach 4 Grundschul jahren und 9 Jahren Gymnasium nach dem Abitur (allgemeine Hochschulreife) mit 19 Jahren die Schule verlassen. Nach dem 15-monatigen Grundwehrdienst studierte er 6 Semester an der Erziehungswissenschaftlichen Fakultat der Universitat Würzburg.

Am Ende des Studiums legte er das Erste Staatsexamen ab; Prüfungsfächer waren Deutsch, Erdkunde, Religion, Musik (Wahlfächer) und Sozialkunde, Pädagogik, Psychologie, Schulpädagogik (Pflichtfächer).

Nach dem Studium folgte die 3-jährige zweite Ausbildungsphase Karl unterrichtete als "Legramtsanwärter" unter Anleitung eines "Seminarleiters" im ersten Dienst jahr eine 5. Klasse mit 18 Wochenstunden an 4 Tagen. Der 5. Wochentag war - auch in den beiden anderen Ausbildungsjahren - Seminar - beziehungsweise Ausbildungstag. Im 2. und 3. Dienst jahr unterrichtete er eine 7. Klasse, die er auch in der 8. Jahrgangsstufe weiterführen durfte.

In den Hauptschulen wird das sogenannte "Klassenlehrerprinzip" verstärkt gefördert, das heißt, daß der Klassenlehrer in möglichst len Unterrichtsstunden, also auch mit möglichst vielen Fächern in seiner Klasse unterrichten soll. Man verspricht sich davon eine größere erzieherische Wirksamkeit des Lehrers und nimmt dafür unter Umständen eine geringere Kompetenz des Lehrers in manchen Schulfächern in Kauf.

In der dreijährigen zweiten Ausbildungsphase wurde dieser hohen Anforderung Rechnung getragen. Im Dreijahresturnus wechseln die Fächergruppen für die Ausbildung an den Seminartagen und für die je drei Unterrichtsvormittage pro Jahr, die der Lehramtsanwärter unter Prü Unterrichtsvormittage pro Jahr, die der Lehramtsanwärter nach diesen 3 Ausbildungsjahren über seine Prüfungsfächer von der Universität hinaus in fast allen Unterrichtsfächern Demonstrationsstunden selbst gehalten und von qualifizierten Ausbildungs lehrern gesehen.

Nach dieser Ausbildungsphase, die Karl seine ganze Kraft kostete (täglich Unterrichtsvorbereitung bis in die späte Nacht), kam die 2. Staatsprüfung, welche über die Anstellung des Lehrers entschied. Je nach Anzahl der neuen Stellen, welche der Staat für junge Lehrer bereitstellte, wurde (und wird) jährlich der Notendurchschnitt neu festgelegt, der für die Anstellung oder das "Aus" entscheidend ist Helmut schaffte diese Hürde und bekam mit knapp 27 Jahren eine feste Anstellung an einer Hauptschule in Würzburg und damit ein monatliches Gehalt von ca. 2500 DM.

Während seines Studiums hatte er in Untermiete in einem Dachzimmer in einem Vorort von Würzburg gewohnt. Nach seiner Hochzeit mit 22 Jahren bezog er mit seiner Frau eine eigene Wohnung. Das war möglich, da seine Frau eine Ausbildung zur Diplombibliothekarin machte, die in den Ausbildungs jahren schon gut bezahlt wurde (ca. 1000 - DM monatlich). Dazu kam ein Jahr später ab dem ersten Dienst jahr als Lehramtsanwärter mit fester Unterrichtsverpflichtung für Karl selbst ein monatliches Gehalt von ca. 1500 - DM.

Karl konnte deshalb bereits zusammen mit seiner Frau während der Ausbildung beginnen, auf beider gemeinsames Ziel, ein kleines Haus, zu sparen. Ein solches kauften Karl und seine Frau mit 25 Jahren (Helmut war noch nicht mit der Ausbildung fertig) und schafften es mit einer waghalsigen Finanzierung und viel Glück (eine Stelle für Karl in seiner Heimatstadt), alles in den Griff zu bekommen. Für Reisen aller Art (ein Hobby vieler Lehrer in Deutschland) und jegliche Art von größeren Anschaffungen war nun jahrelang kein Raum mehr.

Beruflich mußte sich Karl nach der Ausbildung sehr umstellen. Der Schulleiter verlangte auch das Unterrichten in Fächern, die Karl noch nie selbst unterrichtet hatte und in denen sich seine Kenntnisse aus Erinnerungen aus der eigenen Schulzeit beschränkten. Es wurde vorausgesetzt, daß der Junglehrer sich Literatur besorgte, sich einarbeitete und auch schwierige Klassen unterrichtete. In seinem ersten Berufsjahr nach den Prüfungen wurde er Zunächst Lehrer ohne Klassenführung und bekam an seiner neuen Schule alle Fächer und Kurse, welche die Lehrer des "Stammpersonals" nicht oder nur ungern unterrichten wollten. Nach der wohlbehüteten Ausbildungszeit kam ein harter "Praxisschock". Bei 28 Wochenstunden in den unterschiedlichsten Fächern (auch Physik) blieb nicht mehr so viel Zeit wie während der Ausbildung für die Unterrichtsvorbereitung; gleichwohl nahm die Routine zu. Häufig beendete Karl seine Unterrichtstage sehr frustriert über eigene

Unzulänglichkeit, Disziplinschwierigkeiten in manchen Kursen und dem Gefühl "sein Gehalt nicht wert zu sein".

In den folgenden Jahren konnte er seine Position an der Schule festigen; er wurde bei den Schülern recht beliebt und hatte großen Rückhalt im Kollegium und der Schulleitung. Mit 30 Jahren wurde er Beamter auf Lebenszeit.

Seit 1985 ist Karl Praktikumslehrer und damit an der Ausbildung von Studenten für den Lehrerberuf beteiligt. Diese Arbeit macht ihm sehr viel Freude und bietet eine gute Abwechslung zum Alltag des Lehrers. Gleichzeitig wird Karl dadurch immer wieder gezwungen, über seine tägliche Arbeit nachzudenken und sein Verhalten in der Klasse zu überprüfen.

Auch der Computer ist nicht spurlos an Karl vorübergegangen; nach dem Besuch von Informatiklehrgängen und Fortbildungen für ein neues Fach, die "Informationstechnische Grundbildung", hat sich Karl nun selbst einen PC gekauft und erledigt einen großen Teil seiner Unterrichtsvorbereitung am Computer. Mit zunehmender Routine im Umgang auch mit Graphikprogrammen kann er so viel Zeit und Arbeit einsparen und erwirbt sich schrittweise die Qualifikation für ein neues Unterrichtsgebiet.

Seit 5 Jahren hat Karl auch das Amt des Beratungslehrers an seiner Schule übernommen. Er betreibt Schullaufbahnberatung für Schüler und deren Eltern, hält Informationsveranstaltungen an der eigenen und an anderen Schulen, überall, wo Interesse an Informationen über die Schulart "Hauptschule" besteht.
Obwohl Karl zusammen mit Rektor und Konrektor an der Stundenplangestaltung an einigen Ferientagen mitarbeitet und sich für manche Verwaltungsarbeiten durchaus interessiert, hat er nicht den Wunsch, selbst einen Posten in der Schulleitung anzustreben. Er ist der Meinung, dadurch würde sein lockeres, gutes Verhältnis zu den Schülern getrübt und er müßte manches etwas ernster nehmen. Zu Dienstvorschriften hat er gelegentlich ein etwas legeres Verhältnis; er ist bereit, sich gewisse Freiheiten durch großes Engagement über das "Soll" hinaus zu erkämpfen und erwartet dann Toleranze. Hoffentlich hat er immer verständnisvolle Vorgesetzte.

Karl hat nun mit 35 Jahren Familie mit 2 Kindern (4 1/2 und 6 1/2 Jahre alt), ein eigenes Haus mit Garten, einen kurzen Schulweg (max. 20 Minuten mit dem Auto) und sehr viel Freude an seinem Beruf. Er verdient nun 3700 - DM, ein Gehalt, mit dem recht gut leben kann.

Karl is a secondary school teacher and teaches the following subjects: German, Maths, Biology, Geography, History, 'workskills', Music and Physics or Chemistry. How such a collection of teaching subjects came about will be explained in the following description of his training for the secondary school.

Karl left school at 19 after spending 4 years at primary school, 9 years at High School and after completion of the general high school leaving exam (i.e. the Abitur). After a basic military service of 15 months he studied at the University of Würzburg in the faculty of education for 6 terms (half-years).

At the end of this period of study he took his first state exam: the subjects were German, Geography, Religious Education, Music (chosen subjects) and Social Education, Education, Psychology, Teaching (compulsory subjects).

This period of study was followed by a 3 year second period of training. Karl taught as a trainee teacher under the direction of a tutor with class 5 for 18 periods for 4 week days. The fifth day was - as in the two later years of training - a seminar or tutorial day. In the second and third year he taught class 7, which he also had to continue with into their class 8.

In the secondary schools the so-called "class teacher principle" was strongly emphasised, i.e. the class teacher had to take his class for as many subjects as he could possibly manage. This system was supposed to lead to maximum educational efficiency in the use of the teacher and as a result a lowering of standards in certain subjects, depending on the all-round competence of the teacher.

In the three year 2nd phase of the training, provision was made for the above demands. During the three years the subject groups were rotated for the tutorials and for the 4 mornings of teaching in each year; in each of these subjects the trainee teacher was tested during the seminar in front of the group under exam conditions. In this way each trainee teacher left the 3 year training period after having given demonstration lessons individually in nearly all the subjects, taken at university, and had also seen lessons given by qualified specialist training teachers.

After this period of training, which sapped all Karl's energy (daily preparation of lessons until late in the night) came the state exam which decided the placing of the teacher. The appointment of a trainee teacher to a teaching post was dependent on the number of appointments that the state education authority made available - these were fixed on an annual basis according to requirements.

Karl managed to overcome this obstacle and at just 27 he got a permanent appointment at a secondary school in Würzburg and a monthly salary of approximately 2500 D.M.

During his years of study he had rented an attic room in a suburb of Würzburg. After his marriage at 22, he and his wife moved to their own flat. That was possible, as his wife was training to be a librarian and was already, during the training years, quite well paid (approximately 1000 D.M. per month). A year later when Karl was doing his first in-school training year with all the teaching demands made on him, he was receiving an income of approximately 1500 D.M. per month.

As a result of their earnings, Karl and his wife were able to start saving for a small house - both of them having the same goal in view. At 25 Karl and his wife were able to buy such a house (Karl had not yet completed his training) and managed by means of (a) funding and a lot of luck (his job was in his own home town) to get everything to work out. Any kind of travel (an activity popular with many German teachers) or other more ambitious schemes were now completely out of the question for many years.

In his teaching Karl had to be very flexible and this was immediately after his training. This meant that Karl had to teach in subjects that he had never taught and the knowledge of which was limited to what he himself had learnt at school. The headmaster made these demands and took it for granted that the young teacher concerned himself with literature, familiarised himself with the school routines and also taught difficult classes. In his first year of teaching after his exams he was a teacher without a class and got whichever classes and courses that the members of staff in his school did not want to, or taught unwillingly. After the well protected training period came the hard shock of real teaching. After 28 periods of teaching in all kinds of subjects (also in Physics) there was not as much time left as previously was the case as a student teacher for the preparation of lessons; yet in the daily routine there was more and more work. Frequently Karl felt very frustrated at the end of the teaching day over his own short-comings, discipline problems in some classes and the feeling that "he did not deserve his salary".

In the following years he was able to secure his position in the school; he was really popular with his pupils and was highly regarded by his colleagues and the school administration. At 30 he was in a school - where he would be for the rest of his life.

Since 1985 Karl has occupied a position as a teacher sharing responsibility for student trainees in the school. He enjoys this work very much and it gives him a change from the everyday teaching routine. At the same time Karl is forced again and again to assess his daily work and consider afresh his teaching methods in the classroom.

Also the computer has not escaped Karl's attention; after attending a computing course with a view to introducing a new school subject "Basic information technology", Karl has bought a new personal computer for himself on which he prepares a lot of his schoolwork.
With an increasing amount of work using graphics done on the computer, he can save so much time and extra work and is gradually obtaining qualifications for this new area of teaching.

For 5 years Karl has also been responsible for guidance in his school. He gives advice on careers for both the pupils and their parents, holds meetings in his own and other schools to pass on information on careers and also to publicise the type of schooling offered by the secondary school.

Although Karl works alongside the head and deputy headmaster on time-tabling in his own holiday time and is also very involved in the administration of the school, he has no desire to acquire a position in the administration of the school. He is of the opinion that his good, relaxed relationship with the pupils would be spoilt as a result and that he would have to become somewhat serious. As regards the school authorities, he is on quite a friendly footing; he is ready to pressure certain 'freedoms' by fighting for them and against unthinking compulsion and expects more tolerance as a result. It is to be hoped that he continues to have understanding superiors.

Karl at 35 has now a family of 2 children (four and a half and six and a half years old), his own house and garden, only a short distance away from school (maximum 20 minutes by car) and enjoys his profession a great deal. Now he earns 3,700 D.M. a salary that he can live very well on.

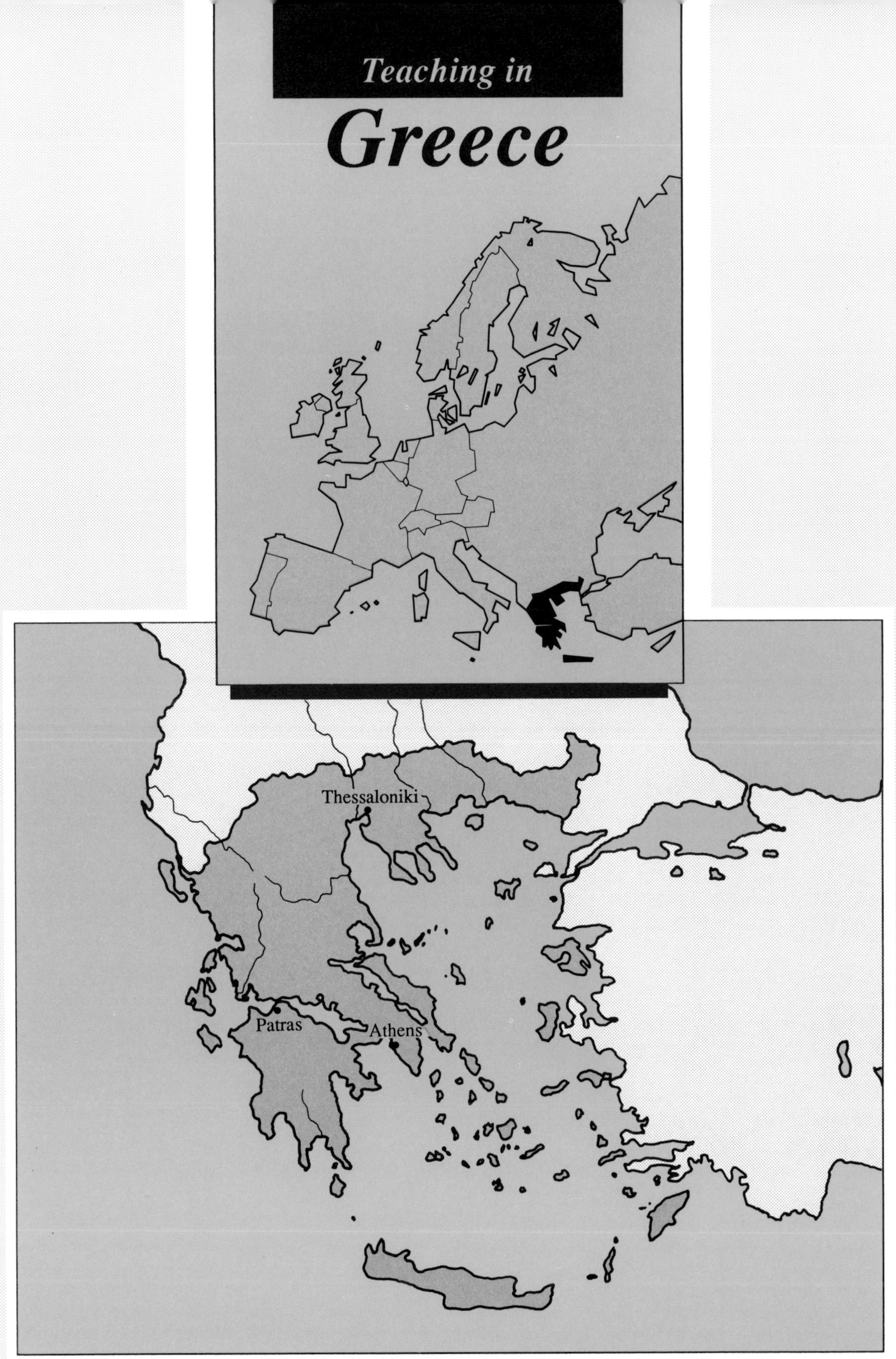
Teaching in
Greece
Thessaloniki
Patras
Athens

TEACHING IN GREECE

Greece stands apart from other EC countries. Situated to the south and to the east, it shares frontiers with Turkey, Bulgaria, Yugoslavia and Albania. Also, in a religious sense, as the main representative of the Eastern Orthodox Church, Greece differs from other Christian countries. At the same time, history puts Greece at the centre: the roots of much that characterises Western European civilization begin there.

The population of Greece is about 10 million. In common with other peripheral areas it is a poor country, with the second-lowest GNP of the EC. The harsh realities of geography and climate are major factors. It is a country of small, unprofitable farms and of small family businesses. The economic life of the country is dominated by Athens - Piraeus where almost one-third of the population lives. Large numbers of Greeks have sought a better life as migrant workers to the wealthier countries of Western Europe.

Educational provision in Greece is the responsibility of the Ministry of National Education and Religion; the regional services for Education; and the various organisations responsible for school buildings and school books. The levels of education include Primary; Secondary; and Higher Education.

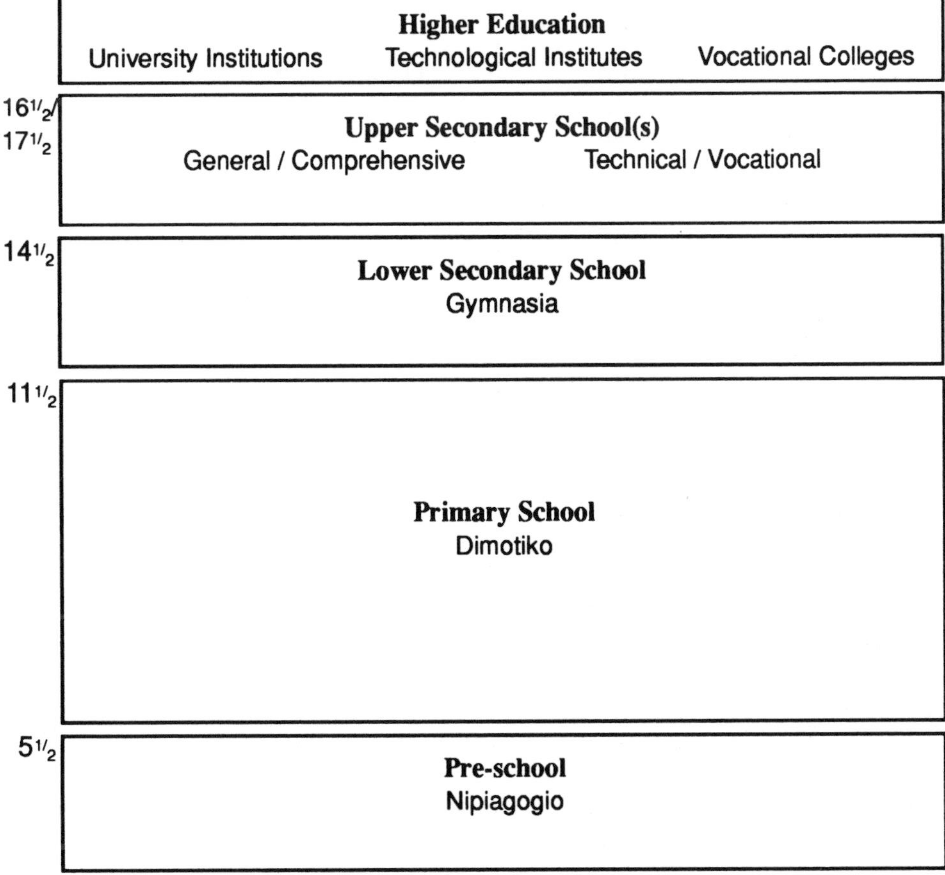

The structure and functioning of the primary and secondary education levels is regulated through the 1566/1986 educational law. In this law are defined the basic educational issues - such as the aims of Greek education; the structure and levels of provision; issues related to the training and education of teachers; the organisation of school life, and other matters. Thus, within the context of the law, the Ministry of National Education and Religion exerts significant influence upon the educational system.

Educational provision at compulsory level lasts for 9 years. Whilst children are not obliged to attend nursery school it is possible for a nursery to be established when more than 8 children wish to go. Law 1566/85 has sought to establish new centres, and some new buildings have been constructed. Primary schools accept children of $5\frac{1}{2}$ - $11\frac{1}{2}$ years, and the main regulations concerning the organisation and functioning of the schools are decided by the Ministry. The subjects which are taught include: Religion; Greek language; Mathematics; Social Subjects; Arts and Crafts; Music and Physical Education.

In particular, the primary school aims to 'build up the abilities that help pupils to assimilate knowledge; to be developed physically; to improve their natural and mental health; and to practise their motor skills'.

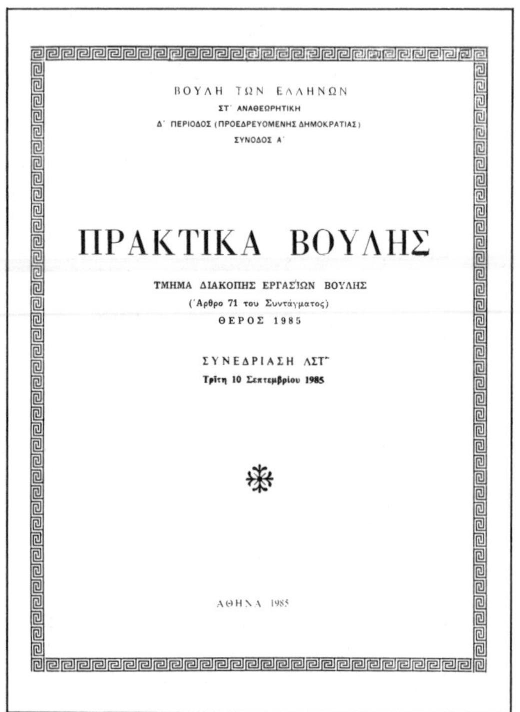

ΒΟΥΛΗ ΤΩΝ ΕΛΛΗΝΩΝ
ΣΤ΄ ΑΝΑΘΕΩΡΗΤΙΚΗ
Δ΄ ΠΕΡΙΟΔΟΣ (ΠΡΟΕΔΡΕΥΟΜΕΝΗΣ ΔΗΜΟΚΡΑΤΙΑΣ)
ΣΥΝΟΔΟΣ Α΄

ΠΡΑΚΤΙΚΑ ΒΟΥΛΗΣ

ΤΜΗΜΑ ΔΙΑΚΟΠΗΣ ΕΡΓΑΣΙΩΝ ΒΟΥΛΗΣ
(Άρθρο 71 του Συντάγματος)
ΘΕΡΟΣ 1985

ΣΥΝΕΔΡΙΑΣΗ ΛΣΤ΄
Τρίτη 10 Σεπτεμβρίου 1985

ΑΘΗΝΑ 1985

Secondary education is provided in two cycles. The first level includes the Gymnasia, which provides a three year course for pupils aged $11\frac{1}{2}$ - $14\frac{1}{2}$ years. The upper level includes the Lycea (General; Classical; Church; Technical-Vocational; and Comprehensive) and the technical and vocational schools. Pupils attending the gymnasium will follow a course which includes a foreign language; scientific subjects; ancient Greek and modern Greek. Pupils are expected to attain a mark of at least 10 (out of a maximum of 20) for each subject studied. Successful completion of their course will lead to the award of a leaving certificate and automatic right of admission to upper secondary education.

Key educational aims include:
- to broaden the pupils' system of values so that they regulate their behaviour accordingly;
- to complete their knowledge and relate it with social problems, and to face successfully various situations and to seek solutions to the difficulties of life with responsibility...;

On entering one of the lycea attendance will last for three years and successful completion of the course will lead to a certificate (Apolitirio). Selection for university and non university tertiary level institutions is closely related to marks obtained throughout the upper secondary school, and in national written examinations.

Teacher Training

Intending nursery school and primary school teachers are trained in one of eight Pedagogical Departments of the Universities, taking a university degree (*Ptjhio*) after completing a four year course.

These university departments started in session 1984-85. Until that time the training of nursery and primary school teachers was in the two year non-university post-lyceum Colleges of Education. The change to a four year course, and integration into a university campus has - as in certain other countries - sought to improve the quality of training; the social status of teachers; and provide a salary scale for nursery/primary school teachers on the same level as that for secondary school teachers.

To enter training it will first be necessary to obtain a leaving certificate from a lyceum; it is also essential to obtain a pass in the national examination for entry to universities and higher technological institutes. Once admitted to the four year course studies will be mainly concentrated upon Education (including Educational Theory; Psychology; Sociology; and History of Education); Teaching Methods (including both theory and teaching practice); and a range of general education subjects related to both personal choices and to the subjects taught in the schools.

The proportion of time allocated to teaching practice varies from university to university, but is estimated - on average - to be between 15%-25% of the course.

The education of teachers for the Gymnasium and Lyceum (i.e. lower and upper secondary education) takes place in the universities and according to the specialisation of the student. Once again, for entry to the university, candidates must obtain a school leaving certificate (apolitirio) and also a pass in the national entry examinations for universities.

Subject teachers (e.g. of Mathematics, or Geography) will be educated in their specialisation in the appropriate university department, over a period of 4-5 years. Intending technical school teachers will also be educated in a university department, or possibly in a Higher Technological Institution.

For teaching it will also be necessary for students to attend lectures on Education, Psychology, and subject teaching methods at Departments of Education and Psychology in the Universities.[1] Teaching methods will be taught separately from subject content and such practical, and pedagogical elements usually take place in the 3rd and 4th years of the university course.

All graduates following this route will normally have the right to be appointed as secondary school teachers.

Entry to Teaching

All graduates from the Pedagogical Department, as well as those from university subject departments, will normally have the right to be appointed as teachers if they are below the age of forty years. Those who have obtained a university degree from another country would submit this to the Inter-University Centre of the Ministry of Education to be recognised.

In the application process teachers submit their application forms for appointment to the local Directorates of Education. In the application form candidates can declare up to 15 Directorates, in order of preference, as well as listing details of education and family circumstances. Such matters can affect the appointment of candidates to a school closer to - or further away from family and relations.

Thus, such qualifications as University degree; Certificate of Greek nationality; Certificate of marital status; Health certificate; and Army certificate will be required. Applicants for teaching posts will then be enrolled on an Appointment Waiting List (Epetirida) based upon the date of their application. Those who have a postgraduate degree; are war victims; resistance victims; or have a large family (i.e. more than three children) will obtain priority on the list. Certain other criteria can also define the order in the list, and affect location. Such criteria include marital status; number of children in the household; children with special needs; and health conditions.

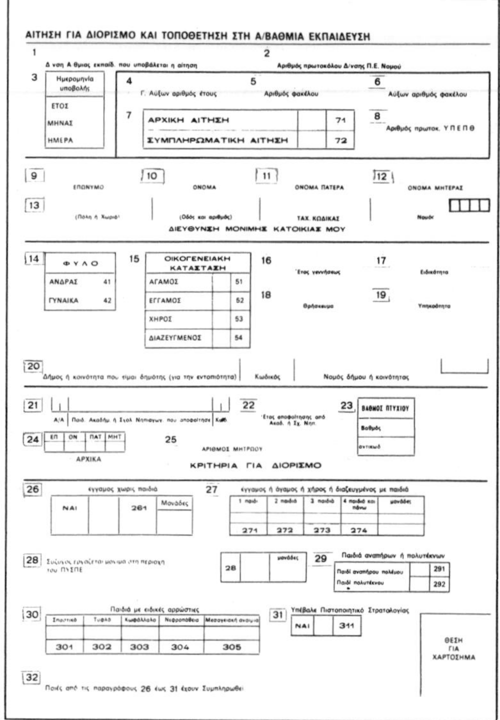

ΑΙΤΗΣΗ ΓΙΑ ΔΙΟΡΙΣΜΟ ΚΑΙ ΤΟΠΟΘΕΤΗΣΗ ΣΤΗ Α/ΒΑΘΜΙΑ ΕΚΠΑΙΔΕΥΣΗ

1 Δ νση Α θμιας εκπαίδ. που υποβάλεται η αίτηση

2 Αριθμός πρωτοκόλου Δ/νσης Π.Ε. Νομού

3 Ημερομηνία υποβολής: ΕΤΟΣ / ΜΗΝΑΣ / ΗΜΕΡΑ

4 Γ. Αύξων αριθμός έτους

5 Αριθμός φακέλου

6 Αύξων αριθμός φακέλου

7

ΑΡΧΙΚΗ ΑΙΤΗΣΗ		71
ΣΥΜΠΛΗΡΩΜΑΤΙΚΗ ΑΙΤΗΣΗ		72

8 Αριθμός πρωτοκ. ΥΠΕΠΘ

9 ΕΠΩΝΥΜΟ | 10 ΟΝΟΜΑ | 11 ΟΝΟΜΑ ΠΑΤΕΡΑ | 12 ΟΝΟΜΑ ΜΗΤΕΡΑΣ

13 (Πόλη ή Χωριό) | (Οδός και αριθμός) | ΤΑΧ. ΚΩΔΙΚΑΣ | Νομός

ΔΙΕΥΘΥΝΣΗ ΜΟΝΙΜΗΣ ΚΑΤΟΙΚΙΑΣ ΜΟΥ

14

ΦΥΛΟ	
ΑΝΔΡΑΣ	41
ΓΥΝΑΙΚΑ	42

15

ΟΙΚΟΓΕΝΕΙΑΚΗ ΚΑΤΑΣΤΑΣΗ		
ΑΓΑΜΟΣ		51
ΕΓΓΑΜΟΣ		52
ΧΗΡΟΣ		53
ΔΙΑΖΕΥΓΜΕΝΟΣ		54

16 Έτος γεννήσεως

17 Ειδικότητα

18 Θρήσκευμα

19 Υπηκοότητα

20 Δήμος ή κοινότητα που είμαι δημότης (για την εντοπιότητα) | Κωδικός | Νομός δήμου ή κοινότητας

21 Α/Α | Παιδ. Ακαδήμ. ή Σχολ. Νηπιαγων. που αποφοίτησε | Κωδ.

22 Έτος αποφοίτησης από Ακαδ. ή Σχ. Νηπ.

23

ΒΑΘΜΟΣ ΠΤΥΧΙΟΥ
Βαθμός
αντικωδ.

24

ΕΠ	ΟΝ	ΠΑΤ	ΜΗΤ

ΑΡΧΙΚΑ

25 ΑΡΙΘΜΟΣ ΜΗΤΡΩΟΥ

ΚΡΙΤΗΡΙΑ ΓΙΑ ΔΙΟΡΙΣΜΟ

26 έγγαμος χωρίς παιδιά

ΝΑΙ		261	Μονάδες

27 έγγαμος ή άγαμος ή χήρος ή διαζευγμένος με παιδιά

1 παιδί	2 παιδιά	3 παιδιά	4 παιδιά και πάνω	μονάδες
271	272	273	274	

28 Σύζυγος εργάζεται μόνιμα στη περιοχή του ΠΥΣΠΕ

28		μονάδες

29 Παιδιά αναπήρων ή πολυτέκνων

Παιδί αναπήρου πολέμου		291
Παιδί πολυτέκνου		292

30 Παιδιά με ειδικές αρρώστιες

Σπαστικό	Τυφλό	Κωφάλαλο	Νεφροπάθεια	Μεσογειακή αναιμία
301	302	303	304	305

31 Υπέβαλε Πιστοποιητικό Στρατολογίας

ΝΑΙ		311

ΘΕΣΗ ΓΙΑ ΧΑΡΤΟΣΗΜΑ

32 Ποιές από τις παραγράφους 26 έως 31 έχουν Συμπληρωθεί

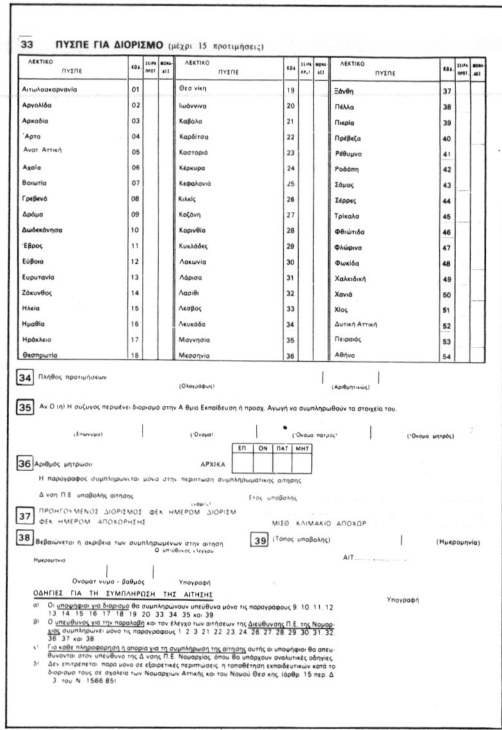

33 ΠΥΣΠΕ ΓΙΑ ΔΙΟΡΙΣΜΟ (μέχρι 15 προτιμήσεις)

ΛΕΚΤΙΚΟ ΠΥΣΠΕ	ΚΩΔ.	ΣΕΙΡΑ ΠΡΟΤ.	ΜΟΝΑΔΕΣ	ΛΕΚΤΙΚΟ ΠΥΣΠΕ	ΚΩΔ.	ΣΕΙΡΑ ΠΡΟΤ.	ΜΟΝΑΔΕΣ	ΛΕΚΤΙΚΟ ΠΥΣΠΕ	ΚΩΔ.	ΣΕΙΡΑ ΠΡΟΤ.	ΜΟΝΑΔΕΣ
Αιτωλοακαρνανία	01			Θεσ νίκη	19			Ξάνθη	37		
Αργολίδα	02			Ιωάννινα	20			Πέλλα	38		
Αρκαδία	03			Καβάλα	21			Πιερία	39		
Άρτα	04			Καρδίτσα	22			Πρέβεζα	40		
Ανατ. Αττική	05			Καστοριά	23			Ρέθυμνο	41		
Αχαΐα	06			Κέρκυρα	24			Ροδόπη	42		
Βοιωτία	07			Κεφαλονιά	25			Σάμος	43		
Γρεβενά	08			Κιλκίς	26			Σέρρες	44		
Δράμα	09			Κοζάνη	27			Τρίκαλα	45		
Δωδεκάνησα	10			Κορινθία	28			Φθιώτιδα	46		
Έβρος	11			Κυκλάδες	29			Φλώρινα	47		
Εύβοια	12			Λακωνία	30			Φωκίδα	48		
Ευρυτανία	13			Λάρισα	31			Χαλκιδική	49		
Ζάκυνθος	14			Λασιθι	32			Χανιά	50		
Ηλεία	15			Λέσβος	33			Χίος	51		
Ημαθία	16			Λευκάδα	34			Δυτική Αττική	52		
Ηράκλειο	17			Μαγνησία	35			Πειραιάς	53		
Θεσπρωτία	18			Μεσσηνία	36			Αθήνα	54		

34 Πλήθος προτιμήσεων (Ολογράφως) | (Αριθμητικώς)

35 Αν Ο (η) Η σύζυγος περιμένει διορισμό στην Α θμια Εκπαίδευση ή προσχ. Αγωγή να συμπληρωθούν τα στοιχεία του.

(Επωνυμο) | (Όνομα) | (Όνομα πατρός) | (Όνομα μητρός)

36 Αριθμός μητρώου

ΑΡΧΙΚΑ

ΕΠ	ΟΝ	ΠΑΤ	ΜΗΤ

Η παράγραφος συμπληρωνεται μόνο στην περιπτωση συμπληρωματικης αιτησης

Δ νση Π.Ε υποβολής αιτησης — Ετος υποβολης

37 ΠΡΟΗΓΟΥΜΕΝΟΣ ΔΙΟΡΙΣΜΟΣ ΦΕΚ ΗΜΕΡΟΜ ΔΙΟΡΙΣΜ
ΦΕΚ ΗΜΕΡΟΜ ΑΠΟΧΩΡΗΣΗΣ — ΜΙΣΘ ΚΛΙΜΑΚΙΟ ΑΠΟΧΩΡ

38 Βεβαιώνεται η ακρίβεια των συμπληρωμένων στην αιτηση
Ο υπεύθυνος ελέγχου

Ημερομηνια

Ονοματ νυμο - βαθμός | Υπογραφή

39 (Τόπος υποβολής) | (Ημερομηνία)

ΑΙΤ.......

Υπογραφή

ΟΔΗΓΙΕΣ ΓΙΑ ΤΗ ΣΥΜΠΛΗΡΩΣΗ ΤΗΣ ΑΙΤΗΣΗΣ

α) Οι υποψήφιοι για διορισμό θα συμπληρώνουν υπεύθυνα μόνο τις παραγράφους 9. 10. 11. 12. 13. 14. 15. 16. 17. 18. 19. 20. 33. 34. 35 και 39

β) Ο υπευθυνος για την παραλαβή και τον έλεγχο των αιτήσεων της Διεύθυνσης Π.Ε. της Νομαρχίας συμπληρώνει μόνο τις παραγράφους 1. 2. 3. 21. 22. 23. 24. 26. 27. 28. 29. 30. 31. 32. 36. 37 και 38.

γ) Για κάθε πληροφόρηση ή απορία για τη συμπλήρωση της αίτησης αυτής οι υποψήφιοι θα απευθύνονται στον υπεύθυνο της Δ νσης Π.Ε. Νομαρχίας, όπου θα υπάρχουν αναλυτικές οδηγίες.

δ) Δεν επιτρέπεται παρά μόνο σε εξαιρετικές περιπτώσεις, η τοποθέτηση εκπαιδευτικών κατά το διορισμό τους σε σχολεία των Νομαρχιών Αττικής και του Νομού Θεσ κης. (άρθρ. 15 περ. Δ 3 του Ν. 1566 85)

Ultimately the appointment to a Directorate will be decided by the Ministry. The exact location within the Directorate will be decided by the local education committee on the basis of the needs of the school; the applicant's preference; and other criteria - each estimated in points. For example

to be in the same place as husband/wife	: 3 points
married without children	: 1 point
married with one child	: 2 points
married with two children	: 3 points
married with four children	: 4 points
married with four children or more	: 7 points

All this is significant, given the norm that new teachers are usually located in remote districts and where schools have low numbers of pupils.

Within the state school sector teachers will be employed by the Ministry of Education; be accorded civil service status (this also includes contracted employees in private schools); and are required to be nationals.

Having the status of civil servant means that teachers, once appointed, have a permanent job; they are paid by the state; and have their health insurance and pension paid by the state. Teachers in the private schools are paid by the school manager, and have their health insurance and pension from the social security organisation.

Teacher Probation

The first two years of teaching are typically considered as a probation period. Over these initial two years the teachers are evaluated by the local school advisers, and upon this evaluation being successful they will obtain a permanent position. It is rare not to be offered a permanent post.

No special support is provided for probationers beginning their career although it is possible that other staff may help on an informal basis. It is also possible that the new teacher could be the sole teacher in charge in a small village school. According to the law 10-25 pupils make a one-teacher school, with the average number of pupils for each teacher being 25.

One specific development relates to teachers beginning their work in the 1990's. From 1989 special seminars have been provided for beginning teachers who are now required to attend prior to taking up their teaching post. These can be full or part-time courses designed to help with initial orientation to schools.

Closely influencing the probationer will be the School Adviser. By the law 1304/1984 the school inspectors were replaced by the school advisers, whose task it is to provide guidance and help; to participate in the evaluation and in-service training of teachers; and to encourage research within the schools. Their job description also includes co-operation with school staff in the planning of school work, and the implementation of the educational policy of the Ministry of Education.

It is likely that probationer evaluation will include comment on such matters as: preparation and presentation of lessons; classroom rapport and relationships; knowledge of school rules and school law; professionalism; and general comment on character and attitude.

Professional Development and Career prospects for Teachers

Over the 1980's a number of developments have extended the opportunities for the professional development of teachers. In particular, in 1989, several inservice training centres were established, with plans for courses to begin - in the centres - from 1990-91. These would serve local teaching populations.

Courses would include:
- initial inservice and orientation courses for beginning teachers;
- further initial inservcie training opportunities, with a focus upon pedagogy and classroom management;
- periodic inservice training, on a full time basis, for selected teachers;
- part-time inservice programmes to meet special needs.

Other than professional development through inservice work teachers may advance through the professional grades of C, B, and A level. Teachers are appointed at grade C; after two years' satisfactory work they are promoted to grade B; after six years to the grade A.

Salary scales rise from scale 16 to scale 1 with increases in salary after completing two years in the same scale. Reaching scale 1 would thus take about 30 years from the commencement of a teaching career. Typically Headteachers will be chosen from those who have grade A. In the one teacher primary school the one (sole) teacher is the headteacher also. In larger primary schools the headteacher will normally be the teacher with the higher grade. In the case of teachers with the same grade a decision will be made by the local Directorate of Education. Headteachers and Deputy Headteachers of gymnasium and lycea are chosen from the teachers with Grade A.

Such posts will attract a special responsibility allowance. It may also be noted that such appointments to schools (at the secondary level) are invariably for a period of 4 years. After this period promoted staff may be relocated for a period of one year, or return to their schools as teachers.

Conditions of Work

Primary school teachers will normally teach for 25-30 hours per week (a teaching hour typically lasting for 45 minutes). Headteachers of large primary schools (viz: six teachers or more) will teach for 20 hours per week; those in charge of 4-5 teacher primary schools will have to teach for 24 hours per week.

In the secondary schools teachers will have to teach 21 hours per week, initially. After six years of teaching this will reduce to 19 hours per week, and after 12 teaching years to 18 hours per week. Headteachers will teach in proportion to the size of the school, varying between 3-8 hours per week.

Footnote

1 The duration of such professional courses, and teaching practice is small. The time that is given to pedagogical and practical teaching elements is estimated to be between 5%-10% of the university course, and which is mainly devoted to subject specialisation.

A Greek Headmaster of a Primary School

According to the law 1566/1985, the headmasters are chosen by a special committee for a three-years period. All teachers with 10 years service can be candidates to be headmasters.

The criteria of selection are:

1. *Experience in service.*
2. *Knowledge of educational matters.*
3. *Administrative ability.*
4. *Knowledge of teaching work.*
5. *Social contribution.*
6. *Post-graduate studies.*
7. *In-service training.*
8. *Publications.*
9. *Interview.*

The headmaster is responsible for the good functioning of the school and of the school life and the observance of the laws. He cooperates with the local authorities and the school council. He is the chairman of the staff committee and of the school council. He is also a member of the school committee.

Since the situations are not so good the headmaster has to face a lot of difficulties and has to solve a lot of problems, such as repairing, cleaning, heating, secretarial work, keeping books, issuing certificates, buying materials etc.

He teaches 20 hours per week (5 hours less than the other teachers), and in these 5 hours he has to care for all these things.

The development (i.e. salary grades) of a teacher does not depend upon the evaluation of the headmaster. For this reason the headmaster's status among the teaching staff depends only upon his personality, critical thought, fellowship, and his decisions.

There is no perspective on the development of the headmaster. He only acquires a good experience as a headmaster and this is a criterion to be re-elected as a headmaster.

His salary is not different from the salary of other teachers who have the same teaching time (years). He gets only an extra amount for his extra duties (about 13,000 drachmas).

Greek society respects the school and the school master. Communication and cooperation with parents is always good.

There is not enough time to complete his own duties. There should be a reduction of the teaching hours to 10 at least, so that he may face more easily the various problems of the school.

A Greek Headmaster of a Lyceum (Lykio)

The life of a headmaster in a Lykio in Greece differs from district to district. Generally speaking, however, the conditions are almost the same in every school. There are not enough school buildings, so the students have to attend one week in the morning and the other week in the afternoon. This provides difficulties both for the teaching staff and to the students, particularly when they have to attend school in the afternoon.

The teaching hours for the headmaster is (for my school where there are 14 classes) only 3 per week - but the hours of administrative work are many.

The time for preparation is 2-3 hours for each teaching hours for the next day.

In my career I have 20 years of teaching work. I have been a vice-headmaster for 5 years. Initial training: Degree of a University (Ptihio). In-service training: two years in the In-service Training School for Secondary School teachers (now closed). My salary 140.000 drachmas per month. [1989/90].
Publications: two works on education and one on history.

A Greek Primary School Teacher

I am a teacher in Primary Education for 24 years. All these years I have been working zeolously having a conscience that my work is holy, since the state trusted to me the most valuable: the child.

The conditions were not always ideal: I remember the day I arrived at a remote village of Messinia (a district in the south of Peloponese) as a newly appointed teacher - with my husband. It was December 1965.

My first impression was very disappointing. Poverty both material and spiritual around me. There was nothing to make life somehow human. In that village we had to live for 4 years.

The postman who came twice a week gave us the joy of communication with the rest of the world, with some pedogogical magazines or some newspapers, or the correspondence of the school.

I had no other choice than to devote myself to my work and to reading.

I was working for 30 hours per week, in the morning and in the afternoon. My school work I prepared from the previous day. I was anxious to put in practice what I had learned before in two years at the Pedagogical Academy (College of Education). There were no teaching aids nor school library. Apart from any school work I felt my duty to do something for the parents, e.g. celebrations, speeches, etc.

My first salary was 2.500 drachmas.

Inspite of the problems I was an optimist. Some difficulties were, when I had to combine the role of the teacher with the role of the mother. In these duties my husband helped me. He is an able teacher and a man of understanding. Maternity not only did not prevent me from my work, but on the contrary it helped me to understand and love more the child.

Then I was moved to West Germany. There we faced a new situation. I've adjust easily and we benefited professionaly. There we finished a two-year course.

Today the situations have changed very much to the better. But the abundance, the super-consuming and the mass-media have created other problems.

But again as teachers devoted permanently to the values of our Faith and Tradition we are struggling with love and patience our efforts for advancing the cultural level and quality of life of our pupils and of our nation generally.

A Greek Secondary School Teacher

The secondary school teacher has to teach 18-21 hours per week, if he/she is newly-appointed. After 10 years he/she gets the grade A (starting from the C and B grade) and the teaching hours are reduced to 18. He/she teaches 18 hours until he/she gets away for his/her profession. He/she can leave the service after 15 years, if she is a woman, and after 25 years if he is a man.

The conditions of work in the secondary schools (gymnasia and lykio) are below moderate and in many cases very bad. Most of the schools in the cities share the same building (one in the morning and one in the afternoon). This results in a lot of damage in furniture and it is not possible to find the culpable person. Another disadvantage may be the large number of the students (e.g. 585 students in the school year 1989-90 in the 2nd Gymnasium of Ag. Paraskeri are divided into 18 classes with 32-35 students in each class).

The number of teachers is enough for schools in the cities, but not in remote districts where secondary school teachers are not willing to be appointed, because their salary is about 70.000 drachmas and the living conditions are not good.

The time for preparation for every day teaching depends on the subjects and on the teacher's conscientiousness. Two hours each day is enough, not including in this time the time needed for correction of essays, tests, etc. which may need another two hours. The teacher, apart from the teaching in the school, has also to work at home, in order to fulfil his duties.

The professional development of the teacher seems, today at least, to have not any perspective of advancement. There is no evaluation, and not any recognition. The self-respected teachers work, without expecting any recognition for their work. They feel satisfaction, because they believe in what made them choose the teaching profession. Sometimes they feel disappointment when they see that their work is not recognised by the new teachers. So the teachers of 30 year's service have almost the same duties as a new - comer to the teaching profession.

From 32 teachers of my school 2 have a second degree and 2 have got a one-year course of in-service training. Teachers generally want to have opportunities for in-service training, but this is not enough. You need to have chance, since the selection for going to an in-service training school depends upon lottery. There is no any other kind of in-service training.

The administration of the school is done by the headmaster and vice-headmaster. They have a reduced number of teaching hours, but they have to be at the school all the time.

Those teachers who have completed 10 years of service may apply to be in the list of headmasters and vice-headmasters.

In the school, according the law, must be secretary and building-keeper. In many schools there is not such personnel, so teachers have to do their duties.

School advisers who gradually replaced the School Inspectors are underestimated. Each school adviser has in his jurisdiction about 90 schools, so he has not enough time to visit them at least once a year. Their visits to the schools are only for suggestions about the teaching content and nothing more. Recently some seminars are organised by the school advisers mostly for the newly-appointed teachers. After their lecture a discussion is followed. Participation in the seminars, is not compulsory.

The teaching content is defined by the Ministry of National Education and Religions and the teachers have to plan their teaching content until the end of the school year so that they complete the content that is defined to be taught in each subject.

The level of the students sometimes is disappointing both in their achievement and their behaviour.

The teaching profession has become today very tiring. This is a general feeling of almost all my colleagues. Most of them feel disappointment; tired and they expect anxiously to complete some years of service and then to retire.

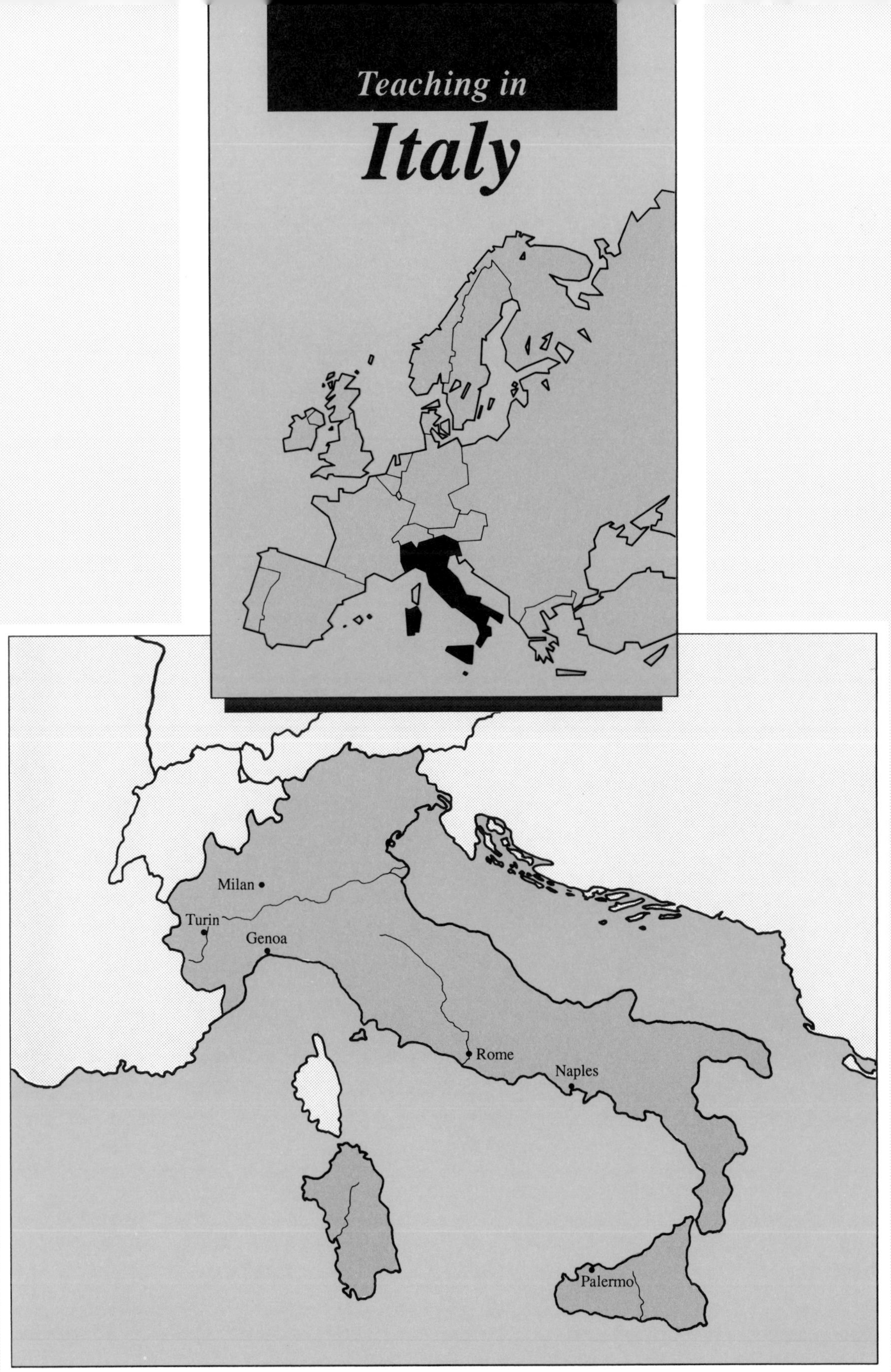
Teaching in
Italy
Milan
Turin
Genoa
Rome
Naples
Palermo

TEACHING IN ITALY

Italy reaches south towards Africa, with coastlines washed by the Adriatic, Ionian, Mediterranean, Tyrrhenian and Ligurian seas. In the north its frontiers are with Yugoslavia, Austria, Switzerland and France. Thus, regular contact with people of varied origins is facilitated by geography.

Geography also determines the contrasts between north and south. The prosperous north with its wealthy industrial cities, notably Milan and 'Fiat City', Turin, has clear economic advantages. Most of the population of some 58 million reside there. In contrast, the peripheral south, the Mezzogiorno, is largely mountainous, often enjoying a harsh climate. Major problems remain there although deliberate programmes of investment since the 1960s have resulted in many improvements. The growth of tourism in the south has also been an important economic factor.

Following a referendum, Italy severed its links with monarchy in 1946, after World War II. The country became a 'democratic republic founded on work'. Laws passed by Parliament apply to all schools, public or private.

The main principles upon which the Italian education system is based are laid down in Articles 3, 33, and 34 of the Constitution. Article 3 states that: "The Republic shall promote the development of culture and of scientific and technical research". Article 33, that: "Arts and science are free, and the teaching thereof shall be free. The Republic lays down general principles and creates schools of all types and of all levels". Article 34, that "State schools shall be open to all. Education shall be compulsory and free of charge for at least eight years".

It is against this background that The Ministry of Education is responsible for the government and administration of the educational system, and all schools (whether they be state or private) must conform to laws, and regulations relating to such matters as curricula, examinations, subject syllabi and so on.

The central administration has its local branches in each province of Italy, where the provincial office, the "*Provveditorato*", is headed by a school superintendent called "*Provveditore agli studi*".[1] This superintendent is responsible for primary and secondary education, the enforcement of laws and regulations related to such education (whether public or private) and the implementation locally of regulations related to teacher recruitment and appointment. In recent years the powers and functions of the "*Provveditore*" have become significantly more important alongside Ministry decisions to implement a policy of greater administrative decentralisation.

The School System

In Italy compulsory schooling is from 6-14 years, with about 60% of the school population continuing beyond age 14 into post compulsory education. Prior to age 6 years non-compulsory schooling is available in the *scuola materna* (nursery school) which is largely run by private groups, or the Catholic church.

Primary education (in elementary schools or *Scuole elementari*) begins at age 6 and includes a wide range of subject study.[2] At this level teaching is usually from 8.30 am - 12.30 pm, including Saturdays, with a teaching contact time of 24 hours per week.

Private education is also available at this level, with more opportunities for private education in the large cities.[3]

On leaving primary school pupils will enter the *scuola media*, or intermediate school, which caters for children from 11 to 14 years. Since 1962 this has been a unified intermediate school for all pupils, and with a centrally prescribed curriculum involving pupils for 30 hours each week, over a period of 3 years. The latest regulations, covering the teaching and curriculum of the *scuola media* were published in 1979, and relate to the content of a wide range of subjects. All pupils will follow courses in: Religion; Italian; Civic and Geographic Education; History; Foreign Languages; Scientific Knowledge and Technical, Artistic, Musical and Physical Education.

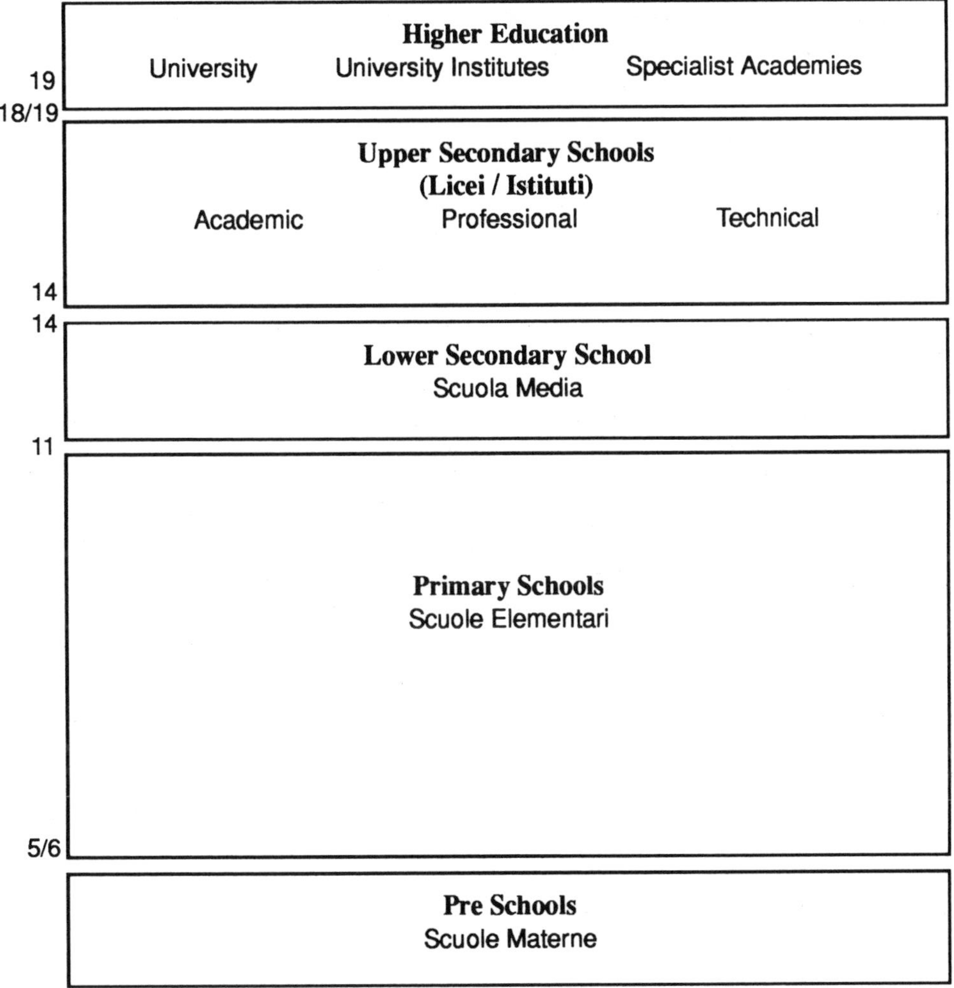

At the end of the three years of study intermediate school pupils are required to take the examination for the intermediate school diploma, an examination normally administered by the school's teachers in conjunction with an external moderator. The possession of this diploma is essential for those wishing to continue their studies.

Higher secondary schooling, which is not free of charge, is available in a range of institutions to pupils mainly between the ages of 14-19 years. It includes classical grammar, and scientific grammar schools (*licei*); teacher training institutes for primary school teachers, and technical and vocational institutes for such sectors as agriculture, commerce, industry, transportation, hotel and catering and tourism.

Each five year course will normally be provided in two cycles, the first lasting for two years. For all students wishing to enter university studies it will be necessary to complete the five year period of study.

Some examples of curricular provision at this level will illustrate the diversity and range of possibilities open to students continuing their education.

i) *Liceo classico:*
Students normally attend the *liceo* from 8.30 a.m. onwards, with the following schedule.

1st period	8.30 - 9.25
2nd	9.25 - 10.20
3rd	10.20 - 11.15
Break	11.15 - 11.30
4th	11.30 - 12.25
....	
5th	12.25 - 1.20 (on certain days)

The course includes: Ancient Greek and Ancient Latin (every year); history of Philosophy; History of Art; History; Mathematics; Italian Literature; Physical Education (all over the last three years); Religion (optional) or History of Religion; Chemistry and Physics (each for one year). In addition, and dependent upon the teacher's demands, up to five hours homework per day could be set.

ii) State professional school for training nursery nurses. (e.g. *Istituto Professionale di Stato "Piero Gobetti"*. Rome)

Typical hours would be:

1st period	8.10 - 9.10
2nd	9.10 - 10.00
3rd	10.00 - 10.50
break	10.50 - 11.00
4th	11.00 - 11.50
5th	11.50 - 12.40
6th	12.40 - 13.30
7th	13.30 - 14.20

Students attending such an institute would normally study a range of 13 subjects, over three years, together with training and practice in nursery schools. For those seeking university entrance it would be necessary to complete the full 5 year course, with further study in psychology, and professional practice. All students would take Italian, History, Psychology, English, Religious Studies, Hygiene, Natural Sciences, Music, Drawing and Painting. Economic development within the local community, as well as nursery school practice and policy, would also be studied.

iii) State professional school for tourist guides/tour operators. (*Istituto Professionale di Stato: Accompagnatori ed operatori turistici*). In this professional institute three years of training leads to a qualifying certificate as a tourist guide. Most students will continue for the full five years to be able to qualify as tour/travel agents.

Over a three year programme students would follow a course including: Italian, Civic Education, English, French, Spanish, History of Art, Hygiene, "Tourist geography", Mathematics, Organisation of Commerce and Industry, Accounts and Accounting; ticketing/vouchers/itineraries; tourist technique; Physical Education; Religious Studies. In each year of study, languages (Italian 4 periods; English 6; French 5; Spanish 3) are compulsory, along with "Techniques of tourism" (6 periods per week).

At the end of their studies in the vocational institutions students will be awarded a qualifying certificate. For those completing studies in the *liceo* there will be a *maturita* examination. Satisfactory performance can be seen as acceptable for continuing study within a university, and to follow a course leading to a degree (*laurea di dottore*).

Teacher Training

As in many continental countries there is a distinction between those teachers possessing a diploma, and entering primary or pre-school work, and those who are university graduates and who wish to enter teaching in the secondary school. In Italy it is policy that intending teachers should compete, in open examination, for vacant teaching posts. It is also the case that teachers are classified in terms of their status, possession of a degree, and in relation to the list upon which their name is placed.

For entry into the nursery school teachers must first possess the diploma awarded by the nursery teachers' training institute, and must then compete in an examination arranged in relation to the jobs available within the province. Primary school teachers will have undertaken a course at an '*istituto magistrale*' for 4 years, and work towards a state examination, and the primary teacher's certificate awarded at the end of these years. As with other teachers, they will be required to sit a competitive examination, organised on a provincial basis.

To enter teaching in the *scuola media*, or in one of the *licei* a teacher must possess a degree, minimally, and pursue a route which may be summarised as follows:

i) Teacher with a university degree: *non abilitate*

ii) Teacher with a degree who has passed the *abilitazione* examination: *abilitate*

This examination is usually prepared for by part-time study. In essence this is a minimal professional preparation with emphasis upon subject competence, together with some focus on teaching methodology and professional studies.

iii) Teachers on a temporary contract; available at short notice; and 'on supply' to cover absences: *precari*

Precari will be placed on lists according to possession of the *abilitazione*. Those without this qualification will be placed on a separate list.

The position or status of a teacher within the lists will relate to such matters as the level of the examination pass in the degree examination, any temporary teaching already undertaken, and other contributions made to school life.

iv) Permanent teacher status, *di ruolo,* accorded to a teacher who has been successful in the *Concorso.*

To obtain a permanent post it is necessary to be successful in the *Concorso,* being an examination arranged by the Ministry of Education and the provincial *Provveditore.* The examination will closely relate to teaching posts available within the province, and be highly competitive. Written tests and an oral examination are included. The status of '*di ruolo*' gives the teacher a placing on the 'permanent list'.

v) Teacher status as - *ruolo straordinario or ruolo ordinario*:

Once successful in the *Concorso* examination a teacher will enter a one year probation period and become a teacher *ruolo straordinario.* A successful probation period (see below) will allow the teacher to become *ruolo ordinario.* An unsuccessful probation period can be repeated for one year only.

Employment and Probation

It will be seen that the matter of permanent employment in Italy is closely related to success in the *Concorso* examination which, in itself, is a means of selection of those applicants seeking jobs that become available within a particular province. Placing within the list of successful candidates can give the teacher a greater or lesser choice from the jobs available.

Teachers' employment conditions are carefully defined. For example, in the secondary schools, teachers must teach 18 hours per week in class. Some subjects are only taught for 15 or 16 hours, which allows the teacher concerned to be available for cover of classes when another member of staff is ill, or absent on a course. Contracts also include time spent with parental meetings, staff meetings and other professional matters. In September, when staff return to their schools, it is expected that they will prepare and present to the headteacher a plan of lessons and activities (*programmazione annuale*) to be undertaken in the school year.

Within the first year of teaching it is necessary that the school headteacher (*Preside*) will watch the new teacher, often informally, and report on professional and other competencies to the provincial office. A number of key issues included in the '*VALUTAZIONE DEL SERVIZIO IN PROVA*' are

Qualità intellettuali
Preparazione culturale e professionale con riferimento a pubblicazione,
diligenza, comportamento nella scuola;
efficacia dell'azione educativa e didattica;

eventuali sanzioni disciplinari;
attività di aggiornamento;
partecipazione ad attività di sperimentazione;
collaborazione con altri docenti;
rapporti con le famiglie degli alunni;
attività speciali nell'ambito scolastico;
ogni altro elemento che valga a delineare attitudini e caratteristiche
in relazione all a funzione docente

Viz:

intellectual qualities;
cultural and professional preparation;
diligence, behaviour within the school;
relationships with headteacher, staff and others;
educational and didactic efficiency;
attendance at courses;
involvement in experimental activities;
special involvement or aptitudes.

A further check on probationer progress is given by members of the school committee (i.e. elected teachers) who will consult the headteacher and present their views. If probation is successful the result will be conveyed to the *Proveddìtore,* and the teacher becomes '*ruolo ordinario*'.[4]

Career development and inservice training

According to the size of the school it is possible that the headteacher will have the help of teachers who are elected by their colleagues, and who can be different persons from year to year. Such a task is unpaid, additional to the minimum teaching load, but considered to be valuable as a preparation for promotion. If the school is large (typically more than 600 pupils) it is possible for a deputy headteacher to be elected, with 50% non teaching time. If the school has more than 900 pupils a non teaching deputy will be fully available for administrative and other purposes.

Such experiences will both provide useful knowledge and also acquire points in terms of experience. Nonetheless, in order to become a headteacher (*Preside*) it is necessary to compete again - in a Headteachers' *Concorso* - and to prepare for this examination in private study and possibly through correspondence work. The opportunity to take the *Concorso* will be available only to those who have been "*di ruolo*" for at least 5 years.

A written and oral examination will test the candidate's knowledge of such matters as: history of education; school laws; psychology; school curriculum appropriate to the level of the school concerned; new teaching strategies; research findings pertinent to the school; and so on.

Other possibilities for promotion might lie in the Inspectorate, whether at national level, under the direction of the Ministry (*ispettori tecnici centrali*) or under provincial direction (*ispettori tecnici periferici*). Both groups work to promote, co-ordinate and control school activities, and teachers' professional development. To become a provincial inspector it is necessary to compete in a further *concorso* (including three written examinations of 6 hours each, and an oral examination). After a minimum of three years permanent service as a provincial inspector one can compete in a further *Concorso* to become a national inspector.

School *Presidi* are expected, as part of their role, to present their school plan and teacher requirements to the *Provveditore*. Similarly opportunities will be available to discuss matters of inservice and priorities for courses to support new developments, or equipment introduced into the schools. Short courses are available, from 3-8 days in total, and school *presidi* are asked to nominate teachers for these. Much of September is generally devoted to preparing for the school year, and becoming involved in inservice developments.

Footnotes

1 *In Italy there are 20 administrative regions, sub divided into Provinces. In 1989 there were 96 provinces in all, with the possibility that subdivisions could create more. The province of Lazio, which includes the area around Rome, is divided into 5 provinces, each with its own Provveditore.*

2 *The subjects studied include: religion; moral and civic education; physical education; history; geography; science; arithmetic; Italian; drawing and design; singing and handiwork.*

3 *Under the law defining the rights and obligations of private schools pupils must be guaranteed treatment equivalent to that of pupils in the state schools. Institutions and individuals have the right to open schools, provided that they are not a charge upon the state. As a result it is possible to find such schools run by religious bodies (generally Catholic), and by private individuals. Every private school must follow the state guidelines in terms of curriculum, and teaching, and obtain permission from the Ministry of Education to become established. A small number of private schools are known for their progressive and 'free' methods of teaching, and ethos.*

4. *Where there are difficulties a provincial school inspector will be called to the school to give advice. Unless there are serious judicial procedings taken against a teacher, or lengthy absences in attendance at work, it is difficult to enforce a teacher 'in ruolo' to leave the profession.*

Teacher in a Lower Secondary School

Maria è un'insegnante di Ruòlo di Materie Letterarie (Italiano, Storia e Geografia) nella scuola media statale.

L'orario di servizio è costituito da h.18 di insegnamento settimanali, h.80 annuali per la partecipazione ai consigli di classe collegio dei docenti e riunioni con le famiglie.

Altre ore pomeridiane sono prestate secondo il piano formula-to dal Collegio dei Docenti per partecipare alle commissioni per la didattica alle attivitá integrative ecc..

L'insegnante di Lettere svolge l'insegnamento per N.18 ore setti manali in due classi e precisamente ad anni alterni
o
Italiano Storia e Geografia nella Terza classe h.11 settimanali

+ Italiano nella 1 classe h.7 settimanali
oppure
Italiano Storia e Geografia nella 2 classe h.11
+ Storia e Geografia nella 1 classe h.4
h.3 (a disposizione per supplenze o altre attività)

I suoi studi
Dopo aver frequentato il Liceo Classico (5 anni dopo il la scuola media) entrò all'università a 19 anni e conseguì la Laurea in Lettere (4 anni).

Appena uscita dall'Università, si preparò per l'esame di abilitazione all'insegnamento (vedi fogli allegati).

In possesso dell'abilitazione lavorò come supplente temporanea e Supplente Annuale a Roma nella Provincia per 4 anni.

Poi partecipò al concorso per entrare nel ruolo ordinario.

Il concorso fu abbastanza difficile da superare sia per il numero dei concorrenti sia per il programma che è molto vasto. (vedi programmi ministeriali allegati).

Vinto il concorso fu nominata insegnate di Ruolo straordinario, cioè in prova, per un anno (il periodo di prova era di due anni prima del 1974) la sede di titolarità fu una scuola alla periferia di Roma.

Nel periodo di prova il Preside visitò più volte le classi a lei assegnate per controllare lo svolgimento del programma e alla fine dell'anno (almeno 180 giorni) preparò una relazione per il comitato di valutazione (formato da insegnanti della stessa scuola eletti dal Collegio dei Docenti all'inizio di ogni anno scolastico) con i seguenti elementi (Vedi foglio allegato).

Il comitato espresse parere favorevole edal Provveditore agli Studi fu nominata insegante di Ruolo Ordinario.

Dopo qualche anno ottenne il trasferimento in una scuola più vicina alla sua abitazione e ha continuato regolarmente la sua carriera che per quanto riguarda i miglioramenti di stipendio è basata soltanto sull'anzianità di servizio e non su ulteriori titoli didattici conseguiti dopo l'entrata in ruolo.

Naturalmente da parte del Ministero della Pubbilica Istruzione, del Provveditorato agli Studi, dell'Università e di altre agenzie educative vengono proposti annualmente, con frequenza volontaria corsi di aggiornamento su temi vari (informatica, ambiente, salute, orientamento; lingue straniere, didattica delle discipline ecc.) ai quali si può partecipare anche durante l'orario scolastico per cinque giorni all'anno ma generalmente sono corsi pomeridiani.

Le condizioni di lavoro sono discrete specialmente nelle scuole con una buona popolazione scolastica, una buona organizzazione e notevole dotazione di sussidi e libri.

Anche lo stipendio, sempre inferiore alle retribuzioni medie italiane ha avuto con l'ultimo contratto un notevole aumento di circa il 35% sullo stipendio lordo.
Esempio:
Insegnante con 30 anni di anzianità percepisce L.32.000.000 lordi e circa 26.000.000 netti.

Mary is a permanent teacher in the secondary state school. She teaches Letters (that is Italian, History and Geography). The contract time for all teachers of any subject is:
18 hours per week to teach in the classes;
80 hours per school year for Class Councils, involvement in the work of the teachers' Council, and for meetings with parents.

Teachers also participate in the Commissions planned by the Teachers' Council for the various activities of the school.

The teacher of Letters teaches for 18 hours, in two classes, alternating every two years; thus:

Italian, History and Geography in the 3rd class	*11 hours*
+ Italian in the 1st class	*7 hours*
or	
Italian History and Geography in the 2nd class	*11 hours*
+ History and Geography in the 1st class	*4 hours*
+ to replace absent teachers	*3 hours*

After attending Liceo Classico, at the age of 19, she entered the University and 4 years later she took a degree in "Letters". Soon after she prepared and passed her abilitation exam and was able to teach as a temporary and annual employed teacher.

To become permanent, she participated in the ***concorso****; that was very difficult both for the number of candidates and the vast programme.*

After winning the concorso, she was appointed teacher on probation for a year. During the probation period (at least 180 days of teaching), the headmaster visited her classes to control her work. At the end of the period, the headmaster prepared a report to present to the Valuation Committee of the school (consisting of the Headmaster and four teachers elected by the Teachers' Council every school year).

After the favourable opinion of the Committee, she was appointed by the Provveditore as a permanent teacher in the list of state teachers. Her first school was in the outskirts of Rome, but a few years later, she was transferred to a school near her house.

Her career proceeds regularly because there are only salary advancements for seniority, and not for qualifications. Only in the last contract there is a little sum for those who attend refresher courses.

She often attends refresher courses that are proposed by the Ministry of Education, The Provveditorato, or the University. Much inservice is also voluntary and generally the courses are in the afternoon after the school time.

Work conditions are fair especially in schools with good school population and organisation. The salary too has increased a lot after the last contract (35% of the gross salary).

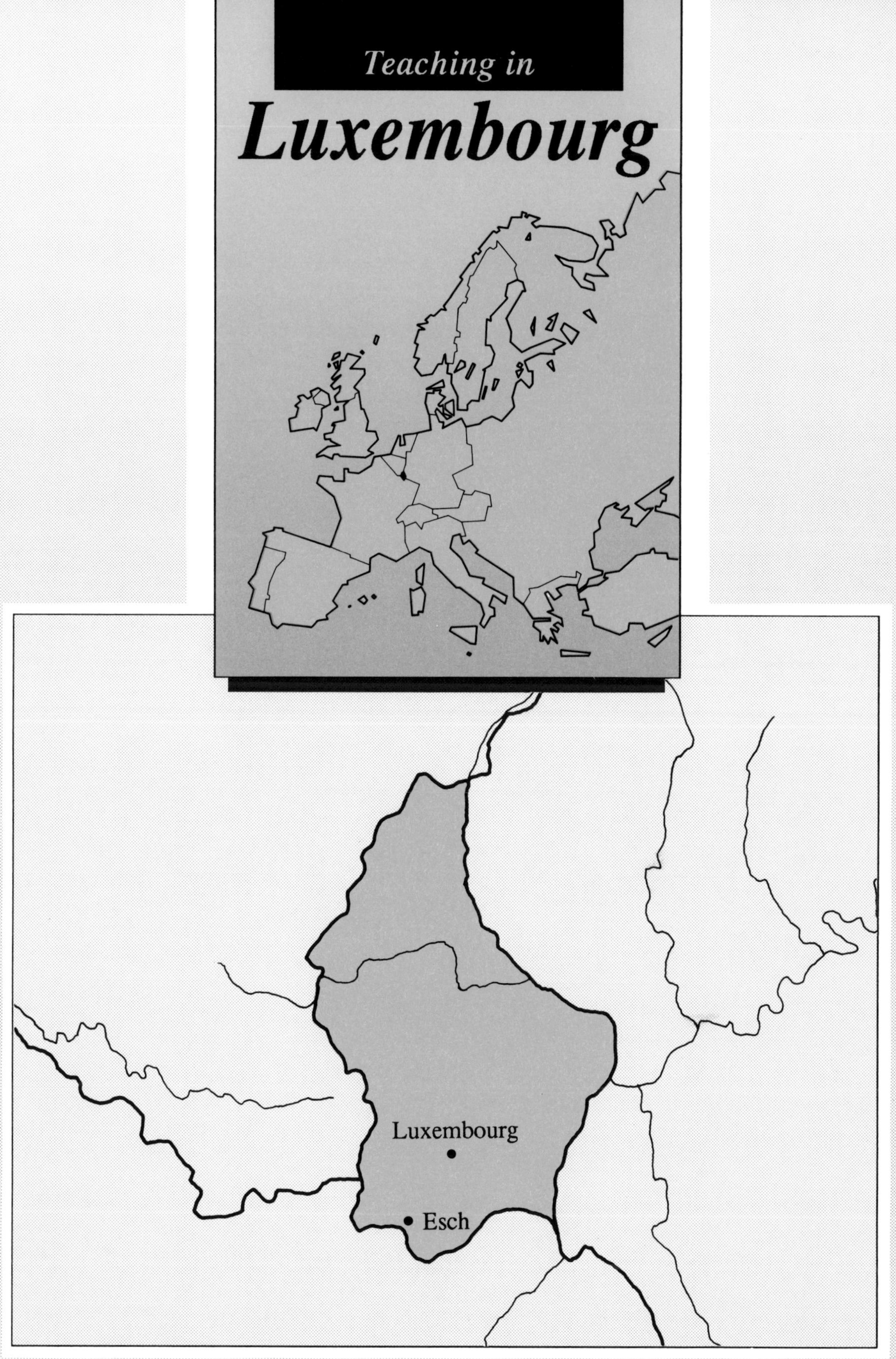
Teaching in
Luxembourg
Luxembourg
Esch

TEACHING IN LUXEMBOURG

The Grand Duchy of Luxembourg (999 sqm. 380,000 inhabitants) is a constitutional monarchy bounded by West Germany, Belgium and France. The people, chiefly Roman Catholic, speak Luxembourgish (*Lëtzebuergesch*), German and French. For entry into higher education it is also necessary to have a working knowledge of English. Even for higher vocational training a certain knowledge of English is required.

Formerly including territories now French, German and Belgian (Luxembourg province of Belgium) the country was a county, then a duchy of the Holy Roman Empire of Germanic Nation, a Habsburg (Austrian and Spanish), and a French possession. In 1815 it became a Grand Duchy as a personal possession of the King of the Netherlands. After the secession of the Luxembourg province to Belgium (nearly twice the remaining area) its present territory (only about 1/5th of that before the partition with France in 1659) was firmly established in 1839. It became really independent in 1890 with Adolph of Nassau as Grand Duc.

The city of Luxembourg was the location for the first institutions of the European Community of Coal and Steel and is now the location for the *Secretariat* of the European Parliament, the European Investment Bank, the Statistical Office and the Office for Official Publications of the European Communities and a number of institutions and offices involved with the European Parliament and the European Commission.

Schooling

Within the Grand Duchy of Luxembourg the basic law on primary education dates from 1912 and the more recent law of 1963 provides for 9 years of compulsory schooling.

The Ministry of Education is responsible for pre-school, primary, post-primary and higher education, and all sectors of education are therefore governed by regulations and directives drawn up and executed by the one National Ministry of Education. The Education Minister may consult the Higher Education Committee[1] for advice on the management and planning of the whole education system.

The direct management of educational institutions is shared between the State, the local councils and some private interests (such as the Catholic Church and the ARBED - Technical School). At primary level the role of the local council is particularly important. In each municipality an education committee gives advice on the functioning of the primary schools, the school buildings and a range of supplementary school activities.

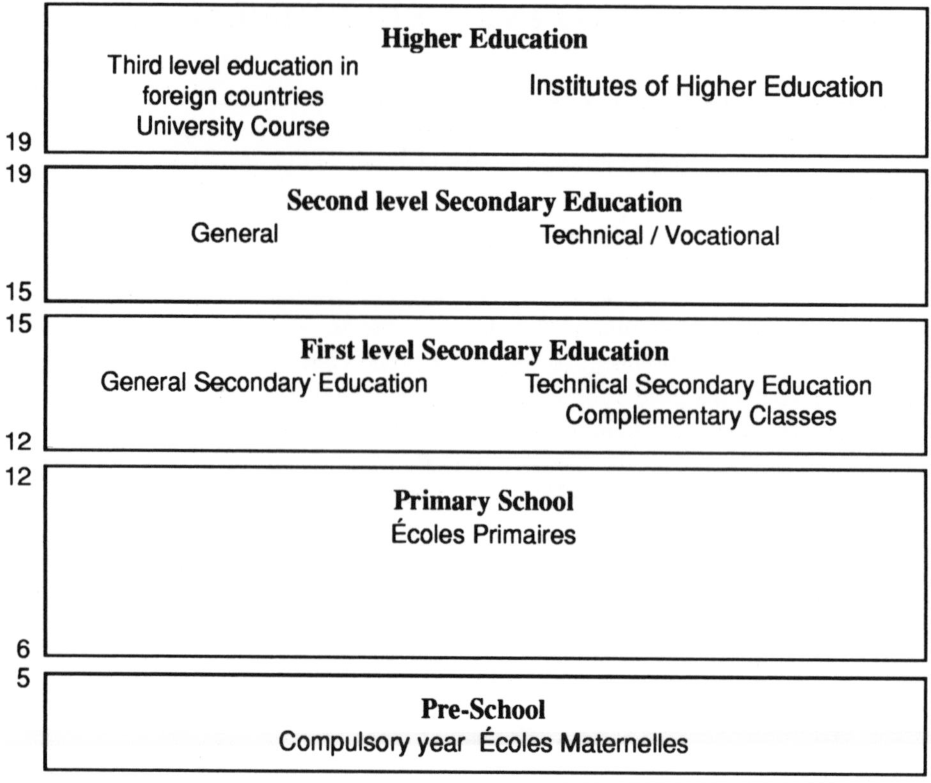

In accordance with the Grand Ducal Regulations of October 1976 pre-school education is compulsory for 5 year-olds (and optional for 4 year-olds). The Ministry of Education contributes to the financing of pre-school establishments but in administrative terms and with regard to maintenance pre-school establishments generally come under the responsibility of the local councils.

Primary education is provided for children of 6-12 years of age. Primary schools are co-educational and free. Teaching in primary schools starts in *Luxembourgish*, which children speak at home, as well as in German which becomes the teaching language for almost all subjects of the primary school. French is also taught from the second term of the second school year.

Other subjects taught include: Religious Instruction, non-religious Moral Instruction, Arithmetic, Literacy, National History, Social Subjects, Music, Art & Craft and Physical Education. Because of the use of three languages, both teaching methods and procedures may be said to be unique, with development in the knowledge about these languages (as well as their use) taking place almost simultaneously.

Teaching is spread over the whole week, with six morning classes (Monday to Saturday), and three afternoon sessions (on Mondays, Wednesdays and Fridays).

Pupils who have completed six years of primary schooling, but who do not want to (or cannot) transfer to some kind of secondary school may remain in the so called complementary classes. Such pupils, aged 12-15 years, continue to be taught General Subjects, but they also have lessons in practically-oriented subjects to help them prepare for working life or possibly to enter technical secondary education.

In order to be admitted to the first year of secondary education pupils must pass an entrance examination comprising written tests in French and German, together with tests in Arithmetic. Two main categories of post primary education are available, viz: General Secondary Education, and Technical Secondary Education.

EDUCATION IN THE
GRAND-DUCHY OF LUXEMBOURG

1987

UNITE NATIONALE D'EURYDICE
MINISTERE DE L'EDUCATION NATIONALE
ET DE LA JEUNESSE
6, bd. Royal
2910 Luxembourg

General Secondary Education begins at the age of 12 years and will last for 7 years. It is divided into two stages, a lower stage lasting three years and an upper stage lasting four years. Provision for general secondary education is in the Lycée. It comprises:

- *la classe d'orientation* (class 7) with a common curriculum for all;
- *la classe de sixième* (class 6) when pupils have chosen between:
  a) Modern Language education (which begins the study of English);
  b) Classical Education (pupils start the study of Latin).
- *la classe de cinquième* (class 5)
  a) continues the same programme;
  b) adds the study of English to the study of Latin.

Considerable changes are being planned. Until 1989-90, and after the third class, pupils could choose one of 6 groups of subjects which were available in upper secondary education.[2] From session 1990-1991 the lower stage will last for 5 years and the upper stage for two years. After the third year there will only be a choice between:

a) general stream-line
b) a scientific stream-line with a stress on mathematics. Both groups will have some optional pre-orientation courses.

The real specialisation will take place only after the fifth year with a choice of seven different specialisations.

After the final year of secondary education pupils must pass a national school leaving examination[3] which is necessary for further study at university, for entry into the civil service and for different other employment.

Technical Secondary Schooling is provided in Technical *Lycées*. It comprises three stages:

- a stage of observation and orientation lasting for three years (thus completes compulsory education);
- an intermediate stage of two years, comprising a full-time technical course, and part-time course leading to an apprenticeship;
- for most successful pupils a higher stage of two years, providing in-depth vocational training and providing a qualification for entry into specialized university studies.

There will also be important changes in this provision, but the overall organisation of Technical Secondary Schools will remain unchanged; the curriculum will be redefined and the streamlining in the first three years will be re-organised.

Teacher Training and Probation

Teacher training is available for those wishing to teach in the pre-schools/primary schools and for those seeking a position in the secondary *lycées*.

To enter training for teaching in the pre-school or primary school it is first necessary to possess the secondary school-leaving certificate and to offer proof of competence in Luxembourgish, German, French and English.

The Teacher Training College (*Institut Superieur d'Études et de Recherches Pédagogiques* - I.S.E.R.P.) located in Luxembourg-Walferdange, provides a three year academic and pedagogical course.[4] Each year the Ministry of National Education will determine the number of candidates to be admitted, according to estimates of jobs available within the Grand Duchy. The level of pass obtained in the school-leaving examination is the decisive factor in the selection of candidates.

Courses at the Institute are run in collaboration with the Luxembourg University Centre, and include both pedagogical and methods study, as well as literary, and scientific studies. The first will focus upon either pre-school or primary education, and comprises common or core courses, pedagogical studies, practical experience and observation in schools. More specific courses in pedagogy and child development/psychology are provided in the second and third years, together with aspects of teaching methodology. The organisation of the courses is in relation to stages of the primary school.

The final examination leads to a *Certificat d'études pédagogiques* (with a pre-school or primary option). Possession of this certificate is necessary in order to be nominated to a post as teacher at pre-school or primary level. Teachers are appointed by the local councils on the recommendation of a school inspector and with the general approval of the government. Where there are several candidates for a post, the inspector will limit the choice to the three most meritorious candidates.

Nominations for teaching positions could be reviewed. They are considered as permanent after a period of two years satisfactory teaching - within the local council concerned.

To enter teacher training for secondary schools minimum requirements include competence in Luxembourgish, German, French and English as well as the possession of the secondary school leaving certificate. At least 4 years academic training is then taken at a university. This training must be concluded by the candidate's taking a degree in his special subject.

Since 1980 teachers of Foreign Languages, Humanities and Science have to spend their first year at the Luxembourg University Centre and then three years in a foreign university. The University Centre was set up by the law of 18 June 1969. Teachers of Economics, Art, Music and Physical Education will spend all 4 years at a foreign university. Titles and degrees of these universities must be recognised and registered by the Ministry of Education.

Regulations concerning the preparation of secondary level and specialist teachers, the rights and conditions pertaining to the *Stagiaire,* and other matters, are embodied in laws (e.g. 18 June 1969; 24 July 1973).

According to the law, for each position and special subject the Minister for National Education will determine annually the number of candidates to be recruited into teaching. It is expected that candidates for teaching in the Grand Duchy will have a working knowledge of the 4 languages used (*Luxembourgish,* German, French and English). If there are more candidates than required it will also be necessary to undergo a competitive selection process.

Courses provided are in accordance with Grand Ducal Regulations, which lay down the syllabus and examination requirements for the secondary general training course, and which also determine the conditions related to the appointment of teachers of specialist subjects. Key elements of the training will include:
Adolescent Psychology, Educational Sociology, School Structures and Legislation on Secondary Education, General Methodology and Subject Methodology. Syllabuses are worked out in detail by the Ministry of Education with the advice of the educational training department.

The student teacher will be appointed as a '*stagiaire*' for a period of three years, and will be expected to act both as a '*surveillant*' in a school, and to teach a minimum of 6 lessons each week. Such general supervision work, and teaching will be remunerated and may vary according to the number of teaching periods.[5]

During the first year as a *stagiaire,* the student teacher will also attend university classes in the key elements of training (see above), and pass an examination in these. In the second phase of the *stage* it will be necessary to complete two dissertations - one of which will be related to the teacher's special subject, and the other related to a practical pedagogical topic.

Responsibility for the supervision of the school experience and apprenticeship lies essentially with the headmaster (*directeur*) who is assisted by two pedagogic counsellors: one for the language and one for the scientific matters. These counsellors are nominated by the government on the advice of the Headmaster. A certain allocation of time is made available for the purpose of supervising and advising the student.

The pedagogic counsellor will arrange for other teachers to help prepare and supervise lessons given by the *stagiaire* in particular subjects. Comments and reports on progress will be co-ordinated by the counsellor and reported to the headmaster.

At the beginning of the third year the candidate has to complete and successfully submit his two dissertations to a special examination board of three members. At the end of the third year another examination board will be appointed to examine the student teacher's competence and performance. Five persons, including a representative of the Government, will observe two lessons taught by the candidate - one in the lower section of the school (12-15 years), and one in the higher level (15+). Once a young teacher has been nominated to a permanent post no further qualification is required. The teacher is now a civil servant with normal rights and pension privileges.

Career Development

Once a permanent appointment has been obtained a teacher will be allocated to a grade (or level) of pay, which will reflect the length of training undertaken and the qualification obtained. Pay will vary according to whether a teacher is a kindergarten teacher, a primary school teacher; or a subject teacher in a secondary *Lycée*.

Typically a teacher would remain as a classroom practitioner, unless seeking to become an assistant Headmaster or a Headmaster. There is also a wide range of inservice opportunities for all teachers who may wish to attend them.

Footnotes

1 The Higher Education Committee is composed of representatives of the Ministry of Education, of religious and private schools, and of the Ministries of Industry and Commerce. There is also a wide range of representation from other interests - including teachers' organisations and parents' organisations and the Headmasters' Council.

2 viz Languages, Mathematics, Natural Sciences, Economics, Music, Artistic Education.

3 Examen de fin d'études secondaires.

4 Prior to 1983, the teacher training course lasted for 2 years. The Law of 6 September 1983 increased the course to three years in length, when the University Centre also became involved in training.

5. Regulations relating to this practical stage are contained in legislation dating from 23rd April 1981. These also refer to such matters as working conditions and remuneration.

A Luxembourg Secondary School Counsellor

En suivant l'évolution de l'enseignement pendant les dernières décennies on peut se rendre compte dans quelle mesure il suit la dégradation des valeurs, des priorités, bref de la conception général de la vie au sein de la société.

Ce qui saute le plus aux yeux c'est de paroxysme de cette espèce de révolution coppernicienne des rapports adultes-enfant. L'adulte ne doit plus, selon l'idée dominante, offrir de modèles de vie aux jeunes. Trop généralement l'enfance et la jeunesse sont considérées comme une qualité en soi, au service de laquelle l'adulte n'a plus qu'à prouver sa valeur en les comblant de biens matériels. Et de ce fait même la place des valeurs affectives se rétrécit. Ces adultes espèrent leur salut des petits qui sont censés réaliser bientôt cette société au bonheur béat dont ils ont eux-mêmes vécu la faillite. Le résultat en est que trop de jeunes se sentent abondonnés et esseulés et essayent de vaincre leurs sentiments de frustration par une recherche effrénée de faux-fuyants. D'un autre côté on doit remarquer qu'une partie de la nouvelle génération de parents fait preuve d'une attitude de plus en plus directive et égocentrique.

Le climat général démontre une espèce de déficit d'humanité, une absence de réelles valeurs spirituelles, au profit d'un matérialisme sans âme adonné à des dehors futiles. Trop souvent les jeunes sont impressionnés par les rêves éveillés de quelques égarés insoupçonnées à l'épreuve pour épanouir leur propre personnalité dans un concours constructif. L'enseignant de son côté suit souvent se laisser-aller. Dans l'impossibilité de faire accepter une objectivité et logique scientifiques, il essaye de ne pas être immergé dans cette mare des subjectivismes irrationnels et sentimentaux. On le considère généralement comme boux émissaire et n'importe qui se juge expert appelé à lui faire la leçon. Si sa situation financière est encore assez bonne par rapport à celle de bien des collègues dans la Communauté Européenne, elle est en train de se dégrader considérablement. Par ricochet la nouvelle génération s'arrange pour y trouver quand même son compte.

Les conditions extérieurs de travail s'améliorent au moins depuis quelques années, mais tant que la situation éducative n'est pas reconsidéré complètement, mêmes les infrastructures les plus valables ne pourront suffir à créer un climat pédagogique adéquat. Et les meilleures conditions de recyclage permanent ne sauront amener la société et done les jeunes àvouloir développer leurs possibilités d'une façon optimale et à rechercher le bonheur dans une conquête ardue de valeurs spirituelles et humaines.

Teaching in The Netherlands

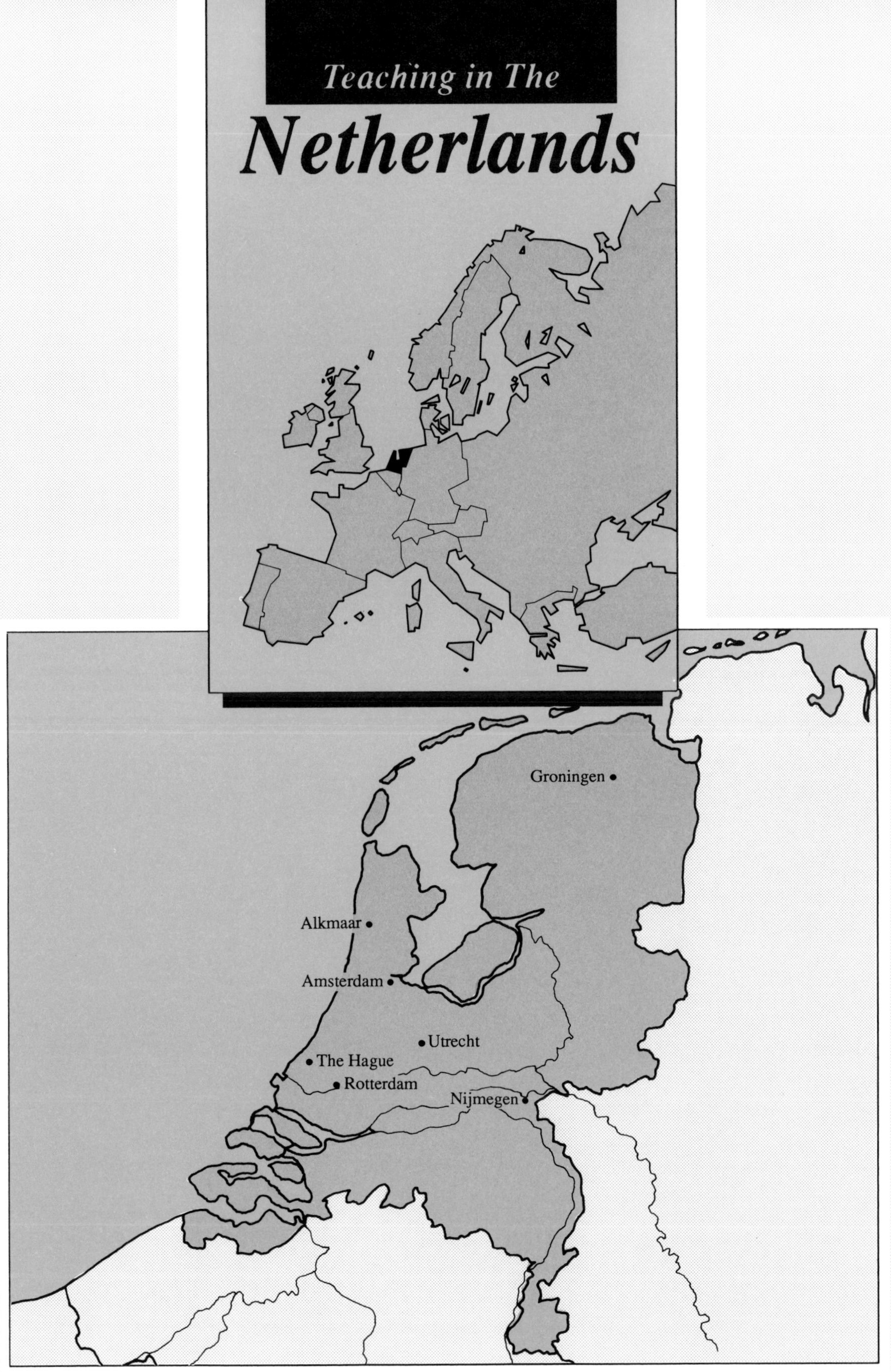

TEACHING IN THE NETHERLANDS

As the saying has it, "God made the world but the Dutch made Holland". The constant struggle with the weather and with the North Sea continues. Land reclaimed in response to population growth has to be defended as other work proceeds. Some 14 million people inhabit this northern, protestant part of the Low Countries.

As is well-known The Netherlands have prospered, through dairy farming and floriculture as well as through tourism. Industry also plays a very important part. One thinks of the multi-national Shell, of the Rhine delta and of Rotterdam - Europoort with its 8 'petroleumhavens'. The electrical giant Philips, 'the largest private employer in Europe', also comes to mind. These capital-intensive, technologically-based industries require a research base and they depend on a modern and effective education system.

Schooling

The major responsibility for education is that of The Ministry of Education and Science, headed by the Minister of Education and Science. Article 23 of the Constitution is central to the educational legislation within The Netherlands, and includes the provisions that:

- Education shall be the constant concern of the Government;
- All persons shall be free to provide education, without prejudice to the restrictions placed on this.

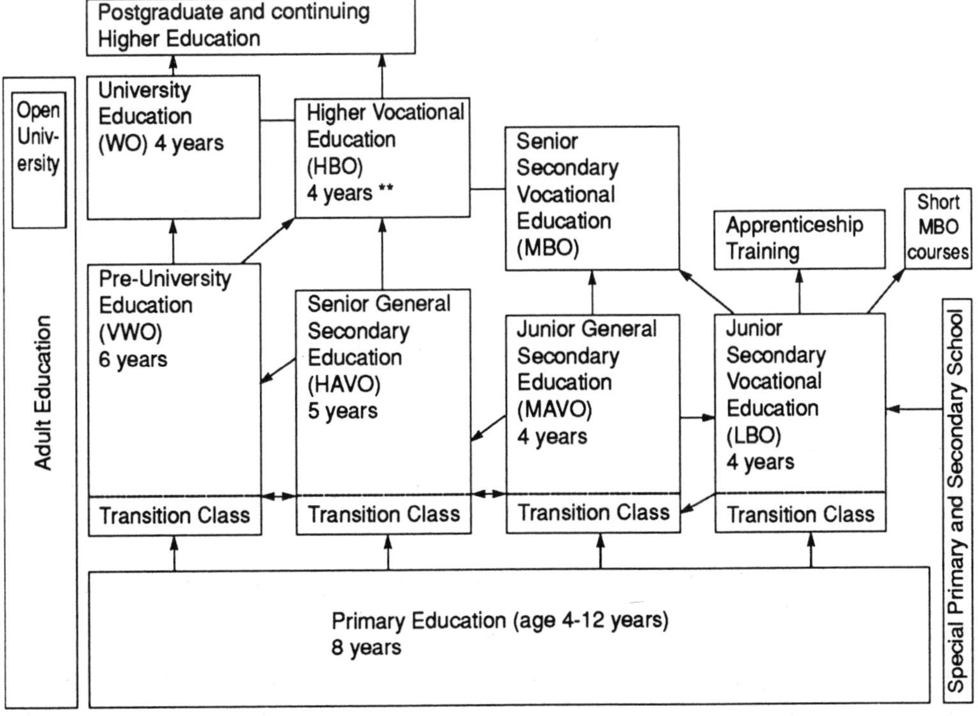

** In 1987 a large merger operation, involving some 400 Institutes of Higher Professional Education, was completed. As a result, more than 60 Institutes called Hogescholen (Polytechnics) were created. These institutes offer a wide variety of courses covering most sectors of higher professional education.

An important element, therefore, is that public-authority and private schools must be treated equally with regard to funding. Public authority institutions which are legally bound to comply with the standards and other rules laid down by law, and private schools which choose to comply with the same requirements and conditions, are financed from public funds according to the same criteria.

All Dutch children attend compulsory school for 11 years. In addition, those who - after their eleventh year at school - are no longer attending school fulltime are obliged to attend school for two days a week for a further year.

Primary (or Base) schools: since 1985 primary schools have been attended by all children aged 4-12 years of age thus providing 8 years of continuous schooling. Prior to 1985 it was quite normal for those aged 4 or more to go to an infant school voluntarily, but from 1985 attendance from the age of 4 became compulsory. The infant school became merged with the primary school, and it was required that the geographical distance between the two sectors be minimised. The high attendance of 4 year olds prior to 1985 is explained partly by a) the high density of population in a small country, and the relatively small distances to be travelled from home to school and b) the long tradition of schooling designed to serve local populations.

Within the Netherlands there are approximately 8,400 primary/base schools and some 69,000 teachers. Schools are generally small (about 140-150 pupils) and parents are closely involved. The average number of staff is 5-7, with a headteacher in charge. Approximately 35% of schools are public authority schools, 30% are Catholic schools and others are private non-denominational institutions.

Typically the base school day lasts from 8.30-11.45 am and from 13.15-15.30 p.m. Each Wednesday afternoon is free and an extra free half day for the infants.

Under various education acts the Minister of Education and Science is charged with the inspection of education, and this is carried out by the Education Inspectors, headed by the Inspector General of Education.

Within the primary school the following subjects must always appear in the curriculum, if possible in an integrated form:

Physical Education, Dutch; Arithmetic and Mathematics; English; Social Subjects; Science; Social Structures and Sivics; Religious Education; Art & Crafts; and Music. Schools in the province of Friesland must also teach Frisian, unless exemption has been given.

Secondary education follows on from primary education and it is designed for pupils aged 12 up to about 18 years. Various types of secondary school exist and, whichever school a pupil enters, the first year is a transition year. This is designed mainly for orientation and adjustment, and for observing and testing pupils - after which they are referred to the type of school best suited to their needs. It is also possible that the transition year (or class) may be repeated by some pupils and some schools have adopted a transition (or "bridge") period of 2 years. After the first year those pupils suited for the type of school already started (e.g.

MAVO secondary) would move to transition class 2A. Those with good results in tests would go to Class 2B. At the end of the second year decisions are finally made regarding the type of school to which the pupil is best suited for the remainder of secondary education.

Secondary education includes the following:

- General Secondary Education of various types (i.e. pre-university education) (VWO)
- Senior General Secondary education (HAVO)
- Junior General Education (MAVO)
- Elementary General Secondary Education (LAVO).

There are also various kinds of vocational schools/courses:

- Junior Secondary Vocational Schools (LBO)
- Senior Secondary Vocational Schools (MBO)
- Short Senior Secondary Vocational Schools/Courses (KMBO).

In theory the parent has a major part to play in the choice of school. This is made in the light of results and advice coming from the primary school and from the transition class. In practice it is sometimes the case that there is difference of opinion between parent and school personnel. Whichever form of secondary education is taken up the pupil may finish, on a full time basis, at the age of 16. As already mentioned if this is the case part-time education will continue until the age of 18 years.

The complexities of the different branches and provisions at the secondary level are reflected in the curriculum provision made, even though it is possible to find different schools existing within the same campus. Thus, within general education, the following provisions are made:
MAVO school. A transition class leading to a four year general education including compulsory Dutch and one modern foreign language plus a choice of 4-5 optional subjects (e.g. Economics; Geography; History and Civics);

HAVO school. This is largely similar to MAVO school, but with the possibility of more choice. There is also the likelihood of a faster pace of learning and a deeper study of subject areas.

MAVO and HAVO education lead to a school examination in 6-7 subjects. Some MAVO pupils will move on to the final class at the HAVO school or to the vocational sector. Some HAVO pupils will move to the final year of the VWO school or to vocational education.

VWO school. Pupils will take 7 or more subjects, with an emphasis on preparation for higher education. A classical emphasis is possible.

Teacher Training:

The opportunities to train as a teacher must be placed against a background of major re-organisation of higher professional education in The Netherlands. In 1987 a large merger operation, involving some 400 institutes of higher professional education, was completed. As a result, more than 60 institutes were created (each called a Hogeschool) with an average of 3000-6000 students. The largest had more than 10,000 students, offering a wide variety of courses covering most sectors of higher professional education.

The grouping of sectors of training inside a Hogeschool may, nevertheless, depend partly upon history and upon chance and some Hogescholen still offer only one type of training (e.g. Economic and Administrative Training; or Primary Teacher Training). Large multi-sectoral Hogescholen can include a Faculty of Education; a Faculty of Technology, Economy and Management; and a Faculty of Liberal Arts. Until the mid 1980s those who wished to enter primary teaching as a career would apply to a Teacher Training College (PABO). Students now entering a Hogeschool for a four year training course are required to possess a certificate from the HAVO school, a VWO school or possibly from an MBO school (i.e. school for Senior Secondary Vocational Education).

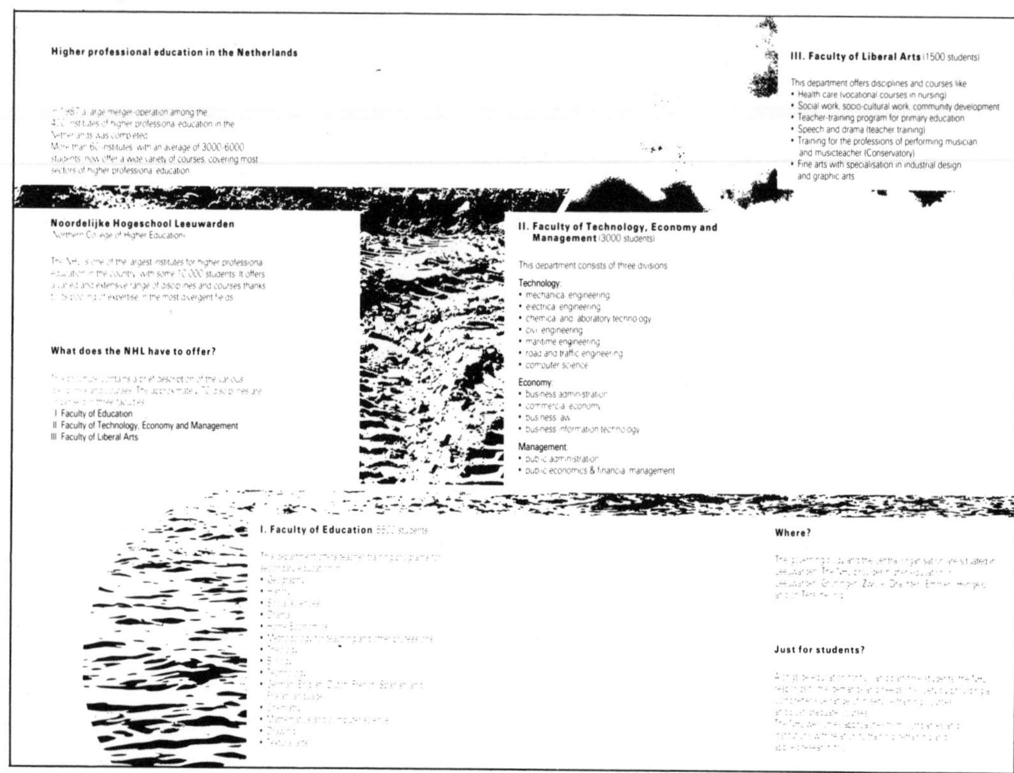

Higher professional education in the Netherlands

In 1987 a large merger-operation among the 400 institutes of higher professional education in the Netherlands was completed. More than 60 institutes, with an average of 3000-6000 students, now offer a wide variety of courses, covering most sectors of higher professional education.

Noordelijke Hogeschool Leeuwarden
(Northern College of Higher Education)

The NHL is one of the largest institutes for higher professional education in the country with some 10 000 students. It offers a varied and extensive range of disciplines and courses thanks to its pooling of expertise in the most divergent fields.

What does the NHL have to offer?

I Faculty of Education
II Faculty of Technology, Economy and Management
III Faculty of Liberal Arts

III. Faculty of Liberal Arts (1500 students)

This department offers disciplines and courses like
- Health care (vocational courses in nursing)
- Social work, socio-cultural work, community development
- Teacher-training program for primary education
- Speech and drama (teacher training)
- Training for the professions of performing musician and musicteacher (Conservatory)
- Fine arts with specialisation in industrial design and graphic arts

II. Faculty of Technology, Economy and Management (3000 students)

This department consists of three divisions

Technology:
- mechanical engineering
- electrical engineering
- chemical and laboratory technology
- civil engineering
- maritime engineering
- road and traffic engineering
- computer science

Economy:
- business administration
- commercial economy
- business law
- business information technology

Management:
- public administration
- public economics & financial management

I. Faculty of Education

Where?

Just for students?

Primary school training courses include theoretical training, (which is given in Dutch), Arithmetic, Mathematics, Science, Social Subjects, Expressive Arts and Writing, and also teaching methods and pedagogy in each subject. General professional training includes the study of aspects of Psychology and Education. Colleges are free to decide upon the total amount of school practice teaching undertaken, provided that this is no less than a minimum amount set by the Minister. Some 600 hours of teaching practice, spread over 4 years, has been possible. A current example involves students teaching about 10 training weeks each year, with 18 teaching hours in each week.

To teach in the lower classes of the LBO, MAVO, HAVO and VWO schools it is first necessary to possess a HAVO or VWO school leaving certificate and then to undertake a 4 year course within a Hogeschool. Until 1990 full-time courses focused upon two subjects but since August 1990 the four year courses have been restricted to one subject. Those who wish to work in the upper levels of the HAVO and VWO schools would have successfully completed VWO education and have obtained a university degree - including two months of educational studies at the undergraduate level. It is also necessary to undertake a one year post-graduate professional course which is centred upon a lengthy period of school practice.[1]

Part-time courses are also available for those who may wish to "upgrade" their level of qualification but this no longer leads to an automatic increase in salary. Salaries are now based upon actual teaching duties rather than upon the number of certificates held by the teacher.

Employment

The Municipalities are responsible for teaching appointments to publicly run schools. Teachers are public employees and not regarded as civil servants, as in Germany or France. Nonetheless, as public employees, teachers enjoy conditions of appointment which are comparable to those of civil servants, viz: in salary schemes; pension schemes; early retirement possibilities; sickness benefits and redundancy pay; and in relation to holidays and allowances.

At the beginning of the 1990s the unemployment rate among primary teachers was high but it was expected to drop in the early years of the decade. Many beginning teachers have had to accept part-time temporary jobs, or job sharing possibilities; some have been recruited to areas of shortage elsewhere within E.C.

Unemployment among secondary school teachers appears to be falling. Many university graduates have found work outside teaching, especially in the western part of The Netherlands. As in some other countries there is a shortage of Science teachers.

Primary school teachers normally work 40 hours per week with teaching contact being between 25-26 teaching units of 50 minutes. The standard workload for secondary school teachers, measured in "establishment units" (viz: lesson units, and duty units) is 29. Non teaching units include staff meetings, supervising student teachers, and maintaining contact with parents. Some activities may be awarded "duty units", instead of lesson units, so that such teachers can be partly released from teaching in order to perform such tasks.

Probation

A period of probation, evident in several E.C. countries, does not exist in The Netherlands. It is possible that a few larger schools may give some form of informal help and supervision, and this will depend largely upon the interest and goodwill of individual teachers. In any case many beginning teachers occupy only temporary jobs, and some have taken up opportunities of working abroad (e.g. in the shortage areas of London).

A school inspector will have regular meetings with individual Headteachers and any cases of teachers encountering difficulties are likely to be raised at these meetings. There appears to be no officially agreed policy whereby Headteachers will keep records or profiles of their staff, related to such matters as teaching performance or professional development.

Career Development

Once a permanent post has been obtained it will take about 20 years for most teachers to go from their minimum to maximum salary. Such progress involves a switch from the initial scales to the highest scale accorded to a Senior Teacher. This new promoted post is awarded to a teacher who has satisfied certain promotion criteria related to inservice training and to recognised professional abilities. Promotion to the position of Headteacher, or Adjunct (Assistant Headteacher) may be possible. No formal training or examination is normally expected for these posts, but, in general, it is expected that the applicant will be an experienced and successful teacher. He/she must possess a degree or certificate relating to the type of school concerned and he/she must demonstrate appropriate personal and leadership qualities. In recent years School Management courses have become available for Headteachers.

Other possibilities for career development may include work in the Education Sector of a Hogeschool.

In 1985 a new salary system (Education Staff Salary Structure Review) came into operation, based on remunerating teachers according to the post they hold. Each post has a maximum scale and one or more preliminary scales. Placing is linked to previous work experience/seniority. The preliminary and maximum scales are the same as those for civil servants.[2]

Inservice Training

Attendance at inservice courses is not compulsory, although this is a condition for promotion to the post of Senior Teacher. In other respects much will depend upon the teacher concerned, and particular interests. Opportunities are available to undertake inservice coursework at the Hogenschoolen, and to up-grade qualifications on a part-time basis. A Headteacher could suggest lines of action to be undertaken by 'poor' teachers.

Footnotes

1 *These professional training courses began on September 1st 1987, and are open to those who have obtained their first degree ("doctoraal") and who have taken the introductory educational studies course as part of their undergraduate work. The main elements will typically include:*

a) preparation for teaching, and teaching practice (as a 'normal' class-teacher, and fully responsible for the teaching of the subject, and the pupils);

b) research on some aspect of teaching, leading to a thesis or completion of a project.

2 *Different salary scales are provided in relation to the level of teaching undertaken. For example, there are separate scales for those teaching in Primary Schools, Lower Level Secondary Schools, Intermediate Level Vocational schools, Upper Secondary schools and in Higher Professional education sector.*

Teacher in a MAVO School

Mijn beroep is leraar aan een Mavo in Nederland. De school is niet groot, een kleine 200 leerlingen in de leeftijd van 12 tot 16 á 17 jaar. De school staat aan de rand van ons dorp en heeft een streekfunktie voor de omgeving. De verst verwijderd wonende leerling woont 12 kilometer van school at. De meeste leerlingen komen op de fiets; een enkeling komt per brommer.

Aan onze school werken 16 killega's die allen les geven in 1 of meerdere vakken. De jongste is 23 jaar en net van de lerarenopleiding; de oudste is 56. De meeste killega's zijn tussen de 45 en 55 jaar (en dus treedt ook hier vergrijzing op).

In 4 leerjaren wordt aan onze school een groot aantal, door de wet voorge-schreven, vakken gegeven. De vier leerjaren zijn in 3 groepen ingedeeld: de brugperiode (= klas 1 en 2); de derde klas en de examenklas (= klas 4). In de brugperiode wordt bezien welke school voor de leerling het geschiktst is. Na klas 1 wordt in klas 2 in twee stromen les gegeven: klas 2A is de Mavo-gerichte kals; klas 2B is de Havo/VWO gerichte klas. In nauwe samenwerking met een grote scholengemeenschap in Assen (waarheen de meeste leerlingen die ná de 2E klas naar Havo/VWO gaan, zullen vertrekken) worden dezelfde toetsen gegeven en dezelfde normering gehandhaafd. De vakken die aan ons soort onderijsinstelling worden gegeven, zijn: de moedertaal Nederlands, de 3 vreemde talen (Engels, Duits, Frans); de sociale vakken (geschiedenis, aardrijkskunde, biologie, maatsc, happijleer); de exacte vakken (wiskunde, natuurkunde, scheikunde), de kreatieve vakken (tekenen, muziek, handvaardigheid); gymnastiek, economic, typen en computergebruik.

Voor ons type onderwijs moet je voor het vak dat je geeft, een bevoegdheid hebben. In Nederland zijn 3 soorten bevoègdheden-eerste, tweede en derdegraadsdie het recht geven om les te geven aan le, 2e of 3e graads scholen. Het Lager Beroepsonderwijs en het Mavo is 3e graads onderwijs; het Middelbaar Beroepsonderwijs en de onderbouw van Havo en VWO is 2e graads onderwijs en het Hoger Beroeps onderwijs en de bovenbouw van Havo en VWO is le graads. De meeste van mijn killega's zijn afkomstig uit het Lager Onderwijs en hebben door avondstudie een 3e, soms een 2e graadsbevoegdheid gehaald. Veel van hen hebben 2 of meer bevoegdheden. Er zijn er een paar die zelfs 4 of 5 vakken mogen geven. Een paar jongere kollega's zijn opgeleid aan de Nieuwe Lerarenopleiding en hebben 2 bevoegdheden.

Er zijn nu zelfs 3 kollega's aan onze school die, en dat is een zeldzaamheid in ons school type, die een universitaire studie hebben afgerond en een titel mogen voeren. Toch krijg je aan ons school type voor je le graads bevoegdheden maar een 2e graads salaris. Het probleem van een groot aktenbezit is dat je over het algemeen ook veel vakken moet geven. Sommigen geven 3 of meer vakken.

Een aantal jaren geleden zijn door de overheid de ambtenarensalarissen gekort (oplopend tot plm.12% per maand). Momenteel is dat percentage iets lager (tot ± 7%) maar nog altijd leveren leraren in (m.a.w.ze krijgen minder uitbetaald dan ze feitelijk verdienen).

Er zijn (bijna) green mogelijkheden om in salaris vooruit te gaan. Hoe ouder men wordt, des te meer gaat men verdienen (tot een zeker maximum). Het bezit van meer bevoegdheden kan, tot zekere hoogte, ook iets meer salaris opleveren. (Maar een le graads akte aan ons schooltype levert geen cent extra.) Men kan, onder bepaalde omstandigheden seniorleraar worden. Dat levert een kleine salarisverhoging op.Maar i.h.a.zullen gevelogde cursussen geen cent extra opleveren.

Promotie in de zin van een hogere funktie is evenmin mogelijk. Als adjunctdirekteur of direkteur benoemd teworden, is de enige mogelijkheid om een hoger salaris te krijgen.

Speciale funkties (brugklasbegeleider, decaan, sectiehoofd) leveren geen salarieel voordeel (hooguit-aan grotere scholen-een taakuur). In vergelijking met het bedrijfsleven verdienen we minder. Daarbij komt dat het aantal uren dat we werken, in werkelijkheid hoger is dan het aantal waarvoor we zijn aangesteld.

Een normale baan in het voortgezet onderwijs is 29 uren (een schooluur heeft 50 minuten). Boven de 45 jaar geef je 28 uren; boven de leeftijd van 53 jaar geef je 26 uren. In de 29 uren is niet inbegrepen: het voorbereiden op de lessen, het korrigeren van gemaakt werk, het volgen van een cursus, enz.

Elke week wordt aan onze school 1 uur in eigen tijd vergaderd en eveneens in eigen tijd 1 uur bijwerkles gegeven. Daarnaast zijn er-alweer in eigen tijdouderavonden, ouderbezoek, werkweken, etc. De rapportenvergaderingen moeten, van de overheid, voor een groot deel in de eigen tijd worden gehouden.

Het lesrooster is meestal aaneengesloten van 8 uur 's morgens tot 3 of 4 uur' s middags, met in de ochtend 15 minuten pauze en tussen de middag 40 minuten pauze. 's Morgens zijn er 5, 's middags 2 of 3 lesuren. Meestal hebben we 2 middagen vrij.

In het lesrooster moeten van de overheid een paar tussenuren zijn, d.w.z. lesuren die men wel vrij heeft, maar die gebruikt kunnen worden om in te vallen en les te geven als een killega absent is.

Het bercoep van leraar heeft momenteel veel minder status dan een aantal jaren geleden. Dit blijkt ook wel uit de grote terugloop van het aantal studenten aan de lerarenopleidingen.

Daar komt nog bij dat veel kollega 's het lesgeven moeilijker vinden dan een aantal jaren geleden: veel leerlingen zijn minder gemotiveerd en moeilijker hanteerbaar.

Het beloningssysteem is in onze ogen onredelijk laag en de werkdruk wordt steeds groter. Onze taken worden steeds omvangrijker. Alle bezuinigingen die de afgelopen jaren in het onderwijs zijn geweest, vallen slecht. Gelukkig zijn er toch nog jonge mensen die, ondanks alles, leraar willen sorden en met grote inzet aan het werk gaan. Juist van hen gaan grote stimulansen uit die het werk toch prettig maken.

My job is being a teacher at a 'Mavo' in the Netherlands. The school is not very big, about 200 pupils, in the age of 12-16/17. The building is situated at the edge of our village and has the function of regional school. The pupil who lives farthest away from school, lives at a distance of about 12km. Most pupils cycle to school; some come here by moped.

At our school 16 colleagues work, who all teach one or more subjects. The youngest is 23 years old and just left college; the oldest is 56 years old. Most colleagues are between 45 and 55 (and so ageing is also occurring here).

In 4 years of classes a great number of subjects (prescribed by law) are taught. The classes are divided into 3 groups: the 'brugperiode' (bridge period) (= the forms 1 and 2); the 3rd form and the examination-form (=4th form). During the 'bridge-period' we determine which type of school is most suited for each pupil. After the first form they will be taught in 2 streams in the second form. Form 2A is the MAVO-form; the teaching in form 2B is directed to Havo/VWO (to which type of school the pupils may leave after their 2nd year).

There is a close cooperation between a large school in Assen (an amalgam of MAVO/Havo/VWO) and our school. The subjects taught at our kind of school comprise: motherlanguage Dutch, the 3 foreign languages (English, French, German), the social subjects (history, geography, biology, humanics), the 'exact' subjects (maths, science, chemistry), the 'creative' subjects (manual work, music, drawing), gymnastics, economics, typewriting and 'how to use the computer'.

In our type of school you must be qualified for the subject you teach. In the Netherlands there are 3 sorts of qualifications: 1st, 2nd or 3rd degree schools. The Lower Vocational schools and Mavo are 3rd degree; the Middle Vocational schools and Havo/VWO-lower classes are 2nd degree schools and the upper classes of VWO/Havo and Higher Vocational schools are 1st degree.

Most of my colleagues are teachers from the Elementary Schools where they taught. Their 3rd and sometimes their 2nd degree they took in evening courses. Many of them have 2 or more qualifications. There are even teachers who have 4 or 5 subjects to teach. Some younger colleagues have been educated at the 'New Teachers Institutes' and have 2 qualifications.

There are now even 3 colleagues at our school who have taken a university degree and are allowed to show this by their title (drs). This is a rarity in our type of school.
And yet you get a 2nd degree pay at our school, even if your qualification is 1st degree.
The problem associated with a large quantity of qualifications in your bag is that you mostly have to teach a lot of subjects. Some teach 3 subjects or more.

Some years ago the government reduced the salaries of the officials or civil servants (up to 12%). At present that percentage is slightly lower (approximately 7%) but still teachers are giving away part of their salary to the government (in other words: they get less than they really have to earn).

There are (hardly) no possibilities in raising your salary. The older one gets the more one earns (up to a certain maximum). That you have more teaching qualifications can lead (to a certain extent) to more salary (but a 1st degree qualification doesn't lead to more pay in our type of school). Under certain circumstances one can be 'promoted' to senior-teacher. The result of it is a slight raise of salary.

But in general: the inservice one did, will not result in higher salary. Promotion in the sense of a higher function isn't hardly possible either. Being the headmaster or adjunct-headmaster is the only possibility to get higher salary. Special functions (being the bridge-class coordinator; sectionhead or the vocational adviser) does not bring more money at our school (in some cases only an hour free from teaching, a so called 'task-hour').

When compared to the salaries in industry we are grossly underpaid. Moreover, the amount of hours worked is in reality higher than the hours we get paid for.

A 'normal' job in advanced teaching is 29 hours; over 53 you teach 26 hours. Not included in those 29 teaching hours are the hours devoted to preparation, correcting the written work, the following of inservice-courses.

Each week there is a 1 hour meeting of the teachers at our school. This is not included in those 29 hours. Giving extra lessons (1 hour a week) is also in our own time. Then there are, also in your own time, the so called evenings for the parents' (meeting with the parents of our pupils), visiting (at home) of pupils, the 'field-work week'. The meetings concerning the reports must be held largely in our own time, according to governmental instructions.

The timetable is mostly from 8 o'clock till 3 or 4 o'clock in the afternoon. In the morning there's an interval of 15 minutes and at noon an interval of 40 minutes. In the morning there are 5 lessons; in the afternoon 2 or 3. The teachers here at our school mostly have 2 afternoons off. In the timetable every teacher must have, according to the government, some 'between-hours', that is: teaching hours that we needn't teach (and so don't get paid) but that could be used to teach children when a colleague is absent during that hour).

The job of a teacher has less status than it had some years ago. This also becomes clear from the ever fewer groups of students at the teachers training colleges. Added the fact that many colleagues think that teaching is more difficult than is was formerly: many pupils have less motivation and are more difficult to handle.

The system of rewarding is unreasonably low in our opinion and the working-pressure is ever growing. Our tasks in school grow bigger. All the reductions in education of the past years have done no good.

And yet, happily, there are young people who, malgré tout, want to become a teacher and work with great enthusiasm.

Teaching in Portugal

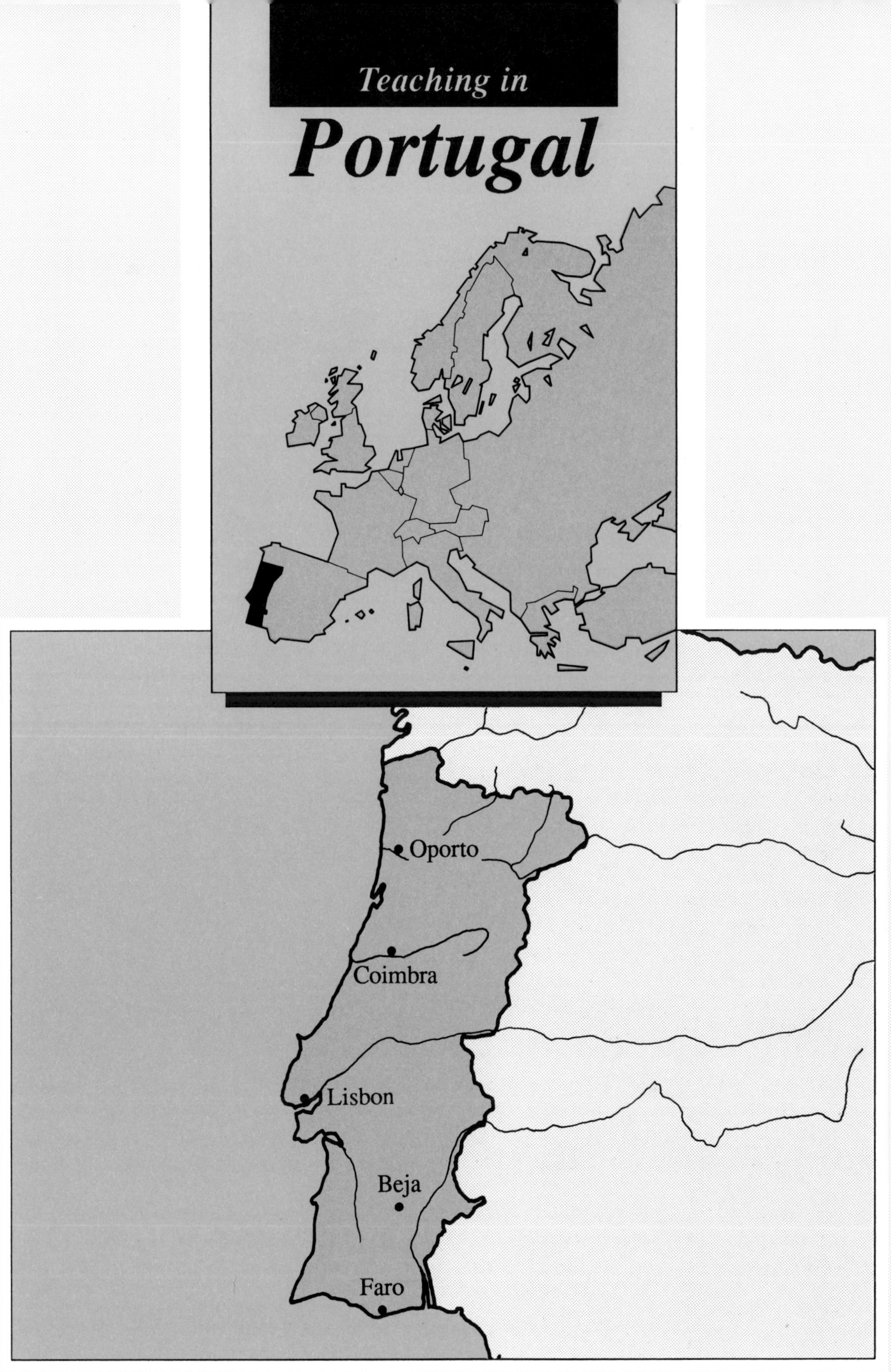

TEACHING IN PORTUGAL

Portugal, including the Madeira achipelago and the Azores, is situated at the south-western extremities of European Community territory, as Greece is positioned in the south-east. Both are among the poorer countries of the EC. With a population of 10 million (and growing) and a GNP of £14bn, Portugal's future is clearly dependent upon much-improved economic performance, in the traditional areas of agriculture, wine production, textiles and forestry as well as in tourism and modern industrial developments.

Education is largely the responsibility of the Ministry of Education based in Lisbon. The functions of central government are concerned with the design, planning, coordination and inspection of the education system. Legislation enacted in 1986 is leading to reform of the system as a whole, and in particular the powers of local and regional authorities are being increased as part of a programme of decentralisation.

The day-to-day management of the schools is the concern of Regional Education Directorates. At a still more local level are clusters of Regional Delegations, responsible to their area Regional Directorate. Finance is largely the business of central government but some funding is provided locally for school building and for special projects etc.

Schooling

Until 1987 there were only six years of free, compulsory education in Portugal, up to a leaving age of 12 years. From 1987/88 this was extended to nine years, with a statutory leaving age of 15. These nine years of basic education now being introduced are organised in three *ciclos*.

Pre-school education is available from the age of 3 in *Jardins de Infancia* (nursery schools). Provision is made partly by the state and partly by private bodies. Fees can be charged.

Formal schooling takes place consecutively in three types of school as follows:

- Primary schools
- Preparatory schools
- Secondary schools

Primary education lasts for four years in two 2-year phases. There is a compulsory basic curriculum, including Language, Mathematics, Social Studies, Physical Education and the Creative Subjects. Pupils' progress is regularly measured on the basis of continuous assessment and at the end of each phase final assessments are recorded.

Preparatory schools have provided two years of education, the teaching being conducted by specialist graduate teachers. Foreign Languages, Natural Sciences, History and Religion/Ethics are among the subjects on offer at this stage. There is some pupil choice of curriculum.

As the new pattern of nine years of basic education takes shape, preparatory schools are sometimes assuming responsibility for the third cycle in which case the school becomes a combined preparatory and secondary school. In other cases the third cycle is taught in secondary schools. For pupils who enrol in secondary schools at age 15, in general the choice is between academic or technical/vocational streams.

The facilities and resourcing of schools vary considerably. Buildings can be old and ill-equipped, possibly with untrained teachers. The newer buildings can be attractive and with better resources. While the teaching is often traditional it can sometimes be child-centred and imaginative.

Smaller, rural communities may be the most disadvantaged and there may not be a preparatory school in the locality. To compensate, there is teaching by television (*Telescola*), under the eye of an 'instructor' (usually a primary school teacher). For *Telescola* there is a structured programme covering a compulsory curriculum of nine subjects. The instructor's task is to conduct a 45-minute follow-up after each broadcast. The need for *Telescola* is fast disappearing as new schools are provided.

Secondary schools are sometimes large, with several thousand students, a few having as many as 5,000. Each day there can be three or more 'schools' in operation, one in the morning, one in the afternoon and one in the evening - evening class provision of courses (usually for adults) is quite common. These large organisations are run by only a small Administrative Council consisting of a President (the Headteacher), a Vice-President and three others, all elected for a renewable term of two years. These positions are not seen as 'promotions' in the full sense, as in the U.K.

As the diagram indicates, only the first three years of what might be called secondary education, (i.e. the third cycle) are compulsory. The curriculum consists of a common core of some ten subjects, with an option in the final year. There are academic or technical and vocational courses for those who wish to stay on. Both the academic and technical streams lead to access to university education. There are lower-level vocational courses giving access to polytechnics, or simply leading to jobs.

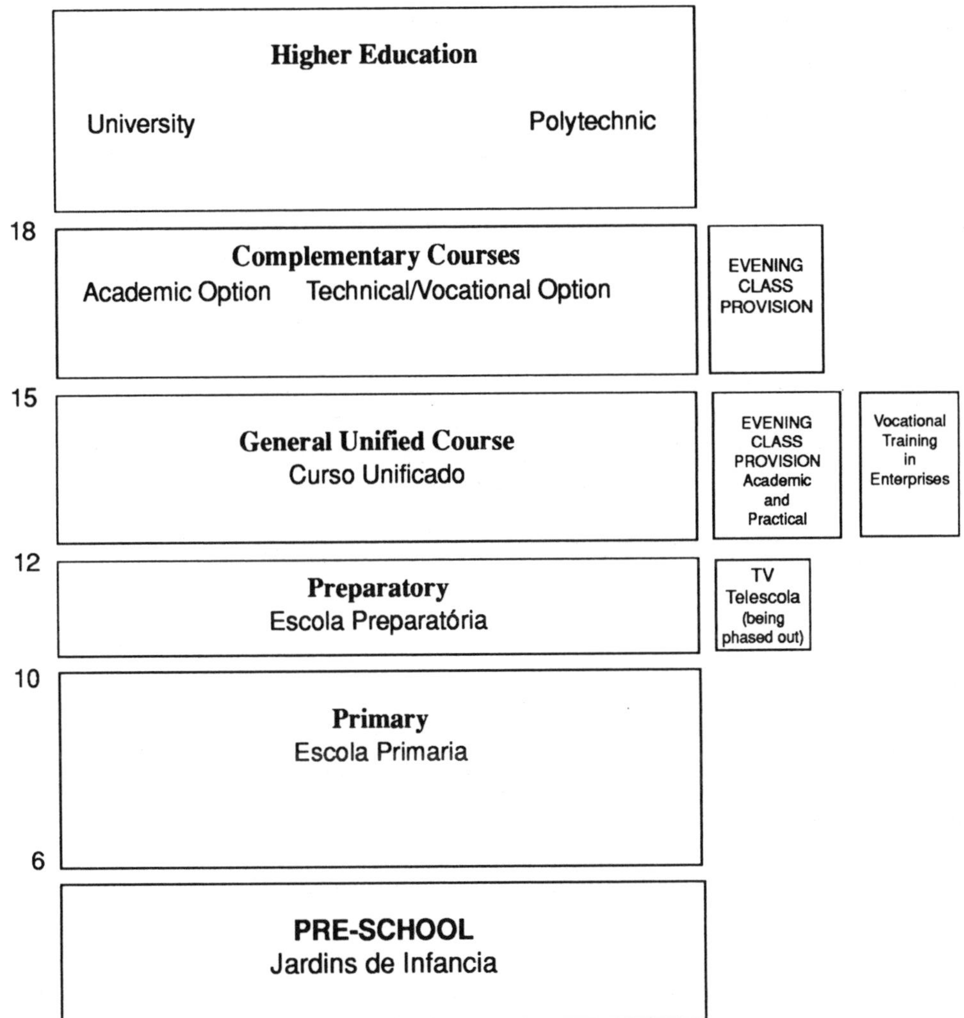

Teacher Training

Any discussion of teacher training in Portugal must be prefaced by remarks about the legacy of the past and about extensive changes that are planned for the 1990s. Prior to 1980 the arrangements for training and for obtaining tenure (i.e. becoming *professor efectivo*) often entailed a kind of apprenticeship (*estágio clássico*). This was monitored by one person, a senior teacher (*metodólogo*) whose judgment was not always seen as impartial. In the 1980s some university faculties instituted a training year (*licenciatura em ensino*) for secondary teaching. This meant that three categories of person were involved - university staff, the teacher trainer (*orientador pedagógico*) who was responsible for a group of trainees and the senior teacher in school in charge of the subject area (*delegado de disciplina*). A parallel school-based system was devised by the Ministry of Education for untrained staff already in post. This lasts for two years and similar kinds of supervisory staff are involved.

Thus, past policy means that Portuguese classrooms have been staffed by substantial numbers of untrained teachers, especially at post-primary level. After completing a degree or other basic course it was a matter of applying for a teaching post when a vacancy occurred. Supply and demand varied and once in post one simply had to wait for a training place to come up. It has been customary to wait for several years and in the late 1980s as many as 1 in 3 members of staff in a school could have been untrained. While remaining untrained a teacher experiences an uncertain future and becoming *efectivo* is a necessary objective. Plans to remedy the situation, in the context of a comprehensive reform of the educational system, were being put in place as quickly as possible following legislation passed in 1986.

Entry into initial training is dependent upon successful completion of full secondary education at the age of 18. Initial training is now required before taking a post in infant, primary and secondary teaching. Courses are available for future teachers of younger age-groups, in a College of Higher Education (*Escola Superior de Educaçao*), leading to the title of *Bacharel em Educaçao* or *Bacherel em Ensino.* Courses for teachers of older pupils are similarly available, leading to the title of *Licenciado em Ensino* in specific subject areas. There are parallel courses for specialist teachers of the vocational and aesthetic subjects.

The content of courses for prospective teachers of younger age groups is made up of three components:-

(i) Personal, social, cultural, technological, technical and artistic studies appropriate to the level of teaching.
(ii) The Education Sciences - Philosophy, History of Education, Comparative Education, Psychology of Learning and Developmental Psychology.
(iii) Practical Pedagogy relating to, and arranged in association with, schools at the level for which the teacher is being trained.

The time devoted to *Práctica Pedagógica* in one course for *Professores do Ensino Basico* is 1 week per semester in year 1, 2 weeks per semester in year II, and 8 weeks and 5 weeks in the two final semesters.

ESEs offer initial training courses along the lines as below:-

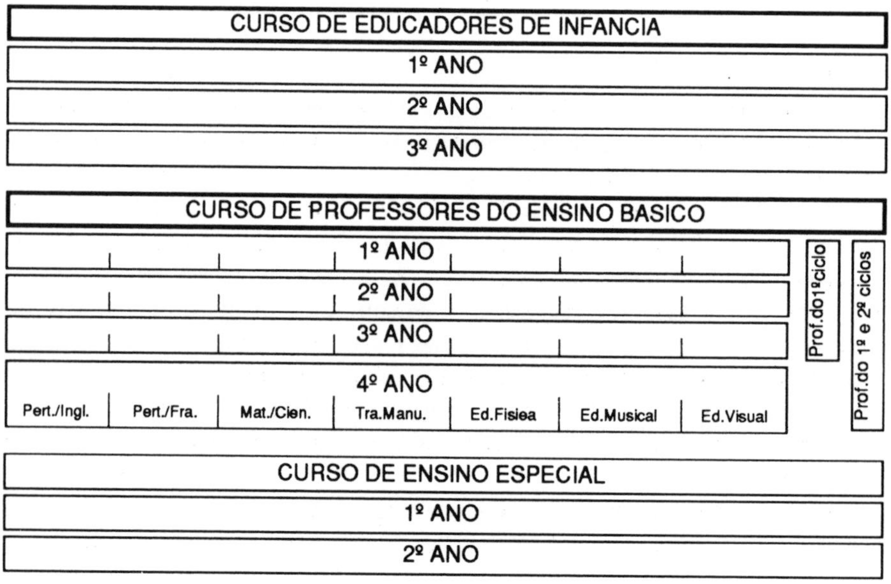

CURSO DE EDUCADORES DE INFANCIA

1º ANO

2º ANO

3º ANO

CURSO DE PROFESSORES DO ENSINO BASICO

1º ANO

2º ANO

3º ANO

4º ANO

Pert./Ingl.	Pert./Fra.	Mat./Cien.	Tra.Manu.	Ed.Fisiea	Ed.Musical	Ed.Visual

Prof.do1ºciclo

Prof.do 1º e 2º ciclos

CURSO DE ENSINO ESPECIAL

1º ANO

2º ANO

In the case of training for secondary school teaching there are two models, one for those already in post, the other for those teachers who enter training immediately on obtaining a university degree.

There is pressure on untrained teachers to become trained. Once a training place has been found the teacher starts a 2 year course. The theory in-put is during year one, on one day a week, in university or college of higher education. Year two is wholly school-based, under the supervision of an adviser (*Orientador Pedagógico*).

For those who train following university studies, there can be faculty differences. In some cases there may be education input during the university course, but mostly the arrangements entail training consecutively in a two-year postgraduate course. Similarly, this course becomes increasingly practical and the later stages are substantially school-based.

In these training courses, assessment is summative and the processes involve both the training institutions and the schools. Theory aspects will be wholly the concern of the ESE or university. The *Orientador Pedagógico* and school staff have opinions to offer as regards practical classroom skills. A scale of 1-20 is still in use, practical skills counting double. One example is:-

Theory	14	=	14
Practical	16	=	32
			46 ÷ 3
Final Mark		=	15

A further attempt is being made to reduce the number of untrained teachers in the classroom, using the organisation of the Open University (*Universidade Aberto*), which was officially launched in February 1990. This new system is for teachers with at least five years service. Course provision is through printed modules and supporting weekly television and radio programmes. The three core modules are (i) Methods and Techniques of Education, (2) Educational Psychology and (3) Educational Communication. There is a unit on Pedagogy related to the particular teaching specialism. There are no face-to-face tutorials nor is the teacher's school involved, beyond some requirements regarding classes taught in a slightly reduced time-table. The course lasts less than one year and assessment is self-operating and formative except for an important final examination. During the first year of operation the focus was on teachers of Portuguese, Mathematics and Philosophy and it is expected that the government will determine priorities each year.

Employment

Success in obtaining a post is dependent upon a number of factors. Some areas of teaching are experiencing teacher shortage, others being well supplied. Getting a post can be by *concurso* and training marks are important. They continue to be important, even to the extent of determining the classes you teach. Thus, for a secondary teacher, university marks, training grade and teaching experience can be combined according to a points system. A good total of points leads to first choice of time-table. The blocks of time left over will be taken up by students or by new graduates who are paid pro rata.

Probation

There is no probation as such. The school-based nature of the training is seen as providing approved basic competencies. Once trained, a teacher can expect to have and retain a job. However, there is an arrangement whereby graduates do get some support from the training institutions during the first year in teaching - *o ano de induçao*, or induction year. In school, help may be given to new teachers by the *Delegado de Disciplina* whose main task is to coordinate the work of all teachers teaching the same subject - in a sense the Head of Department.

However, there are clear indications that this situation will be changed. A supplement to the *Diário da Republica* in April 1990 outlined a new law (*Decreto-Lei n.º* 139-A/1990) concerning the teaching profession. Article 32 refers to the need to verify the adequacy of teachers once they take up a post, in a *periodo probatório*. Support is to be provided by schools during the probationary year. If deemed unsatisfactory (*Não satisfaz*) a teacher cannot teach for a period of two years.

Career Development

As in some other European countries, in Portugal teacher expectations and aspirations are largely restricted to being a good classroom practitioner; there is no dominating career structure.

FEDERAÇÃO NACIONAL DOS SINDICATOS DE PROFESSORES

OS PROFESSORES FAZEM GREVE NO DIA 16 DE FEVEREIRO PORQUE:

- Querem um Estatuto que dignifique a profissão.
- Querem ocupar na Educação o lugar a que têm direito.
- Querem ser excelentes desde a primeira hora.

EXIGEM NEGOCIAÇÕES DIRECTAS COM O MINISTRO

TEMPO DE ANTENA NA RTP - DIA 14 DE FEVEREIRO, A SEGUIR AO TELEJORNAL DAS 19,30h

Not that the rewards of the job are great. Portuguese teachers like others are quick to condemn the low salaries and often the poor working conditions. The first task is to achieve tenure (*efectivo*). For this a teacher must be trained and have taught for a few years. Schools each have a certain number of *efectivo* posts and it is also necessary for the individual to find a vacancy. Good initial marks help both in getting a job near to home and in gaining tenure. Being married to another civil servant can also strengthen the case for getting a job nearer to home. The Ministry decides on tenure, following a *concurso*. The competition can be considerable. Thus, in a large department of 15, 10 may be members of the school's complement of permanent staff while the other five are seeking that, when there is a vacancy there or elsewhere.

Progress after that will mean enjoying, with other civil servants, a salary increase every five years. Successful service over a period of years can also mean reduced teaching hours, perhaps down to 18 per week. There are some promoted posts as mentioned. Responsibility allowances are relatively small (e.g. the *Presidente* receives about 10,000 escudos a month extra, while the *Delegado da disciplina* gets no remuneration and only a little time off for administration). Appointment follows an election and it is for a limited period, renewable. The demand for these posts seems not to be overwhelming. One can speculate that the reform of the education system now underway will place new burdens on school management. Structures and posts might have to be reviewed and management training instituted. In fact, post-graduate diploma courses in school management (*Diploma de Gestão Escolar*) are now being set up although the aims of these courses and their usefulness are as yet unclear.

A Primary School Teacher

The fact that I took a University degree in History almost compelled me to opt for a career in teaching, as the other alternatives (very limited ones) didn't appeal to me. When I was younger I had seldom thought about becoming a teacher but now I don't regret to have followed this career, though this doesn't mean I'm satisfied.

In Portugal, a teacher's life is quite hard because the successive ministers of Education, specially since 1975, haven't been capable of solving the serious problems the system faces. Besides this, teachers have been discriminated towards other professions by the powers that be.

Since the beginning of my teaching career I've dealt with children aged between 10 and 12 (which corresponds, in my country, to the "segundo ciclo do eusino básico, formerly called "eusino preparatorio"). I chose this level because I like to work with young kids. Contrary to what many people think, it's not difficult to work with them, though you do need a certain intuition and liking in what you're doing in order to solve all the problems raised by kids of that age.

That was the reason why the first steps in my profession were a bit complicated because, besides the lack of experience, I didn't quite have the preparation and theoretical basis I needed since in Portugal, at the time I attended the University, there were no teacher training courses. Thus, the first school I worked at was very important. There I was lucky to meet a group of supportive colleagues who helped me to cope with some difficult situations I faced in those days.

During these ten years as a teacher I've been through several experiences, some more pleasant than the others, but mostly I have always tried to give the best of myself so as, harsh working conditions and lack of support notwithstanding, the pupils shouldn't have to pay the penalty.

In spite of the perspectives for a better education not being very bright, as teachers in Portugal are still seen and treated as a second class profession, I'll go on working with my best dedication and to the full of my capabilities.

Professora do Ensino Preparatório

Sou professora do Ensino Preparatório há quinze anos mas só há dois anos é que passei a fazer parte do quadro de professores de uma escola com a categoria de professora efectiva.

Nasci numa aldeia de Trás-os-Montes onde, naquela altura (há 40 anos), não havia água nem electricidade nas casas, nem estrada por onde pudesse passar qualquer tipo de transporte.

Fiz a Escola Primária numa vila do distrito e, para poder frequentar o Ensino Secundário, tive que deslocar-me para a cidade de Bragança, a capital do distrito. Estudei no Liceu de Bragança durante seis anos.

Nestes seis anos estive hospedada num Lar para estudantes naquela cidade, pois ficava a 70 km da residência da minha família. Como entretanto os meus Pais vieram para o Porto, fiz o sétimo ano do Ensino Secundário num Colégio desta cidade.

Ingressei depois na Universidade e, terminada a licenciatura, concorri ao ensino.

Fui colocada numa escola a 250 km de casa e, por razões de ordem familiar, não aceitei o lugar, ficando dois anos desempregada e sem vencimento. Concorri novamente e consegui lugar numa escola mais próxima - apenas a 40 km de casa.

De então para cá, tenho tido sempre lugar em escolas mas, em 13 anos, ensinei em 13 escolas diferentes, sempre com contractos anuais.

Há dois anos consegui finalmente uma vaga para estágio, para poder profissionalizar -me, passar a professora efective ligada ao quadro duma escola e poder enfim ter alguma estabilidade. O estágio teve a duração do Porto e dei aulas numa escola do distrito. Foi um ano difícil, com muito trabalho e muito cansativo pois, além do trabalho teórico ligado ao estágio, tinha aulas para preparar e fazia diariamente três horas de viagem para a escola, que ficava a 50 km do Porto, onde vivo.

Terminado o estágio, fui colocada como professora efectiva noutra escola, também distante de casa mas, por motivos de saúde, pedi para ser transferida para a zona da minha residência. Como a legislação portuguesa prevê casos como o meu, foi-me autorizada a mundaça de escola. Enquanto aguardo um lugar no Porto, espero poder continuar nesta situação.

A Secondary Teacher of Portuguese

My name's Rui and I teach Portuguese in a high school on the outskirts of Oporto. I have been in the teaching profession for quite a while (seven full years) and I thus think I've got a reasonable basis on which to reflect.

I graduated in 1980 from the University of Oporto (Portuguese and English Studies) and I joined the Air Force a few months later to do the compulsory military service. I stayed there for two years (the time then stipulated by law) and when I left I went into teaching not because I wanted to make a career out of it but because there were very few alternatives, if any, available.

I must say that courses at the Faculty of Letters didn't quite prepare students to follow this or that career since it didn't provide either educational training or a specific preparation to become an interpreter or translator, for instance. So when one graduated it was up to him or her to look for a job which (except for a privileged few who knew the right person in the right places and got an attractive and lucrative job) meant going into teaching. One didn't need a specific preparation to become a teacher: a University degree was enough to get a place as "professor provisório".

The first three years of my teaching experience were spent with evening students, people who needed to complete or further their studies in order to get better jobs or promotions within the job they already had. They were generally diligent and well behaved persons with whom I developed a good relationship. However I felt the activity in itself boring and monotonous, always doing the same thing, usually at basic courses level (7th to 9th grades). A good thing was that I was able to remain in the area where I live and thus avoided something that haunted an awful lot of colleagues: moving from place to place every year to distant spots in the countryside, miles from their homes and families.

In subsequent years I've been in charge of two different groups of students: young kids (between 12 and 15 in general) and older ones (16 and above). The former belong to the third stage of general education (7th to 9th grades), whereas the latter follow courses of their own choice called complementary courses and leading to University. Of course these two sets vary sharply not only in their ages but also in the contents of the subject taught: while from 7th to 9th grade language skills and grammar form the basis of the course, from the 10th to the 12th the emphasis is on literature. Because of their different ages and intellectual capacities in relation with my personality and interest the relationship with these two groups of students is clearly distinct. I don't like to teach such young people as they are often childish, often with a negative attitude towards learning and the syllabuses are uninteresting for me to teach. Besides, I also feel very far from these students and there have been a few cases of mutual misunderstandings. On the other hand, with the 15 to 18 age group I've enjoyed a very good relationship since there clearly are some common interests outside the classroom which bind us together which also enables us to work for something worthwhile and get better results.

This being said, I would also like to point out that I am frustrated about not being allowed to teach English. As mentioned above I have done English Studies at the University, Anglo-American culture means a lot to me and I think I could relay interesting and solid things as a teacher of English. As a matter of fact, the "ideal picture" for me would be to teach advanced students (with whom I relate much more easily) in both subjects.

My attitude towards the profession has changed a lot over the years. I didn't become a teacher because I wanted to but rather because I had to. So, in the beginning, I wasn't the least motivated towards this particular profession and I started looking for alternatives. I applied for different jobs without any major success. As time went by, however, I realized there were some positive aspects in the job and so I tried to concentrate on them and improved my professional approach. Nevertheless I continued to try different ways out, once again with modest results. At present I think that I would gladly opt for another career, should the opportunity arise, mainly because I feel I could do better in other areas (like journalism, translations, even educational planning) than get stuck in a classroom for the rest of my life. I have certain capacities and specific knowledge (like foreign languages, for instance) which I don't make any use of in this job. I guess I would also be more motivated to try something new, face new challenges and new realities. I do feel my human potential will never be fulfilled in teaching. But perhaps I am wrong and so I will not take a blind step towards the unknown. Or perhaps it is just a case of "the grass being always greener on the other side", as the saying goes.

A Post-Graduate Student of Education Management

Sou Portuguesa, natural de ´Agueda, mas vivi toda a minha infância na Póvoa de Varzim, onde fiz o ensino secundário. Tive que me deslocar para Coimbra em 1960 por não haver Universidade no local onde residia. Entrei então na Faculdade de Ciências daquela Universidade a fim de me licenciar em Ciências Geológicas. Seduziam-me as matérias leccionadas e principalmente a parte correspondente à sismologia e vulcanologia.

Depois de finalizar a licenciatura, tentei inscrever-me em tudo o que se relancionasse com aquelas ciências, mas todos os esforços foram em vão. Restava-me apenas o ensino.

Depois de um ano sem emprego, comecei em Outubro de 1967 a dar aulas de Geografia e Ciências da Natureza a nível de ensino secundário num estabelecimento de ensino particular. Trabalhei nesse colégio durante dois anos.

Em 1970, já casada e com um filho, fui para a então chamada Província Ultramarina de Angola, onde permaneci durante 4 anos. Aí surgui a possibilidade de ingressar num Departamento do Estado "Geologia e Minas" mas, como não pretendíamos viver definitivamente naquele país, recusei e permaneci no ensino. Dada a enorme falta de professores com habilitaçãoes que se verificava em Angola, tive lugar num establecimento de ensino oficial - um Liceu. Fui colocada como professora de Geografia.

Regressei a Portugal em 1974 e candidatei -me ao estágio. Passei nessa altura para o Ensino Preparatório por ter mais possibilidades de colocação e ser, portanto, mais fácil encontrar lugar numa escola perto da minha residência - Matosinhos. Fiz estágio numa Escola Preparatória do Porto como professora de Ciências e Matemática.

Depois de terminado o estágio, que na altura tinha a duração de um ano, fui colocada como professora provisória numa Escola Preparatória do Porto.

No ano seguinte passei a professora efectiva, mas só tive lugar numa escola a 60km do Porto, que correspondia a quatro horas de viagem por dia. Nunca trabalhei nessa escola porque fui entretanto convidada para pertencer à Comissão Instaladora duma escola do Porto. Estas Comissões Instaladoras são compostas por três ou cinco professores que, ao longo de dois anos, têm que abrir, equipar e gerir uma escola nova. Terminados os dois anos para instalação da escola, esta passa a ser dirigida por um Conselho Directivo eleito pelos professores.

Durante cinco anos fiz parte do Conselho Directivo eleito dessa mesma escola que eu tinha ajudado a criar, embora nunca tenha pertencido ao quadro de professores efectivos. Entretanto, todos os anos ia concorrendo na tentativa de me aproximar de Matosinhos (nos arredores do Porto) onde comprei um andar e passei a residir com a minha família.

Em 1982 consegui finalmente uma vaga como professora efectiva, na Escola Preparatória de Matosinhos. Aí sou novamente eleita para o Conselho Directivo da Escola, onde ocupei o lugar de Presidente até 1990.

Nesta data concorri a um novo curso post-graduação de especialização em Gestão e Administração Escolar na Escola Superior de Educação do Porto - Instituto Politécnico. Fui admitida e vou frequentá-lo. Recebo para isto uma bolsa de estudo durante dois anos, período durante o qual vou ficar totalmente desligada da escola.

Para que vai servir este curso? Não sei e, oficialmente ninguém sabe ainda. Estão previstas alterações na gestão das escolas, mas nada está definido. Penso que com este curso ficarei com possibilidades de fazer carreira dentro da futura gestão escolar.

Esta é, em resumo, a trajectória da minha carreira profissional. Tinha na juventude muitas esperanças de poder vir a trabalhar em áreas que me encantavam, passei pelo ensino de Geografia, Ciências da Natureza a Matemática e talvez venha a terminar numa carreira técnica que nada tem a ver com aquilo que eu sempre quis.

I am Portuguese, born in Agueda, but I lived all my early years in Póvoa de Verzim where I had my secondary education. I had to leave for Coimbra in 1960 because there was no local university where I lived. I enrolled in the Faculty of Science in order to take a degree in Geological Sciences. Course content fascinated me, particularly those parts devoted to seismology and vulcanology.

After completing my degree, I tried to find work in any area associated with these sciences, but all my attempts were in vain. Only teaching was left for me.

After a year without work, in October 1967 I began to take secondary-level classes in geography and the natural sciences in a private establishment. I worked in this college for two years.

In 1970, already married and with a child, I then went to Angola, where I remained for four years. Then there arose the possibility of working for the State Department of Geology and Mines but, as they were not intending to remain in that country indefinitely, I turned this down and remained in teaching. Given the great shortage of qualifications that were recognised in Angola, I took a place in a state school, in a Liceu. I was appointed teacher of geography.

I returned to Portugal in 1974 and I applied for a teacher-traineeship, at the preparatory school level where there were more employment possibilities and where it was easier to get a post in my home area. I did my training in a preparatory school in Oporto teaching science and mathematics.

On completing my traineeship, which at this level lasts a year, I was appointed temporary teacher in the same school. In the following year I was to become permanent, but in a school 60 kms from Oporto requiring four hours travelling each day. I never worked in this school because in the meantime I had been invited to join the Comissão Instaladora of a School in Oporto. Comissões Instaladoras are composed of three of four teachers whose job it is, during a period of two years, to open, equip and run a new school. At the end of the two years the school is then taken over by a Council elected by the teachers (Conselho Directivo).

For five years I was a member of the Conselho Directivo, elected in the school which I had helped to create, although I never belonged to the group of teachers having tenure (the efectivos). However, all this time matters were in tune with my attempts to stay near to Matosinhos where I had bought a flat and where I lived with my family.

In 1982 I finally succeeded in filling a vacancy for a tenured teacher, in the preparatory school of Matosinhos.

I was elected to the Council there, and I was President (Head) until 1990.

At that time I applied for a place in a new post-graduate course in School Management at Administration in the School of Education of Oporto Polytechnic. I was accepted and I am now pursuing this course, I receive a grant for two years during which time I have no connection with the school.

What is the purpose of this course? I do not know and no one knows officially. Changes in school management are envisaged but there is nothing more definite than that. I think that the course has potential for a career in school management in the future.

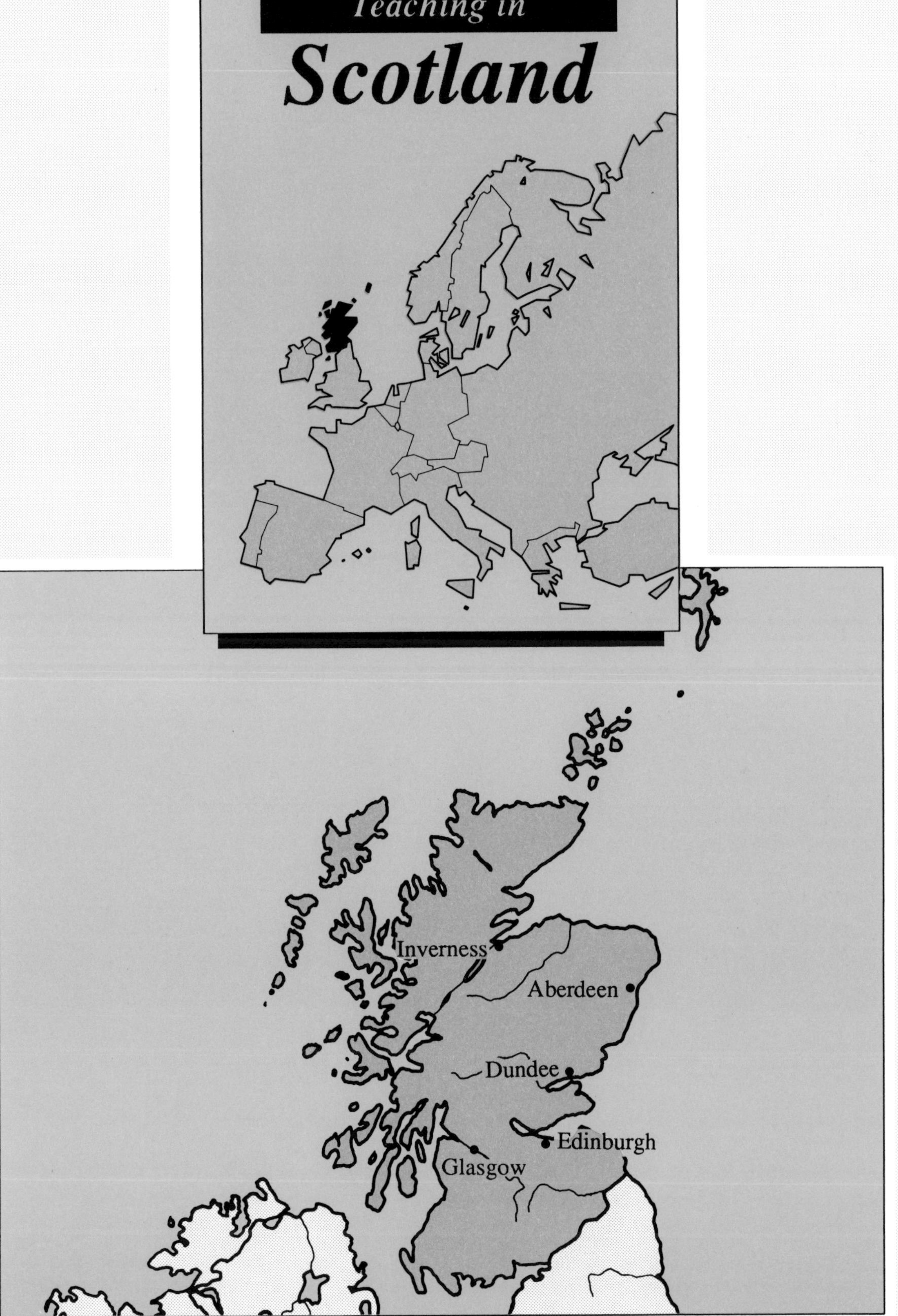
Teaching in
Scotland
Inverness
Aberdeen
Dundee
Edinburgh
Glasgow

TEACHING IN SCOTLAND

The area of Scotland is more than one-third of the United Kingdom and its coastline accounts for more than two-thirds of the UK total. However, less than 10% of the UK population live in Scotland. The country has many islands and it is often mountainous. The greater part of the population is found in the Central Lowlands, more than one-half living in Strathclyde and around Glasgow. Traditional heavy industry has given way to modern industrial development such as electronics, while fishing, agriculture, forestry and tourism continue to be important. The Gaelic language survives in some remote areas in the west.

It is not always appreciated that Scotland, for reasons of history and tradition, has its own church and its own legal and educational systems. The Secretary of State for Scotland, a member of the UK Cabinet, administers education (and all other aspects of government) through the Scottish Office in Edinburgh.

In education there are sometimes sharp differences between Scotland and other parts of the United Kingdom. The process of becoming a teacher in a Scottish school and of being a member of the teaching profession in Scotland reflects some of these differences.

Schooling

In Scotland compulsory schooling begins usually at the age of 5 years. Before that there are pre-school opportunities for some, in nursery schools, day nurseries or playgroups. Of these only nursery schools are likely to be staffed (partly) by trained teachers.

Primary education spans 7 years, from age 5 to age 12. There are a few separate infant schools. Primary curriculum encompasses basic literacy and numeracy and content is often thematic and based on broad areas such as the Language Arts and Environmental Studies rather than on traditional subjects. However, with encouragement from central government, Science and Technology are being given increasing attention in primary schools. Government is also concerned about standards and there are plans to introduce national testing in Language and Mathematics.

At the age of 12 years pupils transfer automatically to secondary schools. These are sometimes called 'Academies' or 'High Schools', or even 'Colleges' or 'Institutes'. Secondary schools are almost always all-through comprehensive schools catering for the 12-18 age groups. Scotland's national curriculum recognises the importance of Language, Mathematics, and Science along with balanced provision in the areas of the Social and Aesthetic Subjects. Government initiatives during recent years have provided extra funding for

Technological Activities, Enterprise Education and Work Experience. Scottish secondary schools provide fully for the personal, social and vocational development of pupils and there is a network of promoted posts called 'Guidance' posts, to accommodate this.

Scotland's examination system, managed by the Scottish Examination Board and the Scottish Vocational Education Council, has pioneered changes which have been taken up by others. At age 16 years pupils sit Standard Grade examinations in selected subjects and at one of three levels appropriate to their ability and attainment. Those who stay on beyond the minimum school leaving age of 16 years may take further examinations. At 16+[1] there are large numbers of short, modular courses of a vocational kind leading to a National Certificate. These vocational courses are available both in secondary schools and in Colleges of Further Education. Pupils who have an academic bent take Higher Grade examinations in subjects appropriate to University entrance or entry to teacher-training courses in Colleges of Education, or entry to courses in the Central Institutions which provide degree-level courses in the fields of Electronics, Commerce and so on.

In fact, many pupils leave school at age 16 either to take a job if one is available, or to take a place on the Youth Training Scheme which has been designed to prepare young people for a job. The staying-on rate has steadily increased since 1985, reaching 59% in 1988, with more than 25% staying for a Sixth year. By 1989 the proportion of 16 year-olds staying on or entering further education or YTS had reached 77%, higher than other areas of the UK.

The private sector in Scotland is very small, educating less than 2% of pupils. Fees are payable and these can be very high. However, a government-funded initiative called the Assisted Places Scheme has enabled some less well-off children to enrol in independent schools, thus extending parental choice. These schools are sometimes similar to state schools in the courses and examinations which they offer; others follow a pattern similar to English public schools.

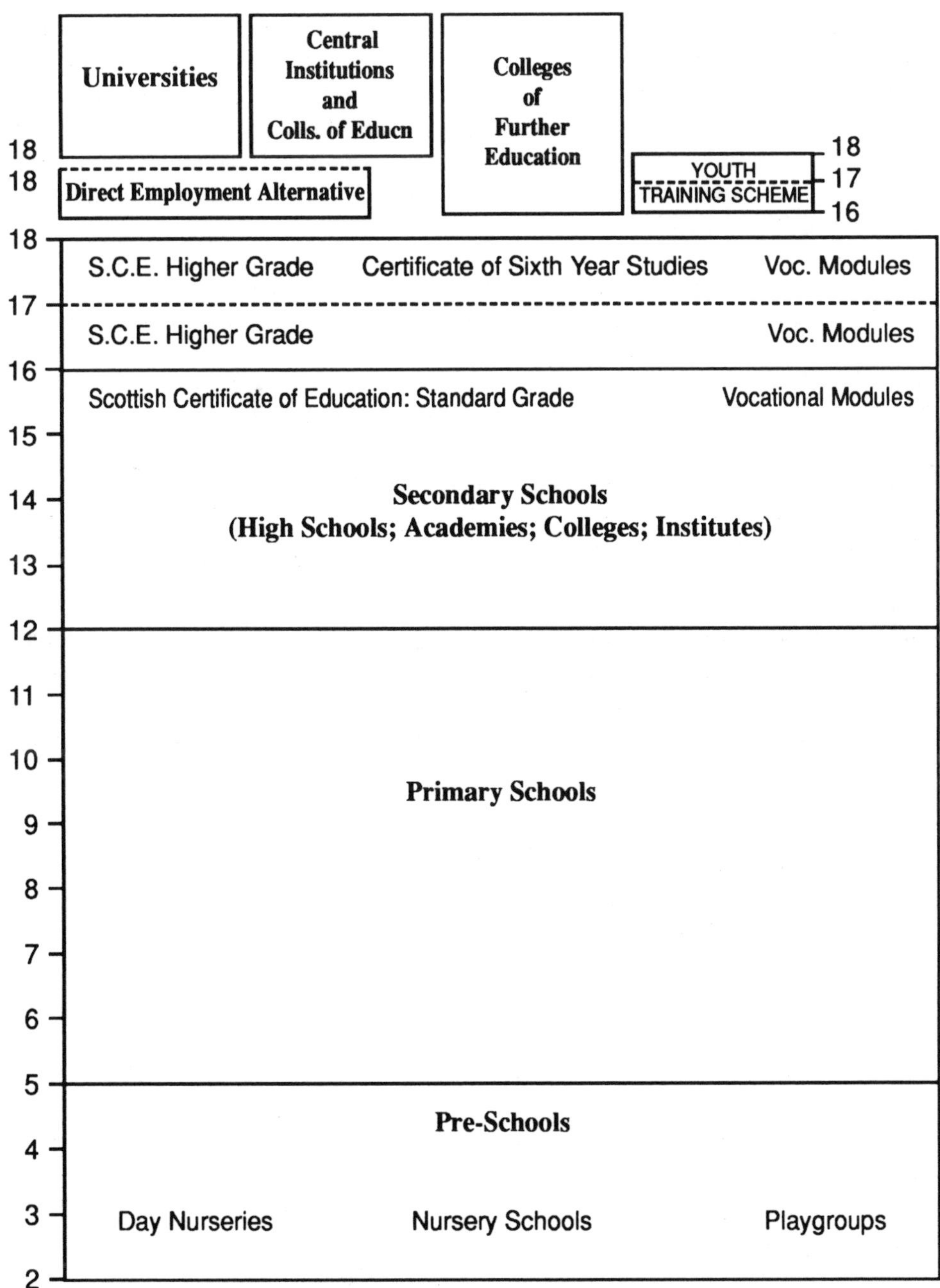

Teacher Training

The principle of professional training for all was introduced in 1906 and today all teachers in public-sector schools in Scotland will have undergone a recognised course of training. Teachers in independent schools are almost certain to have undergone the same training.

As part of the programme of vocational education and guidance, pupils in secondary schools are given information about teaching as a career. Academic entrance requirements are laid down centrally by the Scottish Office Education Department (SOED). In the case of the 4-

year degree course for primary school teaching, the requirements are for at least 3 passes on the Higher Grade of the Scottish Certificate of Education (one of which must be English) plus 2 passes at Standard Grade, including a pass in Mathematics. School pupils will be counselled accordingly when they are making curriculum choices. Some concessions are possible in the case of older applicants, aged 23 years or more. In addition to possessing these academic qualifications, candidates are interviewed by the authorities of the College to which they have applied for a place.

In the case of the one year postgraduate course for secondary teaching, 2 graduating passes in the particular area/areas are the requirement. Again, the interview will have a part to play.

It should be added that, as more employers compete for the services of fewer young people, the authorities are beginning to look for other ways of attracting teacher trainees.

Training takes place in one of the five government-funded Colleges of Education, staffed by experienced and highly qualified staff who are themselves trained teachers. Exceptionally, there are also teacher training courses offered by the University of Stirling.

Many primary school teachers take a 4-year teacher training course leading to a Bachelor of Education (B.Ed.) degree. Others who intended to teach in primary schools take a graduating course in a University, followed by a year's course in a College of Education. Most intending secondary school teachers also go first to a University where they follow a degree course, often in two specialist subjects, e.g. Mathematics and Physics, French and German, English and History, etc. Art, Music, Business Studies and Home Economics are first studied in specialist colleges. After graduation intending secondary school teachers take a one-year course in a College of Education. Teachers who work in Colleges of Further Education, i.e. teachers of vocational education, do not undergo initial training. They must first obtain a post and after that they may be released for professional training in the Scottish School of Further Education. Training is important for their future career development.

Training courses are devised locally by the Colleges, but centrally and rigorously moderated. Standards are high and students must satisfy agreed assessment criteria before completion of the course. There is a national student profile for use by all the colleges. This profile is designed particularly to record student performance in the classroom. Other aspects of the course are assessed through essays, assignments and workshop activities. Once a student has completed all parts of the course satisfactorily he/she is **provisionally registered** with the General Teaching Council for Scotland as a teacher in one of the three areas, primary, secondary or further education. This provisional "licence to teach" is essential and employment in schools cannot be obtained without it. Anyone coming from outside Scotland and wanting to teach must first obtain registration with the G.T.C., and the Council has produced guidelines/leaflets for those wishing to do this (viz: Applications for Exceptional Admission to the Register from Teachers Trained in England, Wales, and Northern Ireland. (Leaflet 5); Applications for Exceptional Admission to the Register from Teachers Trained in European Community Countries and Overseas (Leaflet 6).

Teaching: A Self-Governing Profession

When the General Teaching Council for Scotland (G.T.C.) met for the first time in 1966 it was noted by the Secretary of State for Scotland that "teachers in Scotland have long aspired towards the conception of a self-governing profession". The Secretary of State added that the

G.T.C. "will have wide responsibilities not only in relation to teacher training, but, by its powers of registration and discipline, in the maintenance of the standards of the profession itself". Of the 49 members who form the Council, 30 are registered teachers elected by the teaching profession. The main functions of the G.T.C. are:

1. To keep a register containing the names of all those permitted to teach in Scotland.
2. To keep under review the standards of education, training and fitness to teach appropriate to persons entering teaching.
3. To manage the system of probationary teaching in Scotland.
4. To determine whether in any particular case under its disciplinary powers registration is to be withdrawn or refused.
5. To make recommendations on matters relating to the supply of teachers.
6. To exercise the right to comment upon and to approve all new courses of teacher education.

Election Dates

19 December 1990 (est)
Election results declared

1 February 1991
7th Council takes office

gtc General Teaching Council For Scotland **link**

GTC Dates

Council Meetings

6 February 1991	Edinburgh
6 March 1991	Edinburgh
5 June 1991	Edinburgh
2 October 1991	Dundee
4 December 1991	Edinburgh

ISSN 0142-2162 ISSUE No. 7 WINTER 1990

The Council's informal meeting in Glasgow in October was a great success and well attended as our photograph indicates. Reports of some of the issues raised and discussed appear in this issue of Link.

GTC belongs to you

"THE GTC is funded by you, belongs to you, and is acc[illegible]untable to [illegible]" said Tom Bo[illegible] [illegible]rman. [illegible]

Chairman outlines C[illegible]'s concerns

Teachers 'should be generalists first'

Special education concerns

EMPLOYERS had to be put under pressure not to give fresh probationers jobs in special schools, said Alistair Fulton in response to a teacher's plea to grant full registration to teachers completing two years' service in special schools. Now, they have to spend at least one year in mainstream schools.

There was no registration category for special schools, Ivor Sutherland told the Glasgow meeting. The Council believed teachers had to be generalists first, and so teachers going straight into special education were caught in a trap. The Council had looked at ways to help them, and the decision to accept one year's service in mainstream schooling was itself a concession.

Was it not a bit ridiculous, he was asked, that a Council which complained about probationary difficulties created by supply teaching should prevent probationers taking up permanent posts in special education?

Mr Sutherland r[illegible]ated that the Council was tr[illegible] [illegible]lp the situat[illegible] which [illegible] the primary and secondary categories. The Council's view was that children with special needs were likely to benefit most from teachers who had experience of normal classroom work.

He was supported by a mainstream primary teacher with experience in a school for the profoundly handicapped.

"Quite often," she said, "you are the only teacher there. The head will not necessarily be a teacher. And often when you believe a child is making progress it is because you forget what children in normal schools are doing."

Mr Fulton said inexperienced teachers going straight into special schools put the rest of the staff under a lot of pressure.

The original questioner said it was only recently that teachers had started working with profoundly handicapped children at all. "It is sad when you get good teachers and you have to lose them because of registration requirements," she said. "Instructors with no academic or profess[illegible]onal [illegible]

Teachers in Scotland are not paid by the State; they are employed and paid locally. Scotland is divided into twelve areas, called Regions, and the Regional Councils are currently the employers of teachers. For example, the very large Region to which Glasgow belongs is called Strathclyde, which employs primary school teachers, secondary school teachers and teachers in further education colleges. In accordance with current government policy, parental influence on education is growing. From 1990, if parents wish it, schools may opt out of local authority control, receiving funding direct from central government.

Employment

On achieving provisional registration with the G.T.C. a trained teacher applies to a Region, usually the one is his/her own home area, for a post. Each applicant will be interviewed and, on the basis of the interview and the college grade, a post may be offered. In almost every sector of teaching, posts have been difficult to obtain because of falling school rolls. The first post is likely to be a temporary one, lasting a few months or so, followed hopefully by another temporary appointment perhaps in another school. The lucky ones obtain something more permanent.

Temporary contracts give the employees few rights. Employment can cease at any time. Permanent posts are also seen as vulnerable in these times of falling rolls. Special arrangements for older staff to retire early have helped the situation somewhat. So far surplus teachers have been transferred to other schools and no-one has been declared redundant. This could happen in the future in which case redundancy payments would have to be made.

It has to be noted however, that these circumstances are changing, as we approach the 1990's and as the dip in the birthrate begins to affect the school leaver group. A shortage of young people may well lead to teacher shortage.

Probation

Taking up a post also means starting **probation,** which lasts two years in Scotland. Responsibility for overseeing the probationary period rests with the Headteacher of the particular school. It can be said that there are two main strands to probation. Firstly, throughout the two years the probationer should receive systematic help and guidance so that teaching skills can develop successfully from the base establishing during training. Headteachers and/or other senior staff supervise this assistance to probationers. Secondly, the probationer's progress must be monitored and assessed in accordance with guidelines which the G.T.C. issues to Headteachers. These guidelines highlight the importance of:

BEGINNING TEACHING
Professional development and probation in Scotland
A handbook for probationers and school staff
Edward G. Archer and Bryan T. Peck

a) competence in curricular areas
b) class organisation, management and control
c) conscientiousness
d) relationships with pupils and
e) relationships with colleagues.

At the end of one year of probation the Headteacher must submit a report to the G.T.C. using a standard report form. This is followed a year later by a second report, on which the Headteacher must recommend either full registration, extension of provisional registration or cancellation of registration.

Successful probationers who receive full registration can be said to have been awarded their permanent "licence to teach". No further assessment of performance is required by the G.T.C. but there are suggestions that periodic appraisal of some kind should be instituted to ensure that high professional standards are maintained. The government is very keen that this should happen, and the G.T.C. would like to be involved in it.

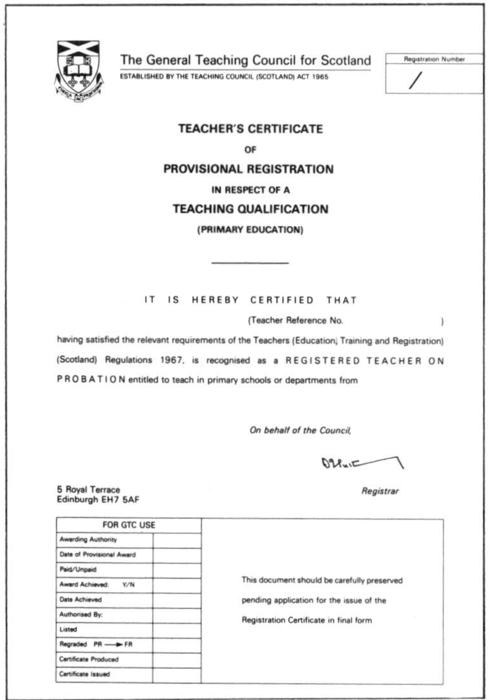

The General Teaching Council for Scotland

ESTABLISHED BY THE TEACHING COUNCIL (SCOTLAND) ACT 1965

Registration Number

/

TEACHER'S CERTIFICATE

OF

PROVISIONAL REGISTRATION

IN RESPECT OF A

TEACHING QUALIFICATION

(PRIMARY EDUCATION)

IT IS HEREBY CERTIFIED THAT

(Teacher Reference No.)

having satisfied the relevant requirements of the Teachers (Education, Training and Registration) (Scotland) Regulations 1967, is recognised as a REGISTERED TEACHER ON PROBATION entitled to teach in primary schools or departments from

On behalf of the Council,

Registrar

5 Royal Terrace
Edinburgh EH7 5AF

FOR GTC USE	
Awarding Authority	
Date of Provisional Award	
Paid/Unpaid	
Award Achieved: Y/N	
Date Achieved	
Authorised By:	
Listed	
Regraded PR ——► FR	
Certificate Produced	
Certificate Issued	

This document should be carefully preserved pending application for the issue of the Registration Certificate in final form

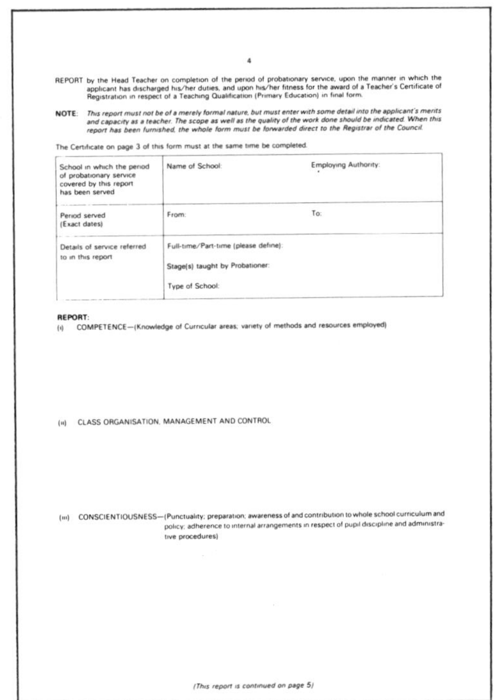

4

REPORT by the Head Teacher on completion of the period of probationary service, upon the manner in which the applicant has discharged his/her duties, and upon his/her fitness for the award of a Teacher's Certificate of Registration in respect of a Teaching Qualification (Primary Education) in final form.

NOTE: *This report must not be of a merely formal nature, but must enter with some detail into the applicant's merits and capacity as a teacher. The scope as well as the quality of the work done should be indicated. When this report has been furnished, the whole form must be forwarded direct to the Registrar of the Council.*

The Certificate on page 3 of this form must at the same time be completed.

School in which the period of probationary service covered by this report has been served	Name of School:	Employing Authority:
Period served (Exact dates)	From:	To:
Details of service referred to in this report	Full-time/Part-time (please define): Stage(s) taught by Probationer: Type of School:	

REPORT:

(i) COMPETENCE—(Knowledge of Curricular areas; variety of methods and resources employed)

(ii) CLASS ORGANISATION, MANAGEMENT AND CONTROL

(iii) CONSCIENTIOUSNESS—(Punctuality; preparation; awareness of and contribution to whole school curriculum and policy; adherence to internal arrangements in respect of pupil discipline and administrative procedures)

(This report is continued on page 5)

Career Development

Once a permanent post has been obtained, assuming a reasonably stable school population, a teacher can remain in the job for many years. Starting salaries are £10647 (April 1991), with yearly increments to a maximum of £17862. After 40 years teaching a teacher can retire with a lump sum and a full pension of about 50% of salary. There are several teachers' unions and these have an important part to play in negotiating salary increases.

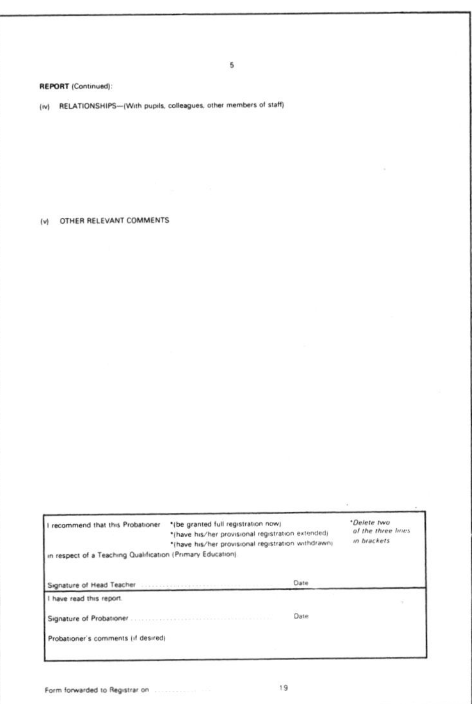

5

REPORT (Continued):

(iv) RELATIONSHIPS—(With pupils, colleagues, other members of staff)

(v) OTHER RELEVANT COMMENTS

I recommend that this Probationer *(be granted full registration now)
*(have his/her provisional registration extended)
*(have his/her provisional registration withdrawn)
in respect of a Teaching Qualification (Primary Education)

**Delete two of the three lines in brackets*

Signature of Head Teacher .... Date

I have read this report.

Signature of Probationer .... Date

Probationer's comments (if desired)

Form forwarded to Registrar on 19

However, a good number of teachers will not be content to remain on the basic scale; they will seek professional advancement in school. About 1 in 3 will obtain a promoted post, some climbing up the promotion ladder to a Headship (salaries increasing quite substantially at each step) and the Head[2] of a large secondary school can earn twice as much as an unpromoted teacher. There is a hierarchy of promoted posts and in larger schools there will be several of these. For example:-

Primary School (Roll 600)		**Secondary School (Roll 1100)**	
Headteacher	1	Headteacher	1
Depute Headteacher	1	Depute Headteacher	1
Assistant Headteacher	3	Assistant Headteacher	4
Senior Teacher	4	Principal Teacher	10
		Assistant Principal Teacher	6
		Senior Teacher	2

Each Regional Council has its own procedures for the selection and appointment of staff to promoted posts. There are special application forms for each level of promoted post. Vacancies are advertised and applicants send in completed forms. Successful experience is a key criterion and candidates will seek references from those who know their work well, e.g. Headteacher, or Head of Department. In times of job shortage, when application lists are long, being able to demonstrate special knowledge and outstanding performance is of crucial importance. The first requirement is to get onto a short-list of candidates which means being called for interview. The interview continues to be a major instrument of selection although questions are more likely to be "situational" nowadays: "What would you do to tackle this problem?" "How would you approach this issue?" etc.

As well as promotional opportunities within schools, there are avenues for advancement in other parts of the educational system viz aiming for:-

an educational Adviser's post
a lectureship in a College of Education
a post as H.M.Inspector of schools
an administrative job in the Regional (or divisional) education offices

Inservice Training

It is essential for professional advancement that teachers build upon initial training and probation in a variety of ways. This is possible in well managed schools where there will be a systematic policy covering the professional development of all staff. In good schools there may also be a staff-development committee and teachers delegated to take on specialist staff-development roles and responsibilities. A major objective would be to cater for both the needs of the school and the needs of individual members of staff.

Since teachers are now contractually required to devote time (a set number of hours annually) in school to staff development, there will be a programme of planned activities (School Focused Inservice Training: S.F.I.S.) to suit the needs of the school. During years of considerable curriculum innovation and structural change such programmes are vitally necessary. The Scottish Education Department and the Regional authorities are encouraging and supporting S.F.I.S. as much as possible and in a variety of ways.

There is also encouragement for attendance at longer courses in the evenings, at weekends and during vacations. These courses may be award-bearing, leading to certificates or diplomas or higher degrees. For the ambitious teacher it is important to acquire extra qualifications if promotion is to be obtained. Usually this would have to be done in one's own time and without financial support, although some Regions do finance attendance at selected courses.

Each Region has a team of specialist Advisers to support the process of innovation and change in schools and they organise courses in Teachers' Centres. The Colleges of Education also have a major part to play. As pre-service work in colleges has declined with falling intakes, so has inservice work increased. The Colleges have many short and longer courses on offer and college staff are also active in schools responding to requests and engaging in consultancy and development work. Some award-bearing courses are also provided by the Education Departments of the Universities. In addition the Open University in Scotland has made a very significant contribution to teacher education and to the professional development of teachers.

The diagram below is an example of how one Region views staff development in its primary schools.

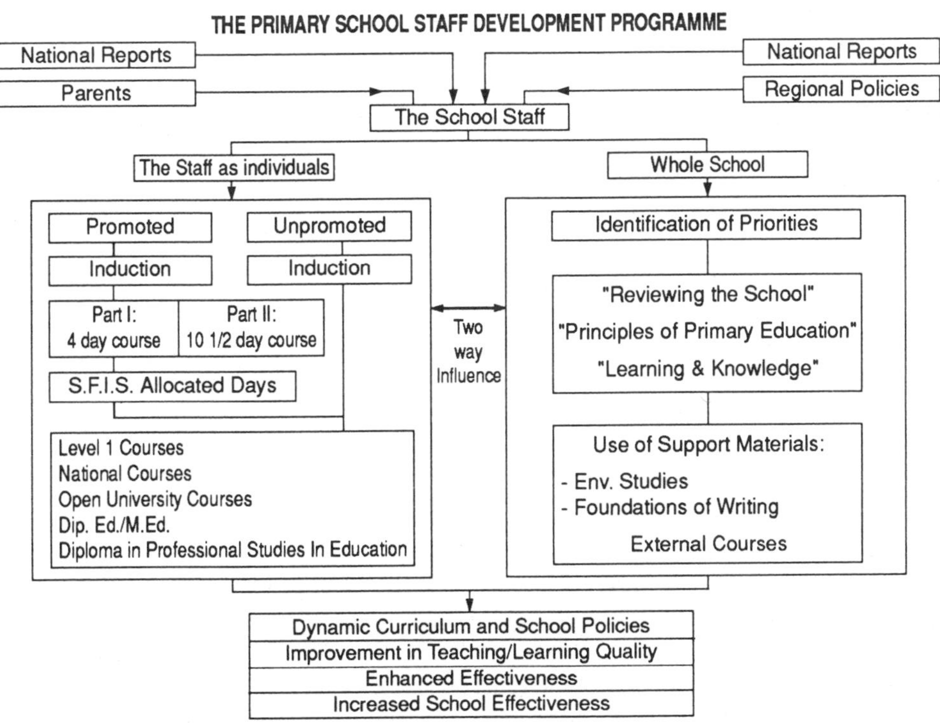

1 Some pupils now take modular courses before reaching the age of 16.

2 Government policy is aimed at attracting very good staff at senior level. There are moves to further increase rewards and incentives for management staff substantially through a separate system of salary negotiations.

A Primary School Teacher Moving from England to Scotland

Eric left school at the age of 17 and went into Chartered Surveying and then moved on to Life Assurance. However by the time he was 20 Eric became rather disillusioned with it all. He sought further career guidance and was steered into teaching.

As a prerequisite for entry into teacher training college in England, Eric had to improve his knowledge of French which was to be his main subject. He worked in Paris for 6 months prior to the commencement of the course.

This course at teacher training college was for 3 years leading to the Certificate in Education. His main subject was primary French (which was in vogue at the time); instead of a secondary subject Eric took a variety of courses suitable for Primary Education (Museum Studies, Physical Education and Games, Writing and Reading). It was also necessary to study basic courses in Mathematics and English.

Towards the end of this course Eric realised he wanted to aim for graduate status. The problem then was that he had already used up a full Local Authority grant and was unable to obtain further financial support. He was lucky, however, to receive a full grant from the Carnegie Trust, sufficient to pay the university fees, and he embarked on a 3 year course at a university in Scotland.

Halfway through the course he applied to the GTC in Edinburgh for teacher registration. He was informed that his English qualifications were not good enough to teach in Scotland! However he would be accepted for registration once he had finished the degree course.

While applying for teaching jobs Eric lived at home with his parents. He applied for jobs as far afield as North Scotland to the South West of England. At the second interview he was offered a job in a large primary school in the West Midlands. At first he lived in a shared flat, but he soon married and, with two incomes coming in, he and his new wife were able to buy a small house. At this school the Headteacher was filling in two sets of probationary forms, one set for the DES in England and one set for the GTC in Scotland. At the end of the first year of teaching Eric successfully completed his probationary period for England; however in Scotland a further year's experience was required. This was also completed and his Head sent the relevant forms off. During these two years very few people actually came to see Eric teach, but the Head and Deputy often gave advice. Especially useful were the schemes of work for each term and the weekly records which staff were obliged to keep.

During his second year of teaching Eric started to do extra school activities outside school hours, and by the end of his third year he was running the Swimming Club (the school had its own pool), and the Rugby Club. He was also organising ski trips abroad. For doing this he was rewarded with a new grade, that of a Scale 2 teacher, earning a higher salary. He was also attending many inservice courses on a wide variety of subjects including DES courses during holidays. His impressions were that DES courses were much more widely recognised than were local courses, and his promotion prospects should have been improved.

In fact promotion opportunities then slowed up. Eric started to look further afield especially Scotland. In the end, having spent five years at one school he took a sideways move and swapped positions with another teacher at a neighbouring school. Also at this time the family moved house to be nearer to work. By then there was a young family to bring up, so money was especially tight.

At his new school Eric taught upper primary classes, but he also did some infant work to broaden his experience. He then started to carefully formulate his career plan. He did not want to aim for the next grade of teaching, Scale 3, as there was a bottle neck of teachers on this grade looking for Deputy Headships in large primary schools. This was necessary if a salary increase was to be obtained. Instead he looked for a deputy head post at a small primary school, and he was fortunate to get one near home.

The workload was heavy at this school: he was full-time class teacher, organiser of field trips, football, rugby, cricket and swimming teams, member of the Governing body, member of Deputy Heads Committee. In addition, being the only male member of staff he was always asked to help with lifting, carrying, etc!

He had once been told, regarding promotion in a school, "in for at least 3 years and be on the move by 5 years". He started planning his next move after 2½ years there. Eric was also still looking towards Scotland; he did part of his training there and his wife came from Edinburgh, while he himself was half Scottish. He had also kept his name on the GTC register even though he had been teaching in England. At this time there were more teaching vacancies and promoted posts in Scotland, and he started to apply for posts north of the border. Ground work was vital to compete with Scottish teachers, this included: a visit to HMSO bookshops and Moray House College of Education, Edinburgh for current printed documents, a visit to a Scottish Primary School for current ideas on trends, a visit to the Scottish Education Department for information on School Boards and the new curriculum. Eric was eventually invited to an interview for the post of Depute Head in a large primary school. He made a pre-interview visit to the school thus giving the Head a chance to see him informally, as well as giving him a chance to see what he was letting himself in for! He was offered the job and accepted it.

Eric expects to be in his present post for about 3-5 years and, he hopes that his next move will be to a Headship. He continues to see it is important to attend nationally recognised courses. Without these courses, further promotion would be less likely.

A Primary School Headteacher

Despite pressure from school and home to delay a career decision I entered a college of education having completed 6th year at school. I wanted to be a primary teacher and rationalised that the primary orientated course would be of greater relevance than the alternative one year post graduate course.

My final teaching practice was at a city school in a renowned area of multiple deprivation, and on qualifying, after the briefest of interviews, I returned to teach a class of 40 seven year olds in August 1974.

During my first few years there was a very high turnover of staff, there still being many job opportunities. At one time there were 14 probationers out of a staff of 20. Adult illiteracy, extreme poverty, theft, violence, child abuse and prostitution were accepted facts of life. In this situation a good learning (and discipline) environment can only be achieved when the children feel you care, not because of an automatic respect for the 'professional' in their midst. Having said that, 'caring' in these circumstances is emotionally and physically draining. With hindsight, I sometimes believe that my full registration by the G.T.C. was awarded on the basis of survival skills!

My second year in teaching signalled the start of teachers' industrial action which resulted in the Houghton Report and the subsequent introduction of a contract of service. From a personal point of view the main effect of this dispute was the welcome reduction of class sizes to a maximum of 33 and a salary increase of £1,000 which in percentage terms was substantial.

The Region met course fees enabling me to return to College during the summer holidays of 1977. I tackled written assignments and practical school based assessments during the following session and returned to College again in the summer of 1978 in order to complete an additional qualification in early education.

By the summer of 1979 I was ready for a new challenge and decided to begin applying for Assistant Head Teacher posts. However a further round of education cuts were implemented and it was agreed that there would be no new Assistant Head Teacher appointments in the city (and this remained the case for the next 3-4 years).

Any euphoria following the Houghton settlement had long since disappeared, subsequent years had been marked by government imposed wage restraint. I now had a mortgage and was struggling financially - I vividly remember calculating that after all basic requirements were met I had the grand total of £11 per month left over for all frivolities e.g. social occasions and holidays. At this point in time there seemed only two possible alternatives, either to leave teaching or to transfer to a post abroad.

Knowing that I was feeling restless my headteacher drew my attention to a post in the islands. I applied, was interviewed, offered the post and in March 1980 moved to join the staff of a new school as Assistant Head Teacher. My financial situation was transformed overnight, I maintained my position on the seemingly never-ending salary scale, but received additional allowances as an Assistant Head Teacher (based on the size of school), an island allowance, a remoteness allowance and most unusual an allowance paid by the council to offset the salary difference between local authority and oil industry workers.

Attitudes in this school were very different to those I was accustomed to meeting previously. This was not a traditional island community, but was made up predominantly of 'south mothers' from all over the country who had taken the 'risk' of moving to the islands to be employed in the oil industry. A sizeable proportion were firemen, technicians and engineers, whilst others were employed in secretarial, cooking and cleaning jobs. All had high expectations and interest/involvement in school and community activities were the norm.

After four years I felt it was time to decide whether to remain in this comfortable situation, perhaps running the risk of becoming stale and somewhat complacent or seek a new challenge. I was also aware that very few promoted posts were being advertised publicly, many regions opting to advertise on an internal basis only. I took the plunge and applied for the post of Assistant Head Teacher in a school on the mainland. Following a successful interview I accepted the post and transferred there in March 1984. I came down to earth with a bump. Although my responsibility allowance as Assistant Head Teacher had doubled, the loss of the other island payments resulted in a considerable drop in salary. At this time house prices in the area were rising literally by thousands of pounds each month, housing assistance was not provided by the local authority and on a salary just over £9,000 per annum it was a nightmare trying to find a mortgage high enough for reasonable accommodation.

Nothing in my previous experience had prepared me for the demands of the new job. There were approximately 300 children in the open plan infant department, yet I had a full time teaching responsibility. Without any induction phase I was expected to take responsibility for the infant enrolment and the annual requisition. The ensuing term was undoubtedly the most stressful I have ever experienced. I was at school by 8 a.m., rarely left before 7 p.m., and still found I had work to do at home. This extra effort paid dividends and I learnt new management skills as I mastered the intricacies of the new post.

As I was in a stable work situation and recognising that I was unlikely to obtain further promotion for a number of years (I was 32 and most new headteacher appointees were in their early 40's). I applied, and was funded by the local authority, to commence the Open University Advanced Diploma in Educational Management in 1987.

At this time several headteacher posts became available in the area and to indicate my interest, rather than anticipating success, I applied for the post at a Community Primary School. I was placed on a short leet with two men and three women and following interview was appointed in April 1987.

Reflecting on my steady career advancement it seems clear that gender has not proved a particular handicap (though possibly this would become a factor if I sought further promotion); rather, I believe personal mobility has been of vital importance. I continue to gain valuable experience in a managerial post and at the same time I am adding to my academic qualifications. In due course I shall look for further career advancement.

An Assistant Headteacher of a Primary School

Having studied History at university like many others in the Arts faculty I was quite unsure as to where my future lay at the end of my four years. At the back of my mind, however, there had always been a vague notion of "working with children" - a notion which came to the fore around the time of my final year. Importantly, the impression and influence which a few teachers had had on me throughout my education never fully left me and having done well and enjoyed studying History I decided to pull all this together and apply to various teacher-training colleges with the idea of teaching History. The truth, however, is that I rather stumbled a bit towards teaching rather than consciously deciding that it was the only life for me!

Unsuccessful in my applications - due to cut-backs in History in-take - my entry into teaching was due to tremendous good luck. A friend who had started work as a primary teacher in an English-speaking school in Madrid found that the school had a vacancy for an English-speaking teacher of History. Term had already begun and so desperate were they, that they telephoned and offered me the job immediately.

I spent two very happy (and at times very trying years there teaching History to upper middle-class Spanish children whose parents had decided that their off-spring ought to learn English by speaking it from the age of 4. I was the sole History teacher taking classes from age 11 to 17, taking some to O'Level and one to A'Level . Being plunged in at the deep end has undoubtedly affected my whole attitude to teaching and the way I tackle the job itself. Children, of course, make few allowances for a teacher's background or training and as such I realised from day one that it was going to be a case of "sink or swim". Similarly I had to "train myself" as I went along if I was to be in any way satisfied and if the children were to receive the education due to them. Though I was semi-oblivious to it then, the management of the school was chaotic and the help given to me negligible.

Two points, finally, are worth stressing. Firstly, the help of colleagues was tremendous; one in particular - the "best" teacher I have ever seen - was a great help and inspiration. Secondly, my answer to the difficulties I faced was to fall back on the methods which I had encountered as a pupil and as a student i.e. "chalk and talk". Hardly ideal, but it got me and the pupils through - at least until my eyes were opened to better things.

Perhaps the most important consequence of my two years in Madrid was a growing sense of there being more to education than the subject which I had chosen to study, that the children themselves were far more important than the subject being taught and that their development involved far more than assiduously prepared and carefully delivered packages of knowledge. Simultaneously, the more I heard my wife talking about her experiences as a newly-qualified primary teacher, the more I began to think that perhaps primary teaching was an option I might prefer. Thus around February 1984 I applied for, and was accepted to do, the Post-Graduate Certificate in Education at St Andrew's College, Bearsden over the year 1984/85.

Teacher training college for me was partly exciting and partly numbing. Based on three terms - theory followed by teaching practice each term - I quickly realised the more I was looking for. Working with 6/7 year olds in Livingston, I saw clearly that ***relationship*** *was vital and that this was what had been missing to some extent in my secondary experience. I was lucky that two of my three class teachers whom I worked closely with were tremendous professionals from whom I learned* ***enormous*** *amounts which I use to this day.*

Being very frank, I must state that the quality of my in-college training was, at least, ***very*** *mixed and at times little short of appalling. Purely coincidentally my own subject History, e.g. was taught superbly. The lecturer obviously had thought things through thoroughly, was able to explain the theory of her ideas, relate them clearly to* ***how*** *children learn, yet never forgot their* ***practical*** *application to the classroom (and the problems which would probably subvert all the preparations which trainee-teachers would put in).*

The quality of the teaching in other areas was little short of disastrous. Luckily, from a selfish point of view, I had learned at least something about teaching in Madrid. How others who did not have this to fall back on managed to survive is a mystery. Why there should be such a differential in standards is something I'm not quite sure of. My ***impression*** *then, (and even yet) was that the management of the college seemed to lack a sense of purpose, of goal and, of vision. Furthermore, the feeling amongst many students was that some of the lecturers did not give the post-graduate course of their best. However, I am not in a position to explain exactly why all this should be.*

Having done well at college, I was lucky enough to get a post in Lothian where I was living at the time, in a small, RC school. I was to spend four happy years there and it was in this school that I can honestly say that I really learned about teaching and education. The reason for this undoubtedly was the management abilities of the Head. Able, experienced and confident, she knew her school, children and parents, as well as teachers, intimately. Aware of everyone's needs, she managed to establish an ethos and culture in the school which made everyone feel needed and confident. At the same time, a very determined individual, she knew what she wanted and how to get it without getting people's backs up. Spending my probationary period here was the best thing that could have happened to me. A healthy balance of "standards" and (child-centredness) the school (and the careful attention of the Head in particular) afforded me the chance to learn, to err, to experiment and get always to keep well within the clearly established, yet invisible boundaries. As I move in to management myself now, my every move is tested against how it would have been done in that school - praise indeed!

This first post was, initially, on a temporary contract and as such meant that I was paid only for hours actually worked. While the hourly rate offered was reasonable, it did mean that I was not paid for holidays - be it occasional, Christmas and even Summer. I found this verydifficult and only the fact that my wife worked for some of this time made it acceptable.

Life, from the start, has always involved bringing work home. At first, this could mean two-three hours per might and at weekends too; corrections, administration, preparations etc. As experience grows, you tend to find ways round some of this but the general concept continues. Social life tends to go, and again, a spouse who is a teacher too at least offers someone who understands the difficulties. Finally, a pervading sense of tiredness tends to come over me - usually over Thursday/Friday. Friends who work longer contractual hours occasionally scoff, yet I'm sure this is due to the sapping, intense nature of teaching and only fellow-teachers know the feeling of exhaustion which comes over you at the end of term.

While I never set out with the idea of getting promotion quickly, I did decide from an early date that if teaching was to be my chosen career I was going to work hard at it, learn my trade, and be in a position to go for promotion when I felt that I was ready to do so. My Head in my first school (I transferred voluntarily to a bigger school in August 1989) was very interested in staff career development and clearly decided that the way ahead for me was to get a good basic grounding in all areas of primary school life. As such, my four years there consisted of four different stages - (i).P.7: 11/12 yr olds. (ii) P5/6: 9/10 yr olds. (iii).P3/4: 7/8 yr olds. (iv).P.1/2: 5/6 yr olds.

I had (as was commented on at a later interview) the almost unique experience of covering all stages of the primary school in my first four years of primary teaching. While I don't know ***exactly*** *the significance of it for others, I do feel that the fact that I spent a year with* *first infants has been something, again, which is almost unique amongst males and which raised eye-brows and interest at the above-mentioned interview. For me personally, I learned in incredible amount in that year, a year which has made me a far more rounded teacher. Again, I thank the vision of my former Head.*

Finally, promotion came my way in June of this year when I started my present post as Assistant Head Teacher in a larger primary school - my remit gives me responsibility for the upper primary stages, classes P.4-P.7. How this will go in the future I cannot say, but study for a post-graduate degree in Education through the Open University - with particular emphasis on management/organisational issues - has already helped me by offering frameworks within which I can try to make sense of the many new duties, ideas and issues which face me daily in this new, challenging position.

A Teacher of Home Economics

Heather is a teacher of Home Economics. After leaving school at the age of 17 she attended a specialist college in Glasgow where she took a three year Diploma Course in Home Economics. On completing this course she trained to be a secondary school teacher. This meant taking a one year post graduate training course in a College of Education alongside others with a variety of specialisms.

Once qualified Heather was registered provisionally with the General Teaching Council for Scotland, and she was able to look for a teaching post. She made applications to various local authorities. Although she lived at home with her parents on the outskirts of Glasgow she was willing to take a post wherever there was a vacancy. After an interview she was offered and took her first job in a medium sized secondary school in a rural town some seventy miles north of Glasgow. Heather was delighted at this prospect.

The two year probationary period went well. She taught a range of classes in Food & Nutrition and Fashion & Fabrics, and she had an Ordinary Grade certificate class from the start. Thus, by the time she was finally registered with the G.T.C. as a teacher of Home Economics she had had broad experience of teaching and she was enthusiastic about her work.

During subsequent years, however, Heather's enthusiasm waned. The industrial action taken by teachers over pay and conditions of service soured the situation. Strike action by teachers had a bad effect on pupil-teacher relationships. Pupils became resentful of authority. Confrontation was too often the order of the day. Pupil's attitude to work also suffered. They became lazier and more apathetic and often would not do homework. Heather's morale slumped and she even considered giving up teaching.

Fortunately a new aspect of work attracted her. She became interested in Guidance matters. In Scottish schools this means providing programmes under three headings: Curricular Guidance, Vocational Guidance and Personal Guidance. A vacancy arose in Heather's school for a promoted post, that of Assistant Principal Teacher (Guidance). Initially this was offered to her on a temporary basis but some eight months later the post became a permanent one. After seven years in teaching Heather is seeing her career develop and she has a new enthusiasm for the work.

Financially the early years as a teacher were a struggle. Accommodation was not easy to find nor was it cheap. She shared an unfurnished house with two other teachers and all spare cash went on making this comfortable. Heather took driving lessons and she took a bank loan which enabled her to buy a second hand car. Unfortunately this was not a good buy and repair bills were high. After five years in teaching she decided to look for accommodation of her own and she bought an apartment in a village a few miles from the school. Two more years of penury followed. Now for the first time, with this promoted post and over £700 in her hand each month, Heather feels that she has some money to spend.

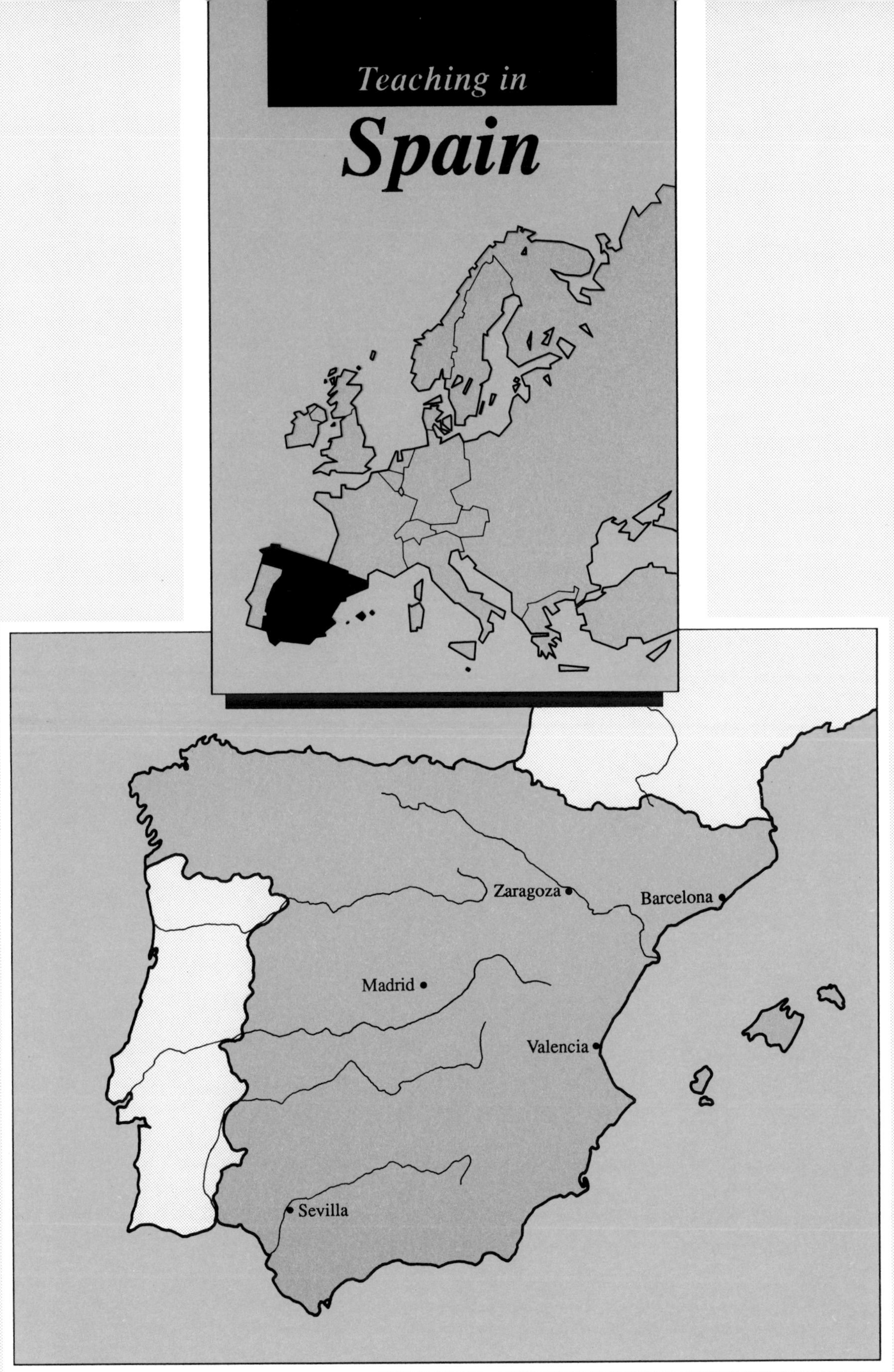
Teaching in
Spain
Zaragoza
Barcelona
Madrid
Valencia
Sevilla

TEACHING IN SPAIN

In recent decades, especially since the death of Franco, Spanish society has undergone a number of very significant changes, all of them affecting education. Politically the main development, of course, has been the remarkable transition to democracy, supported by a popular constitutional monarchy. Part of this process has been the loosening of a strong tradition of central control and administration, albeit underpinned by a socialist ideology. At one extreme the result has been the autonomy which the various regions have obtained (*Comunidades Autónomas*); at the other, is the devolution of some decision-making to the school and the community.

Similarly, there have been big economic changes characterised by rapid industrialisation and the flight from the countryside to the cities. With the great rise in the standard of living, people's expectations have risen. Illiteracy has virtually disappeared and more than 80% of parents want a university education for their children.

Social and educational tensions have built up during these changes. New values and attitudes have emerged. The dominance of the Church has been removed and the role of the family has declined. At the same time, the status of women has improved considerably, as they have joined the labour force and as they have begun to enjoy the new freedoms. However, what has occurred is not another extreme swing of the pendulum. There is a new equilibrium and a new consensus, enshrined in the Constitution of 1978. Since 1986 a truly democratic Spain has been playing its full part as a member of the European Community.

As regards education, the broad principles are determined centrally. These are enshrined in the Constitution of 1978 and in laws and statutes passed by the Spanish Parliament in Madrid, notably in the 1985 Organic Law on the Right to Education. Through these laws the State regulates both investment in education and the overall structure of the system. The state also determines minimum educational standards and it oversees inspection of the system.

However, the Statutes of Autonomy transfer varying amounts of authority and responsibility to the Autonomous Communities. These have their own elected assemblies and their own education department (for example, the *Generalitat de Catalunya* and its *Departament d'Ensenyament*). The Autonomous Communities may have many powers relating to educational matters, including responsibility for buildings, personnel, examinations, teacher training, research, and so on. A particular concern may be the teaching of a regional language alongside Castilian.

Some 75% of schools in Spain are state schools. About 10% belong to the Church and a further 14% are in the hands of private proprietors. The private schools are accommodated within the system and they may receive state funding.

Schooling

As the 1990's run their course the system of schooling in Spain is to undergo further considerable change. Diagram 1 shows the position as it has been. Pre-school education is likely to remain largely unaltered. Provision for the 2 to 5 year olds is optional and free in the public sector, some classes being located in primary schools. More than 90% of Spanish 4 and 5 year olds enjoy the benefits of a nursery school (*escuela de párvulos*).

Currently, compulsory education lasts for 8 years from the ages of 6 to 14 years, now to be extended to 16. The three cycles of basic education (*Educación General Básica*: EGB) have been delivered through seven lines of activity (*ramas de actividad)* in a 25 hour week. Pupils advanced from one cycle to the next only when particular learning outcomes had been achieved. Overall success results in the certificate of *Graduado Escolar* (School Graduate), giving access to secondary education. Those pupils who do not reach the required standards gain the *Certificado de Escolaridad* (School Certificate), leading to the lower level courses in the vocational Training Institutions. This *doble certificación* at the end of EGB has come to be seen as socially divisive and undesirable.

What follows is a dual system of secondary education, some 70% moving into the academic stream and into Integrated Secondary Education (*Bachillerato Unificado Polivalente*), followed by a one-year university orientation course (*Curso de Orientación Universitaria*: COU). The less able have the opportunity to enrol in level 1 of Vocational Training (*Formación Profesional*) courses leading to the title of Assistant Technician (*Técnico Auxiliar*).

Further vocational training is available in the higher levels of *formación professional* and some movement between the academic and vocational streams is possible. On the academic side, tertiary education follows three cycles. The first, leading to a diploma (*diplomado universitario*) in the universities and in the *escuelas universitarias*. The second cycle leads to graduate status (*licenciado o ingeniero*) while the third leads to a doctorate (*doctorado*).

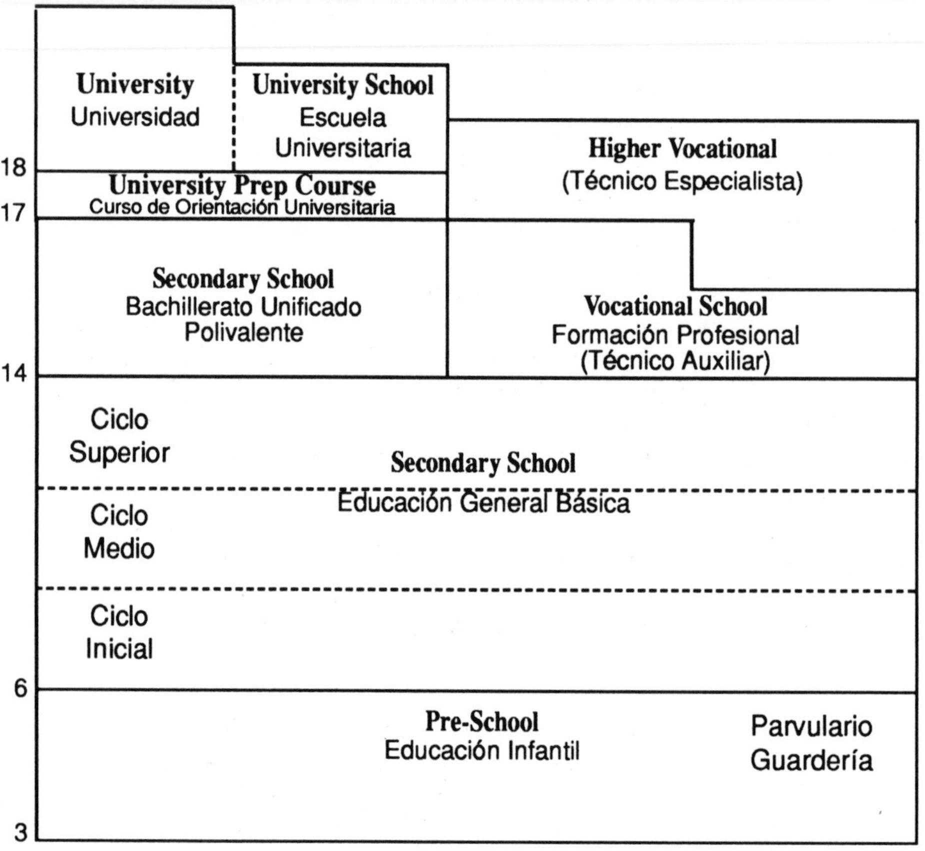

What are the most recent changes and why are they being made?
Among the main reasons given are the following:

1. The system is seen to be under-performing, with a pupil failure rate of 40% - the *fracaso escolar* problem.
2. The system is élitest and socially divisive, the more fortunate taking the high-prestige BUP/COU courses, the rest (apart from the 10% who leave school at 14) following the vocational training route.
3. COU is not a successful course.
4. Many teachers in post are not up to the job; they badly need inservice training. Nor are the pre-service training courses up to standard: they are much too academic and not much concerned with classroom performance.

As Diagram 2 indicates, the new reforms envisage the extension of compulsory schooling to age 16 years, with comprehensive secondary education for all (*Educación Secundaria Obligatoria*). Indeed, the aim is to produce an integrated and more coherent system. Pupils will follow the same basic curriculum but teachers will have the opportunity to programme the tasks to suit the needs of individuals and classes. Pupil choice of options will be offered increasingly to age 16 years and beyond compulsory education into the upper secondary school.

Vocational education will form part of the secondary school curriculum for all and it will be available through a network of modules catering for a range of career needs and specialisms . Aesthetic education will also be given a proper place in an integrated curriculum. The teaching of Modern Languages will start at the age of 8 years instead of 11 years. This new emphasis on Modern Languages and on Information Technology recognises Spain's needs as a member of a rapidly developing European Community.

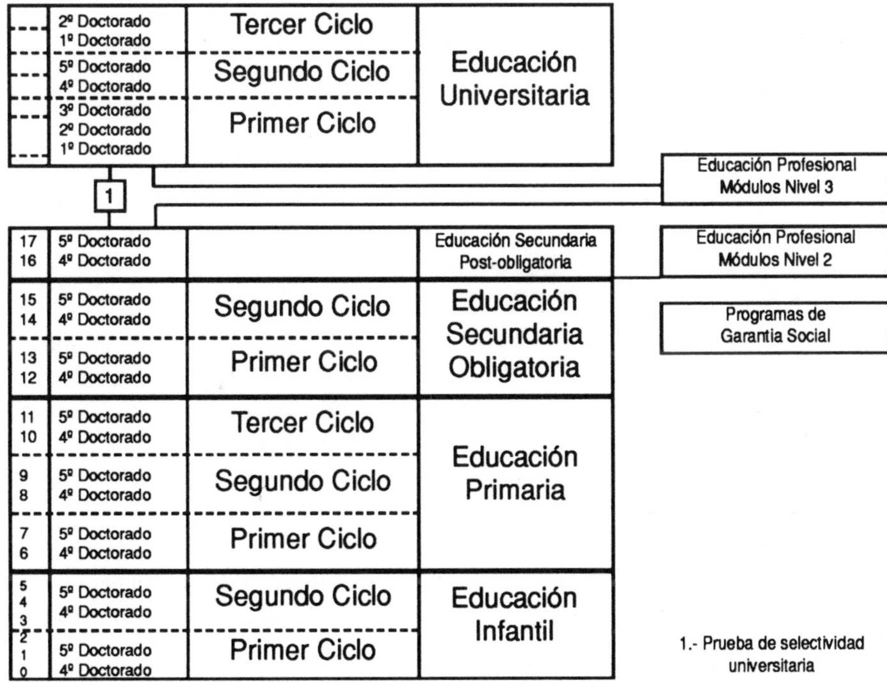

Teacher Training

Primary and secondary school teachers in Spain, as in other countries, have been far apart in training, qualifications and status. Changes begun in the 1970's and continued through the new reforms for the 1990's should produce a more unified profession.

Since 1972 the entry into primary school initial training has been through COU, with an academic content including Spanish and English, plus a group of either Arts or Science Subjects. In addition, an entrance examination is being introduced and the official view is that the procedures should be further tightened in order to improve teacher quality.

In 1975 the former *Escuelas Normales* were incorporated into the university sector as *Escuelas Universitarias de Formación del Professorado de EGB*. Staff in the EUs are traditionally university graduates with experience as secondary teachers. Entry qualifications for EU are low and students often go there as a second choice. On entering EU at age 18 years, primary school teacher trainees take a three-year course consisting of General Pedagogy and a specialist option from areas such as the Social Subjects, Modern Languages, Mathematics and Science, Pre-School Education and Special Education.

All teachers who teach the stages beyond EGB must be university graduates (*licenciados*) i.e. teachers in secondary schools (*institutos*, where BUP is taught), teachers of university preparatory courses (COU) and teachers of vocational education (*Formación Profesional*). University courses last 5 years. They have not been geared to the practicalities of teaching, the emphasis being on academic excellence. Professional training, as far as it goes, is provided in a course of about 6 months duration leading to the *Certificado de Aptitud Pedagógica*. This is taken either concurrently or consecutively within the university, in an Institute of Education. There is general dissatisfaction with the training of all categories of teacher and major reforms are being implemented during the early 1990's.

Substantially these planned changes in teacher education reflect the overall reform of the system of schooling as already mentioned. The idea of secondary education for all and the new place for vocational education both suggest that new kinds of teachers are needed. Changes in curriculum and methodology along with an emphasis on meeting individual pupil needs, will also affect teaching roles and classroom skills. The traditional preoccupation with academic excellence is no longer seen as appropriate.

It is pertinent to mention the government Schools of Languages (*Escuelas Oficiales de Idiomas*) which have been established in most regional capitals and in other centres. The many thousands of students in EOIs have a wide age range. The courses aim at high standards in an increasing number of languages, catering for interpreters, teachers etc. These courses have a high reputation nationally and teachers who have taken a full 5-year course can demonstrate a very high level of proficiency, equipping them to teach advanced courses. EOIs represent an important, alternative model for teacher training.

Entering Teaching

Obtaining a post has become increasingly difficult. In 1988 education graduates accounted for almost one-third of graduate unemployment. With a declining school population, matters are not likely to improve.

Good numbers of teachers have only temporary contracts. to acquire tenure (*agregado*) and have a permanent appointment it is necessary to pass a competitive and predominantly academic examination - the *Oposiciones*. This examination, before *el tribunal* has both written and oral elements. Candidates prepare and submit work relating to chosen themes, such as might form the basis for a sequence of lessions. The selection and use of appropriate materials and teaching methods require to be explained and defended before the panel.

The chance to choose a post in a preferred location is directly related to the order in which the names appear on the pass list. Those with higher gradings have first choice.

When obtained the first appointment is provisional, and a trial period of six months follows. If the Headteacher or Head of Department finds that the probationer is not suited to teaching, the examination pass is declared *inválido* and the Ministry of Education will not admit him/her. This rarely happens but there have been cases.

Career Development

There are few opportunities for career development. Spanish schools have few promoted posts. A teacher may aspire to become Headteacher, Deputy Headteacher, Director of Studies, or Secretary. None of these carries a great deal of status nor much extra pay. They are open to all with tenure and a few years relevant experience. Appointment is for a limited period only and it is the result of an election held by the School Council (*Consejo Escolar*). This body is composed of parents, teachers, senior pupils and a representative of the local authority. A prospective Headteacher requires an absolute majority before his/her name can go forward to the local office of the Ministry for confirmation of appointment. The Headteacher then forms his/her management team from teacher members of the Council. Every two years elections are held again and the Head may or may not continue in office.

Inservice Education

The government began to see inservice training as a priority even before initial training came under the spotlight. The teaching profession concurs. Now the demands of a newly reformed educational system are considerable, especially for those teachers who were inadequately trained in the first place. Many have been under stress - notably those in older, urban schools - "In this profession disaster is always just around the corner", as one commentator put it.

Official thinking is in fact much concerned about teacher morale and professional satisfaction. It is seen as important that teachers should have a sense of belonging to '*la comunidad educativa*' and that they should be fully involved in change and development. For these reasons the creation of Teachers' Centres (*Centros de Profesores, CEPS*) is central to the strategy, Government has established a network of these centres, serving most areas of Spain. CEPs are usually located in well-appointed buildings provided by the Ministry. They are places for teachers and others to go to for educational and social reasons. There are formal courses and workshops relating to curriculum development, to Information Technology (where there is now a major thrust), to Special Educational Needs and so on. Each separate sector or subject may generate its own working group to produce materials and to share experience.

Clearly, the government sees CEPs as having a continuing and vital role to play. Links between CEPs and the schools are to be strengthened. More courses are to be on offer and these must be staffed by sufficient numbers of the best people - the *profesores de profesores*. Furthermore, the universities will have to play their part in the '*renovación de los profesores*'. Thus, it no longer seems reasonable to keep initial training and inservice provision apart. Strong links between the university training departments and secondary schools are to be forged. Therefore, all the various interests are seen as contributing to a national network providing for both initial training and the further professional development of teachers.

It should be added that Spanish teachers may apply for leave of absence (*salidas temporales*). After three years as *agregado*, a teacher may take time (from 2 to 10 years) off without pay for whatever reason. Special reasons for taking a year off would include working in another institution at home or abroad. Five years as a tenured teacher opens the door to an application for a year of study-leave with 80% pay. These opportunities could clearly be of great significance to a professional wishing to remain fresh and alert to new ideas and practice.

A Primary School Teacher

Fernanda es maestra de Primera Enseñanza. Nacida de familia humilde en un pueblo de España en el año 50, pudo ir al Instituto porque sacó becas de estudio, comedor y transporte.

De todas formas las becas no cubrían los gastos de estudio, por lo que a los quince años se tuvo que poner a trabajar. A la vez que trabajaba, estudió por su cuenta sin maestros ni dirección, pues no disponia de medios económicos para sufragarlo, y utilizó las vacaciones laborales para ir a la ciudad a examinarse libre.

La familia se trasladó a la ciudad. La enseñanza era algo que siempre le había atraído, y fué a la Normal a preguntar si era posible cursar estudios nocturnos. Era posible por última vez, y pertenence a la última promoción nocturna del plan 67.

Todos los alumnos de esta clase trabajaban y estudiaban, por lo que la motivación intrínseca era grande y el ambiente muy bueno.

Los estudios consistieron en tres años de teoría, en los que se estudió Didáctica de las diferentes asignaturas, más Sicologiá, Pedagogiá, Historia y Filosofiá de la Educación. El cuarto año fue entero de prácticas.

Las prácticas las hizo en la Aneja de la Normal. El primer trimestre fue de observación de todas los cursos de E.G.B. El segundo trimestre fue un periódo de observación de un curso concreto, donde se podía cuestionar cualquier cosa que surgiera. El tercer trimestre fue de co-responsabilidad, con preparación, programación y realización de todas las clases bajo la supervisión del profesor.

Apenas terminada la carrera tuvo la oportunidad de ir a California, U.S.A., y aunque no tenia ni idea de inglés, (la lengua estudiada habia sido el francés) no lo pensó dos veces y allá se fué.

El primer año lo pasó estudiando inglés. El segundo año trabajó en escuelas en que había alumnos bilingües e inició en la Universidad un Diploma que empezaba entonces, para llegar a ser profesor de una segunda lengua.

Tuvo que regresar a España. Se presentó a oposiciones. Mientras estaba de exámenes en España le llega aprobada una beca del Estado de California para realizar este curso en la Universidad. Aprueba las oposiciones. El Gobierno Español no le concede licencia de estudios sin sueldo que solicitó para poder realizar el curso en la Universidad. Decide quedarse en España y no perder la oposición.

Empieza, pues, la vida profesional esperada, con plenas responsabiliades. Durante los primeros años de ingreso en el cuerpo de profesores de E.G.B., no se tiene un puesto fijo, se está provisional.

Ella tenía la idea muy clara de que queriá conocer todo el proceso de aprendizaje, desde preescolar hasta el Graduado, y para ello fue eligiendo las escuelas en las que había vacantes en aquellos cursos en que estaba interesada. De esta manera fué pasando por todos los cursos de E.G.B., y cada año, bajo su presupuesto y en horas extra-escolares, se matriculó y estudió aquellos aspectos particulares que corresponden a cada curso en concreto, con la ventaja de que siempre pudo poner en práctica lo que se estudiaba.

Cuando le dieron la escuela definitiva, fué en la escuela que ella habiá elegido por conocer al equipo de profesores del que sabía sus inquietudes profesionales. Se organizó un grupo de trabajo, sin ayuda de ningún tipo. El primer año centró su actividad en la orientación escolar y pautas de seguimiento de estudio. Al año siguiente se organizó un seminario con el objetivo de encontrar una metodologiá, que con matizaciones, todo el equipo de profesores estuviera de acuerdo; y su aplicación en las diferentes asignaturas. Al curso siguiente se aplicó la metodología, y por primera vez, el Ministerio ofrece ayuda económica.

Afortunadamente para el país, España, hoy en día las cosas han cambiado mucho y existen muchas mas facilidades en el campo del estudio. No así en el campo de las motivaciones para los enseñantes. Los maestros necesitan motivaciones profesionales aparte de las económicas (que continúan siendo insuficientes) para desempeñar con dignidad y profesionalidad su trabajo. Los maestros han de motivar a los alumnos, ciudadanos del futuro, pero, ¿quién y cómo motiva a los maestros?

Fernanda is a primary school teacher coming from a humble background. She was born in a Spanish village in 1950. Because of a grant towards fees, meals and transport some schooling was possible in the Instituto.

However, the grants in no way covered the costs and when she was 15 years old Fernanda had to take a job. While working she studied on her own without teachers and with no guidance because she had no means of paying for them. She took advantage of any holidays from work to go to town to study.

The family moved to live in town. Teaching had always been attractive to her and she went to the primary teachers' training college to enquire about taking a course in the evening. Eventually this was possible and she joined what was the last evening course, in 1967.

Everyone in the class worked hard and studied well; motivation was strong and the atmosphere was very good.

The course was theoretical for three years and it included didactics of the various curriculum areas, psychology, teaching methodology, and the history and philosophy of education. The fourth year was devoted wholly to practical experience. Practical took place in the college annexe. The first term was taken up by observation of all the EGB courses. The second term was spent observing a particular course, with an opportunity to discuss issues arising. Term three meant some responsibility for a class, including lesson planning, preparation and teaching, under the supervision of the teacher.

As soon as the course was successfully completed Fernanda had the chance to go to California in the USA and, although knowing no English (the language she had studied was French), she never thought twice about it and away she went.

The first year was spent studying English. During the second year she worked in schools where the pupils were bi-lingual. At that time the University was launching a Diploma course for those wanting to be recognised as second language teachers.

Fernanda had to return to Spain. She enrolled for Oposiciones. While preparing for examinations in Spain, she heard, that she had been awarded a grant by the State of California to take the Diploma course in the University. The Spanish government would not allow her leave of absence without pay and rather than give up the chance to take Oposiciones she decided to remain in Spain.

Thus, she began her hoped-for professional career, with full responsibilities. During the early years as a teacher of EGB she did not hold a permanent post, only temporary ones.

She had a clear idea that she should be familiar with the whole curriculum from pre-school to upper school. For that reason she chose schools where there were vacancies to teach the courses in which she was interested. As a consequence she gained experience of all the EGB curricula and every year, at her own expense and in her own time, she took courses to upgrade her own knowledge of each particular subject area. Therefore, she was always able to use the knowledge that she had obtained.

When she was given a permanent post it was in a school which she chose because she understood the staff's professional anxieties there. She organised a working party without any help whatsoever. The first year focussed on pupil orientation and on curriculum guidelines. In the second year she organised a seminar aimed at finding a methodology which, with some variations, all members of staff would accept. This approach to methodology was applied to all areas of the curriculum. The following year she applied the methodology and for the first time the Ministry offered her financial assistance.

Fortunately for Spain, much has changed and today there are many more opportunities for study and development. The same is not true for the motivation of teachers. School teachers need professional motivation apart from economic incentives (which continue to be insufficient) if they are to perform their duties with dignity and with professionalism. School teachers must motivate the pupils, citizens of the future. Who is it who motivates the teachers and how?

A Teacher of Basic Education

Sofía es profesora de E.G.B. Su vocación, quizá debida al ambiente familiar, con abuelos y hermanos dedicados a la enseñanza si no temprano fue decidida al terminar el "Bachillerato Elemental". Atràs quedaban 4 anõs de enseñanza primaria y otros cuatro del bachiller y aún por estudiar, 2 anõs de bachiller superior, una reválida o examen general de los 6 cursos y finalmente el C.O.U. (Curso de Orientación Universitaria). Tomó la opción en el primer curso del bachillerato superior de estudiar ciencias: química, matemáticas, física en lugar de letras: latin, griego y sin embargo la atracción del mundo del arte y de la historia eran grandes por lo que en C.O.U. eligiendo como asignatures optativas matemáticas, historia, literatura, intentó combinear un poco todo. Tras superar las pruebas de acceso a la Universidad (aunque el examen no era obligatório para el ingreso en la Escuela Universitaria del Profesorado de E.G. B.) sus conocimientos matemáticos y linguísticos le serían de gran ayuda pues el espectro de asignaturas de la carrera era muy diverso. El primer fue año teórico y básico, el segundo en el que ya había especializacíon (en su caso lenguas española e inglesa) comenzaban también las prácticas, realizadas una vez por semana en la "escuela aneja" al centro de estudios. Durante el tercer año en el que eligió como optativa francés las prácticas duraban 3 meses: un informe del profesor que las impartía más un examen final decidían la califacación. Al terminar sus estudios le comunicaron que junto a otros compañeros la "Escuela" la propondría para una de las "plazas de acceso directo" es decir, obtendría trabajo en una escuela estatal sin necesidad de realizar las temidas "oposiciones". El premio ANPE (Asociacíon Nacional del Profesorado

Estatal) fin de carrera le garantizaba que sería la primera en pedir escuela. Durante el año posterior a sus estudios y entre tanto no llegara su nombramiento oficial trabajó en una escuela privada; corría el año 1979 y tenía 21 años. En octubre de 1980 llegó su primera escuela oficial y tras ella, en un itinerante viaje que le hizo recorrer no menos de 6 escuelas diferentes (rurales y urbanas) gran número de experiencias en las substituciones a distintos profesores de todos los niveles.

La consciencia del desconocimiento real de la lengua inglesa le hizo pedir un puesto como asistante de lengua española en Escocia. Allí, en Glasgow, (vivió) durante un curso escolar, asistiendo además a clases de inglés durante dos horas y media cada tarde.

Un año más tarde comenzaba, de verdad, su carrera como profesora de inglés en un centro de E.G.B. en Espanã. Sabiendo que su titulación le permitía ser profesora de francés pero considerándose no capacitada para impartir esta asignatura en la práctica pidió un puesto como profesora asistante de lengua española en Francia. Su puesto en Burdeos fue extraordinariamente fructífero pues su misión primordial era compartir experiencias teóricas y prácticas con un grupo de profesores de español, debido a ello su visión de las didáctica del idioma cambió y se enriqueció. Un curso especializado en historia del arte y literatura contemporáneas franceses en la Universidad de Bordeaux III en Talence le daba confianza para impartir la asignatura de lengua francesa.

De regreso en Espanã (1984), 26 años de edad, se integró en un grupo de profesores que en el CEP compartía sus experiencias en el aula y fue propuesta para junto con otra compañera seguir un cursillo como "Formadora de Profesores".

Se le planteaba sin embargo una disjuntiva: seguir su carrera profesional en España o aceptar un trabajo, también como profesora, en Yakaita (Indonesia), independiente del Ministerio de Educación español. Se decidió por esta última opinion y desde enero de 1986 se encuentra en situación de excedencia.

Sofía is a teacher in the basic school. Her career, perhaps because of family influences, with grandparents and brothers dedicated to teaching, if not decided at an early stage, was certainly clear on finishing the elementary course. She completed four years of primary education, another four years for the certificate, two years for the higher certificate, with six examinations passed, then the one-year university orientation course (COU).

In the higher certificate she opted for the sciences (Chemistry, Physics and Mathematics) instead of Latin and Greek. However, she was much attracted to the world of Art and to History such that she took Mathematics, History and Literature as options in COU, wishing to combine a little of everything.

After passing the university entrance examination (although this was not necessary for primary teacher training), her knowledge of Mathematics and Languages was to serve her well because the subjects to be taken for her career were of a very diverse nature. The first year of training was basic and theoretical; in the second year there was already some specialisation (in her case Spanish and English). Practical experience also began at that time, once a week in the school annexe. During third year, when French was taken as an option, school practice lasted three months. A report from the supervising teacher plus a final examination determined the grading. On completing the course she was told that the college had proposed that she (along with some others) should be awarded one of the 'direct access places'; that is to say, that she should have a post in a state school without the need to take oposiciones. The ANPE (Asociación Nacional del Profesorado Estatal) assured here of priority in the choice of a school. In the year following her studies and in the absence of an official appointment she worked in a private school, it was 1979 and she was aged 24 years. In October 1980 she got her first official job an an itinerant teacher covering no less than 6 quite different schools, rural and urban. This provided many varied experiences replacing teachers of all stages.

Awareness of the imperfections in her knowledge of English led her to apply for a post as Spanish language assistant in Scotland. She spent a full school session working in Glasgow schools, attending English classes for two and a half hours every evening.

One year later her career as a teacher of English in a basic school in Spain really began. Knowing that her qualifications also allowed her to teach French, but aware that in practical terms she was not capable of doing this, she applied for a post as a Spanish language assistant in a French school. The post in Bordeaux was extraordinarily beneficial since the basic task was to share experiences of theory and practice with a group of teachers of Spanish. Thanks to that, her picture of the didactics of the language was changed and enriched. A specialised course in the history of contemporary French Art and Literature in the Université de Bordeaux III in Talence gave her the confidence to be a teacher of the French language.

On returning to Spain in 1984 aged 26 she joined a teachers group which met in the CEP to share classroom experiences and it was proposed that she and one other should take a Teacher Trainers course.

She was faced however with a dilemma, either to pursue her professional career in Spain or to accept a teaching post in Indonesia, outwith the jurisdiction of the Spanish Ministry of Education. She chose the latter and since January 1986 she has been outside the system.

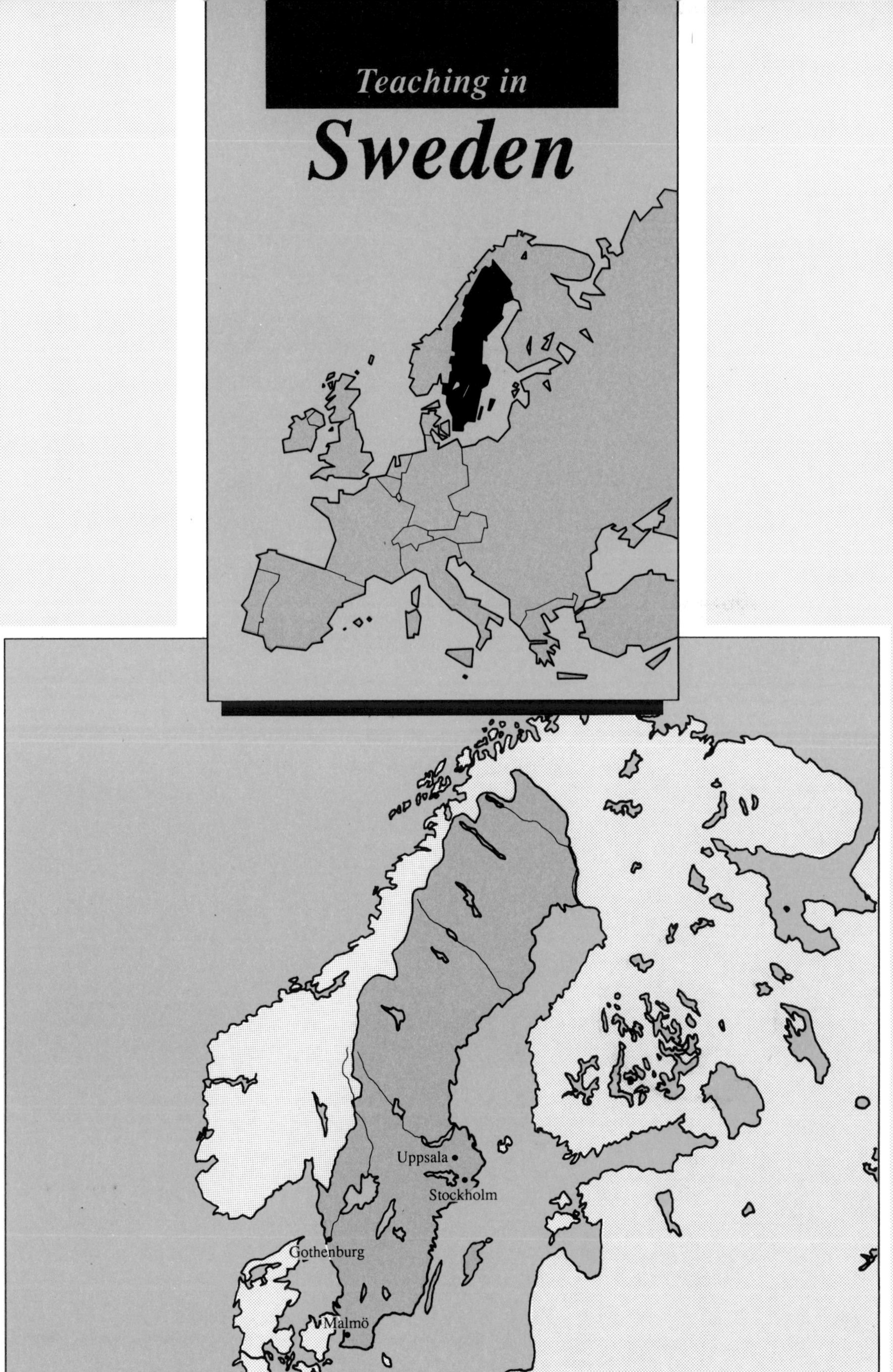
Teaching in
Sweden
Uppsala
Stockholm
Gothenburg
Malmö

TEACHING IN SWEDEN

Sweden is one of the Norden countries, Finland, Denmark, Norway and Iceland being the others. Some areas in the north, where the Sami people live, lie beyond the Arctic Circle. The ancient and eroded rock formations result in a landscape that is generally low and undulating, with numerous lakes.

Sweden is a sparsely populated country. In area, it is the fourth largest country in Europe but with only just over 8 million inhabitants. Occupying the eastern portion of the Scandinavian peninsula, it extends some 1000 miles (1,600 km) from north to south with the majority of the population living in the south. According to the 1980 census 83% of the population lived in cities and urban areas. Greater Stockholm, Göteborg (Gothenburg) and the Malmö region account for over 2.5 million inhabitants.

Economically Sweden has made great progress to become one of the richest countries in Europe. Key sources of wealth are timber, metallic ores, fishing, hydro-electric power and scenic resources. Industrial and commercial success is linked to an advanced educational system.

Over many years the Social Democrats have held power, either alone or in coalition with other parties. One result has been a series of rolling reforms which have expanded the educational system, and opened up opportunities for young people to continue their education beyond the compulsory period. Major objectives include the creation of greater equality in education, closer ties between school and society, and the expansion of recurrent educational opportunity.

The School System

After many years of educational research and investigation, educational reforms set in motion in Sweden during the 1950s have resulted in a compulsory 9 year comprehensive school, followed by an integrated upper secondary school designed to accommodate the needs of all 16 year olds and adults returning to education. All children are entitled to pre-school education for at least one year, before starting school at the age of 7 years.

The guidelines and regulations governing Swedish schools are highly centralised and within the context laid down by the Government for school work. Central planning and implementation are the responsibility of the National Board of Education (*Skolöverstyrelsen, SÖ*) which has the key task of ensuring that the goals laid down for the school sector by Parliament and Government are achieved. Its other tasks include long-term planning, evaluating school activities and encouraging local development work and research.

In terms of administration the country is divided into 24 counties, and 284 municipalities. In many respects the municipalities are independent of the counties and not simply subdivisions. The municipalities will tax themselves according to the different needs, and a local education committee will be appointed to ensure that activities in the schools are co-ordinated, that sufficient facilities are provided and that the curriculum goals are achieved. The county Board of Education will have the duty of checking that these matters are undertaken and executed in accordance with rules and guidelines laid down by the National Board of Education.

One particular issue, in recent years, has been that of increased local autonomy and decentralisation.[1] From the late 1980s, for example, teachers' salaries will be paid wholly by the municipality and not, as hitherto, partly by the municipality and partly by the State. The municipalities will continue to have jurisdiction over school buildings and equipment but it is likely that increased autonomy will be accorded in terms of financial subsidies coming from the state.

Elementary and lower secondary education in Sweden takes the form of a compulsory 9 year comprehensive school, divided into three levels (junior, intermediate, senior). All pupils at the junior and intermediate level take the same subjects ; at senior level a limited range of options is available together with a broad range of compulsory subjects. Across the country there is a compulsory core course including: Swedish, English, Mathematics, General Subjects (including Social Subjects and Science), Sport, Art, Music and Handicraft. Centrally framed goals and guidelines lay down the basic skills and the basic knowledge to be acquired by all pupils.

A further distinguishing feature is the focus on working life, both through instruction and through first-hand experience. Pupils will attend field trips and visits to workplaces of various kinds and to this end there is close co-operation between schools and the employment sector.

There are no examinations, but marks are awarded (on a five point scale) for work assessed in the final years (i.e. grades 8 and 9) of the compulsory school. A school leaving certificate will allow the school leaver to apply for entry into the upper secondary schools.

The upper secondary school (the *Gymnasium*) draws together students from several municipalities which are seen as forming an upper secondary school region. Student numbers may vary from some 300 students to about 1500 but every attempt is made to provide students with access to a wide range of vocational lines (or courses); to specialised courses or to theoretical studies in general subjects and in vocational subjects.[2] With well over 90% of compulsory school leavers continuing into the upper secondary school or *Gymnasium*, together with increasing numbers of 'mature' students returning, the students in every line of study represent a wide range of academic aptitude. Entry to any particular line is nonetheless related to a minimum level of attainment reached in the basic school assessment tests.

Hitherto the great majority of vocational lines have been for two years duration and the theoretical lines for three years. In the late 1980s, however, the reforms proposed for the upper secondary school were that vocational lines would become three years in duration, with some practical work transferred to out-of-school workplaces. By 1992 all two-year vocational lines will become three years in length.

In addition all students have to take a number of compulsory, common subjects. Foreign languages are compulsory subjects in all theoretical lines and many vocational ones also.

As in the compulsory school, marks are awarded on a five point scale, related to the average national level of achievement in each subject. An upper secondary school leaving certificate confers general eligibility for higher education.

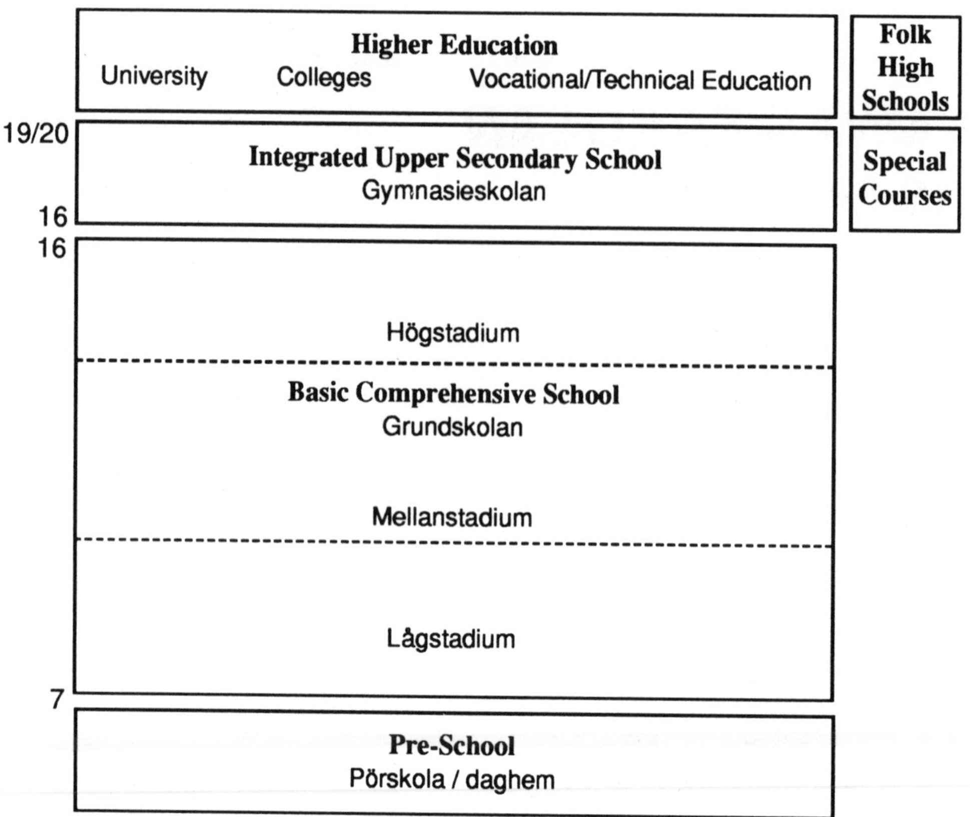

Teacher Training

To understand the process of teacher training in Sweden, it is important to recognise two major routes into the profession, viz:

a) the teacher training programme for teachers in the compulsory comprehensive school (*Grundskollärarlinjen*) and,
b) the training for subject teachers at the upper secondary schools (*gymnasieskolan*), and - until 1988, for subject teachers in the senior level of the compulsory school (i.e. grades 7-9).

a) During the expanding years of the 1960s many new teachers colleges or *Lärarhögskolan* were established, and all pedagogical teacher education was located in these institutions, which had university standing. By session 1985-6 there were 7 such *Lärarhögskolan* in Sweden, all closely associated with universities or forming a department of a university. Teachers who would be involved in teaching pupils in grades 1-6 of the compulsory school would undertake a three year course of training, and typically take a study loan to help with costs of accommodation, books, travel, and general living costs. From January 1989 the Swedish Government had modified its student funding system in favour of increasing grants, in an attempt to increase working class participation in higher education.

The experience of considerable decline in pupil population, a concern for greater flexibility for teaching personnel, and other matters, have led to major changes in the training provided for comprehensive school teachers.[3] Until 1988 class teachers at junior level would undertake a programme whereby points would be accumulated on completion of different elements of their coursework (e.g. subject studies - comprising Swedish, English, Mathematics, General subjects, Art, Music and Sport - 45 points); pedagogics and methodology (25 points); teaching practice and school observation (30 points). Such teachers would complete their course within 2 $^1/_2$ years.

Intermediate level teachers, whose subject studies were extended over a longer period (and awarded 65 points) would complete their course within three years.

The Government, with the authorisation of the Swedish Parliament, determined that a new general study programme be established as from July 1st 1988, and be given the title "The Teacher Training Programme for Teachers in Compulsory Comprehensive School". In summary, the radical reforms incorporated a number of key principles, viz:

STOCKHOLM INSTITUTE OF EDUCATION

HÖGSKOLAN FÖR LÄRARUTBILDNING I STOCKHOLM

A BRIEF PRESENTATION

In connection with the University Reform of 1977, several different lines of teacher training within the Stockholm area were merged into a single new unit, which came to be called The Stockholm Institute of Education (HLS). Work is carried on there today with an extensive programme of education courses and in-service training of teachers. The Institute also encompasses development and research work within the area of education. Approximately 750 employees are responsible for this work, and a further 2,000 teachers act as advisors or are in a similar capacity connected with the teacher training programmes.

TEACHER TRAINING at HLS is carried out in 13 study programmes, of which several have different directions and extents within the study programme. Almost all the teaching professions which exist within child care and the school are represented within the training program of HLS. The lines of teacher training study differ from each other as regards the length and content of the training as well as the previous knowledge, age and professional experience of the students. In addition, the work of HLS is spread geographically over all of Stockholm, its suburbs of Solna and Södertälje and the city of Uppsala. Despite the differences, one finds occuring in all the teacher training programmes four elements, namely pedagogy/psychology, methodology, teaching practice-work experience and subject theory.

Study programme committees answer for the content and organization of the teacher training programmes. Qustions of a more overall nature are handled by the University Senate. The chairman is the Vice-chancellor.

- that teachers should have not only a good and relevant knowledge of subject matter, but also a comprehensive view of children's, and teenagers' development and learning;
- that a common foundation training programme be provided for comprehensive school teachers;
- that comprehensive school teachers must have a shared responsibility for four grades;
- that subjects are organised into blocks and groups;
- that students, as teachers, can contribute to their pupils' understanding of and sympathy with minority groups living in the country.

Such principles, and others, have become incorporated into one study programme for all comprehensive school teachers, with two orientations, viz:

(i) a sub group for teaching grades 1-7 in the comprehensive school, (140 points), and
(ii) a sub group for teaching grades 4-9 (140 - 180 points).

Alternative in-depth studies and subjects specialisations are available within these orientations.[4]

To enter such a study programme the student must satisfy the general requirements for admission to the university while there are additional regulations relating to certain subjects. Successful completion of the study-programme will lead to the award of "Degree of Bachelor of Education in the comprehensive School" for a course of studies covering less than 160

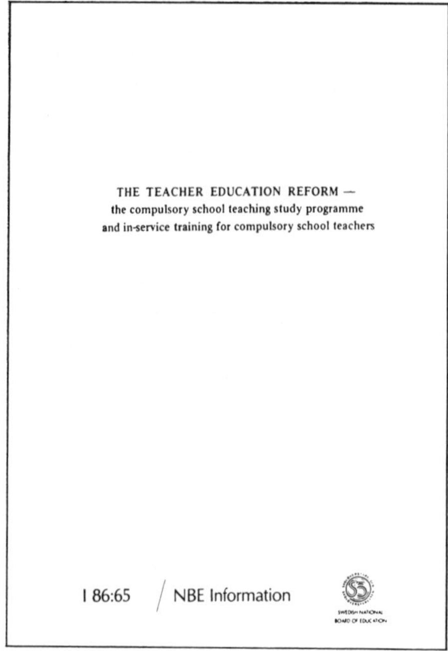

points. For studies covering 180 points the degree title will be "Degree of Master of Education in the Comprehensive School".

b) Until the session 1988-1989 teachers of theoretical subjects in the senior level of the basic comprehensive school were able to undertake one of three study programmes for subject teachers (viz: History and Social Sciences; Scientific Subjects; Languages Education) each with a course in the Theory and Practice of Teaching. Special programmes were also available for certain teachers (e.g. in Sport, Music and Art). From 1988 such senior level teachers will no longer be confined to the grades 7-9 but (as indicated) be responsible for a broader range of pupils, and undertake a considerably revised study programme.

For those seeking to teach in the Upper Secondary School (the *Gymnasium*) it is necessary to undertake a course involving two subject studies at a university, together with practical training and methodology. A total of 40 points will be accumulated for studies in the Theory and Practice of Education, taken at different times throughout the university course.

Employment and Probation

Upon completion of training the student teacher has been accustomed to face the difficult prospect of finding a job. Throughout the 1980s permanent jobs, especially in the major cities and certain areas of Sweden, have been rare and appointments for the most part have usually been made on a temporary basis. Very often considerable travel, or appointment to a teaching post far away from the home area, is involved.

In 1979 the Teacher Education Committee (L.U.T.) set up by the Government had proposed that all newly qualified teachers should have an induction period in school, that they should have the support of mentor or "companion" teachers and that there should be a programme of induction meetings drawn up by school management. In general terms, however, there is no specified probation period, as existing in a number of European countries, nor a requirement for formal assessment of the initial teaching years.

Nor are teachers formally assessed or appraised at later stages of their careers. As in many other countries regional school inspectors do visit schools but usually to report on matters of administration, curriculum, and the development of the school in relation to national goals and guidelines. Comments about particular teachers may be made privately to the school leader, but it is not compulsory - as yet - for such teachers to attend any form of inservice or remediation course.

In the late 1980s considerable unrest and low morale characterised the teaching profession, leading to a prolonged strike in the final weeks of 1989. Until this time teachers' contracts were such that teaching periods were fixed in relation to the grade level taught.[5] Government proposals indicated that teachers should have the same working hours each week as employees in other fields, and that teachers should spend 36 hours at school, including preparation, marking and allocated teaching hours. Further proposals were that separate salary scales should be consolidated into a basic scale.[6]

By 1990 it had become clear that teachers could be obliged to remain in their schools for an extra five hours each week to undertake preparatory work and related matters. Teacher pay levels no longer differentiated between categories or level of teaching, with the result being that a teacher in the comprehensive school, and a teacher in the upper secondary school would receive the same salary, related to years of service.

Career Development and Inservice Training

Readers are reminded that the 9-year school is seen as an administrative unit, as one local organisation and part of the municipality or *kommun*. Within the municipality's school management (*rektorsområde*) there are often several school sites and the Headmaster, or School Principal will be the administrative and pedagogical leader of a school which can consist of several buildings and range over several levels (i.e. 1-3; 4-6; 7-9 grades). Under the authority of the School Principal are Study Directors who will have particular responsibilities for day to day decisions, and who will direct the teacher's work.

Career development may therefore include the possibility of becoming a School Leader, of several working units; to be a Director of Studies, and - more recently - to be promoted to a new rank of *Studieledare*. This is a teacher who also takes on certain duties regarding the ordering and organisation of school materials and books, and other administrative tasks as may be required.

The training of School Principals has been extensively documented,[7] and especially so for Sweden. Government emphasis on this training was manifested in 1976, and revised programmes have been introduced in 1984 and again in 1986. A 12 year experimental inservice training programme has now led to a five year on-the-job training for new School Principals, and a continuous inservice training programme for all those in such posts. Given the recent changes in the teacher training for the compulsory school it is likely that further refinements will be made in the training available for school leaders.

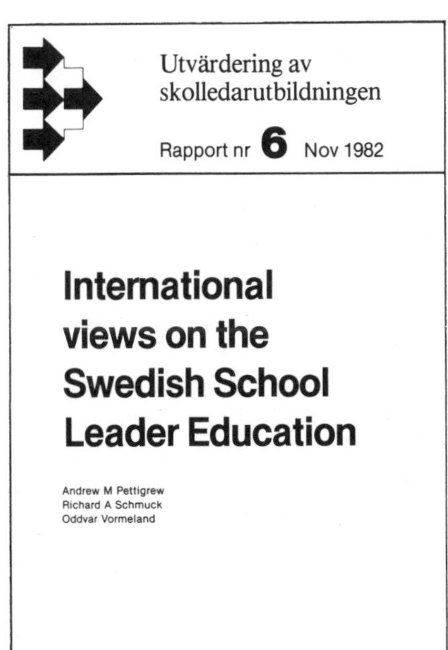

School Principals will not have the same holidays and working conditions as teachers, with fewer days of paid leave normally allocated to such posts of responsibility.

For the majority of teachers inservice training is related to short part-time courses and to the provision of 5 study days, which form part of the teacher's contract. New national curricular developments, regional or county programmes, and specific changes in relation to such matters as learning difficulties, work with immigrants, and health education may be identified.

In the 1980's there has been considerable emphasis upon special educational needs, and issues of pupil performance and personal relationships.

For the 1990's the new study programme for teacher training is seen as the first part of a continuing development of professional skills and lifelong inservice support and provision. In this respect it is inevitable that further study days will be allocated to the inservice training of teachers. Indeed, from 1990 an extra 8 days has been allocated for such inservice development, and each municipality will arrange this according to local needs and priorities.

Until 1900 teachers have been State employees but, as from 1st January 1991 they became employees of the municipalities. It is the duty of the municipality to employ trained teachers and to ensure that staff receive the requisite in-service training. The State will be responsible for the provision of opportunities and for in-service provision prompted by centrally enacted reforms.

Footnotes

1 *More local influence was a key feature of a bill presented to the Swedish parliament in 1988. Each locality should draw up its own plan for schooling at least every three years, and local influence with regard to the appointment of teachers was to be strengthened.*

2 *In 1986 the main sectors of study in the Upper secondary school included:*
Languages, Social Sciences, and the Arts (5 lines);
Caring Professions, Social Services, and Consumer Education (3 lines);
Economics, Commerce, and Office Work (4 lines);
Industry and Crafts (8 lines);
Technology and Science (4 lines);
Agriculture, Forestry and Horticulture (3 lines).

3 *In 1978/79 there were more than one million pupils attending the basic school. In 1985 this figure had declined considerably, and by 1993-94 it will have dropped by more than 200,000. According to the National Board of Education the number of pupils at the junior level of the comprehensive school will be at its lowest in the school years 1991/92, and 1992/93. The equivalent of more than 2000 full time jobs would be superfluous at the junior level of the comprehensive school and at middle level about 2500 jobs. For specialist teachers most of the decline would take place between 1987 and 1992. By the year 2000 the number of pupils in the comprehensive school is likely to be more constant.*

4 *For those students training to teach grades 1-7 there are two alternatives for in-depth studies; one alternative concentrates on Swedish and Social Subjects; the other alternative concentrates on Mathematics and Science subjects.*

For those students training to teach grades 4-9 there are five alternative combinations of subjects, viz:

(i) *Languages: Swedish and English, combined with one of the following: German, French or a home-language (i.e. immigrant or minority language) e.g. Finnish, Lappish or*

Swedish and Swedish as a second language combined with one other language (English, German, French or a home-language) or

Swedish as a second language and a home-language in combination with one of the following: English, German, French.

(ii) *Social Subjects (Civics, History, Geography, Religious Knowledge etc.)*

(iii) *Science Subjects.*

(iv) *Mathematics and Science Subjects.*

(v) *Child-Studies, Visual Arts, Home Economics, Physical Education, Music or Craft in combination with one of the following subjects: Swedish, Swedish as a Second Language, English, German, French, Home-Languages (for immigrant groups), Mathematics.*

Alternative Specialisations
For those training to teach grades 1-7 three specialisations are available. These lead to a basic teaching qualification and a specialist qualification in certain areas e.g. in the teaching of Swedish as a second language.

5 *Viz: Teacher for 1-6 grades: 29 periods per week; (28 from July 1st, 1990)*
7-9 grades: 24 periods per week;
Upper Secondary School: 21 periods per week.

6 *Throughout the 1980s salaries have been related to level of school work (viz: junior, middle, upper or subject teacher) with additional payment for those with MA or Ph.D. degrees a Director of Studies, and School Principal would have separate salary levels.*

7 *See, for example: The Training of Secondary Heads in Western Europe. John Buckley, Council of Europe NFER-Nelson 1985.*

An Upper Secondary School Teacher of Languages

Jag tog realexamen när jag var 17 år och sedan arbetade jag på skatteverket i Stockholm. Efter ett år sökte jag till Folkskoleseminariet för flickor, och där gick jag i fyra år. Under tiden bodde jag hemma hos mina föräldrar. Som utbildad lärare gifte jag mig sedan (med en lärarkollega), och fick lärartjänst i det samhälle som vi bodde i.

Att vara lärare på det stadiet, med elever i åldrarna 10-13 år, var, måste jag säga, ingen lätt uppgift: stora klasser på mer än 30 elever, och hela skalan av olika ämnen, inklusive slöjd, gymnastik, musik och teckning. Men jag gillade det i alla fall.

Efter tre år (år 1959) kunde jag ta tjänstledigt med 3/4 lön. Så jag tog tillfället i akt och började läsa engelska vid Stockhoms Högskola (tror jag att det hette då). Kanske skulle jag nämna, att jag hade varit tvungen att läsa in gymnasiekurserna i latin och franska för att få börja läsa engelska. Därvidlag är det ändrat numera, till det sämre, faktiskt, så nu kan man bara undantagsvis läsa ett valfritt ämne med 3/4 lön, och man "måste" inte kunna latin för att få läsa språk.

Sommaren 1960 gick jag på en sommarkurs i Cambridge på egen bekostnad. Här skulle jag vilja klaga en smula på Skolöverstyrelsen över deras snålhet och brist på förutseende, när de inte hjälper språklärare att komma ut regelbundet och oftare till det land/deländer vilkas språk de undervisar i, genom t.ex. frikostiga stipendier. Själv har jag varit till England bara fyra gånger och i U.S.A. en gång på trettio år; två gånger på stipendium, tre gånger på egen bekostnad och alltid - på min fritid.

Medan våra barn var små tog min mamma eller en au-pair-flicka hand om dem under dagen, då jag arbetade 1/2-tid i en högstadieskola, antingen som klasslärare eller som speciallärare med små elevgrupper för stödundervisning. På kvällstid hade jag ofta engelska för vuxenstuderande.

År 1969 blev jag konsulent i engelska med fortbildning i engelska för lågstadielärare som första och viktigaste uppgift. Enligt 1969 års läroplan för grundskolan skulle ju engelska införas redan i åk 3. på lågstadiet, och många lärare saknade behörighet att undervisa i detta ämne. Fortbildningsprojektet pågick i tre år, men mitt arbete som konsulent (1/2 -tid) kom att fortsätta till 1981. Parallellt läste jag svenska på kvällarna och tog min fil.kand. och fil. mag. 1975.

Jag blev ordinarie 1976 i svenska och engelska i en högstadieskola nära där vi bodde, och tre år senare fick jag en ännu bättre ordinarietjänst i det gymnasium där jag fortfarande arbetar. Termen "ordinarietjänst", förresten, är avskaffad numera, eftersom alla är garanterade anställningstrygghet genom lagstiftning.

Jag år mycket glad och nöjd med mitt liv. Jag tycker om att undervisa äldre elever och jag tycker om att arbeta i en stor skola med teoretiska och praktiska linjer. Min senaste erfarenhet gäller undervisning av invandrare. För att meritera mig tog jag en 5-poängskurs på universitetet.

De flesta lärare är med i "facket", mindre av övertygelse än av lojalitet och grupptryck. Men de flesta är ganska missnöjda med lärarfackens oförmåga att verka för en bibehållen reallön. Sedan 60-talet har lärarnas (gäller adjunkterna) reallön enl. uppgift sjunkit med 20%. Som en jämförelse kan Finland nämnas, där (också enl. uppgift) en svensklärare har 18.000 kr/mån (mot i Sv. 14.000) förutom att de dessutom har fördelaktigare tjänstgöringsförhållanden. Allt detta påverkar dessvärre också läraryrkets prestige i allmänhetens ögon. Glädjande nog, har emellertid folk i allmänhet ställt upp på lärarnas och skolans sida, eftersom undervisningens kvalitet är något som angår alla. Myndigheternas ständiga nedskärningar och sparprogram har mött allt större motstånd och de har nu börjat dra örenen åt sig och lovat bättring.

Likaså glädjande är, att det nu har blivit "fint" att plugga. Eleverna, åtminstone på gymnasiet, det är mitt intryck, är mer seriösa och målmedvetna nu än, låt säga, för 10 år sedan. Detta är en trend som jag optimistiskt nog tror ska fortsätta och som kommer att göra det lättare och roligare att arbeta med undervisning.

I graduated from High school at the age of 17 and then I took a job as an office employee at the local tax department in Stockholm. After one year I applied and was admitted to the Teachers' Training College (for girls) and studied there for four years. Meanwhile I lived at home with my parents.

As a qualified teacher I then got married (to a colleague), and got a teaching post (there was some competition!) in the community where we lived.

Being a teacher at that level, age group 10-13 years of age, was, I must say, not an easy task: big classes of more than 30 pupils, and the whole range of various subjects, including handicraft, athletics, music and art. However, I enjoyed it all the same.

After three years (in 1959) I was entitled to leave of absence for studies with $^3/_4$ of my salary. So I took the opportunity to start studying English at the Stockholm University. Perhaps I should mention that I had to take evening classes in Latin and French to qualify for my English studies. Things have changed since then, however, for the worse, I am afraid , so that only exceptionally can we study a subject we choose with $^3/_4$ of our salary, and we do not have to know Latin in order to study languages.

In the summer of 1960 I attended a language course in Cambridge at my own expense. Here I should like to put in a small complaint about the meanness and lack of foresight on the part of the Education Department when they do not help teachers of languages to get out regularly and more often to the country/countries whose languages they teach here in Sweden, by e.g. generous scholarships. I, for one, have been to England only four times, and in the U.S.A. once, in thirty years, twice on scholarships, three times at my own expense and always - in my leisure time.

While our children were small, my mother or an au-pair girl took care of them during the day when I was working $^1/_2$-time at a secondary school, either as a class teacher or had small groups of students for remedial instructions. In the evenings I usually had classes in English for adults. In 1969 I was appointed to lead an inservice programme for school teachers at basic level who were to qualify to teach English in grade three of "their" level, i.e. Junior, in accordance with the new curriculum of 1969. The project went on for three years, but my job as adviser of English lasted until 1981. In the evenings I studied Swedish and got my B.A. and M.A. in 1975.

I got a permanent post in 1976 as a teacher of English and Swedish at a secondary school near where we lived, and three years later I was appointed for an even better (permanent) post at the Upper Secondary School where I still work. This term, "permanent" post, by the way, is abolished now, as "security of employment" is guaranteed everybody by law.

I am very happy and pleased with with the way things have turned out for me. I like teaching grown-up students and I like working in a big school with academic as well as vocational lines. My latest experience is teaching Swedish to immigrants, mostly from Chile and Iran. I took a class in the subject to qualify myself.

Most teachers are members of a Teachers' Union, (there are two of them) not so much of conviction as on account of loyalty and peer pressure. I do not think, however, it is too much to say that there is a widespread discontent among the members with the Unions. The fees we pay to the Union, c.1.600 Sw Cr/year, make it tempting to leave the Union, especially as they seem incapable to really do something for us - paywise or otherwise. Compared to what it was like in the 60's, which was a good decade, we - they say - lag behind by 20% in real wages. In Finland, where they have a school system very similar to ours, the terminal pay amounts to 18.000 Sw Cr/month while in Sweden a teacher of a comparable status has 14.000 Sw Cr/month, not to mention that there are other differences as regards professional prestige in the eyes of the public and differences in the actual working conditions.

Education concerns everybody individually and the society as a whole. Therefore it was particularly gratifying to experience the massive support from the press and the general public in their manifestations for the school against the continuous cut-downs and savings programmes over the years. There were even large demonstrations by students, conscious of the importance and standard of education. Studying is becoming more and more prestigious apparently, which will make it easier and all the more fun to teach. At least there are signs pointing to such an optimistic development within the field of education.

Teaching in Switzerland

Basle
Zürich
Berne
Lausanne
Geneva

TEACHING IN SWITZERLAND

"Ce n'est qu'en collaborant avec le monde extrascolaire - qui est plein d'enseignements pour l'élève - qui l'enseignant peut remplir son mandat"

(Rapport National de la Suisse Sur la Formation des Enseignants. Berne 1985)

Switzerland is a mountainous country, much land being over 1000 m. A central plateau lying between the Jura range and the Alps, and the valleys of the Rhine and the Rhone, provide most of the lower land. Here one finds the major cities - Basel, Berne, Geneva and Zürich - and the large lakes. Its borders are with France, Germany, Austria and Italy.

With a population of some 6.5 million, including about one million foreigners, Switzerland has the highest GNP of all the countries in Europe as well as a very healthy current-account balance. Its wealth derives from manufacturing, tourism and, of course, from banking and financial services; in recent years there has been a marked swing away from the manufacturing to the service industries. Consistent with its politically neutral stance, Switzerland is a member of the European Free Trade Association, not the EC at present.

The location and geography of Switzerland, as well as religious differences, determine its diverse nature. In some respects it is a divided country; physical barriers are a factor, and proximity to other states is another. About one half of the citizens are Roman Catholics, the others Protestants. Four languages are officially recognised: German is spoken by 75% of the population, French by 20%, Italian by 4% and Romansch by less than 1%. Within these there are different dialects - Romansch has five! Thus language divides, and attempts to produce bilingual or multilingual Swiss are not as advanced as some would wish. Here lie some important problems facing the government.

The Education System

Politically, Switzerland is made up of 26 cantons, united by a federal constitution (*confederatio Helvetica*). The result is a diverse and highly devolved system. There is no Swiss federal department of education. Control rests with the cantons and these vary in size, wealth and resources. So much of the decision-making takes place at cantonal level that it is extremely difficult to generalise about Swiss education. In a real sense there can be said to be 26 education systems in Switzerland, the Federal Government having a coordinating and financial role in one or two areas, notably in higher education and in vocational education. Each canton has its own legislation recognising its responsibility for:

- the setting up, financing and administration of its schools, colleges and universities
- the overall structure of the schooling, including the length of compulsory education
- its own version of the *Matura* examination
- teacher training
- teachers' salaries

Since the early 1960s increasing attempts have been made to harmonise the various school systems. Particularly important in this respect is the Conference of Cantonal Directors of

Education, which meets regularly in order to implement the 'Concordat on School Coordination'. These meetings, and parallel meetings of different categories of officials, aim to secure some degree of uniformity across the cantons, including mutual recognition of examinations and qualifications.

It has to be added that a considerable amount of influence rests at the community level: local school boards have a significant part to play. Furthermore, it is in the nature of the Swiss system that important matters will be subject to direct popular vote, and not left to officials nor committees.

Because of the variety between cantons, the diagram below gives only a general picture of the system. As in the other levels, **preschool** provision varies although one can reasonably assume that the early years of all Swiss schooling have benefited from the ideas of Pestalozzi, Claparède, Montessori, Piaget and Dévaud etc. Attendance is not compulsory although take-up in some areas is very high.

Primary education is compulsory for all from the age of 6 years although its length in relation to compulsory lower secondary education, which follows, varies.

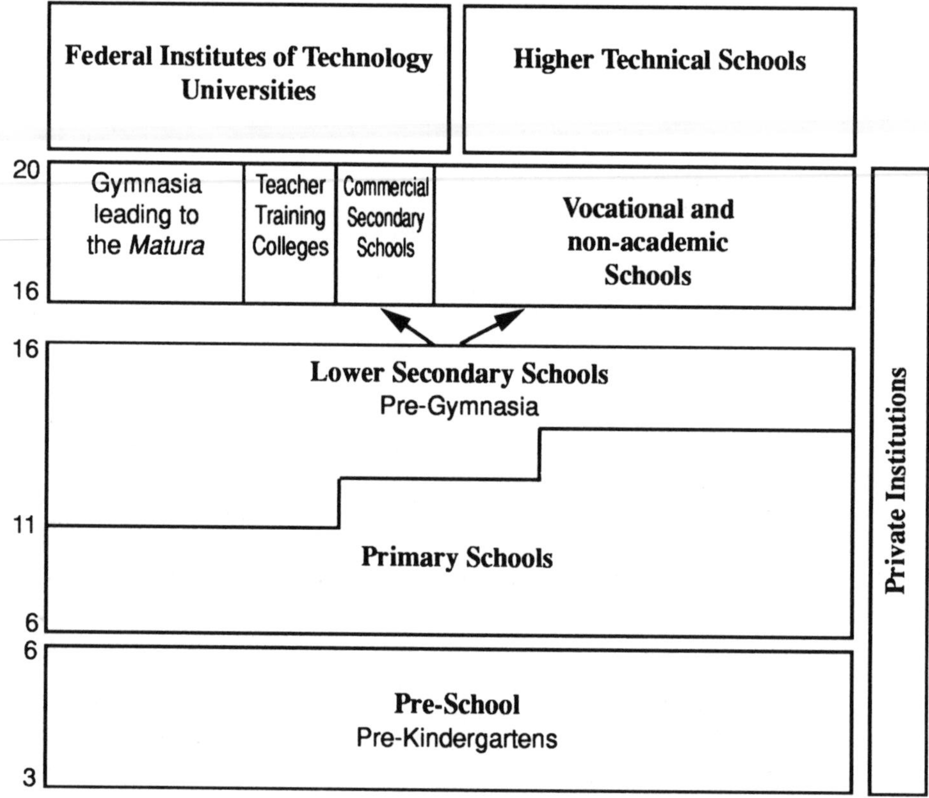

Curriculum and aims may differ from canton to canton but within national guidelines. In general the first year is concerned with socialisation and with the foundations of number and language. During the next two years basic skills, knowledge and understanding are further developed through a balanced curriculum of language study (area mother tongue), mathematics and the social and aesthetic subjects. Afterwards, there is a transition period when pupils either seek access to secondary education in academic courses or settle for more practical courses suited to their aptitude and ability.

Lower secondary schools are organised on a subject basis, with specialist teachers (of Languages, Mathematics, the Sciences, History, Music, Physical Education etc.). These schools prepare pupils for entry into vocational courses, commercial courses or teacher training. Also at this level are pre-gymnasia, providing a transition to the Gymnasia which are **Higher Secondary Schools**, offering different types of *Matura*. The Gymnasia in turn prepare pupils for university entrance. For those seeking vocational alternatives to the Gymnasium there are full-time **vocational schools** of various types. These may be run by the canton or the State, subsidised by the Federal Government. The eight Swiss **universities** are in a similar position: they are cantonal institutions but they receive state subsidies. Most types of *Matura* permit entry to the universities and to the two institutes of technology.

Teacher Training

Teacher training is also the responsibility of the cantons. They control the admissions policy, the course content and the examinations.

Kindergarten teachers are trained in cantonal, communal or private centres. In some areas candidates must be aged 17 or 18 and they must have completed ten years of schooling. An additional requirement is that they have completed a period of practical experience in a family, in a day-nursery or in a children's home. Selection tests to gauge motivation and some basic skills are also used. Successful candidates take a 2-3 years training course with theoretical and practical content.

In other areas, training is conducted in a primary school teachers' training college, (*École Normale*) in a special section. Courses last 3 or 4 years and again content combines theory and practice. Only in Geneva is the *Matura* a pre-requisite. There the training is of a post-secondary/university type and the arrangements are the same as for primary school teachers.

In general (apart from Geneva and Basel) **primary school teachers**, traditionally have been trained in *Écoles Normales*. These are effectively alternative secondary-type institutions, operating in parallel with Gymnasia. Candidates have been selected on the basis of various criteria - intellectual, aesthetic, practical. Content has combined personal education with practical and professional training in a course lasting four or five years, and leading to the *Brevet d'Enseignement Primaire*.

However, there has been disatisfaction with this course. There is evidence that, while a sound personal education has been provided, practical and professional aspects have not been dealt with effectively. Reforms have been set in motion governing the two routes to primary teaching. The first, in *Écoles Normales* is now intended to last six years. The second, after the *Matura*, takes two years to complete. Year I consists of a basic training course for various categories of teacher; Year II courses differ according to the level and type of teaching chosen.

Secondary teacher training reflects cantonal differences and it is further complicated by the use of different terminology relating to Lower Secondary Schools (*Sekundarschule,*

Realschule, Abschlussklassen; Cycle d'Orientation, Classes Préprofessionnelles). Basically there are two types of teacher in Lower Secondary School:

(i) the *Reallehrer* whose pupils are taking practical or vocationally-orientated courses and
(ii) the *Sekundarlehrer/Maîtres d'École Secondaire* whose pupils are likely to move on to advanced courses.

Entry to training requires either the *Matura* or a primary teacher's certificate. The 3-year courses reflect different specialisms and there are theoretical and practical elements. Training takes place either in a University department or in an Institute of Advanced Pedagogy and it leads to the Secondary Teachers' Certificate (*Le Brevet de l'Enseignement Secondaire/Sekundarlehrerpatent*).

Teachers in the Gymnasium (*Professeurs de Gymnase*) must be university graduates in appropriate school disciplines; they usually teach two or three subjects. Training takes place either in the university or in courses specially arranged by the Canton, lasting for 1-2 years.

Vocational teachers are trained on a full-time or part-time basis, with courses incorporating both theory and practical experience. Federal influence is apparent and the *Institut Suisse de Pédagogie pour la Formation Professionnelle* (ISPFP) is increasingly involved. The ISPFP also organises training courses for **teachers in Higher Technical Schools**.

Within this general framework, special training arrangements operate for **teachers of general subjects** in **vocational schools** (*Gewerbelehrer*); for **specialist teachers of the aesthetic subjects** i.e. Music in the Conservatoires, and in the Schools of Art, PE in the *Écoles de Sports;* and for **teachers of pupils with special educational needs** (*Maîtres d'Enseignement Spécialisé*).

Teaching and Probation

It is clearly understood that decisions are largely taken at the level of the cantons. Generalising across cantons cannot safely be done. The power rests with each cantonal Ministry of Education.

On completion of training teachers apply for posts to the appropriate authorities. In the case of primary school teaching, application will be to the School Board as set up by the local (*commune*) council. In the case of lower secondary school teaching, the procedures are likely to be similar but upper secondary school teachers are employed and paid by the cantonal Ministry of Education. Legislation passed in the canton determines salaries and conditions of employment. There are no formal contracts of employment.

The first post might be of a temporary kind. Vacancies for established posts are advertised in the press. The choice might be between a rural post and one in town; the latter would pay a higher salary. Selection could include going to a strange school and teaching a lesson with the school board (*Aufsichtscommision/Commission Scolaire*) watching, perhaps 8-10 people!

Probation varies according to local circumstances and according to level. Usually the three-year probation for primary teachers includes compulsory attendance at courses during summer vacations. For secondary teachers probation lasts two years.

The school board and the headteachers are responsible for operating the arrangements. Heads will visit classrooms and probably cantonal school inspectors will play a part. The area inspectors might be expected to visit every teacher in his schools anyway and probationers would be visited in the normal course of events. There are no agreed criteria for teacher assessment or appraisal. An inspector would be expected to engage in a discussion with a probationer after observing a lesson. In principle this seems to be a good idea since valuable help and advice could be forthcoming. In addition the system overall should benefit since the school inspector also reports (in very general terms) to both the headteacher and to the Ministry. However, evidence from teachers in some cantons is that the work of the inspector is valued by some but not by others.[1]

On the face of it the situation does not seem well geared to support the young teacher in her/his early years of teaching. The Headteacher supervises all staff and he should be in a position to give help and encouragement; often this will happen. In secondary schools where there is a deputy headteacher he may have a role in respect of staff development although this seems not to be formalised. Nor are *provisors* (in the large schools where they are appointed) likely to be involved.

Inservice Training

Some considerable emphasis is placed on inservice training and on further professional development in Switzerland. As noted, for primary school teachers it is compulsory for them to attend a one-week course each summer vacation for three years. In addition, all primary and secondary staff are expected to attend courses regularly, especially when there are changes in curriculum or education innovations to contend with. Substitute teachers may be hired to make attendance possible during school hours. Other courses may take place on free afternoons or in the evening, in which case attendance is voluntary.

As regards primary inservice training, this remains within the orbit of the cantons. For other categories of teacher, Swiss organisations have been established e.g. as follows:

> *Centre Suisse pour le perfectionnement des professeurs de l'enseignement secondaire/Weiterbildungzentrale* (WBZ)
> *Secrétariat Suisse de pedagogie curative;*
> *Institut Suisse de pédagogie pour la formation professionnelle.*

These organisations, along with the various subject teachers associations, run courses for their members and others at various times throughout the year. Thus, teachers of modern languages, of science, of geography etc., attend courses at national or area centres. Contributors will be university staff or other specialists or experts.

Career Development

As described above, entry into training depends on the possession of the *Maturité*. Grants could be available from the canton for the less well-off during training but parental support is likely to be necessary. These could be for a long training period, perhaps as long as 6 years and longer in some cases.

After a period of temporary teaching, the first priority is to obtain an established post and tenure. Obtaining a permanent post depends on a vacancy occurring and after that it depends essentially on the Headteacher; he proposes you for permanency.

Opportunities for promotion are few. The emphasis is more on professional growth as a teacher. Salaries are relatively high and obtaining extra qualifications can enhance monetary rewards.

Where there are opportunities for promotion, these are restricted to the posts of Headteacher or Deputy Head teacher. The post of *provisor* (a kind of head of department) exists in some large secondary schools, and it may be disappearing. In any case the duties are not of a high order nor are there high monetary rewards. In the primary sector there are advisory or staff tutor posts, *coordinateurs*, with responsibility for a subject (e.g. Craft) in a group of schools.

There are opportunities for some teachers in *Gymnasia*, especially in city areas, to teach for 2 or 3 periods each week in the university. This might be seen in career development terms although there is no fixed ladder of promotions in Switzerland as exists in the UK.

1 *In one canton legislation defines the 'Obligations de l'inspecteur'* as follows: *L'inspecteur est chargé de la surveillance des écoles de son arrondissement. Il guide et contrôle le personnel enseignant dans l'accomplissement de sa tâche et l'application du programme. Il contrôle et appuie les commissions scolaires, veille à la bonne exécution de la loi et des règlements.*

A Teacher of English as a Foreign Language

Adrienne is a teacher of English as a Foreign Language. After her "maturity" diploma (end of secondary school diploma that allows 19-20 year olds to enter any Swiss university), she spent 3 months in Oxford at a school of English. She then passed the Cambridge Certificate of Proficiency in English. At the same time she began a 3-year degree course at the University of Fribourg (CH) in English Literature, English Philology and Latin. After her degree, she was offered a teaching job, but she chose to spend a school year in England as a French Language Assistant. Then she obtained a Graduate Teaching Assistantship at the University of Alberta (Edmonton), where she completed a Master's Degree in Comparative Literature.

She began teaching at a Girls' High School near her home town in Switzerland and remained in the same job for 13 years, until the school closed down.

In her Canton, no training in Education is required, and very few teachers attend Education courses at University during their studies. Young teachers have to "sink or swim" in their first job. An Inspector comes once a year and gives advice, but the role of supervisor is left to the Headteacher.

Adrienne imitated the teaching methods she knew from her own schooldays and those used at the School of English she had attended in Oxford. She was sent by her Headteacher to various workshops, but she still found it very hard to cope with discipline problems. She gave particular care to her lesson-plans and never accepted a full teaching load. She learned proper teaching techniques on a Summer Course in London and went on attending summer courses in Britain, on her own initiative.

After the Girls' High School closed down, pupils and teacher were relocated in a large co-ed Grammar School, where she taught for 3 years. She felt again like an inexperienced teacher in these very different surroundings. She took less periods at the Grammar School and found a part-time job teaching evening classes at the Open University. When a new Business School for adults opened in the same town, she applied for the part-time position of Teacher of English and is now doing her second year there. She has kept her job at the Open University because she enjoys its friendly unstressed atmosphere. Teaching small groups of young adults (up to 18) suits her much better than controlling large forms of teenagers (up to 32).

Although she has been teaching for 16 years, she has never been appointed on a permanent basis. Most teachers who have joined the profession in her Canton in the past ten years have not been appointed, because of the decreasing trend in demography.

Moneywise she finds she can easily earn her living even by teaching only part-time. Teachers at the Business School have a shorter teaching week and a higher salary than secondary-school teachers. Salaries are periodically adjusted to the inflation rate, and from 1992 on all the civil servants (including teachers in State Schools like Adrienne) will receive a thirteenth monthly salary. Unemployment and accident insurances as well as a retirement pension scheme are compulsory, paid partly by the employer (the State) and partly by the employee. Teaching at the Open University on the other hand is closer to a free-lance activity.

A Secondary School Teacher

Mon nom est Monique. Je suis enseignante dans une école secondaire du canton de Genève en Suisse. Mes élèves ont entre 13 et 15 ans.

J'ai passé ma maturité, c'est-à-dire le diplôme de fin d'études secondaires à 19 ans. Je me suis inscrite tout de suite à la faculté des lettres de l'université de Genève après avoir passé 3 mois en Angleterre. Un peu par hasard mon choix s'est porté sur la philosophie, la littérature anglaise et l'histoire, trois branches que j'avais étudieées et appréciées au collège secondaire.

Immédiatement après le début de mes études, une amie me proposa de remplacer sa mère à l'école primaire. Le désir d'une vie active me poussa à tenter l'expérience. Mon premier contact avec une classe de petits enfants m'enchanta. Le travail n'était pas stressant et surtout, la confiance et l'affection des élèves me touchèren beaucoup.

Je donnais également des cours privés à des élèves âgés de 10 à 14 ans et cet enseignement, quoique différent, était très enrichissant.

Aprés l'obtention de ma demi-licence, j'avais le droit d'enseigner au niveau secondaire. Je commençai presque immédiatement avec un remplacement d'une durée de deux mois dans une classe d'élèves âgés de 17 ans. J'étais bien entendu terrorisée et, pour m'en défendre, j'étais exagérément autoritaire. Cependant j'étais assez sûre de la branche que j'enseignais grâce aux trois mois que je venais de passer aux Etats Unis.

Puis s'enchaînèrent différentes propositions de "remplacement maternité" d'une durée de 4 mois. Les enseignantes que je remplaçais me contactaient directement et notre collaboration a dans certains cas bien contribué à mon expérience.

Ces longs remplacements m'évitaient de me faire réveiller chaque matin à 7 heures pour un remplacement urgent souvent effectué dans des conditions disciplinaires pénibles pour moi. La discipline ne posait pas trop de problèmes dans ces classes "à long terme" mais le contact était parfois difficile car je n'étais pas "la vraie prof." Comme je l'ai mentionné, la discipline était souvent un problème crucial lors de mes remplacements d'un ou de deux jours. Le bon salaire offert était alors ma seule compensation pour un travail de "baby sitting".

Après avoir réussi ma licence en lettres à l'université de Genève, je m'inscrivis aux études pédagogiques, institut de l'état qui forme les enseignants tout en leur donnant un salaire et grâce auquel, une fois terminés les deux ans, les enseignants obtiennent le droit au travail. Ce n'est que l'année suivante que ma candidature a été acceptée et je poursuis maintenant ma deuxième année.

Mes nombreuses années d'expérience dans les remplacements m'ont donné une assurance qui me permet d'enseigner avec une certaine aisance dans mon contact avec les élèves.

Comme je connais bien mes élèves que je garde toute l'année scolaire, ma discipline s'est assouplie et j'accentue le côté affectif du rapport professeur-élève. J'éprouve ainsi plus de satisfaction dans mon travail et dans celui des élèves.

Au point de vue financier, je suis payée à 95% du plein salaire et je bénéficierai du 100% quand je serai nommée par mon directeur d'école et d'autres membre d'un groupe. J'ai choisi d'enseigner dans un poste de 13 à 15 heures par semaine ce qui me donne un salaire très suffisant car il s'additionne à celui de mon mari. J'aurais pu prendre un poste avec plus d'heures mais j'ai préféré me donner le plus de temps possible pour la préparation de mes cours, comme je suis toujours "en formation".

J'ai constaté qu'il faut parfois beaucoup de temps pour l'élaboration d'un cours et un cours bien préparé me permet d'aborder mes élèves détendue et sûre de moi.

Aprés ces nombreuses années de remplacement et de status de rempliçante, j'apprécie d'autant plus mon poste d'enseignante et la stabilité qu'il implique. Je suis heureuse d'enseigner, heureuse de retrouver mes élèves et de planifier mon travail avec eux sur une année entière.

My name is Monique. I am a Secondary school teacher in the Swiss Canton of Geneva. My pupils are in the age-group 13 to 15 years.

I passed my Maturité, the diploma taken at the end of secondary school, when you are 19.

Immediately afterwards I enrolled as a student in the arts faculty of Geneva University after residing in England for three months. Somewhat by chance my choice of subjects was Philosophy, English Literature and History, three areas which I had studied and which I had liked during my secondary schooling.

Straight after completing my studies, a friend suggested me as a replacement teacher for her mother who worked in a primary school. My wish for some form of activity caused me to try the experience. The first contact with a class of young children delighted me. The work was not stressful and above all the trust and affection of the pupils touched me greatly.

I was also giving private lessons to pupils aged 10 to 14 and this teaching, although different, was very rewarding.

After completing half my degree course, I was able to teach at secondary level. I began almost immediately as a replacement teacher - teaching 17 year olds. I was understandably anxious and I reacted by adopting an exaggeratedly authoritarian manner. However, I was quite sure of the level I wanted to teach, thanks to the three months I had just spent in the United States.

Then followed various spells as 'maternity replacement teacher' lasting some 4 months. The teachers I replaced kept contact with me and sometimes this collaboration added significantly to my training.

These long spells as replacement teacher meant that I did not have to go at short notice to fill in for an absent teacher; then there could be trying disciplinary problems. Discipline did not present too many problems in these long-term commitments but relationships were sometimes difficult because I was not the 'real teacher'. As mentioned, discipline was often a problem during one or two-day replacements. The good pay was the only consolation for work as a 'baby-sitter'.

After passing degree examinations in the university I enrolled for teacher training in the cantonal college. While training you receive a salary and once the two year course is completed you have the right to a job. I was not accepted until the following year and I am now in the second year of the training course.

My various years experience as a stand-in for absent teachers has given me an assurance which serves me well in my relationship with pupils.

As I know my pupils well when I have them throughout the year, my discipline is relaxed and I stress the caring aspect of teacher-pupil relationships. Therefore I experience a great deal of satisfaction from my work and from the work of the pupils.

From a financial point of view, I am paid 95% of full salary and this will increase to 100% when I am 'nominated' by my Headmaster and by other members of the board. I chose to teach for 13-15 hours each week. This provides me with sufficient income to supplement that of my husband. I could have taken a post with more hours of teaching but I prefer to give myself as much time as possible to prepare my work as I am still learning.

I have learnt that sometimes a good deal of time is needed for the development of a course, and a course well-prepared allows me to face my pupils relaxed and confident.

After those years as a replacement teacher, I appreciate my present post all the more and the stability which goes with it. I enjoy teaching and I enjoy meeting my pupils again and planning my work with them over a whole year.

A Teacher of English at a High School (*Kantonsschule*)

Excerpts from interviews answering students' questions:

Mr Wagner, we have often wondered how old you really are. With a grey moustache like yours?

I was born in 1935.

Tell us something about when you went to school.

Well, I was born in Stuttgart. My parents weren't exactly rich, but we always had what we needed. That is, except chocolate. My father, together with his cousin, had a chocolate factory.

I went to primary school for about two and a half years out of the regulation four - the rest was wasted on air raids and hiding in cellars while the French and German armies took several turns conquering the village where we lived after our house and factory had been bombed.

After the war I managed to get into a well-known Stuttgart *Gymnasium* - we did Latin, a lot of music (no books needed to read or write in) and all the rest of it. And later Greek, which I rather liked, especially Nausicaa, the pretty princess, sneaking up on shipwrecked Odysseus with not a stitich on him.

When I passed my *Abitur* exam in 1955 - I was 19 then - I couldn't make up my mind as to whether to go in for some sort of engineering or for a teaching career. So, for a change, I followed my father's advice and learned the respectable trade of a micro-electro mechanic.

Do you mean you became an ordinary apprentice after you Abitur exam?

That's right. The training was supposed to last three years and a half, but they granted me the diploma called *Facharbeiterbrief* a year earlier.

But you didn't really go into engineering, did you?

Apparently not. I found out that in the economic world you had to use your elbows ruthlessly if you wanted to stay in the rat race and get promoted in the hierarchy of the company you worked for, and that you always had to do what other people told you to do. I didn't like either, and so I decided on a schoolmaster's career.

Do you mean to say you actually wanted to be a teacher in the first place?

Yes, I did. Crazy, isn't it? And I haven't even regretted it so far. After my apprenticeship I went to the university of Tübingen near Stuttgart, where I started reading English, German and Latin: English because of good marks; German because I already knew German, didn't I? and Latin because I couldn't choose Greek. Within a year, however, I found out that Latin was no substitute for Greek; that reading German included learning Old High German and studying Adalbert Sifter, two terrible bores; and - worse still - that I couldn't even understand the Londoners who kindly and patiently tried to show me the way. So I gave up Latin, decided to like English and German for other reasons, and to move a little further away from my dear family, spending the next year at Freiburg in the Black Forest.

But doesn't changing universities cost a lot of time?

It doesn't shorten the time you spend studying for your degree, if that's what you mean. But it's extremely interesting and educating.

I applied for a very lavish scholarship at Edinburgh university. I was lucky to get it (mainly because the important people were so impressed by my apprenticeship) and spent my third year there.

So that's where you learnt your English?

Yes, I think so. Mainly by translating Thomas Mann's *Zauberberg* into English at the German Department, like my English speaking fellow students, which was terribly unfair!

On returning to Switzerland I went to Zurich for a semester or two to do semantics, hoping to be able to do a doctoral thesis in this field one day. That was in 1960. I decided to stay a little longer, as I had grown fond of Zurich, its university (about 4500 students then!) and a sweet Swiss lass who played second fiddle in the students' orchestra, where I played the bassoon sitting right behind her pretty neck. Music has always played an important role in my life, so why shouldn't it here?

I decided not to go back to Germany. Besides, I needed money to have my old *Isetta* car repaired. So I decided to try and teach English and German to two classes at the then *Töchterschule*, which meant girls only. Just imagine me, after nine years at boys' school!

Was it awful?

No, not really, I had done my teacher training at that high school and survived it. If "teacher training" is the right name for a one-semester course in which eight students sat in on a number of English classes and taught two lessons. Well, the teacher who ran the course was fantastic: she positively lived either in England (the one before 1939) or in her classroom - that was her life, besides gardening, of course. For her, teaching English wasn't a job, rather a vocation to her. I'd say it was her way of life, the only worthwhile way of living. Although I didn't learn a lot of useful teaching techniques and tricks from her, her attitude has had a great influence on me.

When did you become a teacher at our school, then?

In 1961. The time before the spring of 1964 was somewhat busy: my headmaster had advised me to apply for a permanent position at his and "my" school, which meant preparing for my degree exam within four months, a year earlier than planned; it meant preparing for the *Diplom für das Höhere Lehrant,* the teaching diploma; it also meant having lots of surprise visitors in my lessons who wanted to see me teach before they appointed me to a permanent post. (Well, *permanent* here means for six years, not for life as in Germany). Besides, I wanted to marry the neck - you remember? - which took a little preparation, too. The doctorate had to wait till 1967: a full teaching load doesn't leave you enough time for such luxuries.

What was your thesis about?

Five English adjectives meaning more or less the same as German *frech.*

Where did you get your professional training, apart from that one-semester course you've mentioned?

In those days that was all, and only very few candidates bothered to take the teaching diploma, too. I took it because I was a foreigner then and wanted to stay on. Nowadays the training course takes a whole year and includes at least 30 lessons taught by the candidate under close supervision of experienced teachers, and many more periods to sit in. Quite a few schools appoint a *Mentor* to supervise and advise a young teacher during her or his first semester of regular teaching. But it's still not an impressive lot of formal training, is it?

You can say that again - if you think of the two years of training my sister had to undergo to become a primary school teacher! And it'll soon be three years.

That's right. It's also very little compared with the training in, say, Germany. But funnily enough, pupils who came from German *Gymnasien* to our school agreed that teachers here weren't so much worse than their former teachers. I wonder why...

Perhaps with Swiss teachers it's in the blood. They're sort of born to be teachers.

That's it, of course! Another reason might be that high school teachers are usually (or: unusually?) well paid in Switzerland and enjoy a lot of leeway to choose what they want to do in their classes. That attracts people with initiative, love for their subject and classroom work to the profession - although there *will* be others, too, as in every other walk of life. And since the mid-sixties there have been an increasing number of in-service training opportunities to choose from. Teaching has definitely become much more professional than it used to be - whatever that may mean.

You've been at this school since 1961. Isn't that terribly boring? And don't you want to be promoted?

Well, there's no need for me to get promoted: our salaries rise with our experience (ehem!)

for a number of years, and I'd hate the life of a headmaster: I want to teach young people, not to bargain with old politicians and settle petty disputes among the staff or personnel. And here in Zurich most heads are nominated by and from among their former staff, which means no change of school for them, either, for better or worse.

Is that boring? Let me put it like this: if you feel you're teaching *the same subject matter* every year, the answer may well be Yes. But it's No if you are aware you teach a *different bunch of people* every year. Perhaps this has something to do with the attitude I mentioned when I told you about my teacher training. and anyway, at upper level we can read different things with every class, if we like; there are no lists of books we have to "do".

Besides, like most of my colleagues, I've done quite a few things alongside my teaching: I studied and introduced language labs in the early seventies, trying to suggest *meaningful* ways of using them - our lab is still used successfully by quite a number of colleagues. I was in charge of the *Swiss Association of Teachers of English* for a term of three years. I introduced video at our school and took part in our courses in *Medienkunde*, i.e. education towards a better understanding of the media. I was one of the first teachers at our school to own a computer, which is the main reason why I am now a member of our computer science department, by the way the only language teacher among them. And in the spring of 1988 I went into the training of future teachers of English, which is a great challenge to me as well as a welcome change in a long teaching life.

What training have you received for that?

That's a very clever question. The answer is: none. I have to draw on the experience of almost thirty years of teaching and of writing a textbook (I am one of the authors of *English, of Course!*, which is used fairly widely in this country), and I'm desperately trying to squeeze in some reading between my other duties. In a few years we may have some training for teacher trainers, too, but at the moment all depends on personal initiative - which is still alive, perhaps owing to the relatively high degree of autonomy high school teachers are enjoying here - still.

So you haven't done any in-service training yourself?

I wouldn't say that. In course of time I've attended - and organised - quite a number of in-service training courses - my next will be a week in Thomas Hardy's "Wessex" on the South Coast of England - but I haven't attended any courses on teacher training yet.

I must say we envy you a little. At least I do. Talking about your ten-year-old beard again: am I right it'll be another ten years or so to your pensioning?

....retirement.....

Of course: retirement; pension is what you get when you are retired, isn't it? Anyway, how do you feel about those ten years ahead of you?

I think if I hadn't had the chance of starting something new like this teacher training job recently, the thought would have worried me. As it is, however, I'm not worried at all. You know, young people like you have a healthy way of asking awkward questions. That's a powerful challenge that will not let you sit back and be pleased with yourself. Actually, I feel that it is this challenge that I'll miss most after I've made room for a younger colleague.

Vocational education and the teacher

VOCATIONAL EDUCATION AND THE TEACHER

This volume has taken as its focus that of teacher and teaching in primary/elementary schools; in lower secondary schools; and in upper secondary schools - where such patterns exist. A specific issue relates to vocational training and the teacher, and, as the foregoing chapters have illustrated, the distinction between education and vocational training can be very sharp or blurred. In some countries (Sweden is an example) vocational skills and experiences are built into basic or compulsory education for all children. At the post-compulsory level every attempt is made to integrate in one building those students who specialise in specific vocational skills and take occupational 'lines' with other students who prepare for university entry and other forms of higher education. In some countries (such as The Netherlands) vocational subjects are introduced early in the educational system, and in a vocational/technical school existing at the first as well as the second stage of secondary education. At LBO level vocational subjects are assessed in school-based examinations. Some countries (such as Belgium, Luxembourg and Italy) have created a new system of vocational education. Developments in Belgium have allowed some young people to follow more flexible course patterns. In the new Spanish curriculum, based on modules, all pupils will experience vocational education; what was a bi-partite approach has been abandoned as divisive and ineffective.

Various models become apparent. The comprehensive model, evident in Sweden, will try to bring together academic and vocational programmes under one roof. In Sweden the upper level Gymnasium School is a good example of this. Academic and Vocational 'lines' provide for a wide range of subjects, taken by those who continue their schooling following on the basic comprehensive school, and by adults returning to education.

The bi-partite model, the traditional model for many European countries, shows academic and vocational schools coexisting, but largely parallel to each other. In the Federal Republic of West Germany the dual model is one which provides the academic pupils with a university-preparing Gymnasium, and - for the remaining pupils - an apprenticeship system with part-time formal instruction and practice in various industrial and commercial enterprises.

It is also evident that many countries are preparing their pupils for future vocations by providing a solid, and prolonged general education and, increasingly, incorporating work orientation courses into these programmes. The Swedish example has been quoted. In the Danish Folkeskole the class teacher is responsible for imparting the necessary information relating to vocational guidance. In the 7th-9th classes the teacher can call in not only the educational and vocational counselling teacher, but also guest instructors and experts. The class teacher can also conduct study tours and send pupils out to job practice.

Within the UK many students are involved in specific schemes of work promoted and sponsored by the Technical and Vocational Education Initiative, or TVEI, and using their secondary school as a base. A vocational strand is therefore integral to the secondary curriculum, as a whole. After completing their compulsory education some pupils will enter Further Education colleges, on a full or part-time basis, for further general education, or for specific vocational skills.

Such examples serve to remind us of the complexities of provision, and of the difficulties involved in defining - or separating a "vocational" teacher from others. In many respects the class teacher is intimately involved; there are teachers of particular subjects or skills, who may feel more obviously 'vocational' than 'academic'; there are those who work specifically in secondary level vocational schools, and upper secondary or post compulsory technical-vocational institutions. There are also those who are, increasingly, recruited from trades and industrial experience, and for work at different levels of the school systems.

Additional to the models described above, comparative studies carried out by the European Centre for the Development of Vocational Training have shown that the EC Member States can be grouped by 'type' of initial vocational training, as follows:

a) those countries where initial vocational training is predominantly based in companies, with supplementary school-based elements (as in the dual system of West Germany, and also in Denmark);
b) those countries where initial vocational training in predominantly school-based, and where such training is largely concerned with basic and foundation skills. Subsequent training in specific skills will usually be provided later in companies, and via specific training programmes (as in The Netherlands, and in France);
c) those southern Member countries where no regular vocational training system yet exists, but where vocational training will start after the completion of a general education, and is company based. Greece and Portugal provide us with such examples.

Within the context of this study, and of particular interest and relevance to all teachers, are the developments leading towards a vocational training policy for the European Community; the work and contributions of CEDEFOP; and the recognition and/or comparability of non-university vocational training qualifications obtained in the different Member States.

Article 128 of the Treaty of Rome refers to the fact that:
"The council shall, acting on a proposal from the commission and after consulting the Economic and Social Committee, lay down general principles for implementing a common vocational training policy capable of contributing to the harmonious development both of national economies, and of the common market."

In addition Article 118 calls for close cooperation, and particularly in matters related to basic and advanced vocational training. Further articles relate to policy action in the field of vocational training (article 59); the right of establishment (article 52); and to the free movement of workers (article 48).

From 1963, with the Council decision to lay down general principles for implementing a common vocational training policy, further decisions or resolutions have been made concerning an action programme for the vocational training of young people.

In 1982, for example, in the preamble to the Draft Resolution of the Council (concerning Vocational Training Policies in the European Communities in the 1980's) the Council of the European Communities re-emphasized the 'vital place of training' within public policies generally and considered that 'a new commitment is required to develop convergent policies throughout the Community which place a much higher premium on the importance of investment in human resources'. In the Draft Resolution Member States were invited to develop their vocational training policies, and to take the necessary measures to ensure that all young people who so wish, may receive as a minimum:

a) a full-time programme of social and vocational preparation for working life during an initial one-year period immediately after the end of full-time compulsory schooling;
b) an entitlement to the equivalent of a further one-year period of vocational training to be used on a full-time or part-time basis before reaching the age of 25.

Substantial subsidies for initial or continuing training projects have been contributed from the European Social Fund, and also by the European Regional Development Fund.

Particularly significant is the European Centre for the Development of Vocational Training (CEDEFOP).[1] As well as serving as a centre for initiating and coordinating research, and disseminating these research findings, CEDEFOP is also a platform for national authorities, trade unions, associations of employers and other organisations involved in initial and continuing training. In addition some current activities include matters relating to the comparability of vocational training qualifications; and programmes of study visits for vocational training specialists.

By the end of 1988 preliminary findings were available on the comparability of vocational training qualifications in six occupational groups (covering some 100 occupations).[2]

The implications of 1992, reviewed in the earlier chapters of this book, are unlikely to change, overnight, the educational structures, programmes, or vocational training. Nonetheless, the exchange flows of peoples with particular skills; the growing number of exchange schemes; the action programmes promoted by ERASMUS and COMETT; and the variety of transnational training projects will undoubtedly encourage greater mobility in the education and vocational training systems. The acceleration of developments related to initial and continuing vocational training will be of particular importance to teachers, along with increasing competence in Community languages; and a concern that vocational training, and qualification, is valid and convertible within the different states of the European Community.

The goal of free movement of persons and services by 1993, and the possible introduction of a European Vocational Training Pass[3], are matters about which all teachers - whether specifically concerned with vocational knowledge and skills, or with more general subjects - should be increasingly aware.

Footnotes

1 *CEDEFOP was established by a decision of the Council in 1975. It incorporates some 30 work projects, and is based at: Jean Monnet House, Bundesallee 22, D-1000 Berlin 15.*

2 *See also Information sheet on the comparability of vocational training qualifications between the Member States of the European Community. 89/C 209/01. Official Journal of the European Communities 14 August 1989. Priority has been given to "occupations which most frequently give rise at present or in the future to the movement of workers*

within the Community on account, for example, of a geographical imbalance between vacancies and applications or the foreseable consequences of completion of the internal market".

In spite of the complexity and difficulties involved in this work the Community is determined to meet the target date of 31 December 1992. The timetable has been set as follows:

In 1990
- *textiles - clothing*
- *textiles - industry*
- *metalworking*
- *office work/administration*
- *chemicals*
- *commerce*

In 1991
- *tourism*
- *transport*
- *agro-foodstuffs and food processing occupations*
- *public works*

In 1992
- *printing*
- *woodworking*
- *iron and steel*
- *leatherworking*

3 *The idea of a European Vocational Training Pass was advocated by the committee for a People's Europe in its report delivered in March 1985. In the Council Decision of 16 July 1985 on the comparability of vocational training qualifications between the Member States of the European Community it was affirmed that "The Commission is to continue studying the introduction of the European vocational training pass".*

Further information available to teachers involved in vocational subjects and vocational training may be obtained from:

1) EURYDICE European Unit, Rue Archimède 17/Bte 17, B-1040 Brussels
The Education Structures in the Member States of the European Communities (1986)

2) IFAPLAN, 32 Square Ambïorix, B-1050 Brussels
Newsletter, for all those participating or interested in The European Community Action Programme *"Transition from Education to Working Life".*

3) O.E.C.D.
Education in O.E.C.D. Countries (1986-1987). A Compendium of Statistical Information (1989)

4) UK Centre for European Education, c/o Seymour House, Seymour Mews, London, W1H 9PE.
Publications include *EVE. European Vocational Education (1988)*

5) Youth Forum of the European Communities, Rue de La Science 10, Wetenshapstraat, B-1040 Brussels.
Publications include *"A European Perspective on Vocational Training for Young People"*.

Part 3

Looking Forward

LOOKING FORWARD

Voir loin et préparer l'avenir: c'est l'objectif que se sont fixé ceux qui, en 1956, ont créé l'AEDE. Ils avaient conscience de l'importance qu'aurait, pour les nouvelles générations, une connaissance approfondie des problèmes européens et ils ont donc considéré, dès cette époque, que les enseignants auraient la mission importante de préparer leurs élèves et leurs étudiants à faire face âa des situations nouvelles.

Il semble bien, par contre, que les négociateurs des Traités n'aient pas prévu que les systèmes éducatifs auraient un rôle important à jouer dans la construction de l'Europe.

Une seule clause du Traité CECA concerne la formation: l'article 56 prévoit "une aide non remboursable" pour contribuer "au financement de la rééducation professionnelle des travailleurs amenés à changer d'emploi" (dans les industries du charbon et de l'acier, s'entend).

Le Traité CEE va un peu plus loin, puisqu'il se fonde sur les principes de libre établissement et de mobilité. Il a donc prévu à l'article 57 qu'il fallait prendre des directives "visant la reconnaissance mutuelle des diplômes, certificates et autres titres".

L'article 128 charge aussi le Conseil (des Ministres) d'établir "les principes généraux pour la mise en oeuvre d'une politique commune de formation professionnelle qui puisse contribuer au développement harmonieux tant des économies nationales que du marché commun". Dans cette politique commune de formation professionnelle, on n'est pas encore très loin; de toute façon quand on en discute, c'est davantage au Comité des Ministres du Travail qu'à celui des Ministres de l'Education.

Pendant longtemps, les systèmes éducatifs eux-mêmes se sont donné un rôle mineur dans cette vaste entreprise que constitue la réalisation d'une Communauté européenne. Il est significatif que la première réunion des Ministres de l'Education de la C.E. n'ait eu lieu qu'en novembre 1971, que la deuxième se soit tenue en juin 1974, soit deux ans et demi plus tard, et que le premier programme d'action en matière d'éducation ait été adopté en février 1976, vingt-trois ans après l'entrée en vigueur du Traité CECA, dix-huit an après l'entrée en vigueur du traité CEE. Ce traité a été interprété de manière très stricte et l'on considère encore, officiellement, que l'éducation n'est pas une matière communautaire. Tout ce qui s'y fait, au niveau européen, relève donc de la **coopération.** On comprend le souci des gouvernements nationaux - et dans beaucoup de pays, des gouvernements "regionaux" - de préserver leurs compétences dans un domaine aussi délicat dans une société qui entend fonder son développement sur la responsabilité individuelle et sur le respect, voire la promotion de la diversité. La société européenne perdrait certes une bonne partie de sa richesse culturelle, de son efficacité à répondre aux défis multiples que lui pose son développement, si elle se lançait dans une politique d'uni formisation systématique de l'enseignement. Mais les faits eux-mêmes ont fait apparaître qu'une position 'maximaliste" dans ce domaine présentait quelques inconvénients et suscitait des problèmes.

L'Europe des citoyens (A People's Europe)

A la fin des années soixante il devient clair que le marché commun ne s'établira pas par la vertu des seuls mécanismes des Traités, et qu'il y faudra une vision et une volonté politiques. On va, dès lors, avoir recours aux "Sommets", c'est-à-dire aux réunions des chefs d'Etat et de Gouvernement, dont on attend qu'ils définissent les grands objectifs à moyen terme et dénouent les situation de blocage. Le premier Sommet s'est tenu à La Haye en 1969. Il y a été souhaité que la jeunesse soit "étroitement associée" aux "actions créatrices et de croissance européenne" dont il a décidé. Le Sommet de Paris (décembre 1974) a fait un pas de plus et a exprimé la volonté d'assurer une coopération plus grande dans le domaine de l'éducation. Entretemps, la Commission avait créé au sein de son administration un "Groupe enseignement et éducation, qui est devenu, en 1973 la "Direction Générale Recherche, Sciences et Education". (Toutefois, un remaniement postérieur a replacé ce service au niveau d'une direction de la Direction Générale des Affaires sociales). En février 1976, les Ministres de l'Education ont enfin approuvé un programme d'action en matière d'éducation.

Voilà donc le bateau enfin mis à flots, vingt-cinq ans après. Encore la résolution de 1976 ne vise-t-elle pas à mener ce bateau très loin. Elle est axée, en effet, sur la notion de "correspondance": il s'agit essentiellement d'améliorer l'enseignement en assurant "la confrontation permanente des politiques, des expériences et des idées entre les Etats membres". On ne peut pas dire que ce soit là un objectif révolutionnaire, puisqu'il était déjà, celui du conseil de l'Europe, et même de l'UNESCO et du BIE.

Toutefois, les événements vont se charger de bouleverser ce shéma de pères tranquilles. J'en retiendrai trois: la crise économique, qui commence dès 1973, la situation politique, la recherche scientifique qu'elle a suscités.

La crise économique

La crise économique, l'accroissement du chômage, placent les responsables des systèmes éducatifs européens devant un nouveau problème: la liaison entre l'école et la vie active.

En 1976, il n'est plus possible, dans l'examen de cette question, de limiter la perspective au seul enseignement professionnel.

Ce sont les liens entre l'ensemble du système éducatif et l'environnement économique et social qui, cette fois font l'objet des réflexions, et, surtout, des récriminations. Le rôle social et économique de l'école est ainsi mis en évidence. C'est, pour un enseignement qui, dans l'ensemble, reste encore attaché, à cette époque, à la notion européenne traditionnelle de la culture, une situation assez neuve et inconfortable.

Dans les années soixante, on avait beaucoup parlé de l'école comme facteur de développement. Comment dès lors échapper, dix ans plus tard, en période de crise, à cette question insidieuse: l'ecole pourrait-elle être un facteur de non-développement?

Les Ministres de l'Education se sont donc réunis une deuxième fois pendant l'année 1976, le 13 décembre, et ils ont adopté une résolution "concernant les mesures à prendre en vue d'améliorer la préparation des jeunes à l'activité professionnelle et de faciliter leur passage de l'éducation à la vie active". Cette résolution comprend une liste de mesures que les Etats membres s'engagent à prendre. Il vaut mieux de ne pas les énumérer, car il faudrait constater qu'elles restent toutes pertinentes, quatorze ans plus tard mais que bien peu a été fait pour les mettre en pratique.

La résolution comprend cependant une disposition en quelque sorte révolutionnaire: pour la première fois, la Commission est chargée, de mettre en oeuvre, au niveau communautaire, des projets pilotes que l'on peut appeler: intégrés. Certes, les autorités nationales se réservent le droit de choisir le écoles et de définir les thèmes précis des expériences. Mais celles-ci doivent s'inscrire dans un plan d'ensemble et être soumis à une équipe internationale; elles seront suivies par celle-ci et le programme fera l'objet d'un rapport d'ensemble. Ce projet a été reconduit plusieurs fois et s'est poursuivi de 1977 à 1987.

Les conclusions ont été soumises au Conseil des Ministres du 24.5.1988 et ce projet a été prolongé, en quelque sorte, par le projet PETRA (1).

La Situation Politique

Au début des années soixante-dix, il devient évident que l'Europe ne se réalisera pas mécaniquement par le jeu des traités, mais qu'il y faudra une volonté politique. D'où le recours de plus en plus fréquent aux "Sommets" des chefs d'Etat et de Gouvernement chargés de dépanner, de donner des orientations, de fixer des délais. Ces "Sommets" finiront par être institutionnalisés en 1986, par le traité appelé "Acte Unique", sous le nom de: Conseil européen.

Parallèlement, l'Assemblée parlementaire se voit accorder plus de pouvoirs. En 1976 un pas important est franchi: cette assemblée est dorénavant élue au suffrage universel et reçoit le nom de Parlement Européen. Ce Parlement Européen prend l'initiative d'étudier une réforme des institutions afin d'accroitre le caractère suprantational de celles-ci.

L'Acte unique réalisera sur ce point un compromis entre les Gouvernements et la majorité Parlementaire.

Le Sommet de Paris (1972) qui a marqué son accord sur le premier élargissement (intervenu en 1973 par l'adhésion du Danemark, de l'Irlande et du Royaume-Uni), s'était aussi donné pour objectif de réaliser l'Union Européenne en 1980. On comprend donc que, de 1975 à 1985, les Sommets se soient beaucoup préoccupés de l'image de la Communauté Européenne dans l'opinion.

Ils s'attachent à définir les grands objectifs politiques, ou plutot, de civilisation, de la Communauté: Déclaration sur la démocratie (Copenhague, 1978), Déclaration solennelle sur l'Union européenne (Stuttgart, 1983), l'Europe des citoyens (Fontainebleau, 1984 et Milan 1985).

Le sentiment se précise que la promotion d'une conscience européenne est, aussi, affaire d'éducation. Les systèmes éducatifs se voient donc de plus en plus sollicités de faire une place, dans leur enseignement, à l'Europe.

Cette sollicitation s'est fortement accrue depuis que l'Acte Unique (1986) a inséré dans le traité CEE un article 8 A qui dispose: "La Communauté arrete les mesures destinées à établir progressivement le marché intérieur au cours d'une période expirant le 31 décembre 1992".

(1) lère phase: 1989-1990 - budget prévu en 1990: 90 M ECU.

Les institutions peuvent rester lettre morte, les décisions ne s'inscriront pas dans la réalité si la volonté de réalisation n'est pas présente, si les mentalités adéquates font défaut.

Sur ce plan, on peut dire que la problématique européene n'est qu'un cas particulier (mais qui a le grand avantage de présenter les problèmes avec un verre grossissant) d'un phénomène général: des sociétés qui connaissent une accélération importante du rythme du changement exigent, pour maintenir la cohérence et l'harmonie de leur développement, que les institutions, mais surtout les individus aient la capacité:

- de détecter le changement;
- de l'orienter, de s'en servir, de s'y adapter.

Discuter de l'apport de l'Europe à l'école et de l'école à l'Europe, c'est attirer l'institution scolaire sur le terrain de l'actuel, du mouvant, du conflictuel. Or notre école reste encore fort attachée à une image d'elle-même comme d'un lieu où l'accent est mis sur ce qui est permanent et sur ce qui vient de la tradition. Et si elle fait une bonne place à la discussion, elle ne dispose pas d'une pédagogie bien assurée dès qu'il s'agit de s'engager sur le terrain de la prospective, de l'indéterminé, du choix ouvert.

Revolution Technologique et Recherche Scientifique

C'est dès 1964 que la Commission est intervenue dans le domaine de la recherche.

Cette intervention a été institutionnalisée en 1974 par la création du Comité de la Recherche scientifique et technique (CREST).

A noter que l'article 24 de l'Acte Unique (1986) inclut la recherche et le développement technologique dans les matières communautaires par l'ajout, dans le traité CEE, d'un nouveau titre VI.

Le programme-cadre 1987-1991 prévoit, pour une période de quatre ans, un budget de 5.396 millions d'écus (2).

Les Universités sont souvent concernées par ces programmes de recherche, et on peut considérer que, par ce biais, le système d'éducation bénéficie non seulement de cet apport de ressources, mais aussi des progrès, dans le savoir, qui en résultent, des possibilités d'équipement et de collaboration avec d'autres institutions.

(2) **Exemples de programmes:**

ESPRIT (European Strategic Programme for Research and developement in Information Technology).
RACE (Research and development in Advanced Communication technology in Europe).
BRITE (Basic Research in Industrial Technologies for Europe).
BAP (Biotechnology Action Program).

JET (Joint European Torus) devenu **NET** (Next European Torus).
FAST (Forecasting and Assessment in the field of Science and Technology).
SPRINT (Strategic Programme for Innovation and Technology Transfer).

Au reste, c'est au niveau de l'Université que la Commission a pu développer le mieux ses initiatives en matière d'éducation.

Cela tient au fait que dans tous nos pays les Universités bénéficient d'un statut qui leur laisse une bonne marge d'autonomie et d'initiative.

Dès 1976, la Commission a lancé un double programme: l'un destiné, par un système de bourses, à encourager le personnel enseignant, le personnel administratif et les chercheurs à effectuer de brefs séjours d'étude dans d'autres Etats membres, le but étant d'augmenter à long terme les possibilités de collaboration entre les établissements; l'autre visant à encourager le développement de programmes d'études en commun entre établissements d'enseignement supérieur de plusieurs Etats membres, l'objectif étant d'inciter des établissements à développer des programmes semblables sur des sujets déterminés et d'échanger, ainsi, professeurs et étudiants.

Un réseau d'établissements a pu être constitué et un système européen de crédits académiques transférables (European academic credits transferable system - ECTS) a pu être développé. Il ne fait pas de doute que ces activitiés ont permis de préparer le programme ERASMUS qui a débuté en octobre 1987.

La Formation Professionnelle

La place de la formation professionnelle au sein de la CEE n'est pas très claire. D'abord, parce qu'elle est en quelque sorte un "mixte". Il est question d'elle dans le Traité, et le Conseil, la Commission, le Comité Economique et social s'en sont occupés bien avant qu'on ne pense à réunir les Ministres de l'Education.

Des directives et des résolutions sont donc prises, maintenant encore, par le Conseil des Ministres du Travail et/ou des Affaires sociales.

Les Ministres de l'Education et les Ministres du Travail et des Affaires sociales ont tenu une fois une réunion commune, le 3 juin 1983, au sujet du passage des jeunes de l'éducation à l'âge adulte et à la vie active.

Mais, sur ce plan aussi, l'Acte Unique a changé les persepctives. Il a inséré, en effet, dans le Traité CEE, un chapitre V intitulé: La cohésion économique et sociale.

La réalisation du marché intérieur suppose, en effet, "un développement harmonieux de l'ensemble de la Communauté", selon les termes du nouvel article 130 A. Ceci implique que la cohésion économique et sociale soit renforcée afin de rendre possible la mobilité et la liberté d'établissement.

Mais comment y arriver si on n'adapte pas, en conséquence, les systèms d'éducation et de formation? Non seulement en prenant les mesures qui permettront de créer un système de

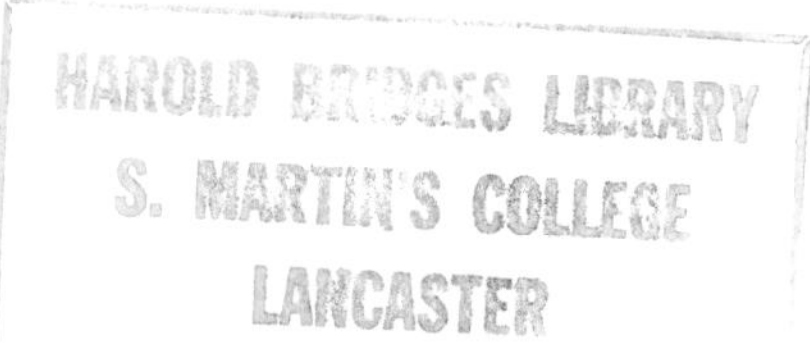

recconnaissance et de correspondance des qulifications à tous les niveaux, mais encore en introduisant une réelle dimension européenne dans l'enseignement et en promouvant l'apprentissage des langues.

Si l'on donne cette ampleur au problème (et comment ne pas le faire?) il paraît bien difficile d'établir une distinction précise entre formation professionnelle et éducation; il devient aussi impossible de nier que tout en restant, au terme des traités, du domaine de la coopération, l'éducation est devenue, en fait, une composante importante des politiques communautaires.

La Commission l'a bien senti et son action dans le domaine de l'éducation s'élargit et se fait de plus en plus insistante. Elle se rend bien compte toutefois que, sur ce terrain, il faut savoir ne pas aller trop loin.

Parce qu'il serait "contreproductif" de trop globaliser et d'uniformiser au moment même où l'on s'aperçoit qu'un des grands problèmes des systèmes éducatifs est contitué par leur manque de souplesse face à des situations régionales et locales qui se diversifient, et par une longueur trop grande de leur temps de réaction face à l'accélération du changement.

La Commission a donc déclaré qu'elle entend agir dans le respect de la diversité. Elle a aussi mis en avant, pour définir son rôle, la notion de subsidiarité: elle se donne donc essentiellement une mission de catalyseur et de coordonnateur.

La Dimension Europeenne Dans L'Enseignement

Ce qui est arrivé à la notion de dimension européenne permet de mesurer le chemin parcouru ces dix dernières années.

En juin 1978, la Commission a soumis au Comité de l'Education un rapport intitulé: "Activités pédagogiques comportant une dimension européene". Constatant les lacunes dans ce domaine, la Commission proposait d'établir à ce sujet un programme cohérent et de définir une stratégie globale tant au niveau national qu'au niveau communautaire.

Ce document ne donna pas lieu à des discussions importantes et fut bien vite classé. Ce n'est que sept années plus tard, et non sans difficultés, que les Ministres de l'Education adopèrent, le 27.9.1985, des "Conclusions" "relatives à une meilleure mise en valeur de la dimesnion européenne dans l'éducation".

Ce document, très succinct, prévoyait toutefois que le Comité de l'Education devait présenter tous les deux ans un rapport "sur l'état d'avancement des travaux au niveau des Etats membres et à celui de la Communauté".

Cette disposition a permis de maintenir cette question à l'ordre du jour, de sorte que les Ministres ont adopté le 24 mai 1988, sur le même sujet, un autre document qui a pris, cette fois, la forme d'une "résolution". Ce document de trois pages, définit les objectifs et l'action à entreprendre, au niveau des Etats membres et au niveau de la Communauté Européenne.

L'Acte Unique

La conclusion de l'Acte Unique a constitué dans le domaine de l'éducation comme ailleurs, un facteur décisif dans le renouvellement de l'approche des problèmes et de la recherche de solution.

Une comparaison entre la Déclaration du 27/9/1985 et la Résolution du 24 mai 1988 est éclairante à ce propos.

En 1985, l'idée de base reste, comme en 1974, d'assurer une meilleure connaissance réciproque.

En 1988, l'accent est mis sur la préparation de 1992, celle-ci étant présentée comme un défi pour les Etats membres, l'économie, les entreprises, les personnes et la Communauté, mais aussi sur la nécessité de réaliser l'"Europe des citoyens".

Deux concepts émergent dès lors. Celui de développement (développement économique, social, technique, scientifique, culturel) qui sera favorisé par la réalisation du Marché Commun et par la création d'un espace de civilisation où les relations sont fondées sur un ensemble de valeurs (affirmées explicitement à plusieurs reprises par la Cour de Justice): la paix, l'unité, l'égalité, la liberté individuelle et les droits fondamentaux des personnes, la solidarité, le besoin de sécurité.

Celui de cohésion, cohésion économique et sociale, qui doit favoriser la mobilité et la liberté d'établissement, elles-mèmes sources de progrès.

Le Programme A Moyen Terme

Profitant de ce changement de climat, la Commission s'est enhardie à préparer un projet de programme à moyen terme (1989-1992) en matière d'éducation. Elle l'a soumis dès février 1988 à une réunion informelle que les Ministres de l'Education ont tenue à Münster.

En novembre de la même année, a été obtenu un élargissement du programme COMETT (1990-1994) en même temps que l'association, à ce programme, des Ministres de l'Education, a été acquise; vers la même période, la deuxième phase d'ERASMUS (1991-1995) a été acceptée, avec des moyens accrus et la Commission a mis en chantier le programme LINGUA, en même temps qu'elle annonçait que le programme YES serait opérationnel au 1/1/1989.

Au surplus, au Journal Officiel de la Communauté du 24/01/1989 paraissait la Directive relative à l'équivalence, sur la base du principe de confiance mutuelle, des diplômes du niveau: enseignement secondaire + trois ans.

Le deuxième semestre de 1988 apparaît donc comme une période décisive pour ce qui conerne la place accordée à l'éducation dans les mécanismes de développement de la Communauté.

Ajoutons-y qu'après plus d'un an de consultations, la Commission a été à même de présenter un document intitulé: "L'éducation et la formation dans la Communauté européenne - Lignes directrices pour le moyen terme: 1989-1992".

La Commission y définit les principes qui la guideront dans son action et dans le domaine de l'éducation et de la formation, ses méthodes de travail et les priorités qu'elle se fixe.

C'est la première fois qu'un document aussi précis a été élaboré.

Tout laisse penser que de nouvelles étapes pourront être franchies dans la reconnaissance mutuelle des diplômes et des qualifications à des fins professionnelles en matière de mobilité des étudiants de l'enseignement supérieur, dnas le domaine d'une meilleure préparation au changement technologique et d'une meilleure utilisation des nouvelles technologies à l'école.

L'enseignement des langues garde, cela va de soi, une priorité particulière pour la Commission.

La Communaute Europeenne et L'Education

Ainsi une phase décisive quant à la place à accorder à l'éducation dans la politique communautaire a été entamée en 1988.

Les objectifs ont été clarifiés, les méthodes précisées, les moyens accrus.

Une image de ce que peut être un enseignement européen se dégage: il n'est pas question de coiffer le centralisme national par un centralisme européen; il convient au contaire d'accroitre la souplesse du système afin de raccourcir le temps de réponse, d'adaptation ou de parade aux stimuli extérieurs, d'enrichir les expériences des personnes et des institutions en créant un réseau de relations inter-personnelles et entre les institutions d'enseignement.

Par contre, il y a une tendance très nette à créer un climat général qui fasse des institutions d'enseignement des moyens puissants de progrès pour la société européenne: en préparant les jeunes générations à maîtriser les méchanismes délicats d'équilibre que suppose un régime démocratique, en précisant le rôle de l'éducation dans le développement économique et le progrès social, en favorisant un sentiment d'unité tout en préservant la richesse qu'apporte la diversité.

Aujourd'hui une série impressionnante de programmes fournissent, dans une multitude de secteurs, des moyens d'action nouveaux qui doivent permettre de créer un véritable tissu éducatif européen.

Les rapports indispensables entre la CEE et les pays de l'AELE (Association européenne du libre-échange), ceux de l'Europe centrale et orientale ne sont pas oubliés. Les premiers ont la possibilité de participer aux grands programmes, tels ERASMUS et COMETT; en faveur des seconds, une Fondation européenne pour la formation a été créée, conformément à une décision du Conseil Européen, qui s'est tenu les 8 et 9 décembre 1989, à Strasbourg.

Bref, le branle semble être donné, avec le réalisme mais aussi l'ambition et la largeur de vues qui conviennent.

Poursuivre l'intégration européenne, tout en maintenant l'ouverture sur le reste de l'Europe et sur le monde: tel semble bien être le cap, et il faut souhaiter que nous soyons capables de le garder.

Le Nouveau Rôle des Enseignants

En fait, la "problématique européenne" n'est qu'un cas particulier de phénomènes plus généraux qui se manifestent dans le développement des sociétés humaines en cette fin du IIème millénaire; et elle a l'avantage de nous permettre de mieux saisir les grands mouvements qui sont à l'oeuvre dans l'histoire contemporaine de l'humanité et qui nous forcent à une réflexion en profondeur au sujet de la mission des enseignants.

C'est dans les années soixante que nous avons pris conscience d'un phénomène d'accélération de l'évolution dans nos sociétés. Le rythme du développement des sciences 'et des techniques, de la transformation des modes de production, des biens et des services et des courants d'échanges, de l'évolution des mentalités, des moeurs, des valeurs s'est accru de manière telle qu'il a imposé le changement et l'innovation comme des données sociologiques fondamentales.

Au début des années soixante-dix, plusieurs sociologues se sont mis à étudier le phénomène de manière théorique; on a parlé alors d'une "société de changement", en la définissant comme une société où un changement significatif se produit dans les modes de production et dans les modes de vie en **une** génération.

Aujord'hui, vingt ans après, nous en sommes à considérer que des changements significatifs se produiront au moins deux, sinon trois fois au cours de la même génération.

Cette donnée sociologique fondamentale place nos systèmes d'enseignement devant des problèmes difficiles. Une longue tradition nous a fait considérer l'école comme étant essentiellment la gardienne des traditions, comme une institution vouée à mettre l'accent sur la permanence, les valeurs sûres, l'"identité" des nations et de groupes.

Depuis les années soixante-dix, nos systèmes éducatifs se trouvent dans une situation inconfortable: ils sont bousculés, harcelés pour qu'ils s'adaptent aux changements, mais ils se font critiquer par rapport à une tradition prestigieuse dès qu'ils s'engagent dans des réformes.

Nos systèmes éducatifs hésitent donc entre conservatisme et réformisme, ce qui ne satisfait personne. Par dessus le marché, les exigences s'accroissent.

Les réformes des années soixante et soixante-dix avaient pour objectif d'adapter l'école aux changements intervenus.

Aujourd'hui, on exige de l'éducation de s'organiser pour **promouvoir le changement** (songeons au rôle qu'on lui demande de jouer dans le changement de la condition féminine, dans la réalisation de l'égalité des chances etc..; on est allé jusqu'à parler de "discrimination positive"), et même pour devenir **un agent de développement**.

Or, en se donnant pour objectif de "faire progresser concrètement l'Union européenne" (article ler de l'Acte Unique) nos pays se sont placés résolument dans une optique de transformation fondamentale de nos sociétés en se référant à un ensemble d'options politiques et de valeurs définis dans plusieurs documents.

L'Union européenne est un devenir. Elle ne se réalisera concrètement que si les nouvelles générations sont capables de faire preuve d'imagination et de détermination. Tout est donc affaire d'information et de caractère (spirit) c'est-à-dire de culture, et par conséquent d'éducation.

Les enseignants européens ont, par conséquent, un rôle fondamental à jouer dans la construction de cet avenir commun. comment doivent-ils s'y prendre pour assumer ce rôle?

A ce jour, personne n'a la recette. Mais ils doivent se persuader qu'elle ne viendra pas d'ailleurs et qu'il leur appartient de définir ensemble les voies et moyens par lesquels ils pourront s'acquitter de leur mission.

Souhaitons-leur courage et bonne chance!

Pierre Vanbergen
Président International de l'AEDE

Part 4

Appendices

Appendix I

The European Association of Teachers AEDE/EAT

Appendix I
The European Association of Teachers AEDE/EAT

The Foundation of The Association

The European Association of Teachers was founded in Paris in 1956, by a group of French and German professors, many of whom had worked in wartime resistance groups, and were resolved to take effective action as teachers to develop a sense of European citizenship in their students, and prevent another catastrophe. Looking to the future of this continent, they believed a more united Europe could not come into being, unless its people were inspired by a European 'consciousness', which would have to start in schools staffed by teachers who supported this ideal. Within a decade the European 'Association of Teachers had spread to eleven Western European countries, and had recruited some 30,000 teachers, coming from all levels of teaching, and owing loyalty to its conception of European citizenship.

Since its foundation in 1956, National Sections have been formed in: AUSTRIA, BELGIUM, DENMARK, FRANCE, GREECE, IRELAND, ITALY, LUXEMBOURG, THE NETHERLANDS, PORTUGAL, SAN MARINO, SPAIN, SWITZERLAND, the UNITED KINGDOM and WEST GERMANY.

Aims and Structure of The Association

The aims of the Association as stated in the European Statutes are as follows:

a) to create among teachers an awareness of European problems, and to disseminate information which has a bearing on European unity.
b) to work by all available means towards a deeper understanding of those essential qualities which are characteristic of European civilisation, and to ensure their preservation: notably by increasing the number of international contacts at the personal level.
c) to develop a similar understanding among students and pupils, and in all other fields where the teacher may exert an influence
d) to support any valid initiatives directed to these ends.

The International Structure

The International Status of the Association requires that an International Congress be organised, as decided by the European Committee, at intervals of not less than one year, and not more than three years. In practice this Congress has been organised every three years, and has become known as the INTERNATIONAL TRIENNIAL CONGRESS.

The EUROPEAN COMMITTEE is charged with the execution of the decisions of the Congress. It directs the Association and controls the actions of the Executive Bureau, and co-ordinates the work of the National Sections by decisions taken at its meetings. The Officers who form the EXECUTIVE BUREAU, are elected at the Congress, for the ensuing three years, as under:

THE PRESIDENT • THREE VICE PRESIDENTS • THE SECRETARY-GENERAL • THE TREASURER • THE ASSISTANT SECRETARY-GENERAL

In addition three members are elected to the European Committee. THE EUROPEAN COMMITTEE is composed of the above ten elected members, plus the CHAIRMAN or SECRETARY of each of the National Sections. Three other members may be co-opted for special tasks. The European Committee is required to meet at least once a year, and the Bureau at least three time a year.

NATIONAL SECTIONS are administered by a National Committee. Each section is free to draw up its own regulations in accordance with European Status.

Appendix II

Resolution of the Council and Ministers of Education Meeting within the Council

on the European Dimension in Education, May 1988

Appendix II

RESOLUTION OF THE COUNCIL AND THE MINISTERS OF EDUCATION MEETING WITHIN THE COUNCIL

on the European Dimension in education 24 May 1988

In summary, this Resolution had a number of key objectives, viz:

- to strengthen the European dimension in Education, and by launching a series of concerted measures over the period 1988-1992. These measures would help to:
- strengthen a sense of European identity amongst young people;
- prepare young people to take part in the social and economic development of the Community;
- make them aware of the advantages and the challenges which the community represents;
- improve their knowledge of the Community and its Member States.

Levels of Action

In terms of the Member States:

- the incorporation of the European Dimension in educational systems;
- the encouragement of initiatives aimed at strengthening the European dimension in education;
- the development of the European dimension in schools curricula;
- the promotion of the European dimension within teaching materials;
- the increased emphasis given to the European dimension in teachers' initial and inservice education;
- the encouragement of contacts and meetings across borders between pupils, and teachers;
- the organisation of particular events, such as colloquia, seminars, school events, competitions and school twinning.

At the level of the European Community, the Commission was invited to:

- promote and exchange of information on concepts and measures in the different Member States;
- to prepare teaching materials and documentation;
- to encourage a range of initiatives related to teacher training; cooperation and exchange; and by specific additional measures.

Subsequent to this resolution we may also note the CONCLUSIONS OF THE COUNCIL AND THE MINISTERS FOR EDUCATION MEETING WITHIN THE COUNCIL 6 October 1989 on the matter of cooperation and Community policy in the field of education in the run-up to 1993.

Five key objectives were identified as a basis for future cooperation activities, and which will contribute to drawing the States closer together in the field of education and training, viz:

- a multicultural Europe;
- a mobile Europe;
- a Europe of training for all;
- a European of skills;
- a European open to the world.

Such shared objectives produced a wide range of recommendations, including:

- the progressive achievement of genuine multilingualism;
- drawing educational and training establishments closer together;
- supporting youth exchanges, and training periods abroad for teachers, instructors, pupils, students, and educational administrators;
- the development of procedures providing teachers with the opportunity to teach temporarily in educational establishments of other Member States;
- the development of appropriate teaching and training for disadvantaged children and of measures to combat failure at school;
- providing young people with a better preparation for working life;
- increased cooperation with international organisations dealing with education and training.

Appendix III

School ages; school weeks; school days

Appendix III

Compulsory School Ages		Length of School Week		School days per year	
		Primary	Secondary	Primary	Secondary
Belgium	6-18 (a)	5 days	5 days	182	182
Denmark	7-16	5 days	5 days	200	200
FRG	6-15/16	5 or 6 days	5 or 6 days	226/200	226/200 (c)
Greece	$5\frac{1}{2}$-$14\frac{1}{2}$	5 days	5 days	175	175
Spain	6-14	5 days	5 days	185	170
France	6-16	5 days	5 days/6 days (b)	316	316 (d)
Ireland	6-15	5 days	5 or 6 days	min. 184	min. 180
Italy	6-14	5 or 6 days	6 days	min. 200	min. 200
Luxembourg	5-15	6 days	6 days	216	216
Netherlands	5-16	5 or 6 days	5 or 6 days	200 240 (e)	195
Portugal	6-14/15	5 or 6 days	5 or 6 days	175 208 (e)	164
U.K.	5-16	5 days	5 days	190	190

a. includes part-time compulsory schooling
b. collèges/lycées
c. acc. to Länder
d. half days
e. 5 or 6 day system

Extracted from:
Tables on the School Year in the Member States of the European Community. Eurydice European Unit 1987

Appendix IV

Useful addresses

Appendix IV
USEFUL ADDRESSES

Association Européenne Des Enseignants / European Association of Teachers

Committee Members (1989)

President
Pierre Vanbergen
21, Rue St. Sébastien
B- 1420 BRAINE L'ALLEUD
(T.: 02/384.94.50)

Vice-President
Christos Collocas
10a, rue Zalongou
GR - 10678 ATHENES
(T.: 1.36.13.229)

Vice President
Jürgen Kummetat
Julius-Brechtstrasse, 16
D - 6231 SCHWALBACH
(T.: 06196-5515)

Vice President
Yves-Henri Nouailhat
61, rue F. de Pressensé
F - 44000 NANTES
(T.: Dom. 40.74.74.80
Prof. 40.74.74.01 ext. 337)

General Secretary
Guus Wijngaards
Koningsholster 64
NL - 6573 VV BEEK-UBBERGEN
(T.: 08895/42854)

Assistant General Secretary
Pierre Kernen
Longchamps, 42
CH - 2014 BOLE
(T.: 038.42.59.21)

Treasurer
Edmond Pepin
100, Rue C. Merjai
L - 2145 LUXEMBOURG-BEGGEN
(T.: 35.2.43.22.90)

Elected Members
Pierino Amadori
Via Euclide 23
I - 74100 TARANTO

John Jeffery
26 Loxley Road
Wandsworth
UK - London, SW18 3LJ

Lino Venturelli
Viale Riviera 283
I - 65100 PASCARA
(T.: Facoltà 085 - 389212
Instituto 085 - 21254)

Co-opted Members
Antoine Morimont
Avenue du Roi Albert, 145
B - 1080 BRUXELLES
(T.: 02/468.05.54)

Georges Peyronnet
80, Avenue de Suffren
F - 75015 PARIS
(T.: 1.43.06.49.75)

Representative of Section

Germany

President
Wolfgang Mickel
Heuchelkeimerstr. 122
BRD - 6380 HOMBURG

Secretary
Jurgen Kummetat
Julius-Brechtstrasse 16
BRD - 6231 SCHWALBACH a.d. T.
(T.: 06196/5515)

Ausrria

President
Leo Leitner
Zentrum für Schulversuche
Strozzig 2/V
A - 1080 WIEN

Secretary
Fritz Mairleitner
Zentrum für Schulversuche
Strozzig 2/V
A - 1080 WIEN

Belgium

Enseignement libre

President
Elie Joseph
Rijschoolstraat 9
B - 3300 TIENEN

Secretary
Claire Petit
Parc de la Sablonniere
Pavillon 5 - Bte 30
B - 7000 MONS

Belgium

Enseignement official

President
Pierre Vanbergen
21, Rue St. Sébastien
B - 1420 BRAINE L'ALLEUD

Secretary
Suzanne Rober
Avenue Winston Churchill, 143
B - 1180 BRUXELLES
(T.: 02/345.29.53)

Spain

President
Fdo Angel Sabin Sabin
p.o. della Castellana, 211
E - 28046 MADRID
(T.: dom. 4.48.19.58
prof. 7.33.07.55)

Secretary
Jose Angel Martin
c/Leneros, 38 - 4.D
E - 28039 Madrid

France

President
Roger-A. Lhombreaud
Le Parc de l'Ile Verte
28, avenue Gambetta
F - 78400 CHATOU

Secretary
AEDE France
Boite postale, 43
F - 78401 CHATOU-CEDEX

United Kingdom

President
Bryan Peck
10 Middleton Drive
Milngavie
Glasgow G62 8HT - GB

Secretary
Mary E Duce
20 Brookfield
Highgate West Hill
London N6 6AS - GB

Greece

President
Christos Collocas
10a, rue Zalongou
GR - 10678 ATHENES
(T.: 1.36.13.229)

Secretary
Georges Sotiriou

Italy

President
Francesco Giglio
10, Via Viviani
I - 85100 POTENZA

Secretary
Paolo Farnararo
Via Parmelide, 38
I - 84100 SALERNO
(T.: privé 089.334838
école 081.8664949)

Luxembourg

President
Eugene Linster
59, Rue de la Faiencerie
L - 1510 LUXEMBOURG

Secretary
Kitty Deville
9, Rue des Champs
L - 1323 LUXEMBOURG
(T.: 2.48.59.88)

The Netherlands

Secretary
Paul Minnee
Kroonsingel 126
NL - 6581 BP MALDEN
(T.: 080/580011)

Huub Koster
Spoorstraat 29
NL - 7003 DX DOETINCHEM

Portugal

President
Luciano Ravara
Avda da Liberdade, 229
P - 1200 LISBONNE
(T.: 570.524)

Secretary
Zita Magalhaes
Rua Coutinho de Azevedo, 214
P - 4000 PORTO

Switzerland

President
Pierre Kernen
Longchamps, 42
CH - 2014 BOLE
(T.: 038/42.59.21)

Secretary
Jean-Pierre Thibaud
La Riollaz, 5
CH - 1530 PAYERNE
(T.: 037/61.11.52)

Former Presidents

Andre Alers (1956-1974)
Président foundateur; président d'honneur de la Fondation A. BIEDERMANN
Populierenhoflaan Bus 8A
B - 3030 HEVERLEE (Leuven)
(T.: 016/206.771)

Jean Kamille Kech (1974-1981)
Av. de la Rousselière, 6b
B - 4500 JUPILLE s/Meuse

Alwin Westerhof (1982-1985)
Mahlerestr. 5/48
A - 1010 WIEN
(T.: dom. 022/512.22.81
prof. 022/97.32.16)

WHO'S WHO IN ATEE?

Association for Teacher Education in Europe (A.T.E.E.)
Rue de la Concorde 60
1050 Brussels, Belgium
Secretary General: M. Yves Beernaert
(March 1990)

1. BUREAU

Mr D Hellawell
President
8 Kidderminster Road
BROMSGROVE
UK Worcs. B61 7JW
Tel. 21 331 6130

Mrs F Vaniscotte
Vice-President
Av. Victor Cresson 56
F 72130 Issy-les-Moulineaux

Mr P Coppieters
Treasurer
UFSIA
Prinsstraat 13
B-2000 Antwerpen

Mr F Buchberger
Engerwitzdorf 56
A-4210 Gallneukirchen

Mrs A L Hostmark-Tarrou
Statens Yrkespedagogiske
Hogskole
Skedsmogt 25
N-0655 Oslo 6

2. ADMINISTRATIVE COUNCIL

Mr E Foldberg
Tangevej 80
DK-6780 Ribe
Tel. 05 420 194

Mrs M Jordana
Major de Sarria 125
E-08017 Barcelona
Tel. 3 3226411

Mr E Maurice
TR UFSIA-IDEA
Prinsstraat 13
B-2000 Antwerpen
Tel. 03 2204685

Mr Per-Erik Michaelsson
University College of Falun/Borlange
Box 2004
S-79102 Falun

Mrs M Montane
Trav. de les Cortes 265 6 2a
E-08014 Barcelona

Mrs M Odete Valente
Dept de Educacao da Faculdade de
Ciencas
Universidade de Lisboa
R. Ernesto Vasconcelos
Edificio C 1-3
P-1700 Lisboa
Tel. 351 1 7583141

Mrs N Plate-Bartels
1e Swelindestraat 66
NL-2517 GG Den Haag
Tel. 010 4008388

Mr A Poly
EURYCLEE
Grille d'Honneur le Parc
F-92211 Saint-Cloud

Mr M Todeschini
Inst. di Pedagogia
Universidad degli Studi
Via Festa des Perdono 7
1-20112 Milano

Press and Information Offices of the European Communities

Australia
CANBERRA
Franklin Street
P.O.Box 609
Manuka ACT 2603
Tel. 95 50 50

Belgium
1040 BRUXELLES
Rue Archimède 73
Tel. 23511 11

Denmark
1004 KØBENHAVN K
Højbrohus, Østergade 61
Postbox 144
Tel. (01) 14 41 40

France
75782 PARIS CEDEX 16
61 rue des Belles-Feuilles
Tel. 45 01 58 85

Germany
53 BONN
Zitelmannstrasse 22
Tel. 23 80 41

1 BERLIN 31
Kurfürstendamm 102
Tel. 8 92 40 28

8000 MÜNCHEN 2
Erhardstrasse 27
Tel. 2399 2900

Greece
106 74 ATHENES
Vassilissis Sofias 2
Tel. 72 43 982-3-4

Ireland
DUBLIN 2
39 Molesworth St.
Tel. 71 22 44

Italy
00 187 ROME
Via Poli 29
Tel. 678 97 22 à 26

Japan
102 TOKYO
Kowa 25 Building
8-7 Sanbancho
Chiyoda-Ku
Tel. 239-0441

Latin America
CARACAS (VENEZUELA)
Quinta Bienvenida
Calle Colibri
Valle Arriba
Caracas 106
Adresse postale:
Apartado 67076
Las Américas
Tel. 95 50 56 - 91 47 07

SANTIAGO DE CHILE
Avenida Américo Vespucio
1835
Santiago 9
Adresse postale:
Casilla 10093
Tel. 228 24 84

Luxembourg
LUXEMBOURG
Bâtiment Jean Monnet B/O
Rue Alcide de Gasperi
Luxembourg-Kirchberg
Tel. 43011

Netherlands
LA HAYE
29 Lange Voorhout
Tel. 070-46 93 26

Portugal
LISBONNE
56, rua do Salitre
1200 Lisboa
Tel. 54 11 44

Spain
28001 MADRID
C/. Madrid
5a Planta
Tel. 435 17 00

Switzerland
1211 GENEVE 20
37-39, rue de Vermont
Tel. 34 97 50

Turkey
ANKARA
15, Kuleli Sokak
Gazi Osnan Paca
Tel. 27 61 45/46

United Kingdom
LONDON SW1 P3AT
8 Storey's Gate
Tel. (01) 222 81 22

Belfast
Windsor House
9/15 Bedford Street
Belfast BT2 7G
Tel. 40708

CARDIFF CF1 9SG
4 Cathedral Road
Tel. 371631

EDINBURGH EH2 4PH
7 Alva Street
Tel. (031) 225 2058

United States
WASHINGTON D.C.
20037
2100 M Street, N.W.
Suite 707
Tel. (202) 872-8350

NEW YORK, N.Y. 10017
245 East 47th Street
1 Dag Hammarskjold Plaza
Tel. (212) 371-3804

University Associations of European Studies

Denmark
Dansk Selskab for Europaforskning
Handelshøjskoler institut for Markedsret
Rosengørns alle 9
DK - 1970 COPENHAGEN V
Tel. (01) 35 37 35

France
C.E.D.E.C.E. (Commission pour l'étude des Communautés européennes)
61 rue des Belles-Feuilles
75782-PARIS CEDEX 16
Tel. 4501 58 85

Germany
Arbeitskreis Europäische Integration
Zitelmannstrass 22
D-5300 BONN
Tel. 23 80 41

Great Britain
U.A.C.E.S. (University Association for Contemporary European Studies)
U.A.C.E.S. Secretariat, King's College
Strand G.E.
LONDON WC2R 2LS
Tel. 01-240 0206

Ireland
Irish Association for European Studies
c/o Mrs Laffan
NIHE
LIMERICK

Italy
Associazione Universitaria di Studi Europei (AUSE)
c/o Prof. A. Papiscadi
Dip. Studi Internazionali
Università di Padova
Via del Santo, 28
351 00 PADOVA
Tel. (049) 65 61 47

Japan
Nihon EC Gakkai;
c/o Prof. R. Taira,
Ofice No. 717, Keio Gijuku University, 2-15-45, Mita,
Minato-Ku, TOKYO
Tel. (03) 453-4511, ext. 3317

Netherlands
I.S.E.I. Interdisciplinaire Studiegroep Europese Integratie
Alexanderstraat 2
DEN HAAG
Tel. 60 22 73

The European Community publishes a variety of information brochures and magazines on education, training, youth and technological change.

These include:

EURYDICE Info
Published by the European Unit of the education information network in the European Community. EURYDICE is responsible for the exchange of information on education and youth policy.
Contact address: EURYDICE European Unit, Rue Archimède 17 (Bte 17), B-1040 Brussels

ERASMUS Publications
Information on the development of the ERASMUS Programme.
Contact address: ERASMUS Bureau, Rue d'Arlon 15, B-1040 Brussels

EURYCLEE Publications
EURYCLEE: Information network specializing in the field of new information technologies in education.
Contact address: National Council for Educational Technology, 3 Devonshire Street, UK-London W1N 2BA

COMETT Publications
Community programme for education and training in new technologies and cooperation between universities and industry.
Contact address: COMETT Technical Assistance Unit, Avenue de Cortenbergh 71, B-1040 Brussels

PETRA Publications
Community action programme for the vocational training of young people and their preparation for adult and working life.
Contact address: IFAPLAN, Square Ambiorix 32, B-1040 Brussels

Information on YOUTH EXCHANGE programmes
Information on the various youth exchange programmes.
Contact address: ECYEB, Place du Luxembourg 2-3, B-1040 Brussels

Information on the programme of European cooperation on the INTEGRATION OF HANDICAPPED CHILDREN INTO ORDINARY SCHOOLS
Contact address: HELIOS, Avenue de Cortenbergh 79, B-1040 Brussels

Euro Tecnet News
News bulletin of the European Community's programme on new information technologies and vocational training.
Contact address: EUROTECNET Technical Assistance Unit, Avenue de Cortenbergh 66 (Bte 13), B-1040 Burssels

IRIS Bulletin
Information bulletin on the IRIS Network, Community network of training programmes for women.
Contact address: CREW, Rue Stévin 38, B-1040 Brussels

Informisep
Publication on developments in employment, training and related policies in Member States.
Contact address: European Centre for Work and Society, P.O. Box 3073, NL-6202 NB Maastricht

CEDEFOP Publications
Information from the European Centre for the Development of Vocational Training.
Contact address: CEDEFOP, Bundesallee 22, D-1000 Berlin 15

SOCIAL EUROPE
The main information outlet for developments in social affairs at European level.
Contact address: Office for official Publications of the European Communities, L-2985 Luxembourg

Appendix V

Glossary

DEUTSCH

A

abroad: Ausland
accountability: Verantwortlichkeit
administration: Verwaltung
adviser: Berater
ambitions: Ziel, Ehrgeiz
application: Bewerbung
appraisal: Bewertung
appointment: Ernennung
assessment: Beurteilung
authorities: Behörden
award: Leistungsnachweis
award-bearing course: Kurs mit Leistungs - nachweis

B

bad report: Schlechtes Zeignis

C

career: Laufbahn
career development: Laufbahnentwicklung
certificate: Zeugnis
civil servant: Beamter
checklist: Prüfliste
class organisation: Organisation der Klasse
classroom: Klassenraum
co-educational: Koedukation
colleague: Kollege/Kollegin
competence: Kompetenz
communication: Kommunikation
composite classes: gemischte Klassen
conscientiousness: Sorgfalt
control: Kontrolle
course: Kurs
curriculum: Curriculum
curriculum planning: Planning des Curriculum

D

delegate:
depute headteacher: Stellvertretender Schulleiter
diploma: Diploma
discipline: Digziplin
distance-teaching: Fernunterricht
duties: Pflichten

E

education: Erziehung
effectiveness: Effektivität
employing authorities: arbeitgebende Behörde
employment protection: Arbeitsschutz
European Association of Teachers: Europäischer Lehrerverein
evaluation: Auswertung
extra-curricular activities: Wahl-und Freizeitkurse
examination: Prüfung

F

fees: Gebühren
form: Klasse
further college education: Weiterführende Erziehung in College-Form

G

guidance: Beratung
guidance system: Beratungssystem

H

head of department: Abteilungsleiter
headteacher: Schulleiter
HMI reports: Schulratsgutachten

I

increments: zuwachs
independent school: Privatschule
induction: Einführung
infamous conduct: ungebührliches Betragen
initial training: Grundausbildung
inservice education: berufliche Fortbildung
inservice training: Ausbildung in Beruf
interview: Bewerbungsgespräch

J

job: Beruf
job description: Berufsbeschreibung

L

leisure education: Freizeitpädagogik

M

management: Management
Master's Degree: Graduierung
maternity leave: Mutterschaftsurlaub
mentor: Mentor
methods: Methoden
mixed-ability class: Leistungsheterogene Klasse
mixed-ability teaching: Unterricht in Leistungs = heterogenen Klassen
motivate: motivieren
multi-disciplinary: inter-bzw. multidisziplinär

N

nationality: Nationalität
native language: Muttersprache
needs: Bedürfnisse

O

open university: Offene Universität

P

parents: Eltern
pastoral: beaufsichtigend
performance: Leistung
performance indicators: Leistungsindikatioem
permanent appointment: Ernennung auf Dauer
preparation: Vorbereitung
primary school: Primarschule
Principal: Leiter, Leiterin
principal teacher: Leitender Lehren
private school: Privatschule
probation: Bewährung
professor: Professor
professional competence: Professionelle Kompetenz
professional development: Professionelle Entwicklung
proficiency: Behernschung
profile: Profil
promotion: Befönderung
prospectus: Prospekt
provisional registration: Vorläufige Aufnahme
post: Posten

Q

quality: Qualität
qualification: Qualifikation

R

regent: Studienleiter
relationships: Verbindungen
relations with pupils: Verbindungen zu Schülern
retirement: Ruhestand

S

salary: Gehalt
schemes of work: Arbeitsplan
school: Schule
school council: Schulbeirat
school policy: Schulpolitik
selection: Auslese
self-assessment: Selbsteinschätzung
seminar: Seminar
service: Dienst
social education: Sozialerziehung
staff development: Kolleginmsbetreuung
staff appraisal: Kolleginmsbeurteilung
staff hand book: Lehrerhandbuch
staff meeting: Lehrerkonferenz
staff tutor: Kollegiumsberater
standards: Leistungsstandards
state school: Staatsschule
status: Status/Stellung
stresses: Belastungen
student: Student/Schüler
syllabus: Lehrplan

T

talent: Talent

target setting: Zielsetzung
teacher: Lehrer
teacher's centre: Lehrerzentrum
teacher training: Lehrerausbildung
teacher tutor: Lehrerberater
teacher's unions: Lehrergewerkschaften
teaching ability: Lehrbefähigung
technical: technisch
temporary appointment: Ernennung auf Zeit
temporary employment: Zeitweise Beschäftigung
tenure: Dauerstellung
term: Trimester
timetable: Studenplan
trainee: Trainee (in Aus = bildung Befindlicher)
Treaty of Rome: Römische Verträge
tutor: Tutor

U

university: Universität

ESPAÑOL

A

abroad: en el extranjero
accountability: responsabilidad
administration: administración
adviser: asesor
ambitions: ambiciones
application: solicîtud
appraisal: valoración
appointment: puesto
assessment: valoración
authorities: autoridades
award: título
award-bearing courses: un curso por el que se obtiene un título

B

bad report: voloración insatisfactoria

C

career: carrera (docente)
career development: progreso de carrera
certificate: certificado
civil servant: funcionario del estado
checklist: lista de control
class organisation: organización de clase
classroom: aula
co-educational: mixto
colleague: colega
competence: competencia
communication: comunicación
composite classes: clases que continenen alumnos de varias edades
conscientiousness: diligencia
control: control
course: curso
curriculum: plan de estudios
curriculum planning: organización del plan de estudios

D

delegate: delegado
depute headteacher: subdirector
diploma: diploma
discipline: disciplina
distance-teaching: enseñanza a distancia
duties: obligaciones

E

education: enseñanza
effectiveness: eficacia
employing authorities: delegaciones de educación
employment protection: seguridad de empleo
European Association of Teachers: Asociación Europea de Enseñantes
evaluation: valoración
extra-curricular activities: actividades extracurriculares
examination: examen

F

fees: derechos de matrícula
form: forma
further college education: colegio de educación postescolar

G

guidance: orientación
guidance system: sistema de orientación

H

head of department: jefe del departamento escolar
headteacher: director
HMI reports: reportaje del inspectorado

I

increment: aumento de sueldo anual
independent school: escuela libre privada
induction: iniciación
infamous conduct: sinvergüenceriá
initial training: orientación elemental
inservice education: formación profesional para profesores practicantes
inservice education: cursos de formación profesional para profesores practicantes
interview: entrevista

J

job: empleo
job description: especificaciones de un puesto

L

leisure education: educación para ocuparse durante los ratos libres

M

management: dirección
Master's Degree: Doctorado
maternity leave: licencia de maternidad
mentor: mentor
methods: métodos
mixed-ability class: clases de aptitudes diferentes
mixed-ability teaching: enseñanza de grupos de aptitudes diferentes
motivate: animar
multi-disciplinary: de varias disciplinas

N

nationality: nacionalidad
native language: lengua materna
needs: necesidades

O

Open University: Universidad a Distancia

P

parents: padres
pastoral: pastoral
peformance: ejercicio de un cargo

performance indicators: índice de habilidad
preparation: preparación
primary school: escuela primaria
Principal: Director
principal teacher: jefe de departamento
private school: escuela privada
probation: periodo de prueba
professor: catedrático
professional competence: competencia profesional
professional development: progreso profesional
proficiency: competencia
profile: perfil
promotion: promoción.
prospectus: programa
provisional registration: certificación profesional
post: puesto

Q

quality: calidad
qualification: calificacion

R

Regent: Director de Estudios profesionales
relationships: trato con los otros
relations with pupils: trato con alumnos
retirement: jubilación

S

salary: sueldo
schemes of work: planes de estudios
schools: escuela
school council: consejo de una escuela
school policy: filosofiá
secondary school: instituto de segunda enseñanza
selection: selección
self-assessment: evaluación personal
seminar: seminario, clase de discusión
service: servicio
social education: educación social

staff development: entrenamiento del profesorado
staff appraisal: evaluación del profesorado
staff handbook: manual del profesorado
staff meeting: reunión del profesorado
staff tutor: consejero pedagógico
standards: niveles
state school: escuela estatal
status: posición social
stress: tensión
student: estudiante
syllabus: programa de estudios

T

talent: talento, habilidad
target setting: previsión de objectivos
teacher: profesor
teacher's centre: centro de profesores
teacher training: formación de profesores
teacher tutor: consejero pedagógico
teacher's unions: sindicatos de profesores
teaching: enseñanza
teaching ability: aptitud profesional
technical: técnico
temporary appointment: puesto de poca duración
tenure: estabilidad de empleo
term: trimestre
timetable: programa de clases
trainee: aprendiz profesional
training: formación profesional
Treaty of Rome: Tratado de Roma
tutor: profesor que tiene a su cargo un pequeño grupo de estudiantes

U

university: universidad

V

vocational: profesional

FRANÇAIS

A

abroad: à l'étranger
accountability: responsabilité
administration: administration
adviser: conseiller
ambitions: ambitions
application: application
appraisal: évaluation; appréciàtion
appointment: nomination
assessment: évaluation
authorities: 1. les autorités
2. les services administratifs
3. l'Administration
award: récompense
award-bearing course:

B

bad report: mauvais bulletin

C

career: carrierè; profession
career development: développement de carrierè; déroulement de carrierè
civil servant: fonctionnaire
checklist: (liste de) contrôle
class organisation: organisation scolaire
classroom: classe
co-educational: (école) mixte
colleague: collègue
competence: compétence; attributions
communication: communication
composite classes: classes mélangées
conscientiousness: conscience (professionnelle)
control: contrôle
course: cours
curriculum: programme d'études

curriculum planning: organisation du programme

D

delegate: déléguer
depute headteacher: directeur adjoint
diploma: diplôme
discipline: discipline
distance-teaching: télé-enseignement; enseignement-par correspondance
duties: service

E

education: éducation
effectiveness: efficacité
employing authorities: le Ministeré de l'Éducation nationale
employment protection: sécurité d'emploi
European Association of Teachers: Association Européenne des Enseignants
evaluation: évaluation
extra-curriculum activities: activités périscolaires
examination: examen

F

fees: droits; frais de scolaritè
form: classe; division
college of further education: Établissement d'enseignement postscolaire; d'éducation continue

G

guidance: orientation
guidance system: l'orientation scolaire

H

head of department: Chef (ou directeur) du département
headteacher: directeur; principal; proviseur

I

increment: augmentation; progression
independent school: école libre; privée
induction: admission
infamous conduct: conduite scandaleuse; mauvaisè conduite
initial training: formation initiale
inservice education: éducation permanente
inservice training: stage de formation
interview: "interview"; entretien

J

job: travail; poste de travail
job description: organisation du travail

L

leisure education: éducation aux loisirs

M

management: gestion
Master's Degree: maîtrise
maternity leave: coupé de maternité
mentor: conseiller
methods: méthodes
mixed-ability class: classe hétérogènes
mixed-ability teaching: enseignement en classes hétérogènes
motivate: motiver
multi-disciplinary: pluridisciplinaire

N

nationality: nationalité
native language: langue maternelle
needs: besoins

O

open university: centre télé-enseignement universitaire

P

parents: parents
pastoral: pastoral
performance: performance
performance indicators: indice de performance
permanent appointment: nomination á poste fixe
preparation: préparation

primary school: école élémentaire
Principal: directeur
principal teacher: professeur principal
private school: école privée
probation: épreuve; période stagiaire
professor: professeur d'université
professional competence: competénce professionnelle
professional development: niveau de développement professionnel
proficiency: capacité; competence
profile: profil
promotion: promotion
prospectus: prospectus; programme
provisional registration: poste intérinaire/provisoire
post: poste

Q

quality: qualité
qualification: compétence; qualification professionnelle

R

regent:
relationship: relations
relations with pupils: rapports avec les élèves
retirement: retraite

S

salary: salaire; traitement
schemes of work: plans de trávail;
school: école; établissement
school council: conseil d'établissement
school policy: projet d'établissement
selection: sélection
secondary school: école secondaire
self-assessment: auto-estimation; auto-évaluation
seminar: séminaire
service: service
social education: éducation en sciences humaines
staff development: perfectionnement des personnel
staff appraisal: notation du personnel
staff handbook:
staff meeting: réunion du personnel
staff tutor:
standards: niveaux
state school:
status: statut
stresses: tension
student: enseigné; élève/ étudiant
syllabus: programme (d'une discipline)

T

talent: talent
target setting: recherche des objectifs
teacher: enseignant; instituteur/professeur
teachers' centre: centre de formation des enseignants
teacher training: formation des maîtres; des enseignants
teacher tutor: counseiller pédagogique
teacher's unions: syndicats (d'enseignants)
teaching ability: aptitude professionnelle
technical: technique
temporary appointment: nomination prassoire
temporary employment: poste provisoire
tenure: stabilité (d'emploi)
term: trimestre
timetable: emploi du temps
trainee: stagiaire
training: formation
Teaty of Rome: Traité de Rome
tutor: conseiller; répétiteur; directeur d'études

U

university: université

V

vocational: professionnel

ITALIANO

A

abroad: all'estero
accountability: responsabilità morale

administration: amministrazione
adviser: consigliere
ambitions: ambizioni
application: domanda di lavoro
appraisal: valutazione
appointment: nomina
assessment: valutazione
authorities: autorità
award: premio
award-bearing course:

B

bad report: cattivo endiconto

C

career: carriera
career development: progressione nella carriera
certificate: certificato
civil servant: impiegato statale
checklist:
class organisation: organizzazione di classe
classroom: classe
co-educational: istruzione mista
colleague: collega
competence: competenza
communication: comunicazione
composite classes:
conscientiousness: sconsideratezza
control: controllo
course: corso
curriculum: curriculum
curriculum planning: piano di curriculum

D

delegate: delegato
depute headteacher: collaboratore
diploma: diploma
discipline: disciplina
distance-teaching: insegnamento a distanza
duties: doveri

E

education: istruzione
effectiveness: efficacia
employing authorities: Autorità Provinciale
employment protection:
European Association of Teachers: Associazione Europea di Insegnanti
evaluation: valutazione
extra-curriculum activities: attività extra-scolastiche
examination: essame

F

fees: tasse
form: classe
further college education:

G

guidance: direzione
guidance system: sistema di direzione

H

head of department
headteacher: preside
HMI reports: relazioni di ispettori

I

increment: incremento
independent school: scuola privata
induction: insediamento
infamous conduct: cattiva condotta
initial training: addestramento iniziale
inservice education:
inservice training:
interview:

J

job: lavoro
job description: descrizione del lavoro

L

leisure education: istruzione per il tempo libero

M

management: management

Master's Degree: laurea
maternity leave: assenza per maternità
mentor:
methods: metodi
mixed-ability class: classe composita
mixed-ability teaching: insegnamento composito
motivate: motivare
multi-disciplinary: pluri-disciplinare

N

nationality: nazionalità
native language: madrelingua
needs: bisogni

P

parents: genitori
pastoral:
performance: esecuzione
performance indicators: indicatori di esecuzione
permanent appointment: impiego permanente
preparation: preparazione
primary school: scuola elementare
Principal: preside
principal teacher:
private school: scuola privata
probation: periodo di prova
professor: professore
professional competence: competenza professionale
professional development: miglioramento professionale
proficiency: abilità
profile: profilo
promotion: avanzamento
prospectus: prospettico
provisional registration:
post: impiego

Q

quality: qualità
qualification: qualifica

R

regent: preside
relationship: relazioni
relations with pupils: relazioni con gli studenti
retirement: pensionamento

S

salary: retribuzione
schemes of work: programmazione di lavoro
school: scuola
school council: consiglio scolastico
school policy: politica scolastica
selection: selezione
secondary school: scuola media - istituti
self-assessment: autocontrollo
seminar: seminario
service: servizio
social education: istruzione sociale
staff development: miglioramento del corpo insegnante
staff appraisal: autocontrollo del corpo insegnante
staff handbook: registro degli insegnanti
staff meeting: riunioni degli insegnanti
staff tutor:
standards: standards
state school: scuola statale
status: status
stresses: tensioni
student: studente
syllabus: programma di studio

T

talent: talento
target setting: fissazione di obiettivi
teacher: insegnante
teacher's centre: centro per docenti
teacher training: addestramento per docenti
teacher tutor:
teacher's unions: associazioni di docenti
teaching ability: abilità all'insegnamento
technical: technico

temporary appointment: impiego temporaneo
temporary employment: impiego temporaneo
tenure: durata in carica
term: trimestre
timetable: orario scolastico
trainee: apprendista
training: addestramento
Teaty of Rome: Trattato di Roma
tutor: istitutore

U

university: università

V

vocational: professionale

Appendix VI

The Staff Development Europe project

Appendix VI

The Staff Development Europe Project

This investigation of entry into the teaching profession, and of the early career development of teachers, seeks to make comparisons between a number of European countries.

Comparisons are being made in terms of:-

- (i) preparation for teaching
- (ii) control of entry to the profession and control of the profession generally
- (iii) the process of beginning to teach
- (iv) roles of staff in the processes
- (v) support for teachers provided through inservice training and in other ways
- (vi) the assessment of teacher performance
- (vii) teacher records
- (viii) career structures for teachers
- (ix) salaries, rewards and status.

We should be pleased if you would respond to each of the questions which follow. Please give separate information for primary and secondary teaching, and for teaching in further education, when necessary.

Please write responses on the pages enclosed for that purpose and return only these to the researchers.

Section One

Preparation for Teaching

In Scotland all primary teachers (for 5 to 12 year olds) and all secondary teachers (for 12 to 16 or 18 year olds) **must** receive teacher training before they are allowed to teach.

Primary teachers take a special 4-year degree course which includes teacher training (Bachelor of Education Degree). Secondary teachers take a one-year teacher training course after having first obtained a university degree.

Teachers in colleges of further or higher education and lecturers in universities are not required to have training.

1.1 In your country is teacher training obligatory for

- (a) primary teachers?
- (b) secondary teachers?
- (c) further (vocational) education teachers?
- (d) university teachers?

1.2 Please give a brief statement on how and where teachers are trained and prepared.

- (a) primary teachers?
- (b) secondary teachers?
- (c) further (vocational) education teachers?
- (d) university teachers?

Section Two

Control of Entry into Teaching and Control of the Teaching Profession Generally

In Scotland central government, local government and the teaching profession itself all play a part in the control of the profession.

2.1 Please explain what part if any is played in your country in controlling entry to the profession and in the control of the profession generally by:-

(a) central government

(b) local government (please identify what this is)

2.2 In Scotland the affairs of the teaching profession (apart from salaries) are managed by the profession itself through the General Teaching council for Scotland. Is there such a body in your country? If so give details.

2.3 Which authority (e.g. central or local government; school district; etc.) employs and pays teachers?

2.4 Are there agreed conditions of service for teachers? Please provide a copy if possible.

2.5 Do teachers sign a contract of employment? Please attach a copy if possible.

2.6 Give the names of any teacher unions which exist. Please give brief statement of their powers and functions.

Section Three

The Process of Beginning Teaching

In Scotland there is a two-year period of probation normally following completion of training and covering the first two years of appointment. During probation teachers must demonstrate satisfactory teaching performance. Various staff are involved in helping and assessing probationers.

3.1 Is there a formal period of probation in your country? Give details of its length and how it operates.

3.2 Is there a member(s) of the school staff with special responsibility for teachers who are starting their careers? Give details.

3.3 Are any officials from outside the school involved? (e.g. from the training institutions and/or from central or local government). Please give details.

3.4 Give details of any programmes of support (lectures, discussions, demonstrations etc.) which are provided especially for new teachers. Please indicate where and when these occur.

3.5 How and by whom are new teachers assessed? Give details including details of criteria.

Section Four

Roles and the Management of Staff

Some information about roles has already been requested in Section Three. Here we extend the area beyond the first years of teaching to ask about the management of all teaching staff.

4.1 Briefly outline the Headteacher's or Principal's role and responsibilities with respect to the management of staff.

4.2 Does the Head or Principal sometimes delegate any of these management tasks to a senior member of staff? If so, to whom? Please give details, including job description if available.

4.3 Are there Principal Teachers or Heads of Department or any others with particular responsibilities for staff? Please give details, including job description if available.

4.4 Please give details of how the School Inspector carries out duties with respect to staff in the school.

4.5 Are there others from outside the school who have duties and responsibilities with respect to school staff?

Section Five

Further Professional Training

5.1 Is there an in-school programme of inservice training for teachers. Give brief details - timing, staffing, content. Enclose specimen programme if possible.

5.2 Is attendance at this programme compulsory?

5.3 Is there an out-of-school programme of inservice training for teachers? Give brief details - timing, staffing, content. Enclose specimen programme if possible.

5.4 Is attendance at this programme compulsory?

5.5 Give brief details of award-bearing courses available, with examples.

5.6 Is attendance at courses (a) essential, or (b) desirable or (c) not necessary for career development and promotion.

5.7 Is attendance at courses linked in any way to salary or salary bonuses? Give details.

5.8 Are Heads or Principals and other senior staff required to attend courses? Give details.

Section Six

The Assessment of Teacher Performance

6.1 Are all teachers regularly assessed?

6.2 Is this a recent development? Give date when this practice was introduced.

6.3 By whom is it carried out?

6.4 Give details of the assessment criteria that are used.

6.5 Does the assessment affect salary, mobility, or conditions of service? Give details.

6.6 Are Principals/Heads and any other promoted staff regularly assessed? Give details.

6.7 Is assessment (a) liked by teachers (b) disliked by teachers (c) accepted by teachers without much feeling either way.

6.8 What do the unions think about assessment? Have official statements been made?

Section Seven

Teacher Records

7.1 Which authorities outside school keep records relating to a teacher's service and career? Give brief details.

7.2 What records are usually kept in school, and by whom, relating to a teacher's service there?

7.3 Do any of these records include assessments of performance? Please give details.

Section Eight

Career Structures of Teaching

8.1 Describe the opportunities for career advancement and promotion available to teachers. Please include the titles and/or a short description of any promoted posts.
(a) Primary teaching.
(b) Secondary teaching.

8.2 Give details of the selection procedures for promotion.

Section Nine

Salaries, Rewards and Status

9.1 Please attach details of salary as operating for primary and secondary teachers.

9.2 How does a teacher achieve higher salaries or higher payments? Is it simply a question of service?

9.3 Give details of the higher scales for promoted staff.

9.4 Are teachers rewarded for 'better performance' or heavier teaching time-table in any other ways?

9.5 How do teachers' salaries compare with those paid to the police, nurses, and doctors? Give brief details.

9.6 What is the status of the teaching profession? i.e. How highly are teachers regarded in society?

9.7 If possible, please provide two or three examples of teachers actual income and expenditure.

Section Ten

Key Texts, Reports and Documentation

Please list any key items which provide important background information and illustrations.

10.1 Legislation

National reports

Local reports

Union position statements

Reference works or texts

Any other relevant materials in print.

Section Eleven

Current Issues and Developments

Please explain, and comment briefly upon, any current issues regarding the teaching profession which you see as pertinent to this investigation.

Appendix VII

Entry into Teaching in European Community Countries;

A summary of basic requirements

SOME GENERAL TRENDS AND ISSUES

1. In most countries closer attention is now being paid to entry requirements and to selection, thus countering the argument that teaching is a soft option.

2. There is increasing evidence related to the lengthening and upgrading of teacher education courses, and especially for primary teachers. Examples of these processes may be found in Belgium, Ireland, France and Greece.

3. A further development is the closer relationship being forged between the teacher training institutions and universities, especially in connection with educating and training primary school teachers. Examples may be found in: Ireland; France; Greece; and Spain.

4. Many countries provide evidence of the tension which exists when designing and developing initial teacher training courses, leading to graduate status and a degree, yet with an increased emphasis on practical skills, classroom observation, and teaching practice. A common problem is that of how best to integrate theory and practice.

5. The means whereby teachers are fully recognised varies from country to country. In many countries this is controlled by the Ministry of Education. In Scotland it is necessary to obtain provisional Registration with The General Teaching Council, and to obtain full registration after a satisfactory period of probation. There are proposals for a Teaching Council in England and Wales, and in Ireland.

6. The process of probation is one that is interpreted in various ways. In Scotland, where probation lasts for two years, there are provisions made both for supporting and assessing the beginning teacher. Probation is a trial period, but one during which the probationer teacher can expect support and help. In England and Wales where probation lasts for one year, there are similar expectations. Some other countries (Greece, for example) are trying to provide more support for the beginning teacher. By contrast there are many countries (such as The Netherlands) where there is no specified support for the beginning teacher.

7. The mechanisms for acquiring permanent posts and tenure vary from country to country. In some cases it is necessary to secure nomination to a permanent post which occurs only after satisfactory employment as a *'stagiaire'*, and subject to a satisfactory report from the inspector. In some countries teachers must first succeed in competitive examinations before they can be made permanent.

8. With the pool of possible entrants likely to be reduced for demographic reasons, alternative modes of entry are being considered (e.g. in England and Wales).

9. There is an increasing emphasis in most countries on inservice training, both for experienced teachers who need to be brought up to date and for the new generations of teachers who are more aware of the need for properly planned career development.

COUNTRY	ENTRANCE REQUIREMENTS	LOCATION	LENGTH/STRUCTURE OF COURSE	QUALIFICATION	PROBATION PERIOD
BELGIUM					
Primary	Upper Secondary School Certificate	*École Normale*	3 years concurrent academic/ pedagogical. Teaching observation/practice increasing over the 3 years.	Teaching Diploma as *Instituteur/Institutrice*.	All intending Teachers are obliged to serve a period of 240 days as temporary teachers before entering a post as *stagiaire*. A satis-factory report related to teaching the temporary post, and as a *stagiaire* is required, prior to nomination.
Lower Secondary	Upper Secondary School Certificate	*École Normale*	3 years compulsory professional and pedagogical courses; specified subject study and further optional practice increases over 3 years to about 50% in final year.	Teaching Diploma (*Diplôme d'Agrégé de L'Enseignement Secondaire Inférieur*).	As above
Upper Secondary	University Degree (*Licence*), plus a course in pedagogical studies typically beginning in third year of university studies.	University and school visits/ some teaching in school(s).	4-5 years academic and pedagogical training which can be simultaneous (two year part-time pedagogical training is also possible, after completing the degree course).	Teaching Diploma (*Diplôme d'Agrégé de L'Enseignement Secondaire Supérieur*).	As above

COUNTRY	ENTRANCE REQUIREMENTS	LOCATION	LENGTH/STRUCTURE OF COURSE	QUALIFICATION	PROBATION PERIOD
DENMARK					
Primary and Lower Secondary	Certificate of general education *Studentereksamen* or *HF-eksamen*.	Teacher Training College (*Seminarium*)	4 year common core of professional and *Folkeskole* teaching subjects, and observation and teaching in schools for at least 12 weeks. Initial school experience, for a few hours per week, will increase as the course progresses.	*Folkeskole* Teaching Diploma	2 years (for a state civil servant)
Upper Secondary	University Degree	University based post-graduate course (*Paedagogikum*)	Short, 5 month course in education theory, pedagogical studies and at least 120 hours teaching practice in upper secondary school (*Gymnasium*).	Upper Secondary (*Gymnasium*) Teaching Diploma	2 years

COUNTRY	ENTRANCE REQUIREMENTS	LOCATION	LENGTH/STRUCTURE OF COURSE	QUALIFICATION	PROBATION PERIOD
ENGLAND AND WALES					
Primary	(i) Successful completion of secondary school courses with examination passes including English Language and Mathematics; individual interview to assess personal qualities and commitment.	Polytechnic or College of Higher Education	4 years concurrent training, combining curriculum, pedagogical and educational studies; substantial practical experience of teaching, amounting to about 20 weeks in schools (including one day a week serial practice).	B.Ed. Degree Registered with the Department of Education and Science as having Qualified Teacher Status (TQS).	1 year
	(ii) University degree in appropriate subjects; individual interview to assess personal qualities and commitment.	University Department of Education, Polytechnics or Colleges of Higher Education	1 year's intensive pedagogical and practical training; teaching practice totalling about 100 days in school observation and teaching practice.	Post-graduate Certificate in Education (Primary); registered with the Department of Education and Science as having Qualified Teacher Status (TQS)	1 year
Secondary	University degree in one or two teaching subjects; individual interview to assess personal qualities and commitment.	University Department of Education, Polytechnic or College of Higher Education	1 year's intensive pedagogical and practical training; teaching practice amounting to about 15 weeks in school observation and teaching practice.	Post-graduate Certificate in Education (Secondary); registered with the Department of Education and Science as having Qualified Teacher Status (TQS).	1 year

COUNTRY	ENTRANCE REQUIREMENTS	LOCATION	LENGTH/STRUCTURE OF COURSE	QUALIFICATION	PROBATION PERIOD
FRANCE					
Primary	*Baccalauréat* and (from 1984) first cycle university education, leading to *Diplôme d'études universitaires* (D.E.U.G.), including a professional module. Competitive entry examination to school of Higher Education	School of Higher Education (*École Normale*) [Note I.U.F.M. developments. Due to open in 1991]	2 years DEUG: 2 years professional preparation in pedagogy, subject knowledge, teaching practice and observation.	Diploma in Primary Education (*Diplôme d'instituteur d'institutrice*)	As a *stagiaire*
Secondary	*Baccalauréat* and University '*licence*' or *Baccalaureat* and University '*maîtrise*'.	University and School Observation/ teaching experience	3 years university (*licence*) or 4 years university (*maîtrise*) and competitive examination leading to one year of lesson observation, class duties, and teaching in school as a *stagiaire*.	(Competitive examination for) *Certificat d'Aptitude Professionelle à l'Enseignement Secondaire*.	As a *stagiaire*

COUNTRY	ENTRANCE REQUIREMENTS	LOCATION	LENGTH/STRUCTURE OF COURSE	QUALIFICATION	PROBATION PERIOD
GERMANY (Arrangements vary between the *Länder* and **one** example is provided in these columns).					
Primary and Middle School	Pass grades in the *Abitur* examination	University; then Training Centre for Teachers (*Studienseminar*)	4 year university course combining academic and pedagogical aspects, including 8 weeks teaching practice (4 in Primary; 4 in Middle School) leading to the First State Examination. Then a $1\frac{1}{2}$-2 years classroom orientated course based on the *Studienseminar*, leading to the Second State Examination.	Pass grades in the First and Second State Examinations	The period between the First and Second State Examination.
Secondary	Pass grades in the *Abitur* examination	University; then Training Centre for Teachers (*Studienseminar*)	4 year (or longer) academic course with education and 8 weeks teaching practice (4 in Middle, 4 in Upper), leading to the First State Examination. Then a $1\frac{1}{2}$-2 years classroom orientated course based on the *Studienseminar*, leading to the Second State Examination.	Pass grades in the First and Second State Examinations	The period between the First and Second State Examination.

COUNTRY	ENTRANCE REQUIREMENTS	LOCATION	LENGTH/STRUCTURE OF COURSE	QUALIFICATION	PROBATION PERIOD
GREECE					
Primary	School (*lyceum*) leaving certificate (*Apolitirio*)	University Pedagogical Department	4 years: Educational theory/ Teaching methods; General education subjects. 15%-25% of total time is devoted to teaching practice.	University degree (*Ptychio*)	2 years
Secondary	School leaving certificate (*Apolitirio*) University degree in subject specialisation	University	Teaching methods and pedagogical elements in 3rd-4th year of university degree course.	University degree (*Ptychio*)	2 years

COUNTRY	ENTRANCE REQUIREMENTS	LOCATION	LENGTH/STRUCTURE OF COURSE	QUALIFICATION	PROBATION PERIOD
IRELAND					
Primary	Competitive Examination, and passes in 6 subjects in the School Leaving Certificate, of which the following three are obligatory: Irish (oral and written), English, Mathematics. Minimum grades required are as follows: Honours (Grade C) on a higher level paper in 3 subjects including Irish. Pass (Grade D) in three other subjects. Grade C on a lower level or Grade D on a higher level paper in English. Interview: Oral Irish and Music Tests	College of Education	3 year concurrent course, including Theoretical, Curricular and Practical Elements. Specialisation in one subject. 15 weeks teaching practice.	B.Ed. Degree	Not less than 1 year
Secondary	University Degree Oral Irish	University + University Education Department	3-4 years degree; 1 year pedagogical including: Educational theory; Subject methods; Elective courses; at least 100 hours teaching practice.	Degree + Higher Diploma in Education (H.Dip.Ed.)	Not less than 1 year

COUNTRY	ENTRANCE REQUIREMENTS	LOCATION	LENGTH/STRUCTURE OF COURSE	QUALIFICATION	PROBATION PERIOD
ITALY					
Primary	Intermediate School (*Scuola Media*) leaving certificate	Upper secondary Institute (*Istituto Magistrale*)	4 years Academic and Pedagogic Studies. Teaching observation and practice in the final two years, mainly assisting the classroom teacher.	State examination leading to Primary Teacher's Certificate (*Maturità Magistrale*)	1 year (for those who are successful in the *concorso*)
Secondary	Upper Secondary School Leaving Certificate (*Maturità*)	University	3-4 years academic study.	Degree	1 year (as above)

COUNTRY	ENTRANCE REQUIREMENTS	LOCATION	LENGTH/STRUCTURE OF COURSE	QUALIFICATION	PROBATION PERIOD
LUXEMBOURG					
Primary	Secondary school leaving Certificate; linguistic competence in Letzeburgesch, German, French, English.	Teacher Training Institute (*L'Institut Supérieur d'Études et de Recherches Pédagogigues*) in collaboration with Luxembourg University Centre.	3 years academic/pedagogical study, comprising common courses; pedagogical studies; practical experience and observation in schools. Focus upon either pre-school or primary education and teaching.	*Certificat d'Études Pédagogigues.*	None: (provisional or temporary nominations are considered permanent after a period of two years, within the commune concerned).
Secondary	University degree, normally obtained by attending the Luxembourg University Centre for one year, and by completing university studies in another university, (e.g. London, Paris). Working knowledge of Letzeburgesch, German, French, English. Competitive examination (*Concours d'admission au stage*).	Appointment as *stagiaire* in school for three years, and paid as a *'surveillant'* and for at least 6 hours teaching per week.	During period as stagiaire, part-time attendance at university for first $1^1/_2$ years for academic and professional studies, with examination. Successful completion of two dissertations related to teaching; practical examination at end of *'stage'*.	Secondary Teaching Certificate	None: (Nomination required for permanent post)

COUNTRY	ENTRANCE REQUIREMENTS	LOCATION	LENGTH/STRUCTURE OF COURSE	QUALIFICATION	PROBATION PERIOD
THE NETHERLANDS					
Primary	School leaving certificate from the HAVO school; the VWO school; or possibly from an MBO School.	Institute of Higher Professional Education (*Hogeschool*)	4 years in general subjects, professional studies, and teaching experience (minimum amount set by Minister of Education).	*Hogeschool* Primary Teaching Diploma	None
Lower Secondary	HAVO or VWO leaving certificate	*Hogeschool*	4 years subject and professional studies/teaching practice.	Teaching Diploma	None
Upper Secondary	HAVO or VWO leaving certificate, and University Degree (which must include educational studies).	University	(From 1987) one year post-graduate course, university based. On average 50% of the post-graduate course is spent on school experience and teaching practice, building up over the year.	Teaching Certificate	None

COUNTRY	ENTRANCE REQUIREMENTS	LOCATION	LENGTH/STRUCTURE OF COURSE	QUALIFICATION	PROBATION PERIOD
NORTHERN IRELAND					
Primary	At least 2 A levels and normally Maths O level	University	4 year concurrent course including Educational Studies (e.g. social psychology of learning; education ideas; institutions). Students specialise in curriculum areas of language and creative arts, or environmental studies, or maths and science. Practical work includes: school observation; small group teaching; periods of teaching in schools (minimally 18 weeks).	Degree (B.A. or B.Sc.)	1 year
Primary/ Middle or Secondary	Normally 3 A levels	College	All students take concurrent 4 year course in education and professional studies, including classroom skills and curriculum planning. Students following primary phase courses take one main subject; those following secondary phase courses take one main subject and an appropriate subsidiary subject. Courses include at least 18 weeks practical experience in schools. (A one year post-graduate course is available for those wishing to teach in primary schools.)	B.Ed. degree	1 year
Secondary	Degree	University	1 year post graduate course combining professional and subject studies. About 50% of the course is spent in schools.	Graduate Certificate of Education	1 year

COUNTRY	ENTRANCE REQUIREMENTS	LOCATION	LENGTH/STRUCTURE OF COURSE	QUALIFICATION	PROBATION PERIOD
PORTUGAL					
Primary and Preparatory	Successful completion of secondary schooling and college entry examination.	School of Education (*Escola Superior de Educação: ESE*)	3 years for infant and primary teachers, 4 years for preparatory school teachers.	Primary Teaching Diploma or Preparatory Teaching Diploma in two specialist subjects.	None
Secondary	University degree in teaching subjects	University	(a) Concurrent: Education option during years 4 and 5 of the course, with extensive classroom responsibilities in the final year.	Degree including Education option *(Licenciatura em Ensino)*	None
		University/ESE	(b) Consecutive: A 2 year theoretical and practical course.		

COUNTRY	ENTRANCE REQUIREMENTS	LOCATION	LENGTH/STRUCTURE OF COURSE	QUALIFICATION	PROBATION PERIOD
SCOTLAND Primary	(i) Specified secondary school examination passes, including passes in English and Mathematics; also an individual interview to assess personal qualities and interests.	College of Education	4 years concurrent training combining academic studies with theoretical, curricular and practical elements; school experience throughout, in total amounting to about 29 weeks.	B.Ed. degree provisional registration with the General Teaching Council for Scotland.	2 years
	(ii) University Degree in approved subjects; individual interview to assess personal qualities and interests.	College of Education	A one-year post-graduate course, lasting 36 weeks, combining theoretical, curricular and practical elements; total school experience of at least 16 weeks.	Post-graduate Certificate in Education (Primary); provisional registration with the General Teaching Council for Scotland.	2 years
Secondary	A university degree in one or more teaching subjects; also an individual interview to assess personal qualities and interests.	College of Education	A one-year post-graduate course lasting 36 weeks, combining theoretical, curricular and practical elements; school experience relating to one or more teaching subjects, in total amounting to at least 14 weeks.	Post-graduate Certificate in Education (Secondary); provisional registration with the General Teaching Council for Scotland.	2 years

COUNTRY	ENTRANCE REQUIREMENTS	LOCATION	LENGTH/STRUCTURE OF COURSE	QUALIFICATION	PROBATION PERIOD
SPAIN					
Primary	Successful completion of a secondary certificate (BUP) course followed by a one-year orientation course for entry to higher education. (*Curso de Orientación Universitaria)*	Teacher Training College (*Escuelas Universitarias*)	3 year concurrent course combining academic elements with general pedagogy and a specialist option.	Diploma for teachers of Basic Education (*Educación General Básica)*	A 6 months trial period
Secondary	University Diploma or Degree in teaching subjects	University and (possibly) post-graduate Institute of Science and Education	A 300 hours course available either concurrently or consecutively, involving a small amount of practical classroom work.	Degree + Certificate of Pedagogic Aptitude *(Certificado de Aptitud Pedagógica)*	A 6 months trial period

COUNTRY	ENTRANCE REQUIREMENTS	LOCATION	LENGTH/STRUCTURE OF COURSE	QUALIFICATION	PROBATION PERIOD
SWEDEN Primary and Secondary (Basic school)	University entrance requirements	*Lärarhögskolan*	Concurrent course with subject specialisation, teaching methods, curriculum studies and school experience related to either: a) grades 1-7 of the basic school, or b) grades 4-9.	B.Ed. or M.Ed. Degree	None
Upper Secondary (*Gymnasium* school)	University entrance requirements	University	Two subject studies together with practical training and methodology of teaching. Theory and practice of education is part of the degree course.	Degree	None

FOOTNOTES

This outline of the provisions made for Teacher Education and Training has been made possible through the assistance of many teachers in EC member countries. Inevitably these provisions are subject to review and change, and there are sometimes differences between State and private or secular schools. Special conditions often apply to Technical and Vocational teachers. Some of the changes or special conditions are noted below.

ENGLAND AND WALES
For courses in England and Wales special requirements may apply for mature entrants, possibly with shorter periods of training. New modes of entry, with largely school-based/in-post training, for small numbers of Licensed Teachers and Articled Teachers, are being introduced in the 1990s.

FRANCE
Proposals announced in August 1989 indicate that future '*instituteurs*' would be recruited from those already possessing the *baccalauréat*, and the *'licence'* (obtained after three years of university study). Student teachers would then attend an *Institut Universitaire de Formation des Maîtres* (I.U.F.M.) for a period of two years. During this time students would be part-time teaching as a *stagiaire* in a school, or schools, and under the guidance of a *conseiller pédagogigue*. The remainder of the time would be involved in educational and related studies. The final examination would lead to an appointment as a tenured teacher (i.e. as *titularisé*). Such plans are expected to be in place by 1991.

ITALY
Those who wish to teach in a state secondary school must normally possess the '*abilitazione*' (viz: pass an examination in basic professional knowledge) usually prepared for by part-time study. To obtain a permanent post a teacher must compete in the national examination *('concorso')* and successful teachers will be placed on the permanent list *('in ruolo')*. They will then enter a one year probation period, when offered their first teaching post. Some other countries have the equivalent of the '*concorso*' (e.g. France, Spain, Portugal).

PORTUGAL
The Portuguese educational system is undergoing considerable change with respect to curriculum, teacher training and school management. Priority will be given to the teaching of Modern Languages and to Technological Education. Personal and Social development will also assume a new importance, as will Vocational and Aesthetic Education. Major efforts will be made to enhance teachers' practical classroom skills.

SPAIN
The Spanish educational system is in the process of being reformed along full, comprehensive lines. The school leaving age is being extended from 15 to 16 years. All pupils will follow the same broad curriculum, including the aesthetic subjects and vocational education. Teachers are being encouraged to tailor courses to suit local needs and pupil-choice, which will increase with age. There will be a new emphasis on Modern Languages (starting at age 8) and on Information Technology. Teacher training is also being reformed, with more stringent entrance requirements and greater attention to classroom skills. Inservice training for teachers along similar lines is seen as very urgent.